Fab. 11. City & Country Mouse. P. 8   12. Crow & Muscle. P. 10.

13. Fox & Raven. P. 11.   14. The old Lion. P. 12.

15. Ass & Whelp. P. 13.   16. Lion & Mouse. P. 13.

17. Sick Kite & her Mother. P. 14.   18. Swallow & other Birds. P. 15.

19. The Frogs desire a King. P. 16.   20. The Kite Hawk & Pigeons. P. 17.

Virtue and the Veil of Illusion

Virtue and the Veil of Illusion

Generic Innovation and the Pedagogical Project in Eighteenth-Century Literature

Dorothea E. von Mücke

Stanford University Press
Stanford, California
1991

Published with the assistance of a special grant from the
Stanford University Faculty Publication Fund
to help support nonfaculty work originating at Stanford

Stanford University Press
Stanford, California
© 1991 by the Board of Trustees
of the Leland Stanford Junior University
Printed in the United States of America

CIP data are at the end of the book

Illustrations

Endsheets: Richardson, *Aesop's Fables* (1740?), p. 2
Facing p. 1: Illustration of the letter "s";
from Joachim Heinrich Campe, *ABeZe und Lesebuch* (1807)

Frontispiece: "La matinée à l'Angloise"; Rousseau, *Julie* (1761), Plate 9

We are far more in love with our own fancy than with the object of it. If we saw the object of our affections exactly as it is, there would be no more love on earth. When we cease to love, the person we used to love remains unchanged, but we no longer see her with the same eyes; the veil of illusion falls, and love disappears. But when I supply the imaginary object, I have control over comparisons, and I am able easily to prevent the illusion of real objects.

—Rousseau, *Emile*

Preface

Invoking the familial intimacy so popular in eighteenth-century genre paintings, the picture reproduced as the frontispiece to this book seems conventionally appropriate: with a didactic gesture an adolescent girl addresses two small children, the older of whom is explaining pictures in a book to the younger one. The adults in the background do not interfere with the children: one woman is absorbed in her needlework, the two men seated at a table are perhaps discussing the newspaper; yet their gaze, like that of the other woman, rests on the children. I chose this particular engraving (Plate 9 from the first edition of Rousseau's *Julie*) not only because it introduces the theme of gentle, quasi-natural instruction as the paradigm for a new eighteenth-century pedagogy but also because it marks a decidedly new approach to book illustration in the eighteenth century.

Traditionally books had had decorative vignettes or allegorical pictures as frontispieces, but beginning with primers and collections of fables, books in the second half of the eighteenth century sought a much closer fusion of reading and seeing. Rousseau, the great theorist of the new pedagogy, chose Gravelot, one of the most accomplished engravers of his time, to illustrate *Julie* and gave him detailed instructions for twelve plates that were to be printed facing the page containing the narrative presentation of the same scene. This marks a new approach to book illustration, one in which the pictures collaborate with the reader's imaginary involvement in the fiction.

Plate 9, bearing Rousseau's caption "La matinée à l'Angloise," illustrates a passage in Saint-Preux's first letter describing the household at Clarens. In this letter Saint-Preux celebrates the supreme serenity and calm of the Wolmar household, seeing in the playing children the spectacle that illustrates for him the phrase "the tongues are silent and the hearts speak to each other" (a phrase that could also serve as a miniature definition of the new epistolary novel as the "correspondence of the hearts"). He also describes to his friend Milord Edouard the wise governance and order of Clarens in words that ventriloquize the crucial points from the pedagogical and cultural program Rousseau presents in the *Letter to M. d'Alembert* and *Emile*. A typical example of the new pedagogy of the eighteenth century appears facing p. 1, below. The picture, taken from Campe's *ABeZe und Lesebuch*, attempts to combine "graphic" illustration, the phonetic reading method, and moral instruction (here the peaceful art of the silkworm as opposed to the military art of the spider).

The illustrations in *Julie* are perfectly sealed into the novelistic fiction; nonetheless, they frequently exceed their specific relevance to the plot. Indeed, they encapsulate what might loosely be called "primal scenes" for the mid-eighteenth-century cultural program of combining literary practice and moral improvement. It is for this reason that I have scattered illustrations from *Julie* throughout the first part of this book, which discusses the development of this program. (There are fewer illustrations in the second part because toward the end of the eighteenth century new literary genres became tied to different pedagogical strategies and ideals.)

This preface might also contain a picture, more precisely a group photograph, if Bourdieu is right that in taking pictures of family and acquaintances we want to fix and to show others not so much how those people look but more our specific ties to them. The acknowledgments of a book partly share this function of the group photograph. As most readers will know from their own experience, the writing of a book can put heavy stress on friends, particularly on those who take the most interest in the book and its writer, yet it can also strengthen friendships and become a record of an ongoing engagement. Chris Cullens has been the most selfless and faithful supporter of the entire project. For five years she offered me gentle corrections, forceful readings, and unlimited patience. David Wellbery has been the ideal reader of this book. From the beginning to the end, he has always known the perfect balance between optimistic trust and critical rigor. His brilliantly clear-minded and articulate responses have been invaluable to my argument and have provided me with an enduring example of intellectual exchange that I hope to live up to. Without Philippe Similon's unerring support, I could not have finished this book. His secret file of backups prevented major crises. His companionship, sense of humor, love, and intellectual integrity have given me daily joy. I express my gratitude to David, Chris, and Philippe by dedicating this book to them.

I also acknowledge the larger circle of friends, teachers, and colleagues who gave me encouragement and support. I am greatly indebted to Terry Castle, William Mills Todd III, and Friedrich A. Kittler for helping me to get this book under way. Rey Chow, Elizabeth Heckendorn Cook, Lynn Enterline, Leonard Green, Veronica Kelly, Deidre Lynch, Biddy Martin, Heidi Reiss, Neil Saccamano, and Mark Seltzer have read individual parts and shared their insights with me. I am indebted to Tom Cohen, Julia Cauthorn, Karin and Rüdiger Ohme, Shirley Samuels, Anette Schwarz, Richard Semba, Rajani Sudan, Renate Voris, and Sharon Willis for letting me learn from and with them. I feel fortunate to have been sustained by the intellectual community of these friends.

Helen Tartar of Stanford University Press has not only been a great reader but also a wonderful accomplice and friend. I thank Helmut Schneider and Jochen Schulte-Sasse for insightful readings of the entire manuscript. I am grateful to John Ziemer for his expertise and acumen in his careful editing of the manuscript. The final stages of this book could only have been accomplished in the context of the stimulating, warm, and supportive environment provided by my friends and colleagues. I am particularly grateful to April Alliston, John Archer, Paul Cohen, Andreas Huyssen, Siobhan Kilfeather, Karen Van Dyck, and Susan Winnett for coffee, dinners, and discussions far into the night. I also thank the students in my Seminar on Eighteenth-Century Aesthetics and Semiotics for patience, enthusiasm, and sharp questions, and I am especially grateful to Ehren Fordyce for his careful translations of the Rousseau passages in Chapter 3 and to Andreas Gailus for preparing the Index.

I thank the staff at the Beinecke Library at Yale, the Yale Center for British Art, and the Avery Collection at Columbia for helping me locate and allowing me to reproduce the illustrations in this book. Portions of Chapter 4 appeared in Kurt Müller-Vollmer, ed., *Herder Today* (Berlin: de Gruyter, 1990), pp. 331–44; and *Studies in Eighteenth-Century Culture* 19 (1989): 349–65. Both articles have been revised for presentation here. I thank de Gruyter and the editors of *Studies in Eighteenth-Century Culture* for permission to reprint these materials. I am thankful to the American Council of Learned Societies for providing me with a fellowship in 1991, to the Columbia Council on Research and Faculty Development in the Humanities for summer fellowships in 1989 and 1990, and particularly to Amy and Bud Cohen for their generous hospitality in letting me write at their summer home on Martha's Vineyard.

D.E.v.M.

Contents

Contents

A Note on the
Citation of Primary Sources

The sources of all quotations from, and references to, primary works are identified in the text itself. Numbers in roman type refer to the original versions of the texts, either to the page number in the edition used or, for ease of cross-reference in the case of some plays, to the numbers of the act, scene, and lines being quoted. Numbers in italic type indicate the page number in published translations. If no italic number is given, the translation is mine.

For complete bibliographic data on the works cited in this fashion, see the list of primary sources in the Works Cited, pp. 317–26.

Virtue and the Veil of Illusion

die spin ne und der sei den wurm.

___

spin ne.
ich spin ne, nach ba rin, siel
sei ner doch als du!

sei den wurm.
kann sein; du spinnst sehr
gut; al lein wo zu?

spin ne.
ich spin ne mir ein netz, und
breit' es künst lich aus;
da kom men dann die slie gen
und die mü cken,
und las sen sich da rin be-
stri cken,

s.

Introduction

I

Aus Morgenduft gewebt und Sonnenklarheit,
Der Dichtung Schleier aus der Hand der Wahrheit.

(Woven from morning mist and clearness of the sun,
the veil of poetry from the hand of truth.)

—Goethe, from "Zueignung," 1784

In 1787 Goethe placed the poem "Zueignung" (Dedication) at the beginning of the first volume of his complete works,[1] a position whose promi-
nence suggests "Zueignung" should be understood as a preface and frame
for all his poetry. In effect, the poem sets forth a theory of poetry that
centers, as I hope to show, on the socializing function of poetic illusion.

The poem narrates a young wanderer's ascent of a mountain. As he is
surrounded by the rising morning mist, he gradually loses sight of the landscape, but soon the sun divides and dispels the fog. Although blinded by the
harsh light, the wanderer dares to blink, and there appears to him, carried
on a cloud, the most beautiful of women. Gazing upon him, she asks:

Kennst du mich nicht? sprach sie mit einem Munde,
Dem aller Lieb und Treue Ton entfloß:
Erkennst du mich, die ich in manche Wunde
Des Lebens dir den reinsten Balsam goß?
Du kennst mich wohl, an die, zu ewgem Bunde,
Dein strebend Herz sich fest und fester schloß.
Sah ich dich nicht mit heißen Herzensstränen
Als Knabe schon nach mir dich eifrig sehnen?

(Do you not know me? She spoke with a mouth
from which flowed all the sound of love and fidelity.
Do you recognize me who poured in many a wound
the purest balm of life?
Ah, well you know me as the one, with whom forever
your aspiring heart was closer and closer tied.
Did I not see how with the hot tears of your heart
even as a boy you yearned for me?)

The wanderer responds:

Ja! rief ich aus, indem ich selig nieder
Zur Erde sank, lang hab ich dich gefühlt;
Du gabst mir Ruh, wenn durch die jungen Glieder
Die Leidenschaft sich rastlos durchgewühlt;
Du hast mir wie mit himmlischem Gefieder
Am heißen Tag die Stirne sanft gekühlt;
Du schenktest mir der Erde beste Gaben,
Und jedes Glück will ich durch dich nur haben!

(Yes, I exclaimed, as I blissfully sank down
to earth, I have felt you for a long time;
You brought me peace, when through my young limbs
passion was restlessly raging.
As it were with celestial pinions you have cooled
in the hot days of summertime my brow;
you gave me the best gifts of earth's dominions;
and every kind of happiness I will have exclusively through you.)

After this scene of mutual recognition, the young man insists that he
will no longer speak of her as do the multitudes, who erroneously assume
they can name and possess her; rather, he will enjoy his happiness alone,
within himself. She reproaches him for such selfish arrogance. Eagerly he
listens to her gentle reproof and embraces his duty to share his gifts and
insights with others. And by accepting her pedagogical guidance, he enters
into a more intimate relation with her.

Und wie ich sprach, sah mich das hohe Wesen
Mit einem Blick mitleidger Nachsicht an;
Ich konnte mich in ihren Augen lesen,
Was ich verfehlt und was ich recht getan.
Sie lächelte, da war ich schon genesen,
Zu neuen Freuden stieg mein Geist heran;
Ich konnte nun mit innigem Vertrauen
Mich zu ihr nahn und ihrer Nähe schauen.

Da reckte sie die Hand aus in die Streifen
Der leichten Wolken und des Dufts umher;
Wie sie ihn faßte, ließ er sich ergreifen,
Er ließ sich ziehn, es war kein Nebel mehr.
Mein Auge konnt im Tale wieder schweifen,
Gen Himmel blickt ich, er war hell und hehr.
Nur sah ich sie den reinsten Schleier halten,
Er floß um sie und schwoll in tausend Falten.

Ich kenne dich, ich kenne deine Schwächen,
Ich weiß, was Gutes in dir lebt und glimmt!
—So sagte sie, ich hör sie ewig sprechen—
Empfange hier, was ich dir lang bestimmt;
Dem Glücklichen kann es an nichts gebrechen,
Der dies Geschenk mit stiller Seele nimmt;
Aus Morgenduft gewebt und Sonnenklarheit,
Der Dichtung Schleier aus der Hand der Wahrheit.

(And as I spoke, the high being
looked at me with sympathy and indulgence;
I could read myself in her eyes
what I had failed at and what I had done well.
She smiled, at once I was recovered,
the spirit in me rose to new joys;
now I could with firm confidence
approach her and look upon her close.

She reached her hand out of the streaks
of light clouds and perfume around her;
As she touched it, it could be gripped,
it could be torn and there was no more mist.
Again my eye could scan the valley,
I looked toward the sky, it was bright and high;
I could only see how she was holding the purest veil,
flowing around her and swelling into a thousand folds.

I know you; I know your weaknesses,
I know the good that lives and glows in you!
Thus she spoke, I hear her speak forever—
Receive here what I have long destined for you;
the happy will lack for nothing
who takes this gift with peaceful soul;
woven from morning mist and clearness of the sun,
the veil of poetry from the hand of truth.)

The culminating metaphor of the veil introduces the central concerns of this book. This poem, with its statement about the socializing function of poetry, is part of a long tradition of texts, each of which marks an epochal reformulation of subjectivity. The narrative of an ascent of a mountain and the consequent modification of vision replicates the experience of Moses, Augustine, and Petrarch, to name three prominent figures. It is a tradition in which each textual instance displays a paradigmatic subjectivity, an exemplary relation among the individual speaking subject, his perception, and the truth. Whereas Augustine, alluding to the dying Moses' gaze onto the holy land, uses the view from the mountaintop as a simile for his pseudo-conversion (i.e., the vision of truth attained through his neo-Platonic reading of Scripture),[2] Petrarch describes his ascent of Mount Ventoux as ending in an insight to the futility of worldly desire. Upon reading a randomly selected passage from Book 10 of Augustine's *Confessions*, he repudiates the expansive domain of nature opened to his panoramic view: " 'Men go to admire the high mountains and the great flood of seas and the wide-rolling rivers and the ring of the Ocean and the movements of the stars; and they abandon themselves.' . . . I was angry with myself for admiring the things of this world, when I should have learned long since from the pagan philosophers themselves that nothing is admirable except the soul, besides the greatness of which nothing is great."[3] In Petrarch's text, the view from the mountaintop is interrupted and modified through a process of reading that not only alters the beholder's view of the landscape but also radically changes his subjectivity and his attitude toward the world. The experience on the mountain brings about a transformation of desire.

The textual mediation of perception that characterizes Petrarch's experience reveals what is at stake in Goethe's detailed account of the wanderer's vision. Initially the wanderer, surrounded by fog, loses sight of the landscape. The sun removes this obstacle to vision but proves to be so powerful that the wanderer is blinded and compelled to close his eyes. The wanderer can see only when sunlight and mist blend, when white light, the medium of all visual information, is filtered and refracted. With Goethe's precursors in mind, we can interpret this perceptual dynamics as figuring a problem of textual mediation: language as symbolic order organizes and mediates our access to the world. Hence the sudden rupture and shift within the poem from a "naturalistic" view to the encounter with the beautiful woman, an allegorical personification of truth and language, and indeed of allegory itself.

However—and this qualification takes us to the specific features of Goethe's text—initially this allegory is not presented as such. Far from introducing herself as the instance of mediation and triangulation, the beautiful woman presents herself as that source of happiness and consolation the poet has known and desired from infancy, in brief, as a maternal figure. He responds to her invocation of his infantile longing by affirming her as the guarantor of peace and contentment, sinking to earth as if he were swooning or losing his adult motor control. The strategy by which he hopes to hold on to this state of bliss and to keep the female figure to himself is his refusal to name her.

> Dich nenn ich nicht. Zwar hör ich dich von vielen
> Gar oft genannt, und jeder heißt dich sein.
> Ein jedes Auge glaubt auf dich zu zielen,
> Fast jedem Auge wird dein Strahl zur Pein.
> Ach, da ich irrte, hatt ich viel Gespielen,
> Da ich dich kenne, ich bin fast allein:
> Ich muß mein Glück nur mit mir selbst genießen,
> Dein holdes Licht verdecken und verschließen.

> (I do not name you. Though by many I have heard
> you often named, and each one calls you his.
> Each eye believes its glance at you is aimed,
> for almost every eye your beam is painful.
> Ah, when I was errant I had many playmates,
> since I have known you I am almost alone:
> I must enjoy my fortune all by myself,
> and cover and lock up your gentle light.)

Proudly he announces the insight that distinguishes him from his fellows: no longer does he assume that the name provides direct access to a referent or that the naming of the object secures its possession. He desires to preserve the object of his love by refusing to communicate his newly acquired and symbolically mediated knowledge of her. This effort to seal the beloved object within the privacy and silence of his self elicits Truth's response:

> Kaum bist du Herr vom ersten Kinderwillen,
> So glaubst du dich schon Übermensch genug,
> Versäumst die Pflicht des Mannes zu erfüllen!

> (Scarce master of a childish kind of willing,
> you think yourself already superman,
> and neglect the duty of the man!)

Her lesson turns him away from adherence to his childish imago and steers him toward adulthood and speech.

The pedagogical intervention of the maternal figure proceeds across three stages: (1) she channels his errant desire by fixing it to herself as the source of happiness and contentment; (2) she teaches him that he can love her only by not directly possessing her; (3) she makes him into a poet/pedagogue, who accepts his adult duty of communicating his insights to others. Although the disciplining of the selfish boy into a responsible man involves prohibition and command, it is carried out in the most gentle and loving terms: she needs only to look at him for him to be able to read himself in her eyes. And it is this reading that—as in the texts of Goethe's predecessors—alters the wanderer's view from the mountaintop. Only when he has read himself in her eyes does he gain an unobstructed view of the valley below.

Here we can note the major difference between Goethe's poem and the texts of his predecessors. In Goethe's case, the modification of the wanderer's subjectivity is brought about not by the reading of a particular text containing certain prescriptions but by a specific manner of reading, a reading that treats a symbolical construct, an allegory, as if it were an immediate presence. It is a matter not of reading as decoding, but of reading imaged as the immediate recognition of the self in the eyes of the loving and gentle mother. Thus, when Truth presents the poet with the gift of the text—the veil of poetry—she in fact imparts to him a particular attitude toward language, an attitude that might be termed "illusionistic." The veil of poetry produces the illusion of a quasi-immediate access to the world. It produces a surface of reflection and refraction that offers an object to vision rather than signs to be read and deciphered.

The socializing function of poetic illusion illustrated by Goethe's "Zueignung" constitutes the subject matter of this book. In his appropriation of tradition Goethe substitutes the loving and understanding maternal agency of instruction for a masculine textual authority. The gift of illusionary transparency accompanies the gentle reorganization of the beholder's subjectivity through the imaginary union with the maternal gaze. In Goethe's text, the pedagogical process inserts itself exactly at the threshold of (that is to say, at the individual's moment of entry into) the symbolic order of language. But we should also keep in mind that this imaginary interchange with the maternal figure itself is produced in and through a symbolic construct: she is not the mother but an allegory. This conjunction of poetics, pedagogy, and perception exemplifies one of the major imperatives of Enlightenment culture. The Enlightenment postulates the aesthetic domain as the semiotic utopia of sheer transparency; it seeks to render the signs of art as diaphanous as Truth's veil and thereby to fulfill its educative mission. My hypothesis is that generic innovation in the eighteenth century can be interpreted in terms of this aesthetic-pedagogical program. By transforming the conventions regulating both the experience of texts and the textualization of experience, the eighteenth century developed new instruments for the fashioning of subjectivity. It is no accident that Goethe's allegory of poetic transparency stands at the head of his oeuvre.

II

My study of eighteenth-century generic innovation proceeds through close readings of literary texts that were to become paradigmatic for the epistolary novel, the bourgeois tragedy, Classical German Tragedy, and the bildungsroman. Since I want to understand these innovations as part of specific reorganizations of subjectivity and since, as we have seen in Goethe's poem, this pedagogical function is intimately involved with an ideal of signification, I place these new genres in the context of eighteenth-century theories of language and aesthetics.

In *The Order of Things*, Michel Foucault analyzes the periods traditional intellectual history has called the Age of Reason and the Enlightenment with regard to their more or less explicit relation to the sign. He demonstrates that one model of signification organizes such disparate disciplines of knowledge as natural history, economics, and linguistics.[4] This model of signification is animated by the hope that ideally a sign is a representation, a perfect duplicate of the thing represented. In his reading of Lessing's *Laokoon*, David Wellbery shows how eighteenth-century aesthetics not only is solidly grounded in the semiotics of the Age of Reason but also postulates art as the site where the cultural telos of transparency is proleptically achieved.[5] Although transparency theories of language and art have by no means disappeared, by the end of the eighteenth century they had lost their paradigmatic function of organizing the production of knowledge. In fact, in the "invention" of History and the sciences of Man and Life, Foucault identifies a radical break at the beginning of the nineteenth century.[6] With this epistemic break, semiotics yields to historical philology, and the representational model is replaced by an intransitive model of signification. No longer a perfect replica of the thing represented, the sign is rendered opaque and endowed with depth to the extent that it contains the accretions of its own historical development.[7]

Foucault's periodization allows us to isolate two distinct cultural paradigms organizing the conjunction of pedagogical and aesthetic concerns.

7

These cultural paradigms provide a historical framework for my analysis of generic innovation. I can thereby situate the mid-eighteenth-century emergence of the epistolary novel and the bourgeois tragedy in the context of the dominant concern for transparency, a concern equally compelling in French, English, and German discourse on aesthetics and semiotics. My discussion of Classical German Tragedy and the bildungsroman from the turn of the nineteenth century, however, abandons the European context and attends exclusively to the German preoccupation with the social function of art. Although the intransitive model of signification that marks the end of the Enlightenment paradigm of transparency is generally valid for what comparatists refer to as European Romanticism, the specific generic innovations rooted in this model of signification require that I narrow my focus to a single national context.

Indeed, from the beginning of the nineteenth century, European literatures start to evolve within clearly distinct national traditions. Only as long as the pedagogical function of poetic illusion is firmly situated within the transparency paradigm can we find a fair degree of similarity across European literatures. The reason for this is that the transparency model sees the formation of subjectivity in generic innovation accomplished through an obliteration of the artificiality of the poetic construct. The difference between art and life is canceled in an anti-theatrical fashion by including the reader/audience within the illusionary realm. The corresponding educational scenario is one of gentle integration of an individual into a family, in which paternal authority has weakened if not entirely vanished. By the turn of the century, however, pedagogy has to be understood in terms of its institutional dependency within the framework of the expanding modern state. Thus, the German model decisively departs from its European counterparts; the primary addressee of its pedagogical program is no longer the bourgeois male subject in general but that male subject who must be fashioned into a loyal civil servant within a locally defined state apparatus. In other words, at the turn of the nineteenth century generic innovation in Germany is shaped by the specifics of the German ideal of *Bildung*.

The theme of transparency and its vicissitudes has been treated in several recent studies of the period of concern here. Michael Fried's *Absorption and Theatricality* discusses Diderot's aesthetics of transparency as a theoretical frame for major generic innovations in eighteenth-century French painting. As Fried shows, the development of French painting between 1750 and 1760 can best be understood in terms of how the beholder is addressed by the painting and drawn into its fictional world. Paintings of the period elaborate what Fried calls an "anti-theatrical" mode of address: oblivious to the world around them and fully absorbed in their own activities, the painted figures pay no heed to the fact that they are part of a scene to be displayed. The external beholder is thus invited, as it were, to step into the painting and live the supreme fiction of being part of the world represented. The figures in these paintings behave, according to Fried, in conformity with Diderot's advice to stage actors: perform as if the curtain would never rise. Foucault describes a different (but related) sort of transparency. In *Discipline and Punish*, he sees the penal reforms of the eighteenth and early nineteenth centuries as a transition from a system based on the public spectacle of punishment to a disciplinary system aimed at resocializing the delinquent. The innovation, embodied in Bentham's Panopticon, requires a sophisticated system of surveillance to monitor the individual's internalization of authority. This institutional embodiment of transparency is joined with the aesthetic version discussed by Fried in John Bender's 1987 book, *Imagining the Penetentiary*, which compares the eighteenth-century penal reform movement in England with contemporary innovations in narrative fiction. Bender arrives at the fascinating conclusion that the new modes of novelistic discourse—which establish a closed fictional universe centered on a unified consciousness and thereby render even the details of everyday life meaningful—prefigure the architecture of the modern prison with its devices for the shaping of consciousness.

Finally, Friedrich Kittler's *Aufschreibesysteme, 1800/1900* demonstrates that German literature around 1800 produces and uses the hallucinatory sensuality of fiction exactly at the conjunction of the two institutions of motherhood and the civil service. By 1794, when the Prussian Territorial Law made breast-feeding one's own children obligatory, women were flooded with a wealth of detailed pedagogical advice on how to educate their children: the modern phonetic method of teaching children to read (advertized through this pedagogical literature) became the crucial step in the spreading of literacy. While motherhood was being "professionalized," the modern absolutist state of Prussia, rapidly expanding its bureaucratic net, took over the entire system of primary and secondary education and institutionalized the pedagogical training of teachers, who eventually became civil servants. On the basis of Kittler's research, it can be argued that the Enlightenment ideal of semiotic transparency achieved its institutional realization when the phonetic reading method was implemented.

In the first part of this study, I analyze the theory and practice of aesthetic transparency as it emerges around the middle of the eighteenth century. In particular, I argue that the supreme fiction of illusion—the reader's or spectator's absorption into the represented world—is realized through a set of anti-theatrical strategies that *veil* the materiality of the signifier, the structures of semiotic mediation, and the labor of artistic production. These strategies create the scenario for the formation of a disciplined subject, in Foucault's sense. Aesthetic transparency, in other words, serves an essentially pedagogical function. This point initially appears implausible: transparency, after all, is a model of signification that presupposes the neutrality of knowledge and the immediacy and objectivity of representation, and it therefore seems to exclude questions of the subject, affective economy, and authority. Nevertheless, starting around mid-century, the ideal of transparency found a very practical application in pedagogical reforms that deemphasized authority and tradition in favor of a quasi-natural acquisition of knowledge. Inevitably these reformers—one thinks in this connection of such figures as Jean-Jacques Rousseau (1712–78) and Johann Basedow (1723–90)—based their theories on the immediacy of the child's experiential access to the things of the world. The name given by German reformers to this transparent unmediated experience is *Anschaulichkeit*. My project in the first part of the book is to investigate how the paradigm of Anschaulichkeit is given concrete form through the two major generic innovations of the period, the epistolary novel and the bourgeois tragedy.

By the end of the eighteenth century, transparency no longer functions as a semiotic ideal. The Enlightenment model of the sign is superseded by the concept of intransitive, self-referential signification. Likewise, the aesthetic realm is no longer construed as perfect representation. It becomes, rather, the site of a particular kind of autonomy: the autonomy not only of the artwork itself but also of aesthetic production and reception. The same historical phase also witnesses the increasing national differentiation of literature as well as its dichotomization into high and low, true art and mass culture. Moreover, this dichotomization of art is part of a widening polarization of gender. Thus, the postulate of "autonomy" must be understood within extreme limitations; it can be applied not to all the literature of the period but only in the main to those literary texts later classified as belonging to German Classicism. Nor do I want to contradict the findings of Kittler and Bender that for most of the nineteenth century the transparency model is valid for the realm of fictional literature in general. Nevertheless, with regard to the specific generic innovations of the bildungsroman and Classical German Tragedy, I postulate a fundamentally new conjunction of pedagogy and aesthetics. The second part of my book suggests that the new pedagogical function of art entrusted to these genres emerges exactly at that moment when transparency is absorbed by the institutional reforms of an expanding state bureaucracy.

In order to name this second paradigm for the conjunction of aesthetic/ poetic and pedagogical concerns, I again borrow a term from the language of educational reformers and analyze the emergence of Classical German Tragedy and the bildungsroman as part of the project of Bildung. Whereas Anschaulichkeit as a didactic concept pertains mainly to the levels of primary and secondary school education, Bildung bears on the formation of teachers and civil servants, the primary agents of the state. The term assumes a programmatic function in the neo-humanist discourse of such educational theorists as Johann Gottlieb Herder (1744–1804) and Wilhelm von Humboldt (1767–1835). Inspired by cultural ideals from classical antiquity the proponents of Bildung aim at a "well-rounded" self-cultivation and character formation. In regard to questions of signification, the discourse of Bildung draws on the organicism of the intransitive and self-referential model for the classical/romantic symbol.

By establishing the two paradigms of Anschaulichkeit and Bildung, this book claims that the bourgeois tragedy and the epistolary novel participate in a contemporary pedagogical agenda and that even the bildungsroman and the Classical German Tragedy, two genres so intimately linked with the aesthetics of autonomy, can be understood as part of a scenario of subject formation. Thus, I do not relate individual literary texts to history by reading them as "reflections" of their times, nor do I grant them a privileged position from which they could serve as springboards for an emancipatory or conservative critique of society. Rather, my analyses of the individual texts work to show how emergent literary genres function as discursive models that organize new types of subjectivity.

III

> The slightest alteration in the relation between man
> and the signifier . . . changes the whole course of history
> by modifying the moorings that anchor his being.
>
> —Jacques Lacan, "The Agency of the Letter in
> the Unconscious," *Ecrits*, p. 174

Why would the deployment of a particular model of poetic illusion be such a powerful instrument of historical change? Psychoanalytic theory suggests an answer. Freud and Lacan have demonstrated that it is precisely at the threshold of representation that the affects and drives are organized into desire and specific emotions. At the moment of the individual's entry into language, both the object and the subject come into being through processes of identification and "othering." In his study of the infant's jubilant recognition of his own mirror image, Jacques Lacan shows that what looks like the most simple and fundamental moment of identification is in fact implicated in a complex process of mediation and delusion, which he calls *méconnaissance*, or "misrecognition." He argues that this assumption of the imago provides the matrix for the future functions of the ego. In its seeming unity and permanence as a gestalt, the mirror image furnishes a model for the Ideal I and a source of libidinal normalization. "But the important point is that this form situates the agency of the ego, before its social determination, in a fictional direction."[8]

This méconnaissance of the mirror stage does not merely represent a delusion that, once the infant has entered into discourse as a speaking subject, can be overcome. It is, rather, the basis of an enduring aspect or dimension of the subject's experience, which Lacan calls "the imaginary," that is operative in language insofar as the subject forgets or denies the extent to which the signifier separates it both from the "real things in the world" and from "itself as an entity." In other words, the imaginary asserts itself at that moment when the subject takes a signifier for a signified, mediation for immediacy, triangulated communication for a dyadic encounter—a moment beautifully enacted in Goethe's "Zueignung." To the extent that this book investigates the particular conjunction of the imaginary and the symbolic orders in poetic illusion, it is concerned with exactly that hinge of historical change which Lacan postulates in his dictum that alterations in the relation between man and the signifier have profound historical consequences.

However, it would not be especially fruitful to enter here into the complex and as yet unresolved debate regarding the validity of the various psychoanalytic models claiming to describe the negotiation between the pre-symbolic and symbolic stages in the formation of the ego. A basic premise of this study is that such negotiations are susceptible to historical change, that illusion does not always operate in the same manner or for the same purposes. Thus, I devote primary attention throughout to the actual eighteenth-century conceptualizations of the "veil of illusion" as it serves the implementation of virtue. In other words, I take my theoretical cue from the writers themselves and invoke current psychoanalytic models (especially of sublimation) only when they help to clarify a local issue.

Certainly the historical elaboration of man's relation to the signifier need not focus on the illusionary realm of literature. Why, then, did poetic illusion assume such a prominent position within the meta-semiotics of eighteenth-century culture? No doubt a full answer to this question would have to consider several factors, including the well-documented publishing boom of the period with its important implications for the sociology of reading. The overarching constellation that determined the centrality of poetic illusion, however, can best be glimpsed by considering the particular organization of the classical *episteme*, that relation which eighteenth-century culture entertains with language.

Wellbery has shown that Enlightenment culture holds a deeply ambivalent relationship toward language and the sign. On the one hand, its view is extremely optimistic: "Sign-use allows man to elevate himself beyond immediate sense experience and to grasp the world intellectually; it is the vehicle of cultural progress." The central tenet of this instrumental notion of language is the view that "at its origin, the sign is an arbitrarily selected name for an immediately apprehended mental representation."[9] However, although the arbitrariness frees man from the thrall of immediate sense impressions, it also prevents direct access to ideas and to the perceived world. The Enlightenment hopes that this fundamental ambivalence can be resolved in the aesthetic realm.

In fact, by the 1730's the new discipline of aesthetics begins to displace the traditional discipline of rhetoric. "In one and the same movement, art becomes the subject matter of theory and aesthetic experience is transformed into something that takes place between subjects and their representations, without the mediation of inherited bodies of erudition and independently of a locally defined cultural site." The value of art or literature is no longer discussed in terms of production, performance, or connoisseurship but instead in terms of universal features that relate to the general representational activity of the human soul. In the discourse of aesthetics, art becomes "a special form of representation" and is drawn "into the mental immanence of the ideational realm."[10]

In Wellbery's reading of Lessing's *Laokoon*, narrative poetry becomes the site where the ideal of semiotic transparency is achieved. As opposed to painting, poetry preserves the "advancements and advantages of semiosis . . . the representation remains ideal. But, in contrast to ordinary language, the perfected language of poetry recovers the experience of presence and communicates its contents immediately to intuition."[11] Lessing's fundamental question is: Which organization of signs, the spatial one of painting or the temporal one of poetry, most effectively instantiates the transparent structure of the natural sign? Although Lessing does not explicitly discuss particular genres, his description of poetry as a natural sign implicitly constitutes the matrix for further generic specifications. The manner in which signifier and signified are related distinguishes a natural sign from an arbitrary sign. Whereas for the arbitrary sign the two are merely yoked together by convention, the signifier of a natural sign is informed by the signified.

The signs of painting are motivated both materially and formally. Their spatial structure corresponds to the spatial structure of the corporeal object represented and the individual signs duplicate the material nature of that object insofar as they are solid, colored and fully determined as material things. The motivation of poetic signs, however, is only formal. The sign vehicles bear no similarity to the action-referent except as regards their successivity. The poem replicates only the form of perception, not its content. Poetry is a natural sign only because its signs present themselves to the reader in the same successive form as would the action itself. Poetry, therefore, maintains the advantages provided by its more advanced stage of semiosis; its individual signs remain arbitrary. The distinguishing feature of poetry is that it recovers for language the form of intuitive presence because the poem as a whole attains to the status of a natural sign.[12]

The notion of "the poem as a whole" immediately raises the issue of genre specification, for it is at the level of generic conventions that a text becomes a meaningful entity. The ideal of natural signification can be realized only through strategies that frame and organize an array of arbitrary signs as a coherent whole. Furthermore, since the formal organization or compositional structure of the text simulates an experiential apprehension of reality that is not symbolically mediated, the generic conventions can also be understood as providing a psychological mapping and programming of the recipient.

Hence the question from which my study takes its point of departure: How does the cultural program for the formation of a new type of subjectivity become attached to the production of new literary genres? To answer this question, it is necessary to demonstrate in detail how the interpenetration of pedagogy and aesthetics in the eighteenth century is not merely a matter of a structural homology between the two discursive fields. In other words, it needs to be shown that the aesthetics of transparency entails the question of the subject in a manner that generates the parameters for generic innovation. This is the task of Chapter 1, which outlines the project of Anschaulichkeit in the mid-eighteenth century as it evolves around discussions of the fable. The debate on the nature and function of the fable—in traditional rhetorical theory the genre that combines training in verbal skills with moral instruction and the formation of the student's character—illustrates the transition from a rhetorical culture of spectacle to the new ideological and institutional position of aesthetics and literature. I analyze the fable not as an isolated literary genre but as a node in Enlightenment discourse at which the question of the relationship between subject and sign is articulated. The debate on the fable is a discursive locus at which the concerns of epistemology, semiotics, aesthetics, didactics, and pedagogy intersect, at which discontents with the cultural achievements of rationality are voiced and remedies are sought. By placing Richardson's, Lessing's, and Rousseau's views on the pedagogical efficacy of the fable in the context of semiotic theory (Warburton, Condillac) and aesthetics (Diderot), I show how, on the one hand, the fable, parable, *image sensible*, and hieroglyph are praised for their immediate persuasiveness and yet, on the other hand, are conceived as semiotic constructs to be overcome if analytic reasoning is to progress. This loss of immediacy, however, is not accepted without attempts at recuperation: the abstractness of language is compensated by the hallucinatory effects of silent reading (in Condillac's epistemology), the *tableau* (in Diderot's aesthetics of immediacy), and the image of the ideal woman (in Rousseau's pedagogy).

Nowhere are the strategies and politics of eighteenth-century subject formation more consistently articulated than in the writings of Rousseau. In his reprise of the debate on the fable toward the end of *Emile*, shortly before the construction of Sophie as the ideal woman, he supplements the pedagogical function of the fable with the power of specific fictions, which captivate and control Emile as he is released from his tutor's authority and enters worldly society. In this passage, Rousseau elaborates the metaphor of the veil of illusion ("le voile du prestige"), which I have adopted for the title of this book. As Rousseau's text shows (and as we have already observed with reference to Goethe's "Zueignung"), the veil condenses semiotic, poetic, and pedagogical concerns. The subject of semiotics must be understood in its gendered dynamics. My reading of Rousseau's *Lettre à M. d'Alembert* shows that the anti-theatrical literary genres of the age of transparency are conceived primarily as instruments for disciplining the male bourgeois subject. The woman remains a supplementary fiction.

Chapter 2 analyzes the framing conventions of Richardson's epistolary novel and those of Diderot's and Lessing's bourgeois tragedy as rejections of a "frivolous" performance-oriented theatricality in favor of an aesthetics of illusion that constructs its recipient as a private, absorbed consumer. Although both genres aim at the moral improvement of the reader/audience within the project of Anschaulichkeit, the means for achieving this improvement are quite different. At issue in the epistolary novel is a specific attitude toward writing and reading, a certain semio-technology of documentation; in bourgeois tragedy, the central issue is the affective economy of the subject. In order to localize the differences between these two generic strategies, I focus on how each develops what was to become the anthropological "deep value" of the period: sympathy or pity. In *Clarissa*, pity or empathy plays a constitutive role in the construction of the exemplary woman as well as in the reform of the rake; however, only in the bourgeois tragedy—in particular, in Lessing's theoretization of the genre and in his dramatic response to *Clarissa* (i.e., *Miß Sara Sampson*)—does pity prove to be the central or organizing value of the literary construct.

Chapter 3 analyzes Rousseau's *Julie* as a more complex model for the reorganization of subjectivity than that of Richardson. In *Clarissa*, the heroine's "writing to the moment" is by itself the sufficient condition of "truth" and "virtue." As mirrors of the soul, her letters become instruments of reflection, of critical self-examination before the gaze of an authority that sees through ruse and disguise. Rousseau, however, does not rely on the letter as mirror. For him writing does not produce this smooth surface of reflection. Writing and reading produce only illusions and desire. Therefore, the way to moral reform leads through a superior illusion that channels desire and tames the imagination. Additionally, with Rousseau's novel the focus of the family romance shifts from an "ideal" father/daughter paradigm to one of a tender attachment to a mother/lover figure. With that shift of focus, another dimension comes into play: the paternal authority is replaced by a maternal agency in the service of a new social order, the modern state. Saint-Preux, the tutor of an older, aristocratic order, is reprogrammed to become an educator in a new social order. In this sense, I read *Julie* as a model of the education of the educator in the absence of a primary authorial/educational agency. My reading of the novel examines this process as one that draws its formative force from love and its illusions. I show how Saint-Preux's passion for Julie is an intervention in his psyche at exactly that threshold where the subject comes into being: the threshold that organizes his affective economy and defines for him referentiality in language. But although Rousseau complicates the semiotics of transparency and illusion, his epistolary novel still remains within the larger paradigm of Anschaulichkeit.

By the 1770's, particularly within a German context, a new model of a male subjectivity emerges under the name of Bildung. Chapter 4 charts major shifts of emphasis in the conjunction of the semiotic, aesthetic, and pedagogical concerns described in Chapter 1 as the project of Anschaulichkeit. These changes can be observed in the field of semiotics in the rejection of the arbitrary nature of the sign, and in the field of aesthetics in the privileging of sculpture as opposed to the previously valorized tableau. In addition, the discussion of sensory perception places hearing and the sense of touch above the sense of sight, and in pedagogy and anthropology a stress on freedom and autonomy as *the* markers of Humanity (*Humanität*) replaces the former emphasis on sensibility and pity. The antitheatrical genres of the epistolary novel and the bourgeois tragedy, which tended to veil the artificiality of the aesthetic object, become "trivial literature," and true or genuine art is proclaimed an autonomous institution in a revalorizing of aesthetic distance and the spectacle. I interpret the project of Bildung as the emergence of a new type of "interface," a new type of "suture," between subjectivity and representation. Like Chapter 1, Chapter 4 establishes a model that helps to understand both the rise of two new literary genres (the German Classical drama and the bildungsroman) and a new layer in the genealogy of the modern disciplined subject. This subject is modeled on a particular ideal of sublimation that, in my view, can be understood as a version of male narcissism.

Chapter 4 examines the general model of Bildung as it is elaborated in Herder's theory of language and in the aesthetic theories of Moritz and Schiller, and Chapter 5 focuses on how the more concrete institutional effects of this educational ideal are worked out in Schiller's *Maria Stuart* and Wieland's *Agathon*. I relate the emergence of Classical German Tragedy and the bildungsroman to the reforms that expanded the modern state bureaucracy and educational system. In this light *Maria Stuart* appears as a drama about the loss of spectacle and "transparency" in the political realm, *Agathon* as the script for the sublimation of a "civil servant" in training. In both texts male subjects are no longer disciplined through love and illusion but through a mobilization of their defense mechanisms against a disruptive feminine sexuality.

1

The Project of Anschaulichkeit in the Mid-eighteenth Century

The term *Anschaulichkeit* cannot easily be translated, but a rough English approximation would be "clearness," or "distinctness." For the adjective *anschaulich* English provides "clear," "graphic," "vivid," "evident," or "obvious." When illustrations or examples present a complex issue so graphically that we are led to say "Ah, now I see your point!" we find the same allusion to visual perception preserved in the verb *anschauen* ("to look at," "to view," "to consider"). But what do we see, when we say "I see"? We "see" the meaning, the signified, of a verbal message as if it were given to our visual perception. What we do not see is the medium of the message (book, print, engraving, voice, gestures), nor do we see the system of signifiers (which would engender not a "sight" but only an endless chain of translations). In this sense, Anschaulichkeit is a strategy for anchoring the referential illusion of language. If we consider the function of what is called *Anschauungsmaterial*, that is, the props of modern school didactics (stuffed animals, skeletons, diesel engines, audiovisual equipment), we realize that insights, self-evidentiality, and truth are established not so much through the authority of books or teachers but through a specific placement of students vis-à-vis language and the media of representation. The demand for Anschaulichkeit, then, must imply a dissatisfaction with the way language is perceived to work. I would demand more Anschaulichkeit if I thought that the presentation of certain issues were too abstract or embedded in an inaccessible terminology, or if a text struck me as mere words on the page instead of a meaning that could be assimilated into my experience. Privileging certain perceptual modes and veiling the signifying praxis, Anschaulichkeit becomes an intervention in and a constitutive part of the experience of the subject.

In this chapter I argue that the demand for Anschaulichkeit, or the project of Anschaulichkeit, informed the major literary reforms of the mid-eighteenth century. It led to the production of new literary genres as well as to the reorganization of subjectivity. Anschaulichkeit, as part of the concern for the semiotic ideal of a transparent language, is implicated in the contradictions of this ideal, for Anschaulichkeit is an ideal quality of texts and representations that precisely denies their status as mere representations and ignores textual ambiguities and rhetorical intricacies. What I hope to show in tracing formulations of this project is the mid-eighteenth-century's discontent with the role and function of language and representation, a dissatisfaction that locates Anschaulichkeit in a lost stage of the history of language and attempts to compensate for this loss: a compensatory effort that found its first expression in the Richardsonian epistolary novel and in bourgeois tragedy.

Eighteenth-century formulations about the role and function of representations imply a certain notion of subjectivity, for mid-eighteenth-century aesthetics, poetics, semiotics, and pedagogy—the disciplines involved in the production of Anschaulichkeit—quite explicitly produce the knowledge of an individual psychic constellation. They are concerned with understanding the operations of the soul and the role and function of the lower faculties and with relating this psychic apparatus to language, representations, and knowledge. In fact, the discourses involved in the production of Anschaulichkeit can also be described in terms of their emergence as new fields of knowledge that were to conceive the modern individualized and disciplined subject. Replacing traditional drill patterns, Anschaulichkeit becomes a major objective of a didactics that attempts to bring the world of words and that of things into intimate relation by stressing sense perception and individual experience. Without Anschaulichkeit modern pedagogy would not be able to replace external authority and rules by love and an internalization of authority. And, for the new academic discipline of aesthetics, with its focus on the lower faculties, imagination, and intuitive cognition, Anschaulichkeit becomes a central issue in its displacement of traditional rhetoric. Whereas rhetoric emphasizes public performance and figurative language and implies a public persona or connoisseur as a subject of speech or as addressee, the new aesthetics constructs its subject as a private, absorbed consumer.

Why is the fable a particularly good introduction to the project of Anschaulichkeit? Since antiquity, the fable had been a well-established genre for teaching linguistic and rhetorical skills in conjunction with training the student's moral character. But before the eighteenth century, there were few attempts to write or edit fables specifically for children just as there was no broad and institutionalized concept of school didactics.[1] In the first half of the eighteenth century, the fable aroused a great deal of interest, expressed in theoretical discussions as well as in new editions of traditional fables and in attempts to reform the genre.[2] The scrutiny this popular type of parabolic speech underwent between 1730 and 1760 highlights the formulation and reformulation of questions about the kind of truth that can be produced in discourse and about the subject's position vis-à-vis language.[3] Since it is in this debate over the fable that the ideals of a transparency model of signification are formulated with regard to the position of the subject, the discussion of the fable becomes an exemplary site for the articulation of generic innovation in the context of a new model of subjectivity. In fact, exactly those authors who were to launch the prototypes of the new epistolary novel and the bourgeois tragedy spearheaded the debate about the semiotic and pedagogical efficacy of the fable. Richardson and Lessing undertook to reform the genre. Although Diderot did not address the fable explicitly, his notion of the tableau, which was to become a key term for the anti-theatrical poetics of the bourgeois tragedy, emerges from the fable debate. "Tableau" needs to be understood in the context of Condillac's assessment of the fable and hieroglyph as prototypes of a particularly "graphic" means of signification, which—though left behind by the history of semiosis—can be resuscitated in the contemporary praxis of a silent hallucinatory reading and a theater of identification and illusion. The key to understanding the nexus of pedagogy and poetics can be found in Rousseau's discussion of the use and abuse of the fable for the education of Emile. There he formulates quite explicitly the strategic importance of generic considerations in disciplining the modern subject.

The Limitations of the Fable as a Means of Instruction

Before writing the period's best-selling epistolary novels, Samuel Richardson edited and revised Roger l'Estrange's edition of Aesop's fables. Richardson's duodecimo edition signals an effort to insert the fable into a new context of communication, since it was to be much cheaper and more easily available to a growing reading audience than l'Estrange's folio had been. Moreover, by purging l'Estrange's edition of its open political (royalist and popish) partisanship as well as of any crude or "lewd" diction, Richardson directed l'Estrange's *Aesop* to the general public. Like l'Estrange and l'Estrange's opponent Samuel Croxall, Richardson located the efficacy of the fable in its ability to imprint the moral message onto the tabula rasa–

like mind of the child. John Locke had earlier explicitly mentioned the instructive value of Aesop's fables and emphasized the didactic advantages of illustrations: "If his [the child's] *Aesop* has pictures in it, it will entertain him much the better, and encourage him to read, when it carries the increase of knowledge with it; for such visible objects children hear talked of in vain, and without satisfaction, whilst they have no ideas of them; those ideas being not to be had from sounds, but from the things themselves, or their pictures."[4] In his edition of Aesop's fables, Richardson carried Locke's advice even further than l'Estrange, whose edition had only 250 engravings for 500 fables.

As we are sensible of the alluring force which cuts or pictures, suited to the respective subjects, have on the minds of children, we have in a quite new manner engraved on copper-plates, at no small expense, the subject of every fable; and presume, that the little trouble which children will have to turn to the cuts, as ten of them are included in one plate, will rather excite their curiosity, and stimulate their attention, than puzzle or confuse them, especially as the readers are distinctly referred both to page and fable in every representation.[7]   (preface, p. 12)

And indeed, not only does Richardson not spare himself any expense in trying to achieve a perfect symmetry between illustrations and fables, but he also tries to strengthen the moral impact of each fable by revising l'Estrange's statements of the moral and by amplifying l'Estrange's appended "Reflections" on the application of the moral.[5]

However, the proliferation of commentaries seems to indicate that Locke's mechanism of imprinting moral messages as pictures on the mind does not work as easily as the philosopher supposed: " 'This *Rhapsody of Fables*,' says he [Roger l'Estrange], 'is a book universally read, and taught in all our schools; but almost at such a rate as we teach *Pyes* and *Parrots*, that pronounce the words without so much as guessing at the meaning of them: or to take it another way, the boys break their teeth upon the shells, without ever coming near the kernel' " (preface, p. 2). Richardson excised 58 fables from l'Estrange's collection, in order to avoid redundancy or empty verbosity "as being either of the like nature, and affording the like morals and reflections with others inserted; or from which some pertinent morals could not be drawn" (p. 12). To 96 other fables, "we have presumed to give entirely either new morals or new reflections, as we thought the design of the fables more naturally required, in order to direct them to general use; or to avoid party or political reflections" (p. 13). Another 208 fables from l'Estrange's edition were omitted "as being rather to be deemed witty conceits, facetious Tales, and sometimes ludicrous stories, than instructive apologues" (p. 13). The noise of frivolous language seems to endanger the

Fig. 1. Richardson, Aesop's Fables (1740?), plate 2. Although inserted into the text, the illustrations lose much of their immediate appeal and graphicity because the reader has to turn to the appropriate page to connect each picture with the corresponding fable.

pedagogical efficacy of the fable and necessitate abundant commentaries; an " 'emblem without a key to it, is no more than a *Tale of a Tub*; and that silily told too, is but one folly grafted upon another' " (p. 3; Richardson is quoting l'Estrange).

Twenty years later, Rousseau can no longer grant the fable any role in the instruction of children. In fact he rejects the supposed usefulness of fables and claims that they are potentially quite dangerous in the hands of children: "For the words are no more the fable than the words of history are history. How can people be so blind as to call fables the child's system of morals, without considering that the child is not only amused by the apologue but misled by it? He is attracted by what is false and he misses the truth, and the means adopted to make the teaching pleasant prevent him profiting by it" (*Emile*, pp. 139, 77). In a line-by-line analysis of La Fontaine's "The Crow and the Fox," Rousseau demonstrates the frivolous and even pernicious impact of that fable on the mind of a child. Projecting himself into the naive position of a *puer* entering the age of reason, Rousseau identifies those features of La Fontaine's text that cause bewilderment to block instruction: the syntax is inverted in accord with the practices of poetry, the nouns lack the precision of a specific referent, the diction is arcane, and the actors are codified according to poetic convention: "You must explain what a fox is, and distinguish between the real fox and the conventional fox of the fable" (pp. 141, 78). The action itself lacks verisimilitude, since it distorts the representation of sense perception in presenting the fox as attracted by the smell of cheese. And is it not the last straw that fox and crow are supposed to speak the same language? The fox's use of "monsieur," a title of honor, must teach the child to deride authority before understanding when this title is appropriate. Then, there is the frivolity of redundant formulations: "The child, finding the same thing repeated twice over in different words, is learning to speak carelessly" (pp. 141–42, 78). Thus the child is confused by the complexity of the fable's construction, by the duplicity of its language, and its shifting uncertainty: " 'Without lying.' So people do tell lies sometimes. What will the child think of you if you tell him the fox only says 'sans mentir' because he is lying?" (pp. 142, 78) Furthermore, the fox's flattering suggestion that the crow's plumage could somehow correspond to his voice implies an episteme grounded in a system of resemblances that, in the classical age, was rapidly disappearing.[6] " 'Answered!' What does that mean? Try to make the child compare qualities so different as those of song and plumage; you will see how much he understands" (pp. 142, 78). Although Rousseau rejects the implication of a system of resemblances, he approves of the idea of exchange. " 'No doubt, this lesson is well worth a cheese.'—This is intelligible and its meaning is very good. Yet there are few children who could compare a cheese and a lesson, few who would not prefer the cheese. You will therefore have to make them understand that this is said in mockery" (pp. 143, 79). Yet this exchange requires an abstraction, the differentiation of use and exchange value, that would make the disparate entities of lesson and cheese comparable goods. Furthermore, the cheese can have an exchange value only if its consumption is deferred. Therefore, the operation of abstraction, which implies the deferral of gratification, is too complex for the immediate response of the child. In addition, a child will always identify with the stronger character or the winner, and therefore the child's understanding will pervert the authorial intention: "So from the first of these fables the child learns the basest flattery" (pp. 144, 80).

In brief, the fable is an inadequate means of instructing Emile, the child who will be the prototype of the modern disciplined subject. This new subject will be educated in a gentle way, away from the show and displays of *le monde*; he will learn to deal with immediate situations through his own experience and in accordance with his perceptions and natural abilities.

Young teacher, I am setting before you a difficult task, the art of controlling without precepts, and doing everything without doing anything at all.   (pp. 149, 84)

You leave him master of his own wishes, but you do not multiply his caprices. When he only does what he wants, he will soon only do what he ought, and although his body is constantly in motion, so far as his sensible and present interests are concerned, you will find him developing all the reason of which he is capable, far better and in a manner much better fitted for him than in purely theoretical studies.

Thus when he does not find you continually thwarting him, when he no longer distrusts you, no longer has anything to conceal from you, he will neither tell you lies nor deceive you; he will show himself fearlessly as he really is, and you can study him at your ease, and surround him with all the lessons you would have him learn, without awakening his suspicions.   (pp. 151, 85)

These scenarios for learning are laid out through the invisible guidance of Emile's instructor. Such education will prevent any mutiny by the student; there will be no external and explicit rules against which the student could rebel, since the teacher exercises his influence by manipulating the child's faculties and his soul. The discipline Emile acquires grows invisibly, taking the pupil, as it were, unaware.

Like Locke and Richardson, Rousseau believes that the mind of the child is a tabula rasa, and he also sees the dangers of imprinting empty words on it: "Their shining, polished brain reflects, as in a mirror, the things you show them, but nothing sinks in. The child remembers the words and the ideas are reflected back; his hearers understand them, but to him they are meaningless" (pp. 132, 71). And he proceeds to explain what occasions the child's parroting capacity.

Before the age of reason the child receives images, not ideas; and there is this difference between them: images are merely the picture of external objects, while ideas are notions about those objects determined by their relations. An image when it is recalled may exist by itself in the mind, but every idea implies other ideas. When we image we merely perceive, when we reason we compare. Our sensations are merely passive, our notions or ideas spring from an active principle which judges. . . . As children are incapable of judging, they have no true memory. They retain sounds, form, sensation, but rarely ideas, and still more rarely relations.   (pp. 132–33, 72)

Since the images reflect only the thing itself and not, like the *idées*, the network of relationships among things, there is the danger that Emile will become fixated at the level of symbols, without being able to ground those in a stable set of regulated representations. For this reason Emile must not learn foreign languages, geography, heraldry, or any other code or system of symbolic representation: "In any study whatsoever the symbols are of no value without the idea of the things symbolised" (pp. 135, 73). And it is here that we can locate the most detrimental effect of La Fontaine's fable: since the fox proves to be an unscrupulous manipulator of a societal code as an empty, shifting chain of signifiers, the child has only the two options of either becoming a fox or being utterly confused.

Richardson's attempts at improving l'Estrange's edition of Aesopian fables and Rousseau's critique of the genre display a certain discontent with its ability to make a moral message obvious and immediately understandable. Whereas Richardson gets caught in the paradox of adding more and more commentary in order to purify the moral message of mere frivolous verbosity, Rousseau states the problem outright: the world of our experience of things is separated from the world of language and systems of symbolic representations. On the one hand, this gap is necessary: for language to work as a system of representation, the cheese cannot be devoured. The difference between signified and signifier is crucial. But if the child has not yet learned the necessary deferral of gratification, the mere introduction of a symbolic system without the law governing its point of reference will lead the student into confusion or trickery. Thus, on the other hand, this gap has to be closed; the moral value, the authority and law, governing the system of representations has to become immediate, unquestionably anchored in the student's experience. Emile cannot be introduced to morality via the fable, since the fable, with its explicit literariness, merely emphasizes the gap between experiential reality and a symbolic code. In order to understand better this discontent with the fable, and in a broader sense the critique of language, let us now turn to another attempt at reforming the genre.

Just two years before the publication of *Emile*, Gotthold Ephraim Lessing published his own collection of fables (*Fabeln*) along with a treatise on the genre and an appendix on the heuristic use of the fable in school (*Abhandlungen*). Lessing had previously translated and edited Richardson's edition of Roger l'Estrange's *Aesop* and in a preface had praised Richardson's work.[7] Like the fables of his Richardson translation, Lessing's own fables subsequent to this translation are written in prose as opposed to his earlier use of verse to write fables. Lessing has come to reject all poetic ornament and to demand that the fable aim at utmost economy and perspicuity in illustrating the moral.[8] Lessing's poetics of the fable is summed up in his poetological fable "Der Besitzer des Bogens."

The Owner of the Bow

A man had a perfectly balanced bow that allowed him to shoot far and to aim securely. He treasured it immensely. Once, however, when he looked at it attentively, he said: "And yet you are a bit too plain. Your only ornament is your smoothness. What a pity!" However, he found a means to remedy this. He decided he would go and let the best artist carve pictures into the bow. He went; and the artist carved an entire hunt into the bow; and what would have been more proper for a bow than a hunt?

The man was full of joy. "You deserve all these ornaments, my dear bow!" He wants to try it out; he strings it, and the bow breaks.   (*Fabeln*, p. 219)[9]

The fable has to be "perfectly balanced" (the German reads *trefflich*), like the once beautiful and functional bow. Once it is reduced to an ornament, the bow has become a mere duplication on the level of representations and thereby useless in practical terms. The point is proven when the owner attempts to use the decorated bow; weakened by the ornamental carvings, it breaks. In terms of the practical functionality of the fable, the story teaches that the fable has to present its moral to the reader in the graphic way that Lessing calls Anschaulichkeit.[10] This Anschaulichkeit, however, can no longer be achieved through a mere pictorial representation, as Richardson still hoped to do by including an illustration of each fable.[11] A mere pictorial representation would remain on the level of the signifier, one representation pointing to the other without reaching its aim, the understanding of the reader. The cumbersomeness of the procedure is ironically contained in Richardson's description of how the illustrations are supposed to work: "Readers are distinctly referred both to page and fable in every representation."[12] Nor can Anschaulichkeit be achieved through a proliferation of commentaries. In brief, the fable itself has to be transformed in order to resist its decay into mere ornament and to guarantee that it has its intended effect on the reader.

Lessing, too, does not recommend the fable for mere rhetorical wordplay. In his appendix on the heuristic use of the fable in school, he proposes this genre as a means of exercising the student's critical understanding and judgment and suggests the modification of traditional fables. For instance, the fable of the fox and the crow could be transformed by supposing that the piece of meat is poisoned.[13] And indeed, Lessing followed his own suggestion in this version of the fable.

The Raven and the Fox

In his claws a raven carried away a piece of poisoned meat, which the irate gardener had thrown out for the neighbor's cats.

And he was just about to devour it on an old oak tree when the fox sneaked up to him and called to him: "Blessed be thou, bird of Jupiter!"

"For whom do you take me?" the raven asked.

"For whom I take you?" the fox replied. "Are you not the brave eagle who daily descends from the right hand of Zeus to this oak tree in order to feed poor me? Why do you feign to be somebody else? Don't I see in the victorious claw the prayed-for gift, which your god continues to send to me through you?"

The raven was puzzled and very happy to be taken for an eagle. I must, he thought, not disabuse him of this error. Magnanimously stupid, he dropped his prey and proudly flew away. Laughingly the fox caught the meat and ate it with malign joy. But soon the joy was turned into a painful feeling; the poison started to work, and he croaked.

May you never gain through praise anything but poison, you damned flatterers! (p. 212)

Through this version of the fable, Lessing articulates a radical critique of Aesop and La Fontaine. Particularly aimed at their attitude toward language, it is a critique Lessing largely shares with Rousseau. Rousseau feared a possible identification with the trickster fox as the winner in this story. In Lessing's fable, the fox is cruelly punished for his flattery. The fox no longer flatters the raven for his outward appearance but abuses a code of a social and religious hierarchy by suggesting to the raven that he is the eagle of Zeus, a manipulation of social codes and conventions Rousseau also criticizes (*Emile*, p. 141). Furthermore, in Lessing's version of the fable the raven—like Rousseau's student—learns nothing when he loses the meat. What La Fontaine formulates as a neat exchange (a piece of cheese for the caution against flattery) and what Rousseau approves of as a system of deferral and exchange opposed to the bewildering play of resemblances, Lessing does away with altogether. The quid pro quo of a sign as a representation has totally lost its point of anchorage. The raven is saved from an accidental death by mere chance. Instead of a piece of cheese, he takes something resembling something to eat. The appearances are utterly deceiving: the raven should not have trusted his eyes to begin with. Immediate gratification ends in death. Furthermore, Lessing adds to the Aesopian fable an irate gardener who wants to poison his neighbor's cats. But this piece of meat does not reach its initial destination. The gardener's manipulation of the world of signs with its unintentional effects raises theological questions related to this "irate" gardener, questions about Providence, the course of history, its meaning, and the writing of history, questions of major concern in Lessing's theological battles and disputes about the status of Scripture.

Lessing's fable is situated in a world where seeing, reading, and understanding no longer occupy the same plane.[14] For Lessing, as for Rousseau, signs are no longer marks scattered throughout the world in order to be seen and read; rather, they constitute a realm apart from visible, experiential reality. Similarly, history is external to historiography; as Rousseau states, the words of history must not be confused with history itself. Lessing also doubts the instructive value of historical anecdotes. Deprived of an overall perspective on the general providential design of History, the account of an individual historical incident could easily seem marvelous or insignificant. It tends to lack any persuasive force or *Wirklichkeit*, however true to the facts it might be: "Since you cannot demonstrate historical truth, you also cannot demonstrate something through historical truths. That is to say: accidental truths of history can never become the proof of necessary truths of reason."[15] Lessing introduces the term "Wirklichkeit" in order to negotiate the gap separating the world of individual, concrete things, facts, and events accessible to our intuitive cognition from the realm of abstract reason open only to our symbolic understanding.[16] Wirklichkeit means both the facticity of actual events and the efficacy and vividness of an impression on our imagination. The term indicates the slippage from an actual facticity to the efficacy and vividness of an impression produced by a representation: "Since therefore only and exclusively the internal probability can make me believe in the former reality of a case, and since this internal probability can equally be found in a fictional case, what would be able to make the reality of the first more persuasive for me than the reality of the other?" (*Abhandlungen*, p. 446) Wirklichkeit allows Lessing to fuse a correspondence theory of truth (referentiality) with a theory of coherence (logic of plausibility) in an aesthetic theory of illusion. The illusionist technique becomes the means by which the poet compensates for the lost access to the world outside language: "Since historical truth is not always also probable . . . [since] the poet, however, has the power and liberty to deviate from nature in this respect and to make everything that he claims to be true also probable, therefore I should think it clear that generally speaking fables deserve to be preferred to historical examples" (*Abhandlungen*, p. 446). In terms of a generic classification, Lessing situates the fable between the historical anecdote and the parable. From the former it borrows Wirklichkeit, the illusion of facticity, by narrating an individual incident; from the latter it borrows all the cohesion of a general, symbolic truth without appearing to be a mere illustration or example for the general truth. Whereas the parable always requires the translation into the general maxim via our symbolic understanding, the fable has an immediate impact on our will: "Since, compared to a sentence that is symbolically formulated, our intuitive cognition allows us to gain a quicker overall understanding of a sentence and to recognize more motivations in it, intuitive cognition also has a far greater influence on the will than does symbolic understanding" (*Abhandlungen*, p. 443). Note how Lessing slides from sign motivation to psychological motivation. The fable achieves its vivid and immediate impact on the will by sparing the recipient any necessity of decoding. In other words, the decoding effort becomes "naturalized" by making the moral message of the fable part of the depicted outcome of the particular story. This necessitates brevity and unity of action. Furthermore, the aim of the fable is achieved through its use of animals as characters: "You hear: *Britannicus and Nero*. How many people understand what they are hearing? Who was the first? Who was the latter? In which relationship do they stand to each other?—But you hear: *the wolf and the lamb*; everybody understands immediately what he hears and understands how the one relates to the other. These words that straightaway evoke in us certain images further the intuitive cognition, which is hindered by those names. Even those who are not unfamiliar with those names will certainly not all think of exactly the same thing" (*Abhandlungen*, p. 451). The animal characters of the fable repertoire have a dual advantage: they represent concrete individuals, and they are endowed with stable and universally known qualities.[17] The vocabulary of natural kinds evokes the concreteness of a fully described individual to an extent that proper names never can. Whereas for Rousseau there was still the problem of how the child should know to decode the character of the fable animal, for Lessing the apparently non-decodable, "self-evident" character of the fable animal and the tightly unified action of the narrative bridge the gap between seeing and reading. Generic conventions have become the site for the naturalization of the sign.

Lessing's attempts at reforming the genre of the fable demonstrate the search for a particular signifying economy as the most important feature of the genre under consideration. In the context of the Enlightenment concern for transparent representations, the fable serves, so to speak, as a test case for semiotic engineering. Lessing's reforms of the fable can be thus characterized as the response to the dissatisfaction expressed in Richardson's revision of l'Estrange's *Aesop*, when Richardson tries to free the genre from ambiguity and rhetorical extravagance. Lessing's version of "The Fox and the Crow" addresses the same issues that make Rousseau reject the genre altogether. Like Rousseau, Lessing rejects the rhetoricity of the fable, but he also attempts to rescue the genre by reconceiving it in aesthetic terms. But before we can follow in greater detail how a rhetorics of persuasion is displaced by an aesthetics of illusion, we must gain a clearer understanding of the eighteenth-century semiotic discussion that forms the context for the reconceptualization of the fable traced here. In order to get a more precise understanding of this signifying economy, of how exactly the fable is supposed to achieve its vivid impact on the imagination and will of the recipient, it is necessary to discuss this genre within the context of semiotics and epistemology as developed by Condillac.

The Fable in the Context of Semiotics

Condillac's *Essai sur l'origine des connaissances humaines* (1746), the central text for this and the next section, offers another perspective on the project of Anschaulichkeit.[18] On the one hand, it reveals the fundamental ambivalence of the eighteenth century toward language in the conceptualization of the history of semiosis. In this respect the Anschaulichkeit of the fable is considered an effect of a particular semiotic constellation, which had to be sacrificed for analytic reasoning to progress. On the other hand, the rhetorical strategies employed in the *Essai* attempt to compensate for this loss; that is, Condillac's text itself manages to produce a new form of Anschaulichkeit that draws on the hallucinatory praxis of silent reading as *the* central cultural experience of texts. My reading of Condillac in this section focuses on the second part of the *Essai*, in which he gives a historical account of the development of language and the progress of knowledge, a history in which the fable holds a special position. In the subsequent section, I focus on the first part of the *Essai* in order to draw out the parallel between crucial operations of the soul and that stage in the history of language occupied by the fable. I give particular attention to Condillac's conceptualization of the various media of representation, since specific manipulations of these media are crucial for Condillac's handling of his argument with Locke.

Condillac discusses the fable in the penultimate chapter of part one of the second half of the *Essai*, entitled "Du language et de la methode." His argument about the history of semiosis and the fable follows William Warburton's chapter on hieroglyphics from the *Divine Legation of Moses* (1738–41).[19] What is particularly instructive about Condillac's and Warburton's discussion of the fable is their construction of the discursive genre of the fable as a particular semiotic constellation vis-à-vis a particular code and medium. The semiotic status of the fable is considered comparable to that of the hieroglyph: the fable is to speech as the hieroglyph is to writing. Any mode of expression or communication is grounded in the insufficiencies of primitive human languages. This necessitates a semiotic economy in which various media complement each other. Fable and hieroglyph manage to achieve a momentary transparency by establishing a tenuous and highly unstable balance between reading and seeing, as well as between esoteric and exoteric knowledge. The efficacy of hieroglyph and fable is intricately related to that moment in the history of semiosis when they are the means by which different codes and media can meet and complement each other.

Condillac states the underlying model of semiosis: "It evidently appears, that at the origin of languages mankind were under a necessity of joining the mode of speaking by action to that of articulate sounds, and of conveying their thoughts by sensible images" (pp. 256, 279). And Warburton writes: "Thus we see the *common Foundation* of all these various Modes of *Writing* and *Speaking*, was a *Picture* or *Image*, presented to the Imagination thro' the Eyes or Ears, which being the simplest and most universal of all kinds of Information, (the first [i.e., hieroglyphs] reaching where the arbitrary Characters of an Alphabet could not be deciphered, and the latter [i.e., fables] where abstract Terms were not comprehended,) we must needs conclude them to be the natural Inventions of Necessity" (p. 95). Clearly, we would miss the point of Condillac's or Warburton's sophisticated discussion of the hieroglyph and the fable if we took their invocation

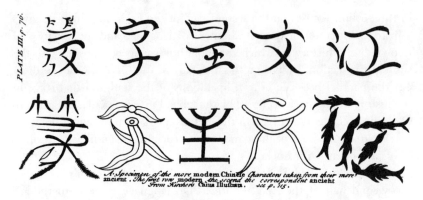

Fig. 2. Warburton, The Divine Legation of Moses *(1738). Warburton uses this illustration from Kirchner's* China Illustrata *to show the gradual growth of abstraction in the development of Chinese characters. For example, the modern sign for river (upper righthand corner) was originally a design composed of six fish.*

of "origins" or their appeal to the "natural Inventions of Necessity" as a reference to a world where language did not rely on codified conventions and where seeing and reading were naturally equivalent. For Condillac and Warburton, both hieroglyph and fable are complex constructs.

Hieroglyphs, according to Warburton, are situated at the beginning of writing, that is, at the transition from the pictorial representation of things to the use of characters to represent words. The hieroglyph fuses both forms; it is a picture and a character. Whereas the Egyptians joined characteristic marks to images, the Chinese "threw out the *Images* and retained only the contracted *Marks*" (p. 76). At the end of this evolutionary chain, we find alphabetic writing, in which the individual marks stand not for words but for individual letters. The Greek language retains some of this history: "Thus the Greek Words ΣΗΜΕΙΑ [*sēmeia*] and ΣΗΜΑΤΑ [*sēmata*] signify as well the *Images of natural Things*, as *artificial Marks or Characters*; and ΓΡΑΦΩ [*graphō*] both to *paint* and to *write*" (p. 79). Neither for Condillac nor for Warburton is there one, unified primal language. Language evolves out of a variety of systems of representation, separated by their specific media. In this sense any concrete language functions like an extension of our bodies: the language of action (gestural language, body language), spoken language, pictorial representation, and writing. Among these various media and their respective codes there is a certain division of labor; each supplements the other and allows for increasing differentiation within each code.

The result of this differentiation is an increase in expressions and words.

Whether this increase produces more specific meanings or mere ornament depends on the degree to which the new signs need to be supported by analogies in other codes and media or are rendered obsolete by more economical modes of signification. Early language was extremely poor and therefore highly equivocal: "This would naturally set them [early men] upon supplying the Deficiencies of Speech by apt and significant *Signs*. Accordingly, in the first Ages of the World, mutual Converse was upheld by a mixed Discourse of Words and Actions; and Use and Custom, as in most other Circumstances of Life improving what arose out of *Necessity* into *Ornament*, this Practice subsisted long after the Necessity had ceased" (p. 83). Just as the hieroglyph fuses reading and seeing in the conjunction of image and character, the fable manages to combine the language of action with speech: "As Speech became more cultivated, this rude manner of Speaking by *Action* was smoothed and polished into an APOLOGUE or *Fable*, where the Speaker, to inforce his Purpose, by a suitable Impression, told a *familiar* Tale of his own Invention, composed of such Circumstances as made his Purpose fully evident and persuasive: For Language was yet too narrow, and the Minds of Men too undisciplin'd, to support only abstract Reasoning and a direct Address" (pp. 87–88). Thus, the Anschaulichkeit of the fable, or its "graphicity," is the product of a certain symmetry and analogy between two codes: action, which derives from the body, and speech, which originates in the voice. These codes are fused by giving each the same purpose and subordinating both to the same logic and teleology.

Condillac marks the point within the evolution of language at which the fable becomes necessary as a stage when the repertoire of logical conjunctions has yet to be fully developed: the narrative logic of the fable compensates at that stage for a deficiency in formal logic. The fable supplies a situational context for the imagination instead of a formal, generalized sign for the operation of the soul.

The particles, for instance, which connect the different parts of discourse, must have been invented very late. They express the manner in which the objects affect us, and the judgments which we frame of them, with a delicacy long unperceived by our dull understanding, which rendered it impossible for mankind to reason. To reason, is to express the relations which subsist betwixt different propositions; now that the conjunctions alone afford us the means of expressing these relations, is evident. The want of these particles could be but very imperfectly supplied by the mode of speaking by action; nor were they in a condition of expressing by names the relations signified by those particles, till they had been fixed by particular circumstances, and a great many different times. We shall presently see that this is the origin of apologue or fable. (*Essai*, pp. 241, 254)

The "image sensible" of the fable appeals to the recipient's imagination and produces the association of ideas within their situational contexts. This becomes unnecessary, however, once we employ particles to designate the logical connection between propositions. In the history of language, Anschaulichkeit yields to more economical formal logic. Once particles provide a means to express the connection between propositions, the more primitive means of producing this connection through particular situational contexts becomes a gratuitous addition to a more economical mode of expression. The fable becomes superfluous by virtue of the logic of rationalization that determines the progress of language and knowledge, and the genre degenerates, having lost its function. This degeneration assumes two forms. On the one hand, through its repeated and generalized use by the broader public, the fable loses its particular meaning and becomes a mere commonplace of received opinion. According to Warburton:

> This was the Birth of *Fable*; a Kind of Speech which corresponds, in all Respects, to writing by *Hieroglyphics*, each being the Symbol of something else understood. And, as it sometimes happened, when a *Hieroglyphic* became famous, it lost its *particular* Signification, and assumed a general one. . . . So it was with the *Apologue*; of which, when any one became celebrated for the Art and Beauty of its Composition, or for some extraordinary Efficacy in its Application, it was soon worn and converted into a PROVERB. (pp. 91–93)

On the other hand, the fable undergoes a decadent and exaggerated artistic refinement that ultimately obscures it and turns it into an enigma. Thus Condillac on the history of the fable: "At length the spirit of refinement, which in all ages has had its admirers, led them into the most abstruse researches. They studied the most singular properties of beings, in order to draw delicate allusions; insomuch that fable was insensibly changed into parable, and rendered at length so mysterious as to be little better than an enigma" (*Essai*, pp. 256, 280). For Warburton the argument about the hieroglyph and the fable was a crucial point in his theological concern to demystify enigmatic and seemingly arcane passages of the Old Testament in order to oppose the Jewish religion to the truly revealed religion of Christianity. Warburton analyzes the parabolic speech of the Old Testament as a once perfectly accessible form of expression that only later degenerated into the secret knowledge of an esoteric priesthood. Condillac adopts Warburton's model of the history of language but not his theological concerns and makes the model of rationalization his overall paradigm for the history of language. Although neither Warburton nor Condillac was engaged in the contemporary debate about the poetics of the fable and its possible reform, the relative importance of this genre for their overall conceptualization of the history of semiosis and their accounts of the fable as a transitory stage in the irreversible evolution of language can be applied to the contemporary argument. Their assessment of the genre corresponds, in a certain sense, to the facts; for despite Richardson's and Lessing's rescue and revival efforts, these authors soon abandoned the fable and took up, respectively, the epistolary novel and the bourgeois tragedy. This raises the question why, after the fable, those two genres were thought to produce most effectively the desired effect of "graphicity." In other words, the decline of the fable, its inability to produce complete "Anschaulichkeit," the effect of "wear and tear," should be understood within the overall Enlightenment model for the progress of language and knowledge.

What is it that makes the fable both an ideal type of transparent signification and a merely transitory phenomenon in the history of semiosis? If the fable easily degenerates into mere rhetorical ornament or an inaccessible enigma, does that mean that Anschaulichkeit, too, needs to be sacrificed to the historical progress of language and analytical reasoning? How does Anschaulichkeit figure within the history of semiosis? In order to pursue these questions, I trace in greater detail what Condillac has to say about the logic of rationalization, which conditions the available modes of expression. Within the architecture of Condillac's epistemological concerns with language and method, the argument of his chapter on hieroglyphs and fables ("De l'origine de la fable, de la parabole et de l'énigme, avec quelques détails sur l'usage des figures et des métaphores") concludes his detailed account of the history of the production of signs, which explicates the range of possibilities of metaphoric language. Since, in Condillac's history of semiosis, the hieroglyph/fable conjunction recapitulates this history *in nuce*, it is useful to turn to the preceding chapters of the *Essai* to gain a more detailed understanding of his account of the particular historical conditions for the production of signs. It is here that Condillac unfolds an intricate account of sign production in conjunction with a theory of media.

According to Condillac, primitive language consisted of gestures and violent contortions of the body (*langage d'action*) that allowed primitive man to communicate immediate needs and some crude sentiments. At that stage, the language of action does not deserve the name of language, since it operates on an instinctual level and is bound to the immediacy of the situation. What distinguishes true language is the repertoire of artificial signs that brings about a controlled use of the operations of the soul: memory, imagination, and reflection. True language is no longer situated in the concrete presence of a situation but can create a presence of its own via the imagination. A system of artifical signs, which deserves the name of language, gradually develops out of a division of labor in the process of signification. Thus, language originates in speech that complements the language of action. It was initiated by an infant who, lacking full control over bodily motor functions, had to have recourse to the tongue, the most flexible organ. Two codes develop, supplementing each other and referring to each other at the intersection of the two media, body and voice. However, it took a long time for primitive man to acquire a sufficient repertoire of articulated sounds to complement gestural language. In the Old Testament one can still find the traces of the "images sensibles" of gestural language supporting the force of the spoken word.

It seems that this mode of speaking was preserved chiefly to instruct the people in regard to matters in which they were most deeply concerned; such as government and religion. Because as it acted upon the imagination with greater force, the impression was more durable. Its expression contained even something elevated and noble, which the language of articulated sounds, as yet poor and barren, could not come up to. This mode of speaking the ancients called by the name of *dance*; which is the reason of its being said that David danced before the ark. (pp. 198–99, 177–78)

Initially the system of articulated sound was poor; men were not able to make subtle vocal distinctions. However, classical antiquity took a decisive step forward in the development of language: in a strict division of labor on the stage of public spectacle, one actor concentrated on the clear and distinctly codified prosody, leaving the other actor free to differentiate the language of gestures and bring about the birth of pantomime. Prosody evolved into chant; the language of gestures became dance. All the arts, music, poetry, and dance have a common origin and purpose in the instruction of the public through "images sensibles" within the context of an oral tradition and a culture of spectacle.

The advent of the new medium of writing changed the nature of verbal language altogether. Its separation of poetry from music led to major innovations in each art. With writing, verbal language is doubled, and the "images sensibles" become obsolete. The "images sensibles" are powerful only as long as they are the exclusive way of representing complex situations by stimulating the imagination to produce an associative context, a matrix for the intended complex of perceptions. Within the hallucination evoked by the "image sensible," representation and perception become indissolubly fused into a complex sign that then appears to be "natural" because of its seeming motivation. Condillac points out, however, that the seeming motivation and naturalness of a sign are merely the accidental effect on a beholder surprised by a strong impression of a certain situation. Here the operations of the soul are not represented but merely provoked through the situational context. Condillac's critique of the naturalness of signs points out the critical advantages of recognizably conventionalized signs. Only when the operations of the soul can be represented independently of an associative, situational context are they subject to analysis.

The connexions of ideas are formed in the imagination two different ways: sometimes spontaneously; and at other times they are the effect of an external impression. The former are generally less vivid, so that they may easily be broke: and it is agreed that they are instituted or artificial. The latter are often so well cemented, that it is impossible for us to destroy them; hence we are inclined to think them natural. They have both their advantages and their inconveniences; but the latter are so much the more useful or pernicious, as they actuate the mind with greater force.   (pp. 143, 79)

Analytic reasoning with its conscious use of arbitrary signs can counteract the ideological dangers of an "image sensible" by dissociating the individual components of a complex of ideas and by foregrounding the artificiality of each connection.

For Condillac, the modern world is marked by a language that has come to follow the rules of logic and that has a full repertoire of artificial signs and thereby the perfect means for analysis. In the background of his history of semiosis is a history of media. Ultimately the medium of writing makes the fable an obsolete genre or from a cognitive vehicle relegates it to one that remains useful only for persuading the masses. As advantageous as this evolution might be for the progress of knowledge and the development of a scientific methodology, Condillac nevertheless expresses a certain nostalgia for the language of the ancients: inversions in Latin or Greek might disobey the rules of logical order, but they can captivate the attention of reader and listener by producing graphic tableaux in a manner that seems forever lost to the moderns. Although Condillac mourns this loss of "graphicity" within the teleology of the second part of his essay, a closer look at the first part of the *Essai* reveals something makes up for that loss.

Anschaulichkeit and Seeing as an Effect of Silent Reading

The first part of the *Essai* treats the material of knowledge and the operations of the soul. Here Condillac does not explicitly discuss Anschaulichkeit, but we can gain more insight into certain discontents with language within the mid-eighteenth-century project of Anschaulichkeit if we focus on the implicit strategy of the production of Anschaulichkeit in this part of Condillac's text. The first part begins and ends with a critique of Locke's *Essay Concerning Human Understanding* (1690). Condillac agrees with Locke's denial of innate ideas, and like Locke he wants to rule out unconscious perceptions. Yet he is immensely troubled by the imperceptible propensity of our judgment, according to Locke, to modify and distort our primary perceptions. By admitting this possibility, we lose the ultimate recourse of grounding our knowledge in sensual perception, because we can no longer distinguish a perception from a judgment. Yet Condillac, like Locke, needs to explain why we are not equally aware of all our perceptions, how a filtering device protects us from being overwhelmed with sensory data. Condillac forces a solution to this problem through his choice of examples. In analyzing these revealing examples, which must be viewed as crucial paradigms of cultural experience in the mid-eighteenth century, we can see how Condillac manages to recover the "image sensible."

Thus, to Locke's argument that our judgment can revise our perceptions without our knowledge, Condillac replies that this is not a matter of revision but merely one of forgetting the details of the entire process of perception.

> If we reflect on ourselves the moment after we have been reading [*au sortir d'une lecture*], it will appear to us as if we had had no consciousness but of the ideas which that reading has produced. We shall no more imagine that we had a perception of every letter, than we have a perception of darkness so often as we involuntarily close our eyelids. But this appearance cannot impose upon us, when we come to reflect that without a consciousness of the perception of letters, we should not have been conscious of the words, nor consequently of the ideas. (*Essai*, pp. 118, 32)

It is Condillac's specific presentation of the example of reading that is so striking. Locke himself used the example of reading, but for Locke reading serves as an example of the result of judgment being mistaken for the actual sense perceptions: "We take that for the Perception of our Sensation, which is an *Idea* formed by our Judgement; so that one, *viz*. that of Sensation, serves only to excite the other, and is scarce taken notice of it self; as a Man who reads or hears with attention and understanding, takes little notice of the Characters, or Sounds, but of the *Ideas*, that are excited in him by them" (pp. 146–47). For Locke perceptions differ from judgment, which has to screen and synthesize the former. Therefore, Locke can use the blinking of the eyes as an illustration of insignificant perceptions: "How frequently do we, in a day, cover our Eyes with our Eye-Lids, without perceiving that we are at all in the dark?" (p. 147)

Condillac's rewriting of Locke's two examples integrates them into one short narrative about the experience of reading. In effect, his rephrasing produces a counterargument to Locke. In Condillac's version, the materiality of the text being read is reduced to the sheer differential marks of the letters comparable to the opposition between light and dark impressions on the retina. Unlike Locke, Condillac does not refer to the material elements of the text as "characters" or "sounds." Rather, just as the continuity of visual perception is unperturbed by the blinking of the eyes, the registration of the individual letters glides into the perception of the text's meaning as a synthesized whole. For Condillac it is "la lecture," not "judgment," that gives birth to ideas. Condillac's "lecture" is not a deciphering but a totalizing experience one enters and leaves as one would a movie theater: it is the scenario of a hallucinatory, visualizing silent reading. In this paradigm for the cultural practice of reading, Condillac manages to integrate the semiotic ideal of transparency: here the sign is transparent and has no exterior qualities; the sign function is a means of controlling the operations of the soul. It is not dependent on a vehicle, a specific material artifact, which needs not only to be perceived but also to be decoded by our judgment.

This insistence on the consciousness of each minute perception forces Condillac to explain how we arrive at a synthetic perception without getting lost in the multitude of individual perceptions. In answer, Condillac cites our faculty of attention. Again, the example he chooses is worth consideration.

Among several perceptions of which we have a consciousness at the same time, it frequently happens that we are more conscious of one than the other, or more strongly apprized of their existence. Nay the more the consciousness of some increases, the more that of others diminishes. Let a person be at a public entertainment, where a variety of objects seem to dispute his attention, his mind will be attacked by a number of perceptions, of which it certainly takes notice; but insensibly some of these will be more agreeable and engaging to him than others, and of course he will more willingly give way to them. As soon as that happens, he will begin to be less affected by others, his consciousness of them will even insensibly diminish, insomuch that upon his coming to himself he shall not remember to have taken any notice of them. *Of this we have a strong proof in the deception [l'illusion] we are subject to at the theatre* [my italics]. There are some moments in which our consciousness does not seem to be divided between the action represented, and the rest of the entertainment⟨, by which I mean, the theatre, the audience, the actors &c⟩. One would think at first that the perception ought to be stronger, in proportion as there are fewer objects capable of diminishing our attention. And yet every man may have observed, that we are never more inclined to think ourselves single spectators at a moving scene, than when the house is full. Perhaps this is because the number, variety, and magnificence of the objects strike the senses, elevate the imagination, and render us thereby more fit to receive the impressions which the poet intends to give us. Perhaps it is also owing to this, that the spectators are mutually encouraged by the example they set each other, of fixing their eyes on the stage. Be that as it may, *this operation by which our consciousness concerning particular perceptions is so greatly increased, that they seem to be the only perceptions of which we take notice, I call attention* [my italics]. Thus to be attentive to a thing, is to be more conscious of the perceptions which it occasions, than of those which other objects produce by soliciting our senses in the same manner; and our *attention* [italics in original] is in proportion greater, as we have less remembrance of the latter.   (pp. 116–17, *30*; the clause in angle brackets was added by the translator)

Again, Condillac argues that rather than a structural opposition between unconscious and conscious perceptions there is a quantitative transition from slightly conscious perceptions to all-encompassing ones; only the latter are retained. Since the multitude of perceptions seems to disintegrate into chaos, he has to find a frame that contains, focuses, and unites them. Whereas in his example from reading this frame is provided by the hallucinatory experience of the "lecture," here the framing device of the mental theater is established through the spectator's identificatory engagement with the events on the stage. In other words, the faculty of attention is a product of an aesthetic illusion. When Condillac describes how the spectator seems to leave physical existence behind among the crowded audience in order to communicate with the mind of the author, we find Condillac—as with his example from silent reading—paying homage to the semiotic ideal of transparency. Yet Condillac's examples of the operations of the soul can also be read as an aesthetic program postulating genres that manage to produce a perfect illusion, an illusion that sustains the continuity of the operations of the soul in its dematerialization of the physical world along with its absorption of the reader/spectator.

And even his third example, of viewing a tableau, which deals with the mechanism of perception and attention and the marking of time, is again drawn from the realm of hallucinatory involvement. As long as we are left with the minute individual perceptions of light and color, we are outside time. There is nothing in the tableau to frame and contain the passage of time. What creates the awareness of temporality is our retroactive engagement with the tableau, the narrative of our experience of how we were affected by its individual elements. And again, this narrative is a hallucinatory re-presentation of the tableau (see *Essai*, p. 119).

One might wonder, however, how Condillac's argument refutes Locke's position that judgments can imperceptibly modify our perceptions, a position that ultimately questions our immediate perceptual access to the world. In fact, Condillac hardly mentions the role of judgment and merely affirms that although we have no unconscious perceptions, we attend to some perceptions more strongly than to others and therefore remember them better. The examples of reading, the theater, and the tableau have to carry all the weight of his argument. His implicit argument, however, lies exactly in his strategic choice and presentation of examples. Most of his instances of visual perception deal with the perception of representations and not with perceptions of things in the world. Yet these representations are not described as codified constructs, which would require that our judgment (or, as Lessing would put it, our "symbolic understanding") know specific conventions before it can translate the perception into the mental image; rather, they are mediated by those signs that in Condillac's terminology are called "images sensibles." The underlying paradigm that alone makes his refutation of Locke possible is that of silent reading: it is within the hallucinatory presence of the mental cinema that the gap can be negotiated, that the signs separated from the world can become transparent, mere representations and artificial at the same time.

When Condillac resumes his argument with Locke in the final chapter of the first part, he argues against Locke's interpretation of William Molyneux's assertion that a blind man, having just gained his sense of sight through a cataract operation, cannot distinguish between a cube and a sphere. For Locke this proves the nonexistence of innate ideas. This example troubles Condillac since he wants to argue the translatability of the tactile perception of space into the visual perception of space. He could not, of course, assert that Molyneux is wrong. Thus Condillac adds two further experiments to his discussion of visual perception. The scenario of the tableau bears the brunt of his argument, which runs as follows. To some extent our perceptions differ from our judgments. Yet, not as Locke would argue, in the sense that they can imperceptibly modify our perceptions; rather, it is in our judgments that consciousness self-reflexively distances itself from the imaginary presence of a primary perception: "I behold a basso relievo, I know beyond all doubt that it is done on a flat surface; I have touched it: and yet neither this knowledge, nor repeated experience, nor all the judgments I can frame, hinder me from seeing convex figures" (pp. 183, *155*). Condillac denies that any picture aiming at a spatial illusion is constructed according to specific codes and conventions that need to be deciphered. For him the primary and consistent perception is the perspectival illusion created by the tableau. In fact, the illusion of the painting assumes for him such an overpowering presence that he is even led to refer to a "bas relief" instead of a painting as the material support of the representation. Thus, Condillac uses the aesthetic illusion of the tableau to contradict Locke: since the blind man had acquired a notion of space through his sense of touch, the man in Molyneux's experiment should have been able to distinguish the globe and the cube through perspectival vision.

Condillac concludes his first part on the material of our knowledge and his argument against Locke's analysis of perception with the discussion of the Chiselden experiment, which seems to contradict his own thesis. A young man who had been given sight by a cataract operation needed two months to acquire perspectival vision and kept confusing his perceptions of sight with those of touch. However, Condillac saves his thesis by pointing out that at the completion of the operation the young man's vision had not yet been fully developed; his cornea, for example, had become too rigid to follow the minute adaptations required by perspectival vision. Of course, the apparently scientific argument of blaming the rigidity of the cornea does not solve the problem that the young man needed two months to learn to decipher the conventions of a perspectivally contructed painting.

Condillac does not render the experiment in his own words but insists on quoting Voltaire: "For it would lose by being rendered in other terms" (p. 188). But what in terms of the experiment (in French, *experience*) would be lost? First, by giving his own version, Condillac would miss the opportunity of presenting his reader with the introduction by which Voltaire prefaces the experiment, and which makes up a good third of Condillac's quotation.

In 1729, Mr. Cheselden, one of those famous surgeons who combined manual skill with the greatest intellectual insights, having fancied that he could give sight to a man born blind, by couching the cataracts, which he supposed to have been formed in his eyes, almost at the very moment of his birth, proposed the operation. The blind man with difficulty consented; for he could not well conceive how the sense of seeing should make any great addition to his pleasures. Were it not for the desire instilled into him of learning to read and write, he would not have wished to see.   (pp. 188, *164*; trans. slightly modified)

Voltaire's introduction celebrates the close cooperative enterprise of the Enlightenment, the desire to read and the acquisition of vision. The enlightened surgeon uses his skills to make the young man able to see/read.

And further, by paraphrasing, Condillac would have missed the chance of performing some cataract surgery on his own reader. Inserting the quotation, he makes his reader "see" an experiment by presenting Voltaire's narrative of the experiment. Somehow it does not matter what Voltaire has to say in detail, nor that he is on the side of Locke and Berkeley. When Voltaire writes: "It was not till after two months' experience that he could perceive that pictures represented solid bodies" (pp. 188, *165*), Condillac's response does not even address the issue. Apparently the young man could see the marks painted on the flat surface; his blindness to the conventions of perspectival illusion cannot be explained in terms of corneal rigidity. What matters is that Condillac's own reader gets "something to see," is drawn into a hallucinatory silent reading. Condillac's peculiar empiricism culminates in the equivocation of an experience of reading with the perception of an experiment, an equivocation possible only because it presupposes a particular practice of reading grounded in an illusionist aesthetics. If Richardson tries to negotiate the gap between reading and seeing by including an illustration of each fable, Condillac negotiates this gap by quoting a description of an experiment that is supposed to affect the reader's imagination graphically.

In the introduction to the *Traité des sensations* (1754), Condillac explicitly states his own method of creating evidence by appealing to the reader's hallucinatory participation and identificatory engagement: "Let me warn the reader that it is very important that he put himself exactly into the position of the statue we are going to observe. He has to begin to exist with it, to have no other sense, nothing that it doesn't have; to acquire only those ideas that it acquires, to take up only those habits that it takes up: in one word: he has to be exclusively what it is."[20] The experiment/ *experience* of the statue translates into a particular reading experience for Condillac's philosophical audience.

Although the analysis of Condillac's discussion of the fable in the context of the progressive development of language and knowledge seemed to point to a loss of Anschaulichkeit, of immediacy and an experiential totality, due to the institution of the artificial signs of a written culture, a loss that nevertheless seemed necessary to the progress of critical understanding, an analysis of the first part of Condillac's *Essai*, focusing on his strategic use of examples, shows that this loss has been recuperated or compensated by a new kind of Anschaulichkeit made possible by silent reading in a print culture. It is on the background of silent reading that we must understand both the transformations of such crucial terms as "seeing" and "images" and the production of the new semiotic constellation of the tableau, which is to supersede the one of the hieroglyph/fable. If the semiotics of Condillac's *Essai* marks the construction of philosophical evidence within the imaginary presence of silent reading—a displacement away from a spectacular organization of signs to one of transparent representations within the mind of the individual that gives all the power to illusion and the imagination—this transition must be all the more strongly reflected in aesthetic discussions. In the following section, I demonstrate that Diderot's *Lettre sur les aveugles* and *Lettre sur les sourds et muets* can be read as indicative of exactly this transition from a spectacular culture to an anti-theatrical print culture, a transition that implies the rejection of traditional rhetoric and poetics in favor of the new discipline of aesthetics.

The Aesthetic Sign of the Soul's Synthetic Totality

I propose to conceive of Diderot's *Lettre sur les aveugles* (1749) and *Lettre sur les sourds et muets* (1751) as a response to the discussion of sense perception, sign, and knowledge in Condillac's *Essai*.[21] Read against the background of Condillac's work, Diderot's letters sharpen our understanding of the role of signs and the changing function of seeing and the imagination within Enlightenment aesthetics and semiotics. It seems almost as if Diderot had separated Condillac's evolutionary account of human signs and knowledge into two issues located in two distinct discursive fields. On the one hand, he goes along with the rationalist conception of knowledge as ascending to pure mathematical reason with the aid of a "langage de calcul," and this is the thrust of the *Lettre sur les aveugles*. On the other hand, in the *Lettre sur les sourds et muets*, he introduces an element of cultural relativism in denying the ultimate privilege to formal logic and by advocating the new semiotic constellation of the hieroglyph/*tableau mouvant*.

Thus, the *Lettre sur les aveugles* centers on the achievements of the blind mathematician Nicholas Saunderson, which Diderot uses to illustrate the knowledge attainable by the sense of touch alone.[22] Since we do not have a tactile system of signs, the blind man's imagination is minimal and his cognitive ability is primarily analytic rather than synthetic. This makes him particularly adept at dealing with abstract issues, because it prevents him from getting muddled up in metaphors, as happens only too easily to his seeing colleagues: "For abstraction merely amounts to the ability to separate in our thoughts the sensible qualities of bodies either from each other or from the body itself, which serves as their material support; error arises if this separation is badly executed or applied; it can be badly executed in metaphysical questions, and it can be badly applied in questions concerned with physics and mathematics" (p. 32). Saunderson became such an eminent mathematics professor because at the age of five he had come across an arithmetical machine that reduced all numbers to a binary system of two needles, one with a big head and one with a small one. With the aid of this most pure and abstract code, he was introduced to mathematical thinking. Indeed, Saunderson represents the prototype of the rationalist atheist philosopher to the extent that he embodies for Diderot a radicalization and critique of Descartes: Saunderson gives, like Descartes, primacy to the sense of touch. His palpable arithmetics makes innate ideas superfluous, however, and his suffering due to his lack of access to the visible world, his monstrosity, does not allow him to postulate a divine order in nature.

Although Diderot demonstrates that the blind man seems not at all deprived in terms of rational insight, he stresses the impact sight has on social behavior and morality: pity and shame seem to depend totally on the sense of sight.[23] Diderot further insists that a blind man is fairly insensitive to threats of physical violence: "The external signs of power, which affect us in such a lively manner, have little impact on blind people" (p. 24). Diderot develops a close nexus between the modes of sensory perception and the development of the individual mental faculties: touch has a privileged relation to abstract reason; sight to the moral and psychic makeup.

The *Lettre sur les sourds et muets* engages in the ongoing eighteenth-century debate over French versus Latin syntax.[24] On the one hand, Diderot accepts the common rationalist position that French syntax lends itself more aptly than that of any other language to logic and the order of reason. On the other hand, he echoes Condillac's nostalgia for a loss of vivacity in language. Instead of placing the hieroglyph/fable conjunction into an irretrievable, obsolete stage of the history of semiosis, however, he proposes a semiotic/aesthetic ideal, the hieroglyph/tableau mouvant, which is still relevant. If Condillac transforms the imagination into a productive faculty and implicitly appeals to the synthetic activity produced by the mental images of a silent reading, Diderot explicitly makes the "cinema of the mind" the central scenario of the soul's activity.

Diderot begins by questioning the primacy of logical order over a didactic or a rhetorical order. He introduces the question of cultural relativism by pointing out that conventions determine what constitutes an order or inversion, thus displacing the traditional question of which syntactic order is more natural. Then, he radicalizes his argument by denying the necessity of an order determined by the successive utterance of sounds that is then analogous to a logical, rhetorical, didactic, or any other "natural" order. At this point he turns from rhetorics to aesthetics. Leaving behind the rhetorical ties to the temporal succession of the spoken word, Diderot focuses on the overall effect of an aesthetic object and correlates it with the multiple sense perceptions it evokes.

The state of our soul is one thing, the account we give of it to ourselves or others is another thing. On the one hand, there is the total and instantaneous sensation of this state; on the other hand, there is the successive and detailed attention we must give to this state in order to analyze it, to express it, and to understand it. Our soul is a moving picture after which we continuously paint: it takes us quite some time to render it with some degree of fidelity, but it exists in its entirety and all at once: the mind does not proceed step by step like verbal expression. (p. 161)

Rejecting Condillac's account of a succession of discrete, individual perceptions, which then are synthesized and analyzed by the operations of the soul, Diderot gives primacy to the simultaneity of a multiplicity of perceptions that constitute the totality of the soul as a "moving picture." When Diderot addresses aesthetic issues, he turns his/the painter's gaze inwardly to this "tableau mouvant" rather than to the exterior material details traced by the painter's brush: "The paintbrush merely executes over time what the eye of the painter embraces in an instant. Linguistic formulations required decomposition; but to see an object, to find it beautiful, to experience an aggreable sensation, to want to possess it, all this is the state of the soul in one single instant" (pp. 161–62). This kind of seeing engages the totality of the operations of the soul, establishing and maintaining the soul's unity and the unity of perception.[25] It is also equivalent to aesthetic approval, a pleasurable sensation, and desire. Furthermore, the aesthetic object loses its materiality since it is equated with its effect on the recipient. Ordinary discourse merely has to render ideas clearly and distinctly, but poetic discourse can recreate the presence of a total state of the soul.

Thus, poetic discourse is touched by some spirit that moves and vivifies all of its syllables. What is this spirit? Only a few times have I felt its presence, but all I know of it is that it is due to this spirit that things are said and represented simultaneously, that at the same time they are grasped by the understanding, the soul is moved by them, the imagination sees them, and the ears understand them. And this discourse is not merely a concatenation of energetic terms, which expose the thought with force and nobility; it is also a tissue of hieroglyphs piled upon each other, that paint the thought. In this sense I could say that all poetry is emblematic. (*Sourds*, p. 169)

The aesthetic sign or emblem is above the order of rhetoric. It does not have to be successively deciphered but is perfectly transparent: "things are said and represented simultaneously." This aesthetic sign is not, however, like the material entity found in Renaissance emblem books; rather, it is the product of the imagination, an illusion located within the recipient's mind.[26] Any piece of art, music, painting, and poetry can become such an emblem as long as the marks employed in its construction lose their artificiality and materiality and create this unified effect on the soul.

Diderot ends the *Lettre sur les sourds et muets* with an attempt to show how poetry, music, and painting should strive to achieve their own emblematic effect. He polemicizes against Charles Batteux's notion of "la belle nature" in the *Beaux arts réduits à un même principe* (1746). Diderot does not, however, completely overthrow a model of mimesis in favor of one of a unified effect of the aesthetic object on the presencing of the imagination. In the *Lettre sur les sourds et muets*, he concludes by reiterating Lord Shaftesbury's and Jean Du Bos's view of a painterly representation as a direct imitation of the object: "Whereas the painter shows the thing itself, the expressions of the musician and the poet are merely hieroglyphs" (p. 185).[27] Diderot's postulate that each art has to find its particular hieroglyphs seems to anticipate the task Lessing sets himself in the *Laokoon* — a fully developed aesthetic theory and program of how artificial signs can become naturalized in each specific artistic medium.[28]

The evolution of the "image sensible" from Condillac to Diderot demonstrates the radical transformation in mid-eighteenth-century semiotics and aesthetics in the view of graphicity or Anschaulichkeit. What still in Condillac's history of semiosis was considered an obsolete mode of signification has become *the* central effect of any aesthetic object. The ideal semiotic constellation of the tableau constitutes the object of study as well as the norms for any aesthetic and poetic inquiry. As demanded in Lessing's theory of the fable, "Anschaulichkeit" is no longer an effect based on the comparison of the general, symbolic truth with a particular example (as in the parable, allegory, or the historical exemplum) but a direct, unmediated insight. The recipient's imagination, which produces this epiphany, actively supplies the motivations for the artifact and thereby naturalizes and appropriates the sign. The vivacity of the effect is created by an inward-turned vision that has the presence of a sense perception without the intervening separation between the materiality of the sign vehicle and the mental idea.

This notion of Anschaulichkeit, as it takes shape in discussions of the fable, Condillac's semiotics, and Diderot's early aesthetics is anything but spectacular or theatrical; its effect is located in the mind of the individual rather than being part of a public performance. In Condillac's description of how the attention is focused, individual absorption and identificatory participation are compared to that moment of theatrical illusion when the members of a crowded audience become reduced to individual spectators who concentrate exclusively on the events on stage as if part of it—or as if engaged in a silent reading of the drama. The actual efficacy of an aesthetic object in producing this Anschaulichkeit, where reading and seeing become homologous, depends on the degree to which artificial signs can be naturalized and any decoding effort can be veiled by the construction of an effect of "immediacy" and "authenticity." And this construction of an effect of immediacy, this naturalization of the process of signification, is precisely the poetics of the genres that Richardson and Lessing employ in their pursuit of putting Anschaulichkeit into the service of morality after abandoning the fable.

Before turning to those new genres, I return once more to the fable, the genre that led me into this discussion of Anschaulichkeit. To this point, I have analyzed the mid-eighteenth-century project of Anschaulichkeit mainly in terms of its formal criteria irrespective of any particular content. It remains to be shown, however, that graphic representations have indeed privileged objects. The contents of Anschaulichkeit relate to the formation of the subject, the internalization of a mode of authority. Again, discussing the fable allows me to trace the project of Anschaulichkeit as it relates to the formation of the subject.

Mediation and Authority

The statement that Rousseau rejects the fable as a means of instruction calls for qualification. In fact, he does so only when Emile is about to enter the age of reason. At that age the boy still lacks the experience to make the fable graphic, and therefore he would easily be misled into the acquisition of empty words and codes. Emile's premature fixation on the symbolic code would make him into a flatterer and deceiver; he would manipulate appearances in a theatrical show. And yet Rousseau does not reject the fable altogether. At a later stage in Emile's development, the fable becomes a convenient pedagogical resource. Once Emile has become a self-sufficient, reasoning adolescent, he must learn not to be proud and not to look down upon those entrapped in obsessions of rank, fortune, or cheap pleasures. To teach Emile humility is not an easy task for the instructor, who has to be careful to leave Emile's amour propre intact, neither to crush his masculine self-confidence nor to make him rebel against his tutor's exhortations. Again, Emile cannot learn of his fallibility through lectures but only through experience: "But do not on this account waste your breath on empty arguments to prove to the youth that he is like other men and subject to the same weaknesses. Make him feel it or he will never know it" (*Emile*, pp. 319–20, 207). But how can the tutor expose Emile to pitfalls without appearing unworthy of his pupil's love and respect? The tutor has to be frank and warn Emile of the dangers he will face: "Warn him of his faults before he commits them; do not blame him when once they are committed; you would only stir his self-love to mutiny. We learn nothing from the phrase, "I told you so" (pp. 322, 209). At this stage of Emile's education, Rousseau acknowledges the instructive value of the fable, since now Emile has sufficient experience to apply the lesson immediately to himself. What makes the fable effective in this educational phase is its unobtrusive presentation of the moral (recall that Lessing pointed out that the moral maxim of the fable must be produced by the fable itself, through its unified action, rather than explicitly stated in a commentary).

Nothing is so foolish and unwise as the moral at the end of most of the fables; as if the moral was not, or ought not to be so clear in the fable itself that the reader cannot fail to perceive it. Why then add the moral at the end, and so deprive him of the pleasure of discovering it for himself? The art of teaching consists in making the pupil wish to learn. But if the pupil is to take pleasure in his learning, his mind must not remain in such a passive state with regard to what you tell him that there is really nothing for him to do but listen to you. The master's amour propre must always give way to the pupil's; he must be able to say, I understand, I see it, I am getting at it, I am learning something. One of the things which makes the Pantaloon in the Italian comedies so wearisome is the pains taken by him to explain to the audience the platitudes they understand only too well already. I do not want that a tutor becomes a Pantaloon, even less so that an author. . . .

What is the sense of the four lines at the end of La Fontaine's fable of the frog that puffed himself up?[29] Is he afraid we should not understand it? Does this great painter need to write the names beneath the things he has painted?   (pp. 323, *210*; trans. slightly modified)

Rousseau and Lessing are arguing that the only good fables are those that do not explicitly state the moral but imply it in its concrete situational context. Thus, they advocate the veiling of authority, explicit laws, and prescriptions. Emile's morality is based not on rule-governed behavior, but on a formal ethic of judging each individual situation in its particularity and acting authentically in accordance with his subjective experience of being part of a fallible and mortal humanity.[30] In this larger scheme the fable, with its ability to produce graphic effects, has been incorporated into an educational plan that aims at the perfect interiorization of authority, a process that leaves no space for the subject to distance himself from the moral authority of the law. However, the fable's instructive value is limited to making Emile aware of common human weaknesses; it cannot make him a responsible *citoyen*.

Faced with a young adult who has to be fully introduced into society, the tutor has to protect him from all of society's corruption brought about by peer pressure and public opinion and supported by Emile's own imagination, which at this point is dangerously inflamed by his libidinal impulses. The easiest way to negotiate this transition would be to marry him off, but Rousseau argues for a delay of marriage. The transitional period itself can be most usefully employed in constructing the citoyen, in programming his behavior for the future when the tutorial authority is absent and Emile is left alone with his wife. Only if the tutor succeeds, at this stage of Emile's education, in forging a link between his pedagogical authority and Emile's future wife will all previous pedagogical efforts be permanently secured.

The first step in this educational stage is the tutor's renunciation of his fatherly and external authority. He confesses his own weaknesses and treats the pupil as another adult and an affectionate friend. He has to refuse Emile any moral guidance until the young man asks him to be his guide and moral authority. When he then speaks to Emile, the manner of his discourse has altogether changed. He no longer uses words in a parsimonious, sober manner and bores Emile with dry precepts; instead he speaks to Emile in a vivid, animated, and even passionate way. Such discourse will keep Emile's inflamed imagination busy and engrave everlasting images in his heart.

There are moments in human life which must never be forgotten. Such is the time when Emile receives the instruction of which I have spoken; its influence should endure all his life through. Let us try to engrave it on his memory so that it may never fade away. It is one of the faults of our age to rely too much on cold reason, as if men were all mind. By neglecting the language of signs which address the imagination we have lost the most forcible mode of speech. The spoken word is always weak, and we speak to the heart rather through the eyes than the ears. In our attempt to appeal to reason only, we have reduced our precepts to words, we have not embodied them in deed. . . .

I observe that in modern times men only get hold over others by force of self-interest, while the ancients did more by persuasion, by the affections of the heart; because they did not neglect the language of signs. All agreements were drawn up solemnly, so that they might be more inviolable; before the reign of force, the gods were the judges of mankind; in their presence, individuals made their treaties and alliances, and pledged themselves to perform their promises; the face of the earth was the book in which the archives were preserved. The leaves of this book were rocks, trees, piles of stones, made sacred by these transactions, and regarded with reverence by barbarous men; and these pages were always open before their eyes. (pp. 420–21, 286; trans. slightly modified)

With beautiful clarity, this passage praises the disciplinary force of Anschaulichkeit over the enforcement of the law by violence and punishment.[31] Rousseau's seamless digression from the Lockean metaphor of imprinting "sensible images" onto the mind of a student to the nostalgia for the lost hieroglyphic "langage d'action" must sound familiar and resonating with the views of Condillac and Warburton. Rousseau, however, does not develop a detailed semiotic or aesthetic discussion of the issue. He avoids the term "hieroglyph" or "langage d'action," preferring instead "langue des signes." By pairing "la parole" with "les oreilles" and opposing them to the pair "la langue des signes/les yeux," he stresses the aspect of visualization. Through his allusion to antiquity, he evokes the open book of Nature, in which reading and seeing are united. His project is to recuperate this lost stage of Anschaulichkeit in the hallucinatory imagination of Emile.

Rousseau, too, stresses the ideological efficacy of hieroglyphic instruction; however, he does not pair it with the discursive genre of the fable as did Warburton and Condillac. In Rousseau's pedagogical scheme the "langue des signes" is to be complemented by the tableau of the ideal Woman. Since the open book of Nature is closed, the instructor needs the image of the ideal Woman as compensation.

By painting for him his future mistress, you may imagine whether I shall gain a hearing, whether I shall succeed in making the qualities he ought to love pleasing and dear to him, whether I shall sway his feelings to seek or shun what is good or bad for him. I shall be the stupidest of men if I fail to make him fall in love in advance with somebody he does not know. No matter that the object I paint is imaginary, *it is enough to disgust him with those who might have attracted him; it is enough if it is continually suggesting comparisons which make him prefer his fancy to the real objects he sees; and is not love itself a fancy, a falsehood, an illusion?* (pp. 430–31, 294; trans. slightly modified; my italics)

The natural state of man has been irrevocably lost. Emile is to be a member of a contemporary civilized society marked by all aspects of alienation from nature, above all by a dazzling multiplicity of codes and conventions, a world where people are ruled by desire and imaginary goods.[32] Any successful socialization has to take full account of this alienation. This means that the authority of the law and morality must not be opposed to the realm of desire but rather that authority has to be fully implemented within the realm of desire.

Desire will be controllable only once it is anchored in the imaginary; only then does morality become part of the individual's motivational deep structure, part of his productive imagination.

> We are far more in love with our own fancy than with the object of it. If we saw the object of our affections exactly as it is, there would be no more love on earth. When we cease to love, the person we used to love remains unchanged, but we no longer see her with the same eyes; the veil of illusion is drawn aside, and love disappears. But when I supply the imaginary object, I have control over comparisons, and I am able easily to prevent the illusion of real objects. (pp. 431, 294; trans. slightly modified)

This passage contrasts two types of illusion: "le voile du prestige" (the veil of illusion) and "l'illusion des objets réels" (the illusion of real objects). The latter term is used pejoratively. It is the illusion of the frivolous lures of *le monde*, a product of the false discourse of Parisian society. By "voile du prestige," Rousseau means the magic charm that gives an illusionary presence to Emile's beloved object. This magic veil creates for Emile a beloved woman as if she were real; the voile du prestige produces the slippage from the figural language of the tutor to an exterior referent Emile is to search for on his trip to Paris. The veil produces an identification of representation and referent, which, of course, is possible only in the imaginary, and which is an illusion. But it is a superior illusion, superior to the mere illusion of appearances, which lacks any referential anchorage. Since the discourse of *le monde* remains on the level of representations, it is in the imaginary that the referential illusion of language has to be grounded. It will be through his attachment to his imaginary beloved that Emile will learn to differentiate between the false discourse of the world and the truth of morally righteous principles of conduct. Thus the tutor proceeds to engrave the portrait of the ideal woman, whom he will call Sophie, into Emile's heart. The veil of illusion hides the authority of the tutor even as that authority asserts control over Emile's soul. His eyes attached to this ideal image, Emile's ears are plugged to the alluring songs of the sirens and he can safely navigate his way through the dangerous waters of *le monde*.[33]

Thus, the male subject is disciplined through an attachment to an ideal Woman. This is the strategy that characterizes Rousseau's modernity, his break with the traditional models of education. He is quite aware of this, for he prefaces *Emile*'s last chapter, "Sophie ou La Femme," with the following words: " 'Since our young gentleman,' says Locke, 'is about to marry, it is time to leave him with his mistress.' And with these words he ends his book. As I have not the honour of educating 'A young gentleman,' I shall take care not to follow his example" (pp. 465, *321*). All a young aristocrat has to learn is to be a skilled performer within the codes and expectations of his class. He is held in check by the code of honor; the quality of his performance is judged by his peers. For the rest, he can be left to his pleasures and enjoyments; *libertinage* will not endanger his social status. For Emile things are more complicated. He cannot rely on inherited social rank; all he can become in life is determined by his education and behavior. He will have to be socially mobile. Destitute of the security of the status and norms of one class, he has to aim at a standpoint above specific class codes. He is to become a representative of humanity, in general, a free citizen who can move in all social circles, judged solely in terms of the righteousness and authenticity of his behavior. Emile's moral conduct cannot be left to chance. He has to become freed from the mimetic temptations of society; he must not be affected by the specific behavioral conventions of the circle in which he happens to be. Therefore Emile's conduct has to be grounded more firmly on levels other than that of performance.[34] His conduct needs to be linked to an interiorized authority that will be his guiding principle.

This "man in general," a free citizen, above the codes of any particular class, guided by universal moral principles, is necessarily structured in relation to the complementary and supplementary "universal woman." "Sophy should be as truly a woman as Emile is a man, i.e., she must possess all those characters of her sex which are required to enable her to play her part in the physical and moral order. Let us inquire to begin with in what respects her sex differs from our own" (pp. 465, *321*). The complementarity of the two sexes is grounded in their different and opposite relation to language, symbolic codes, conventions, and public opinion. The actual woman should be strictly subjected to the authority of public opinion, whereas the ideal/imaginary woman should regulate the male subject's desire and thus make him independent of public opinion. Sophie has to become the supplement of his amour propre (his independent, masculine ego).[35] Her amour propre will be made congruent with the social norms of femininity: "A man has no one but himself to consider, and so long as he does right he may defy public opinion; but when a woman does right her task is only half finished, and what people think of her matters as much as what she really is. Hence her education must, in this respect, be contrary to ours. 'What will people think' is the grave of a man's virtue and the throne of a woman's" (pp. 475, *328*; trans. slightly modified). For

Man to be entirely on the side of authenticity and *être*, Woman must be completely on the side of representations and *paraître*.[36]

From infancy on, women must become totally constructed for the eyes and the pleasures of others; they will be exclusively on the side of representations, however, without any possible mode of distantiation. The woman must be absorbed with herself as she is perceived by others and must never actively intervene in the way she is observed. She has to abandon herself to the regard of others like a doll: "She sees her doll, she cannot see herself; she cannot do anything for herself, she has neither the training, nor the talent, nor the strength; as yet she herself is nothing, she is engrossed in her doll and all her coquetry is devoted to it. This will not always be so; in due time she will be her own doll" (pp. 479, *331*). Her love for jewelry and clothes should be indulged, and she should be trained to find satisfaction exclusively in being pleasing to others. In order to avoid any manipulative use of her coquettish arts, she has to be strictly subjected to parental authority. Her total subjection to an unpredictable parental authority will make her an excellent psychologist.[37] Her happiness will depend on her ability always to divine correctly the desire of others.[38] Her psychology will not be abused in the public realm since she will be kept strictly apart from that realm and she will be trained to renounce any selfish interest or pleasure. Although she must not utter any demands and is unable to define goals for herself or others, her psychological and social sensitivity will enable her to seek the best strategy for realizing certain objectives once these have been defined by men: "A woman's reason is practical, and therefore she soon arrives at a given conclusion, but she fails to discover it for herself. The social relation of the sexes is a wonderful thing. This relation produces a moral person of which woman is the eye and man the hand, but the two are so dependent on one another that the man teaches the woman what to see, while she teaches him what to do" (pp. 492, *340*). Note how the social engineer expresses his aims: the modern disciplined subject, "la personne morale," is described as the result of the complementary gender polarity.

Due to women's strong position in the economy of desire, they will always rule over men. According to Rousseau, they can do so in two ways: in favor of partial interests, which will be shortsighted and in the end against them, or in favor of the common good, the glory of the republic or the "volonté générale," which will be their true rulership. Although their subjection initially amounts to the negation of their own interests, in the end they will prosper by it.

A bold, shameless, intriguing woman, who can only attract her lovers by coquetry and retain them by her favours, wins a servile obedience in common things; in weighty and important matters she has no influence over them. But the woman who is both virtuous, wise, and charming, she who, in a word, combines love and esteem, can send them at her bidding to the end of the world, to war, to glory, and to death at her behest. This is a fine kingdom and worth the winning. This is the spirit in which Sophy had been educated. . . . Let us say just a word about her person, according to the description I have given to Emile and the picture he himself has formed of the wife in whom he hopes to find happiness. (pp. 515–16, 356)

This passage anticipates the transition from the preceeding chapter, concerned with Emile's education, to the final chapter of the book, which focuses on Sophie's and Emile's courtship. Initially Sophie is a pedagogical construct of the tutor, not a character but merely the name for the Woman as the central disciplinary device in the formation of the masculine subject. From there Rousseau moves smoothly into his novelistic account of the courtship between Emile and Sophie. The transition, one could say, marks the end of his pedagogical treatise and announces the beginning of a genre to come: the bildungsroman.

Yet, despite its novelistic features, *Emile* cannot be called a bildungsroman, not even quite a novel. The character of Sophie Rousseau presents to the reader is fairly weak. Nevertheless we can grasp from the manner in which her character is introduced the deployment of an aesthetic program in the service of ideology. Sophie is thoroughly average; there is nothing particular, excessive, or glamorous about her. At first sight she would almost tend to leave a new acquaintance indifferent; only with time does she capture the imagination. The impact of her personality cannot be particularized in a description of her individual features since it consists in the totality of the picture. The narrator's attempt to depict her in a traditional *blazon* has the effect of emptying her of all carnal qualities. "Her eyes might be finer, her mouth more beautiful, her stature more imposing; but no one could have a more graceful figure, a finer complexion, a whiter hand, a daintier foot, a sweeter look, and a more expressive countenance. She does not dazzle; she arouses interest; she delights us, we know not why" (pp. 516, 356). The "image sensible" of Sophie has a profound long-term effect on the beholder's fantasy life. "Her dress is very modest in appearance and very coquettish in reality; she does not display her charms, she conceals them, but in such a way as to enhance them. When you see her you say, 'That is a good modest girl,' but while you are with her, you cannot take your eyes or your thoughts off her and one might say that this very simple adornment is only put on to be removed bit by bit by the imagination" (pp. 517, 356–57). Although *Emile* merely supplies the blueprint for the construction of the ideal Woman, the pedagogical treatise makes it quite clear how the ideal Woman is to be used within the project of Anschaulichkeit. Sophie functions as a decoy for the taming of the male imagination. We can also see from *Emile* that literary discourse will be the main vehicle for the imaginary attachments regulating the behavior of the individual. Sophie has been programmed to fall in love with Emile through her reading of Fénélon's *Télémaque*. Although the role of literature is of crucial importance in *Emile*, it nevertheless leaves undiscussed what must be its proper institutional place and generic shape if it is to achieve its desired effects. Rousseau pursues this question mainly in his letter to Jean d'Alembert on the theater. This discussion of the theater provides conclusive clues for the anti-theatricality of the epistolary novel as well as for Diderot's and Lessing's bourgeois tragedy.

The *Lettre à M. d'Alembert sur les spectacles* (1757; published 1758) examines in detail those effects of the theater detrimental to the construction of a unified, disciplined subject. The preface describes the public nature of the role in which the letter has been written. The letter does not come from Jean-Jacques, the private man of letters, who personally loves drama,[39] nor does he have any personal interest in criticizing d'Alembert's article on Geneva. Rather, he speaks as a republican sincerely concerned with public morality and its institutions. "But consideration outweighs duty only with those for whom all morality consists in appearances. Justice and truth are man's first duties; humanity and country his first affections. Every time that private considerations cause him to change this order, he is culpable" (pp. 43, 3). Before Rousseau broaches the issue of the theater, he defends the orthodoxy of the Genevan ministers against d'Alembert's characterization of them as Socinians. He will not tolerate the depiction of the official church authorities as secret or private sectarians because he will not allow for a difference between their public role and their private beliefs. Thus, the opening paragraphs already display Rousseau's concern with the nature of the public sphere and the institutions and authorities regulating public opinion.

Rousseau analyzes the theater as an institution of public life and a medium determining people's attitudes toward representation. In this sense, the quality of individual plays is of no importance to his main argument against the theater, which is that theater has an effect of distantiation utterly opposed to Anschaulichkeit. It foregrounds codes and conventions and thereby dismantles the authority of its immediate impact: "The more

I think about it, the more I find that everything that is played in the theatre is not brought nearer to us but made more distant. . . . The theatre has rules, principles, and a morality apart, just as it has a language and a style of dress that is its own" (pp. 79–80, 26). Rousseau rejects the theater because it draws attention to the discrepancies between role and actor. Furthermore, the spectacle tends to emphasize the difference between the representation of an ideological program (e.g., Alceste's speech) and the artifice of the drama with all its aesthetic conventions. The distantiating effect of the theater makes the naturalization of ideology problematic since it can "present virtue to us as a theatrical game" (pp. 80, 26). The theater thus subverts "the whole order of society . . . all the most sacred relations on which it is founded . . . the respectable rights of fathers over their children, of husbands over their wives, of masters over their servants" (pp. 94, 35) by making those sacred laws look artificial and conventional and even by exposing them to laughter.

Another reason for Rousseau's hostility toward the theater is that it externalizes and disintegrates what should be united in the subject: intention and action, individual and role: "And I do not precisely accuse him [the actor] of actually deceiving people, but I accuse him of cultivating by profession the talent of deceiving men, of practicing the habit of deception that can be innocent only in the theater and can serve everywhere else only for doing harm" (p. 164). If the actor is not harmful as long as he remains on the stage and if one does not assume the audience should profit from performances as from acting classes, what exactly is meant by the dangers of "cultivating by profession the talent of deceiving men"? Couldn't it mean that an audience trained in distinguishing theatrical tricks and conventions would be less gullible toward other public actors, those not confined to the stage, such as the state authorities, for whom Rousseau insists on a fusion of role and person? Rousseau does not want an orator or public persona perceived as if he were an actor since "he represents only himself; he fills only his own role, speaks only in his own name, says, or ought to say, only what he thinks; the man and the role being the same, he is in his place, he is in the situation of any citizen who fulfils the functions of his estate" (pp. 164–65, 81). Instead of becoming useful as an ideological state apparatus, an institution that naturalizes general ideology,[40] the theater would only too easily work against ideology: the artifice of the theater would make the "natural" and the "obvious" appear artificial and constructed.

The new subject of the republican state has to be defined exclusively by the authority of the state; that is, he must be constituted as a subject through interpellation by the moral/state authority. He cannot gamble or play with his "honor" by dueling, for instance. In this context we can understand Rousseau's fascination with the Tribunal of the Marshals of France, an institution established under Louis XIV to control and gradually abolish the ritual of dueling through its institutionalization. A ritual in which males could define their honor independently of the state authority could not be tolerated under an absolutist regime. In a republican state a subject's responsibility to his country is of even greater importance. Rousseau compares this Tribunal with Geneva's Consistory and its Chamber of the Reformation, composed of pastors and twelve elders who supervised morals (p. 155).[41] The Tribunal, which, according to Rousseau, should have been called *cour d'honneur* to prevent any association with actual force or violence, is an exemplary institution for the disciplining of male subjects (p. 145). It is purely symbolical; the "show" it stages has no "real" effects. As grounded in the highest authority (even above the king), however, it is effective and powerful in changing public opinion and defining male individuals as subjects.[42]

In order to be effective, even an ideological state apparatus like this Court of Honor has to be supported by the institutionalization of the role of women and the ideal Woman in the service of ideology: "I am convinced that we will never succeed in working these changes without bringing about the intervention of women, on whom men's way of thinking in large measure depends" (pp. 151, 72). What Rousseau means by this "intervention of women" is their banishment from the public sphere. This banishment becomes particularly essential in a republican state, where the subjects are ruled through internalized authority and are expected to support the state as "good" citizens: "Whether a monarch governs men or women ought to be rather indifferent to him, provided that he be obeyed; but in a republic, men are needed" (pp. 196, *101*). "Real" men—republican subjects whose first duty is to serve their country—must not be distracted from their duties by an errant desire, or by private considerations, demands, or pleasure. Sexuality has to be controlled in a system of a stable, monogamous heterosexuality, founded upon the ideology of a binary, mutually exclusive and complementary definition of gender: "I add that there are no good morals [manners] for women outside of a withdrawn and domestic life . . . the dignity of their sex consists in modesty" (pp. 168, *82–83*). Feminine modesty performs a crucial double function in the success of the ideological state apparatuses. It not only keeps women out of the public sphere but also determines their special relation to a symbolic code, to representations and the realm of *paraître*. Only by becoming the object of desire for man can the modest woman who passively suc-

Fig. 3. Rousseau, Julie *(1761), plate 2, "L'Héroisme de la valeur." Julie has convinced Milord Edouard to mend his ways. In front of witnesses, he kneels before Saint-Preux to ask his forgiveness and thus averts a duel.*

cumbs to his "attack" define the male individual as a masculine citizen in collaboration with his interpellation by the state as a "real" man (pp. 170–79).

Rousseau's prime example for the realization of the ideal sex/gender system is England. There, the detrimental hedonism and frivolity of the theater has been replaced by the absorption of novel reading. "From this common taste for solitude arises a taste for the contemplative readings and the novels with which England is inundated. Thus both [sexes], withdrawn more into themselves, give themselves less to frivolous imitations, get more of a taste for the true pleasures of life, and think less of appearing happy than of being so" (pp. 167, 82). The novel Rousseau singles out for special praise is *Clarissa*. In brief, Rousseau's anti-theatrical, pro-novelistic argument substitutes the novel for the theater as the literary institution supporting the interpellation of individuals as subjects within a state ideology. Absorption in novels parallels the interiorization of the "eye of power" and the creation of a stable male identity. Novels like *Pamela* and *Clarissa* celebrating feminine modesty and chastity become a constitutive part of male fantasy.

Throughout Rousseau's writing one can find an intricately interwoven argument of how morality and the authority of the law should be implanted into the subject's soul. As we have seen, this cannot be achieved if the subject is confronted with authority. It is possible only if the moral code becomes part of the motivational structure and experience of the individual. On the one hand, there has to be the invisible, unquestionable force of the law and authority (the "invisible" guidance of the tutor or the interpellation of individuals as subjects through an ideological state apparatus like the Court of Honor). On the other hand, the individual subject has to be unified, prevented from defining himself in theatrical terms (appearances, *paraître*). The subject's outward manipulation of signs has to be prevented. Any mental reservation producing a split between his *amour propre* and his *amour de soi* must be eradicated. In brief, theatrical behavior as proposed by Rameau's nephew in Diderot's text has to become impossible for Rousseau's subject.[43] By closing the gap between reading and seeing, between the code and what is signified, Anschaulichkeit cancels the possibility of a mental reservation and radically unifies the subject in the presence of the imagined object.

However, this salutary effect of the imagination is not guaranteed a priori. The imagination has a particular relationship to language and desire. Since it initially is with the aid of the imagination that man produces artificial signs and leaves the realm of immediate, instinctual needs, he is only too easily led into the alienating pursuit of imaginary goods and driven by a desire for appearances. The productivity of the imagination has to be controlled by being focused on one object: the Woman. And the Woman collaborates with the state to the extent that she prevents the male subject from pursuing a frivolous hedonism through her strict morality and chasteness while she perpetuates, focuses, and controls his desire through her inaccessible body. The Woman has to be produced by anti-theatrical genres in order to become the image sensible or the hieroglyph of the law.

2

The Epistolary Novel and Bourgeois Tragedy: An Ideal Daughter and an Ideal Father

The project of Anschaulichkeit within the semiotic, aesthetic, and pedagogical discussions of the mid-eighteenth century calls for a new positioning of the subject vis-à-vis language in order to achieve a particular closure: the fusion of reading and seeing and the unification of the subject as pure interiority. The traditional genre of the fable has come to be considered incapable of achieving those newly defined aims, because any foregrounding of language as a codified construct appears to be an obstacle to the new pedagogy. Furthermore, Rousseau's condemnation of the theater and his approval of private novel reading point to a major shift in the institutional placement of literature. Both the condemnation of rhetorical play with language as well as of frivolous theatricality and contemporary semiotic discussion ask for generic innovation. The epistolary novel and the bourgeois tragedy are responses to this demand for transparency, and both develop a new model of subjectivity. In the following analysis of these new literary genres I shall ask how reading and seeing are related, how the masculine subject is to be disciplined, and how this disciplinary process is mediated by the image of the ideal Woman.

Diderot's and Lessing's programmatic writings about the bourgeois tragedy frequently refer to Richardson's epistolary novels to illustrate how a new, "naturalistic" acting style draws the spectator/reader into the illusionary space of the play. The boundaries between the narrative and the dramatic genre seem to be of little relevance to these authors. If both the epistolary novel and the bourgeois tragedy are understood as responses to the semiotic/aesthetic demand for Anschaulichkeit, their common agenda becomes clearer: they share the anti-theatrical thrust of the new pedagogy.

Yet although both genres aim at the moral improvement of the subject, their methods for achieving this improvement are quite different. The novelistic genre utilizes a specific attitude to writing and reading; the dramatic genre focuses on the subject's affective economy. The differences between the two genres reside in the particular ways language is related to the imaginary and to affects. One way to localize these differences is to trace how each genre develops what was to become *the* anthropological deep value of the period: pity. In *Clarissa* pity or sympathy helps construct the exemplary woman as well as reform the rake; however, only in the bourgeois tragedy—in particular, in Lessing's theorization of the genre and in his dramatic response to *Clarissa*—does pity become the central or organizing value of the literary construct.

This chapter examines first the formation of the epistolary novel and then the formation of the bourgeois tragedy. Each part begins with a characterization of the genre's poetics, the framing of the epistolary or dramatic project in terms of an anti-theatrical presentation of the textual claims to truth. In Richardson's case, I outline those conventions through a brief overview of how his fictional oeuvre establishes anti-theatrical aesthetics. For the bourgeois tragedy, I focus on Diderot's and Lessing's poetological writings about the genre. Each section then analyzes a prototypical text in detail. The guiding questions in this phase of the analysis bear on the role of writing and reading in the construction of plot, the specific ideals of communication posited by the works, the narrated experience of texts, and the processes through which experience itself is integrated into discourse. I hope to show how for both *Clarissa* and *Miß Sara Sampson* the construction of an exemplary subjectivity depends on the particular family dynamics between an ideal daughter and an absent or ideal father.

Richardson's Anti-theatrical Epistolarity

Richardson, in his *Apprentice's VADE MECUM* (1734), thematizes the precarious situation of the young male apprentice as a liminal stage between child and man, servant and master. Finding a successful and efficient means to negotiate this transition is a matter of central importance to the national welfare.

Addressing our selves more particularly to the class of Young Men who are about being apprenticed out to Trades and Business. This, we conceive, is the Subject that has not been hitherto touch'd upon, or consider'd as it ought: And which yet is of very high Importance to the Good of the Community in this great Trading

Kingdom: Since it is from this Source, Members of the Commonwealth are derived; on whose Industry and Labour the Welfare of the Whole almost intirely depends. (p. iv)

Although Richardson advises the apprentice to avoid any entertainment that could distract him from his duties, he seems to believe that the theater is particularly dangerous for the young tradespeople: "1. Because Plays are calculated for Persons in upper Life. 2. Because of the expense of Time and Money. 3. Because of the Resort of lewd Women. 4. Because Trade and Men of Business are the Objects of Ridicule in most Plays" (p. 11).[1] Richardson can recommend only one play, George Lillo's *George Barnwell*, for the moral instruction and recreational enjoyment of the apprentices.

Certainly, Richardson's anti-theatrical arguments are far from original, and, as Jonas Barish demonstrates, they are quite typical for his era.[2] Nevertheless, in Richardson's case, one might also consider these arguments symptomatic of an institution and an ethos against which his own writing, beginning with *Pamela* (1740), tries to establish itself by promoting an entirely new and anti-theatrical genre, a genre based on immediacy.

For, besides the beautiful simplicity of the style, and a happy propriety and clearness of expression (the letters being written under the immediate impression of every circumstance which occasioned them, and that to those who had a right to know the fair writer's most secret thoughts) the several passions of the mind must, of course, be more affectively described, and nature may be traced in her undisguised inclinations. . . . This little book will infallibly be looked upon as the hitherto much-wanted standard or pattern for this kind of writing. (*Pamela*, p. 23)

As this statement from the preface to *Pamela* makes clear, Richardson considers his epistolary novels a new kind of writing. *Pamela* is for him a paradigmatic text founding an anti-theatrical genre; free of disguise and false ornament, it is a transparent representation of the writer's most secret thoughts.

The anti-theatrical edge not only is a constitutive feature of Richardson's moral and poetological statements but also pervades his entire fictional work. It lays the foundation and becomes a legitimizing force for his epistolary fiction. In Richardson's 1741 sequel to *Pamela*, for instance, Pamela writes a long letter to Lady Davers about *The Distressed Mother*, a play she went to see with Lord B. In general she does not object to the theater. She enjoys the drama and the lead actress, and she identifies with the events and emotions on stage. Her indignation at the play stems mainly from the breaking of the illusion after the play.

But the epilogue spoken after the play, by Mrs. Oldfield, in the character of Andromache, was more shocking to me, than the most terrible parts of the play; as by lewd and even senseless *double entendre*, it could be calculated only to efface all the tender, all the virtuous sentiments, which the tragedy was designed to raise. . . . I was extremely mortified to see my favourite (and the only perfect) character debased and despoilt, and the widow of Hector, prince of Troy, talking nastiness to an audience, and setting it out with all the wicked graces of action, and affected archness of look, attitude, and emphasis . . . inverting the design of the whole play, satirizing her own sex, but indeed most of all ridiculing and shaming, in my mind, that part of the audience who can be delighted with this vile epilogue, after such scenes of horror and distress. (*Pamela II*, p. 252)

Her husband grounds this shocking obscenity in the actor's ability to impersonate: "You only see by this one instance, what a character that of an actor or actress is, and how capable they are to personate any thing for a sorry subsistence" (*Pamela II*, p. 254).

The immorality of histrionic actions is emblematically represented by the frivolous countess who attends a masquerade in the habit of a nun.[3] Indeed, virtuous Pamela expresses her views on acting as impersonation in relation to the masquerade: "I thought the dear gentleman no more kept to his Spanish gravity, than she to the requisites of the habit she wore: when I had imagined that all that was tolerable in a masquerade, was the acting up to the character each person assumed: and this gave me no objection to the Quaker's dress; for I thought I was prim enough for that naturally" (*Pamela II*, p. 259). What is so interesting about Pamela's reaction to the masquerade is her shock that people might deliberately fail "to act up to the character" they assume, as if the costume were unable to define its wearer. Pamela demands a perfect congruence among social identity, appearance, and behavior. To foreground any of these as an arbitrarily chosen exteriority seems almost blasphemous. Pamela's virtue does not allow for any play with clothes. She always takes her social position and role entirely seriously. Thus, she is embarrassed at inheriting clothes from Lord B.'s mother and is careful not to be corrupted into seeming more than she is. Pamela labors to make her inner self conform with the demands of being a pious daughter and a dutiful servant. The anti-theatricality both of the character Pamela and of the novel that carries her name is constructed as the ideal of a unified self that adapts itself to her/his persona without reservation, doubt, or ambiguity.

However, the *Anti-Pamelas* and *Shamela*, Henry Fielding's 1741 parody of *Pamela*, indicate that Richardson's contemporaries did not readily accept this presentation of self. One might even argue that the immense popularity of *Pamela* resulted from the novel's carnivalesque plot, the heroine's marvelous gift of transforming herself from a chambermaid into Lady B. by adjusting to the clothes she is given to wear. One might further argue that this popular "misreading" of the novel led to the sequel in which Pamela is at pains to expunge any carnivalesque features from herself and her surroundings.[4] In order to believe *Pamela*'s presentation of an "authentic" self, the reader has to subscribe to an aesthetics of representation and reject the more traditional rhetorical paradigm. And even as modern readers praise Richardson's psychological realism, they are equally as intrigued by his convincing use of the illusionist potential of the epistolary form: the evocation of an imaginary presence, the subject in the act of writing, the effacing of any mediating factor (such as the narrator, or the temporary distance between the I as narrator and I as protagonist in memoirs and autobiographies). As I have argued in Chapter 1, the perfection of illusionist writing techniques together with an Enlightenment aesthetics of representation supports the construction of this rigidly unified subject, defined as pure interiority, as non-mediated presence, as pure voice without body: a non-theatrical aesthetics of illusion and a non-theatrical subject.

The novelty of *Pamela*'s presentation of self can be illustrated by a comparative glance at a contemporary novel, Pierre Marivaux's *La vie de Marianne* (1731–41). The frequent comparisons of these two works suggest many superficial similarities: both novels have a female first-person narrator; both deal with a "from rags to riches" story in the sense that a successful marriage allows both protagonists to ascend socially. But the manner in which the female protagonists tell their stories makes all the difference: Pamela's sincerity versus Marianne's playful and manipulative presentation of self: "I amused myself with all kinds of being pleasing; I knew how to be several women in one. When I wanted to appear roguish, I had the deportment and adornment that achieved this effect for me; the following day I could be found with tender graces; thereupon I would be a modest, serious and nonchalant beauty."[5] Marianne manages to climb up the social ladder by virtue of her histrionic gifts; Pamela's virtue is rewarded not as histrionic talent but as documented authenticity and integrity. Lord B., Lady Davers, and the friends of the family accept her only after her letters have proven her sexual and moral integrity.

The structure of subjectivity implicit in *Pamela* can be characterized in both sociological and aesthetic terms. In terms of aesthetics, it is linked to the category of representation as opposed to the categories of performance or expression. This emphasis on representation with its implicit rejection of performance is also class specific. A performance-oriented culture is rhetorical, theatrical, and action oriented. Its appreciation of artworks is public. "Aesthetic consumption thereby serves to enhance solidarity with a locally defined social group."[6] Richardson, as a spokesman of the industrious bourgeoisie, condemns the pleasure derived from the theater as a sign of the "conspicuous consumption" of the "leisure class": "I cannot forbear observing, that however the Playhouses at the gay End of Town may be tolerated for the Amusement of Persons in upper Life, who would not perhaps as the World stands, otherwise know what to do with their Time, they must be of pernicious Consequence when set up in the City, or in those Confines of it, where the People of Industry generally inhabit" (*Vade Mecum*, p. 16).

Whereas the theater is part of the public sphere and theatrical subjects can construct their subjectivity according to the roles they enact successfully, at the center of representational aesthetics is the receiver's imagination. The work of art is judged by its effect on the emotions and its ability to evoke an illusionary presence. The artistic medium must not draw attention to itself; it should be so transparent that it does not interfere with the work's appeal to the inner eye of the recipient. Clarissa discusses the drama she attended with Lovelace and Miss Horton merely in terms of the ideational realm of the *author's* performance: "It is, you know, a deep and most affecting tragedy in the reading. . . . You will not wonder that Miss Horton, as well as I, was greatly moved at the representation, when I tell you, and have some pleasure in telling you, that Mr. Lovelace himself was very sensibly touched with some of the most affecting scenes, I mention this in praise of the author's performance; for I take Mr. Lovelace to be one of the most hard-hearted men in the world." (*Clarissa*, 2: 372). She does not even mention the actors' performance. She sees the drama as if she were silently reading it. For her the materiality of the medium is effaced, and within the "immediacy" thus produced the subject emerges as pure interiority ("heart" and conscience).

A crucial aspect of Richardson's moralizing anti-theatricality is visible in his description of the duties and behavior of the apprentice. Richardson stresses the importance of the total interiorization of the master's eye and authority: "It will even behove you to double your Diligence in his Absence; for no one can well have a worse Character than he that deserves the Name of an *Eye-Servant*; that is, such a one as no longer heeds his Business, than while he is under his Master's Eye or Observation" (*Vade Mecum*, p. 27). As soon as the gaze of the authority is completely internalized, the subject can no longer manipulate, influence, or persuade an audience.

Fig. 4. William Hogarth (1697–1764), "Strolling Actresses Dressing in a Barn." Note the Medusa's head on the shield behind the left leg of the central figure (see detail).

Losing all backstage/onstage distinctions or possibilities of withdrawal or distantiation, the subject is under constant scrutiny and control.[7]

In *Sir Charles Grandison* (1753), his third epistolary novel, Richardson attempts to portray the perfectly disciplined male subject. The main features of Grandison's discipline are his control of his temper and his rejection of dueling. A large part of volumes 1 and 2 serves to document Sir

Fig. 5. Rousseau, Julie (1761), plate 3, "Ah! jeune homme, à ton bienfaiteur." Suspecting Milord Edouard of betrayal, Saint-Preux wants to challenge him to a duel. Yet the evidence of the letters removes any suspicion. Note the portrait of the woman above the window.

Charles's virtue in terms of his ability to avoid armed confrontation, culminating in the "paper" included in Letter IV (pt. I, vol. 2) from Harriet Byron to Lucy Selby. This paper is based on the minute account of a shorthand writer hired by James Bagenhall to hide in a closet and record the confrontation between Sir Hargrave Pollexfen and Sir Charles. He is supposed to document a conflict expected to lead to a duel in case there should be a legal investigation. Instead of becoming a document in a trial, however, the paper becomes an attestation of Sir Charles's exemplarity for the male sex, proving his magnamity and true heroism in breaking the "evil custom" by showing everyone that "reputation and conscience are entirely reconcilable" (pt. I, vol. 2, p. 256).[8] Sir Charles Grandison, who claims to have given up the sword for the pen, is justified and glorified by those secretly taken notes. He always acts righteously, whether he knows himself to be acting publicly or not; his private persona does not differ from his public persona, and he is unafraid of eavesdroppers. He is the masculine example of an anti-theatrical, radically unified subjectivity: "As I always speak what I think, if I am not afraid of my own recollection, I need not of any man's minutes" (pt. 1, vol. 2, p. 267).

Grandison, however, is the only unblemished example of masculine virtue in Richardson's fiction. Most of the male protagonists are lacking in perfection. Lord B., as he himself admits, has to be corrected and reformed through the exemplary subjectivity of Pamela, who has to expect her intruding husband/master at any time, who has to be at all times "presentable" and pleasing to him, at any time prepared to represent her master's family and estate. She has to construct herself in His gaze, for his eyes.

And when anything unpleasant happens, in a quarter of an hour, at farthest, begin to mistrust yourself, and apply to your glass; and if you see a gloom arising, or arisen, banish it instantly; smooth your dear countenance; resume your former composure; and then, my dearest, whose heart must always be seen in her face, and cannot be a hypocrite, will find this a means to smooth her passions also: And if the occasion be too strong for so sudden a conquest, she will know how to do it more effectually by repairing to her closet, and begging that gracious assistance, which has never failed her; and so shall I, my dear, who as you once but too justly observed, have been too much indulged by my good mother, have an example from you, as well as a pleasure in you, which will never be palled. (*Pamela*, p. 394)

The dutiful wife functions as the invisible medium in a double mirroring process: she corrects her own mirror reflection with regard to the Lord's and her master's expectations of her; smoothing out any uncontrolled passions and expressions, she can offer herself as a guiding mirror to her husband. Thus she can correct her husband's shortcomings as an agent of secondary socialization, a supplement to the maternal influence domesticating the spoiled son, who only too easily indulges in moods and tempers. This passage coordinates the function of the ideal woman and her particular implication in the gaze of authority, a crucial constellation we will examine in greater detail in *Clarissa*.

Richardson's epistolary project can be described as an attempt to establish this rigidly unified and transparent subjectivity, and he seems to have created two more or less convincing examples of it in *Pamela* and *Sir Charles Grandison*. However, his second novel, *Clarissa* (1747–48), is far more complex. Clarissa does not succeed in reforming her suitor or attaining public approval in Pamela's manner; nor is she ever able to tell her "whole story," a failure that denies her access to documented evidence of her integrity in Grandison's manner. Rather, from the beginning she and her writings are threatened by willful misreadings, interruptions, and fragmentations.[9] In other words, Clarissa's long story can be described as her subjection to constant accusations of "inauthenticity" and "plotting." Those accusations put her constantly on trial and transform her into a martyr-like figure, culminating in her death. Like any good martyr, she is justified only after her death, when her own and others' letters constitute her as the image of the ideal Woman and daughter.

Clarissa is organized as a series of "trials" the heroine must undergo at various places: (1) Clarissa's confinement at Harlowe Place; (2) Clarissa's imprisonment by Lovelace, culminating in her rape; (3) Clarissa's self-chosen exile, during which she prepares herself for death. The explicit purpose of these trials is to establish the "truth" about events and characters. Yet each trial alters the conditions of the writers vis-à-vis their epistolary project. Initially Clarissa writes in order to prove the integrity of her heart to her parents; later she is concerned less with the persuasion of others than with her own spiritual state. Lovelace attempts to compensate for his ineffectual seduction schemes by writing to his friend Belford. From a confidant of Clarissa's antagonist, Belford becomes her closest friend and finally even the guarantor of her "authorial intention" as the executor of her will and the editor of her letters. Belford's conversion from a rake into the editor of an epistolary novel provides the key for understanding *Clarissa* as a pedagogical project. It must be understood as exactly that radical change in the attitude toward language that motivates the completion of the novel as a whole and effects the transformation of Clarissa into *Clarissa*.

Clarissa's Aesthetics of Representation

Just as in *Sir Charles Grandison*, where a hidden stenographer tran-
scribes the confrontations between Pollixfen and Grandison in order to
provide evidence for an anticipated trial, so too Anna Howe, in the first
letter in *Clarissa*, requests the heroine to document all the circumstances
leading to any conflict she may become involved in. In this way, the "whole
story" will be brought before the eyes of the public that judges her virtue.

> Write to me therefore, my dear, the whole of your story from the time that
> Mr. Lovelace was first introduced into your family; and particularly an account
> of all that passed between him and your sister; about which there are different
> reports; some people scrupling not to insinuate that the younger sister has stolen
> a lover from the elder. And pray write in so full a manner as may satisfy those
> who know not so much of your affairs as I do. If anything unhappy should fall
> out from the violence of such spirits as you have to deal with, your account of all
> things *previous* to it will be your best justification.   (1: 2)

In both cases the assumption is that a written account is the perfect evidence, beyond any uncertainty or accusation of hearsay. This assumption is
based on an implicit aesthetics of representation and a semiotics of transparency: the text represents the truth, if only it takes in all the details.
Temporal proximity or even simultaneity between the unfolding of the
event and the production of the written document alone can protect the
text from distortions.

Clarissa, as Anna Howe goes on to tell her, is not to establish her innocence in a case in which she is suspected of a transgression—at this point
she is not even fully involved in her family's conflict with Lovelace—but
her trial has to prove her the exemplar of ideal femininity she is reputed to
be: "You see what you draw upon yourself by excelling all your sex. Every
individual of it who knows you, or has heard of you, seems to think you
answerable to her for your conduct in points so very delicate and concerning." Thus Clarissa is faced with the double task of fully representing her
particular individuality as well as her exemplary ideality: "Every eye, in
short, is upon you with the expectation of an example. I wish to heaven
you were at liberty to pursue your own methods; all would then, I dare
say, be easy and honourably ended. But I dread your directors and direc-
tresses; for your mother, admirably well qualified as she is to lead, must
submit to be led. Your sister and brother will certainly put you out of your
course" (1: 2–3). This passage outlines the conditions of Clarissa's "trial"
at Harlowe Place. Her exemplary virtue must be visible to "every eye."
Clarissa is, however, not at all visible to the public. She is confined in Har-

lowe Place and will subsequently be imprisoned under increasingly severe restrictions. Not only is she confined to the private sphere, but she is also not a free agent, since she is subject to her parents. Like Emile's Sophie, Clarissa has to display exemplary virtue for the public without being able to choose her own method.

The parental authority to which Clarissa is subjected is exercised in a complicated web of mutual dependency and want. There is her father's "wounded authority" due to his gouty attacks: "But my father was soured by the cruel distemper . . . which seized him all at once in the very prime of life, in so violent a manner as to take from the most active of minds, as his was, all power of activity, and that in all appearance for life. It imprisoned, as I may say, his lively spirits in himself and turned the edge of them against his own peace. . . . Those I believe who want the fewest earthly blessings, most regret that they want any" (1: 23). And there is her mother's "sensible mind, which has from the beginning, on all occasions, sacrificed its own inward satisfaction to outward peace" (1: 22). Clarissa attributes her mother's failure to assert her parental authority to being too dependent on her children's and her husband's love. Her mother gives in to their demands and thereby affirms her own want of love as a want, which Clarissa dares to criticize in the following words: "Upon my word, I am sometimes tempted to think that we may make the world allow for and respect us as we please, if we can but be sturdy in our wills, and set out accordingly. It is but being the *less* beloved for it, that's all; and if we have power to oblige those we have to do with, it will not appear to *us* that we are. Our flatterers will tell us anything sooner than our faults, or what they know we do not like to hear" (1: 22). Her mother has lost the power to satisfy all demands by satisfying some of them. Giving in to her son's demands, she has entered the realm of appearances; her want has made her dependent on James's flattery. For fear of losing their children's love, the parents have lost their authority over James and Arabella. This situation allows the children instead of the parents to dictate the standards of behavior and interpretation in Harlowe Place.

Despite her clear view of her parents' shortcomings and weaknesses, Clarissa attempts to act as if the order of the family were still intact. At least she does not want to yield to the corrosion of parental control. Instead she tries to prop up their authority at any cost.

My father himself could not bear that I should be made sole, as I may call it, and independent, for such the will, as to that estate and the powers it gave (unaccountably as they all said), made me.

To obviate therefore every one's jealousy, I gave up to my father's management, as you know, not only the estate, but the money bequeathed me (which was a moiety of what my grandfather had by him at his death, the other moiety being bequeathed to my sister), contenting myself to take as from his bounty what he was pleased to allow me, without desiring the least addition to my annual stipend. (1: 54–55)

And, as if her parents were still the ultimate authorities in family decisions, she also attempts to convince them that her opposition to marrying Solmes is not motivated by a secret love for Lovelace. But she is never given the opportunity of persuading them.

Arabella and James construe Clarissa's refusal of Solmes as motivated by her love of Lovelace. They prevent her from meeting those members of the family willing to believe her avowal that her "heart is free." Clarissa is confined to her room and cut off from her parents because of her "perverseness," her ability to move her interlocutors in face-to-face interactions, which her brother describes as theatrical and fashionably conventional behavior: "There was a perverseness, he said, in female minds, a tragedy-pride, such a one as me, risking anything to obtain pity, I was of an age, and a turn (the insolent said) to be fond of a lover-like distress: and my grief (which she pleaded) would never break my heart: I should sooner break that of the best and most indulgent of mothers" (1: 193). The siblings' accusations of Clarissa, their envy, their *invidia*, are occasioned by Clarissa's particular gaze, her ability to make others invisible and insignificant. Arabella describes Clarissa's ecliptic power:

You are *indeed* a very artful one for that matter, interrupted she [Arabella] in a passion: one of the artfullest I ever knew! and then followed an accusation so low! so unsisterly! That I half-bewitched people by my insinuating address: that nobody could be valued or respected, but must stand like cyphers wherever I came. How often, said she, have I and my brother been talking upon a subject, and had everybody's attention until you came in with your bewitching *meek* pride, and *humble* significance; and then have we either been stopped by references to Miss Clary's opinion, forsooth . . . did you not bewitch your grandfather? . . . Why, truly, his last will showed what effect your *smooth* obligingness had upon him! To leave the *acquired part* of his estate from the next heirs, his own sons, to a grandchild. (1: 216).

And indeed, Arabella has a point: Clarissa's "humble significance" has displaced her father and induced her grandfather to place her before his son in his will.

Somehow Clarissa does disturb the order of the family. Her absolute belief in parental authority renders it strangely impotent and creates a conflict between the laws governing intersubjective behavior and interpretation and the child's encounter with parental authority. As her mother's breakdowns prove, in a one-to-one encounter Clarissa is able to move almost everybody. Thus her uncle Harlowe describes to her the effect of her gaze on members of the family and tries to explain their subsequent refusal to see her.

But how can we resolve to see you? There is no standing against your looks and language. It is our love that makes us decline to see you. How *can* we, when you are resolved not to do what we are resolved you *shall* do? I never, for my part, loved any creature, as I loved you from your infancy till now. And indeed, as I have often said, never was there a young creature so deserving of our love. But what has come to you now! Alas! alas! my dear kinswoman, how you fail in the trial! (1: 304)

He accuses her of having failed her trial because she is not moved by her family, a defect that he too takes for a sign of theatricality.

But since you have displayed your talents, and spared nobody, and moved everybody, without being moved, you have but made us stand the closer and firmer together. This is what I likened to an *embattled phalanx* once before. . . . We are all afraid to see you, because we know we shall be made as so many fools. Nay, your mother is so afraid of you that once or twice, when she thought you were coming to force yourself into her presence, she shut the door, and locked herself in, because she knew she must not see you upon *your* terms, and you are resolved you will not see her upon *hers*. (1: 305)

Yet whether Clarissa can be moved is never determined; nor is the family as a group affected. Clarissa manages in many repeated encounters with individuals to win them over as long as she is alone with them. But her mother and her aunt are only intermediaries of her father's will, and as long as he is out of sight, his will is given the unmovable authority of the law. Only if Lovelace had not tricked her away and she had indeed faced her father would the symbolic order of the family have collapsed. This final confrontation would have meant Clarissa's ultimate defeat as well. But this Clarissa can understand only much later, after her aunt tells her that her father had intended to kneel to her and deploy the same gestural language she was going to use: "A father to KNEEL to his child! There would not indeed have been any bearing of that! What I should have done in such a case I know not. Death would have been more welcome to me than such a sight, on such an occasion, in behalf of a man so very, very disgustful to me! But I had deserved annihilation had I suffered my father to kneel in vain" (2: 166). Despite her ambivalence—encompassing both desire and anxiety—about seeing him, in the end she would not have been able to confront her father. If she allowed him to kneel before her in vain, she would destroy his paternal authority forever. His pleading on behalf of the unbearable Solmes would, however, debase his paternal dignity, a debasement that could not be remedied with her giving in to his demand. A loss of paternal authority would mean her own annihilation. As becomes clear in this hypothetical scenario, Clarissa's presentation of self is dependent on the absent father's absolute authority.

Unaware of this paradoxical want of paternal authority, Clarissa imagines possible scenarios of her "heart's" confrontation with her father's will. "I resolve then, upon the whole, to stand this one trial of Wednesday next—or, perhaps I should rather say, of Tuesday evening, if my father hold his purpose of endeavoring, in person, to make me *read*, or *hear* read, and then *sign*, the settlements. That must be the greatest trial of all" (1: 459). What Clarissa fears most, what would break her resistance to the marriage proposal, is a confrontation with her father, hearing or reading the contract and then having to sign immediately on his command. This scenario does not leave her the time and space to resist the law and name of the father, to resist signing her father's name and thereby being inscribed into the legal document. This signature would annihilate her heart. To refuse obedience to her father's command, to destroy his paternal authority by not signing his name, would be an utter defiance of his authority. This she equally cannot face: "O my dear! what a trial will this be! How shall I be able to refuse to my father the writing of my name?—to my father, from whose presence I have been so long banished!—he commanding and entreating, perhaps in a breath! How shall I be able to refuse this to my father!" (1: 439).

Clarissa's hoped-for alternative is a deferral of his demand for her signature, an interruption in the chain of writing that would be a seeing, a space for the language of the heart, a scene where the purity and integrity of her heart could assert itself against the symbolic order of written transactions and substitutions in the immediacy of gestural language: "If I can prevail upon them by my prayers (perhaps I shall fall into fits; for the very first appearance of my father, after having been so long banished from his presence, will greatly affect me) if, I say, I can prevail upon them by my prayers to lay aside their views; or to suspend the day" (1: 495). She expects this interruption in the chain of writing to arise from her physical reaction to the sight of her father. Her fits would affirm his parental authority as a reaction of love and awe at his sight while rendering her incapable of signing. Her reaction might cause him to abstain from his command without wounding his authority.

She also hopes to win over the other members of her family in individual, dyadic, preverbal confrontations: "Perhaps my mother may be brought over. I will kneel to each, one by one, to make a friend. Some of them have been afraid to see me lest they should be moved in my favour; does not this give me a reasonable hope, that I may move them?" (1: 459). In these scenes of seeing, Clarissa hopes to find a way to represent her "heart" and conscience truthfully. Here she hopes to affirm the gaze of paternal authority without corrupting the integrity of her heart by submitting it to a marriage with Solmes, whom she cannot love.

My heart, in short, misgives me less when I resolve *this* way [to confront her parents as described above] than when I think of the *other* [to escape with Lovelace]: and in so strong and involuntary a bias, the *heart* is, as I may say *conscience*. And well cautions the wise man: "Let the counsel of thine own heart stand; for there is no man more faithful to thee, than it: for a man's mind is sometimes wont to tell him more than seven watchmen that sit above in a high tower." (1: 460)

Just as Clarissa's heart and conscience are opposed to her escaping from her father's house with Lovelace, she equally cannot make use of her legal property against her father's will. Her heart is independent only in claiming a veto, not in making any positive demands on her parents or in claiming independence in legal terms.

Hers [Mrs. Howe's] is a protection I could more reputably fly to, than to that of any other person: and from hers should be ready to return to my father's (for the breach then would not be irreparable, as it would be, if I fled to his family): *to return*, I repeat, on such terms as shall secure but my *negative*; not my *independence*: I do not aim at that (so shall your mother under the less difficulty); although I have a right to be put into my grandfather's estate, if I were to insist upon it: such a right, I mean, as my brother exerts in the estate left *him*; and which nobody disputes. God forbid that I should ever think myself freed from my father's *reasonable* control, whatever right my grandfather's will has given me! He, good gentleman, left me that estate, as a reward of my duty, and not to set me above it, as has been justly hinted to me: and this reflection makes me more fearful of not answering the intention of so valuable a bequest. O that my friends knew but my heart!—would but think of it as they used to do. For once more I say: If I deceive me not it is not altered, although theirs are. (1: 490)

Here Clarissa's reflections describe a space for her heart's identity that can be determined only in a negative way, in her refusal to assert her legal rights. Assuming her legal rights over her inheritance would displace her father and sever her dependence on his control over her. She needs a place from which she can always return to her family. Her heart differs from what her family claims it is or should be, but Clarissa cannot make this difference manifest in terms of intersubjective language and behavioral codes. In fact, all the confrontations with her family establish her "true" self, her heart and conscience, exactly as that part of her that always gets lost when she enters the realm of public language, as that which is necessarily repressed when she becomes part of the chain of linguistic substitutions. For whenever she becomes a subject in language, she necessarily refers to her addressee as something beyond the personal interlocutor, that is, as the subject of game theory who knows all the rules and possible strategies; and this Other similarly attributes to her all the strategic knowledge of any possible position within the symbolic code and thereby turns her necessarily and unwillingly into a theatrical and manipulative subject.[10] Her conscience and heart assert themselves in their absolute individuality and integrity only in the refusal to be integrated into the realm of public language and appearance. She can define herself only by demonstrating that she differs from what appearances want her to be. Of course, this demonstration cannot be accomplished in any medium of representation.

Refusing to give herself over to the realm of appearances, Clarissa has found a medium for representing herself in the manner Anna Howe describes in the first letter. She has managed throughout the first volume to establish her individuality, her "purity of heart," as well as her exemplary femininity in the collection of letters "written to the moment." And it is in that medium that she can effect the same impact on the addressee that she can in a face-to-face encounter. Her uncle Harlowe's letter acknowledges that reading Clarissa's letters has the same first impact as seeing her: "For my part, I could not read your letter to me, without being unmanned. . . . Your aunt Hervey forbids your writing, for the same reason, that I must not countenance it" (1: 304). Thus the Harlowes, as they harden themselves against being moved by her sight, also exclude her from a correspondence with them.

Even when Clarissa is altogether cut off from sight and correspondence, she nevertheless goes on writing. In order to subdue her anger against her family, she composes her "Ode to Wisdom." The ode places wisdom in a location beyond deception and disguise, in the lunar light, where the colors of disguise have faded. Wisdom becomes that particular relation to the gaze that can be called "mental sight" (1: 275). In the gaze of wisdom, the mere physical perceptions of color or the sound of names are transcended and become pure intellectual representations. The "Ode to Wisdom" is Clarissa's poetological statement affirming her anti-theatrical, representational aesthetics.

> No more to fabled Names confin'd;
> To Thee! Supreme all-perfect Mind,
> My Thoughts direct their Flight.
> Wisdom's thy Gift, and all her Force
> From Thee deriv'd, Eternal Source
> Of intellectual Light!
> . . . . .
> Beneath her clear discerning Eye
> The visionary Shadows fly
> Of Folly's painted Show.
> She sees thro' ev'ry fair Disguise,
> That all, but VIRTUE's solid Joys,
> Is Vanity and Woe.
>
> (1: 277–78)

Thus Clarissa goes on writing and representing what cannot be seen or represented: her pure heart and conscience.[11]

Lovelace's Rakish Code

If the Harlowe part of Clarissa's "trial" is intended to establish the evidence of her filial piety as part of exemplary femininity, the trial that awaits her after Lovelace takes her away until her rape is meant to prove her absolute resistance to his attempts at seducing her and subjecting her to his interpretations of her. In order to establish the full evidence for this trial, the reader is provided with the letters of Lovelace as her seducer and tempter. The reader is shown how Lovelace plans to assume two roles in her trial, to be both seducer and judge. Lovelace thereby makes himself master over the symbolic order in a theatrical fashion: assuming the roles of playwright, director, star actor, and audience. In contrast to Clarissa, who merely represents in her letters her reflections and trials in her plain and very own language, Lovelace moves about freely and disposes a whole array of symbolic codes and literary conventions.[12] He defines his subjectivity not in terms of a pure interiority but in terms of his mastery of appearances, which he defines as his "life of honour" (1: 147). In his first letter, Lovelace expresses his opposition to Clarissa's subjection to a symbolic order, which she takes to be anchored in the nature of the family.

But here's her mistake; nor will she be cured of it—she takes the man she calls her father (her mother had been faultless, had she not been her father's wife); she takes the men she calls her uncles; the fellow she calls her brother, and the poor contemptible she calls her sister; to *be* her father, to *be* her uncles, her brother, her sister; and that, as such, she owes to some of them reverence, to others respect, let them treat her ever so cruelly. Sordid ties! Mere cradle prejudices! For had they not been imposed upon her by nature, when she was in a peverse humour, or could she have chosen her relations would any of these have been among them? (1: 148)

Lovelace has no respect for any significance unalterably grounded in "nature." He sees himself as an enlightened nominalist above such "cradle prejudices." [13]

However, as much mastery as he claims over the world of appearances, names, and the world as a stage, his letters to Belford show him being mastered by his own language. His letters are playful, extremely digressive; often Lovelace gets carried away by the language he is using. His first letter to Belford is an example of his ability to write "as well without a subject, as with one" (1: 144). He sets out to prove his literary mastery in indulging in the mere frivolous play of language—unlike Clarissa, who subordinates her letters to the unified purpose of representing the state of her heart—but playing with words and literary tricks that are to shape and inform his errant desire as he describes the paradigm of his previous amours: "Those confounded poets, with their serenely celestial descriptions, did as much with me as the lady: they fired my imagination, and set me upon a desire to become a goddess-maker. I must needs try my new-fledged pinions in sonnet, elegy, and madrigal. I must have a Cynthia, a Stella, a Sacharissa . . . and many a time have I been at a loss for a subject, when my new-created goddess has been kinder than it was proper for my plaintive sonnet that she should be" (1: 145–46). Lovelace's love is entirely mediated by traditional generic convention. Still, he claims that with Clarissa he is truly in love. But as soon as he utters his love, it again becomes a literary game: "But now am I indeed in love. I can think of nothing, of nobody, but the divine Clarissa Harlowe. Harlowe! How that hated word sticks in my throat—but I shall give her for it the name of love" (1: 146–47). At this point the editor of the edition used here attaches a footnote to remind us of the writer's name. He thereby criticizes Lovelace's ridicule of Clarissa's respect for her family as a "loveless" gesture since Lovelace refuses to respect Clarissa's integrity, which is defined in her relation to paternal authority. Lovelace believes he can manipulate the symbolic order, yet ironically the name of his father describes his true character beyond art and artifice.

Lovelace first attempts to voice his love for Clarissa in some lines by Otway, but rejects them as "over-tender" and replaces them with two verses by Dryden. The last line, "with Pride it mounts, and with Revenge it glows" (1: 147), captures his imagination and makes him depict his love of Clarissa as informed by revenge toward the Harlowe family. He sees himself involved in a romance: "But was ever hero in romance (fighting with giants and dragons excepted) called upon to harder trials?" (1: 149) Then he again borrows literary quotations from Dryden, Cowley, and Shakespeare to describe Clarissa's perfection, which is supposedly beyond the literary imagination. Thereupon he enters into an imaginary dialogue with a fellow rake, using their convention of inauthentic speech, marked by the second-person singular, the "thou" and the "thee" (see 1: 144n).

Thou art curious to know, if I have not started a new game? If it be possible for so universal a lover to be confined so long to one object? Thou knowest nothing of this charming creature, that thou canst put such questions to me; or thinkest thou knowest me better than thou dost. All that's excellent in her sex is this lady. Until by MATRIMONIAL, or EQUAL intimacies, I have found her *less than angel*, it is impossible to think of any other. Then there are so many stimulatives to such a spirit as mine in this affair, *besides* love: such a field for stratagem and contrivance, which thou knowest to be the delight of my heart. . . . Is it possible, thinkest thou, that there can be room for a thought that is not *of* her, and devoted *to* her? (1: 150)

Trying to affirm the exclusivity of his love, he affirms instead the multitude of motives behind his pursuit of Clarissa. And whereas for Clarissa writing is a scene for reflecting and scrutinizing the purity of her heart, subjecting herself to the "mental sight" of wisdom, Lovelace rambles on at random, without even reading his own writing: "Thus, Jack, as thou desirest, have I written. Written upon something; upon nothing; upon REVENGE, which I love; upon LOVE, which I hate, *heartily* hate, because 'tis my master: and upon the devil knows what besides: for looking back, I am amazed by the length of it. *Thou* may'st read it: *I* would not for a king's ransom—but so as I do *but* write, thou sayest thou wilt be pleased" (1: 151–52). Lovelace can exert his power in his theatrical world only by refusing to read or see what would contradict his plans or interpretations.

In the last letter of the first volume, he tells Belford that he managed to abduct Clarissa only by refusing to read the letter in which he expected her to cancel their appointment, forcing her thereby to appear in person. And quite tellingly he concludes this letter with an affirmation of his errant desire, propelled by his associative writing and subjection to frivolous language: "But how I ramble! This it is to be in such a situation, that I know not what to resolve upon. I'll tell my inclinations as I proceed. The pros and the cons I'll tell thee: but being not too far from the track I set out in, I will close here, I may, however, write every day something, and send it as opportunity offers. Regardless, nevertheless, I shall be in all I write, of connection, accuracy, or of anything but of my own imperial will and pleasure" (1: 516).

Only initially does Lovelace believe that gaining physical control over Clarissa will make her surrender. Soon he has to realize her resistance: "What can be done with a woman who is above flattery, and despises all praise but that which flows from the approbation of her own heart?" (2: 31) Since he cannot simply "have" her, he devises in a long and meandering letter the rationale for what he calls her "trial" and decides: "To try if she, with all that glowing symmetry of parts, and that full bloom of vernal graces, by which she attracts every eye, be really inflexible as to the grand article?" (2: 42) Still, she always rejects his attempts at intimacy, and she enforces a distance upon him. Whenever she manages to turn him away, he sits down and writes to Belford, using frivolous language to elaborate on the corporeality of her body, inflaming his imagination retroactively in the description, and exploiting the ambiguity of words until they fit into his perspective and serve to justify him in another attempt at seducing and finally in raping her.

Well did I note her eye, and plainly did I see that it was all but just civil disgust to me and to the company I had brought her into. Her early retiring that night, against all entreaty, might have convinced thee that there was little of the gentle in her heart for me. And her eye never knew what it was to contradict her heart. . . . By *innocent*, with regard to me, and not taken as a general character, I must insist upon it, she is *not* innocent.

. . . I am convinced that there is not a woman in the world that is love-proof and plot-proof, if she be not the person.

And now I imagine (the charmer overcome) thou seest me sitting . . . she tenders her purple mouth. (2: 250–51).

Thus Lovelace arrives at a stalemate. Although he has physical control over Clarissa, she remains alien to his intentions and he is locked up in his compensatory literary games.

The woman of Lovelace's literary imagination differs utterly from the actual Clarissa. There is something absolutely commanding about her presence; he is aware of this, and it challenges his self-assurance. But at the same time he blocks himself against her influence. Whenever Lovelace faces Clarissa, his schemes and theatrical presentation of self collapse (see also 2: 400). His mastery over the world of appearances is broken as soon as he confronts the purity of her heart, for the confrontation with Clarissa's integrity and purity always implies the Other's gaze—the father's, divine wisdom's, God's—that sees through the world of appearances.

I was upon the point of making a violent attempt, but was checked in the very moment . . . by the awe I was struck with on again casting my eye upon her terrified but lovely face, and seeing, as I thought, her spotless heart in every line of it.

O virtue, virtue! *proceeds he,* what is there in thee that can thus against his will affect the heart of a Lovelace! . . .

He paints, in lively colours, that part of the scene between him and the lady, where she says, "The word father has a sweet and venerable sound with it."

I was exceedingly affected, *says he,* upon the occasion, but was ashamed to be surprised into such a fit of unmanly weakness—*so ashamed,* that I was resolved to subdue it at the instant, and to guard against the like for the future. (2: 315–16)

But Lovelace's resistance to the effects of seeing Clarissa's heart, to the subjection to her gaze, is entirely conditioned by his adherence to the rakish code of honor. Only when Lovelace finally lets himself be driven to drug and rape Clarissa is he forced to acknowledge his ineffectiveness in imposing his interpretations on people and events. Unless the other endorses his code, the confrontation turns into an act of brutal, meaningless violence. "Well, but after all, I must own that there is something very singular in this lady's case: and, at times, I cannot help regretting that I ever attempted her; since not *one power either body or soul* could be moved in my favour; and since to use the expression of the philosopher, on a much graver occasion, there is no difference to be found between the skull of King Philip and that of another man" (3: 199). Having seen Clarissa's heart without being moved by her, Lovelace in his insistence on rakish performance is faced with the mere mortal body. On this level of corporeal materiality, individuality cannot be found. Since he sets himself against Clarissa's presentation of a transparent heart, trying to turn her into a body, her violation is reduced to a mere statistical incident: "But people's extravagant notions of things alter not facts, Belford: and, when all's done, Miss Clarissa Harlowe has but run the fate of a thousand others of her sex—only that they did not set such romantic value upon what they call their *honour*; that's all" (3: 199). Instead of using his letter after the rape as an occasion for reflection, he goes on rambling, writing without reading and seeing, assuming anew his role of playwright and actor for a further trial. When he glimpses the equality in death and death's indifference to individual endorsements of a code of honor, he does not include his own position in this reflection.

With his further scheming and manipulations, he avoids a guilty conscience, the subjection to the Other's judgment. Thus, for instance, when he comes to think of himself as being tried and judged, he depicts the scene in terms of a triumphal performance culminating in a march from prison to courthouse.

> Let me tell thee, Jack, I see not why (to judge according to our principles and practices) we should not be as much elated in our march, were this to happen to us, as others may be upon any other the most *mob-attracting* occasion—suppose a lord mayor on his *gaudy*; suppose (as I began with the *lowest*) the *grandest* parade that can be supposed, a coronation—for, in all these, do not the royal guard, the heroic trained bands, the pendent, clinging throngs of spectators, with their waving heads rolling to and fro from house-tops to house-bottoms and streetways, as I have above described, make the principal part of the raree-show?   (2: 423)

Richardson added a footnote to this mention of the prisoners' march: "Within these few years past, a passage has been made from the prison to the Sessions-house, whereby malefactors are carried into court without going through the street. Lovelace's triumph on their supposed march shows the wisdom of this alteration." Richardson's comment quite explicitly aligns Lovelace with the culture of spectacle, which has to be overcome in favor of the new, disciplined subject. Richardson draws an explicit parallel between the new semio-technology of the penal reforms of the eighteenth century and his own epistolary novel.[14] Lovelace is the subject of a performance-oriented culture, in which the individual can define himself in terms of his mastery of a specific code, in which power is displayed in spectacular ways and enforced in a contestatory manner. To respect an invisible authority and even to judge himself in this light is utterly foreign to Lovelace. In this sense, the subjectivity of Lovelace is diametrically opposed to that of Clarissa. We find this underlined when Lovelace, in the same letter in which he envisages himself as glorified villain, expresses his bewilderment at Clarissa's accusation of herself for having acted against her parents' will and attempts to judge the situation on her terms: "She believes she acts upon her own judgement; and deserves to be punished for pretending to judgement, when she has none" (2: 419). Lovelace's inaccessibility to reform can be described as his refusal to reflect, to read, and to subject his writing to the Other's gaze, as his fixation on the exteriority of codes and conventions, appearances, and the materiality of the body. A truly effective reform would alter his position toward seeing, reading, and writing radically.

The Conversion of a Rake and the Construction of a Work of Art

In her will Clarissa orders that Lovelace be kept away from her body. If he insists, however, the family should not risk a confrontation but instead let him see her corpse.

But if, as he is a man very uncontrollable, and as I am nobody's, he insists upon viewing her dead whom he ONCE before saw in a manner dead, let his gay curiosity be gratified. Let him behold and triumph over the wretched remains of one who has been made a victim to his barbarous perfidity: but let some good person, as by my desire, give him a paper, whilst he is viewing the ghastly spectacle, containing these few words only: "Gay, cruel heart! behold here the remains of the once ruined, yet now happy, Clarissa Harlowe! See what thou thyself must quickly be; and REPENT!" (4: 465)

This paragraph reveals in a single phrase the ineffable "black transaction" she has suffered at Lovelace's hands. It also defines the conditions of true sight and a language of the heart that Lovelace and Clarissa's family have avoided. In order to be reformed, to be open to repentance, Lovelace's errant desire and writing have to be arrested, bent back on themselves, and subjected to a sight that is joined to a reading. And the text to be read comes from an other who is beyond the world of appearances and the mortal flesh. But Lovelace wants to see her dead body no more than her parents do. All he wants are fragments of her body, most of all her heart, as the physical organ to be owned and preserved by him.

Although Lovelace cannot be reformed by this shortcircuiting of reading and seeing, his former fellow rake and later executor of Clarissa's will, Belford, undergoes precisely this process of repositioning with regard to the gaze, the materiality of writing, the body, and reading. At the beginning of the novel, Belford is introduced as a rake and accomplice through his dialogical implication in Lovelace's letters addressed to him. But after Lovelace abducts Clarissa and is planning to "try" her, Belford leaves his passive position as a mere reader and becomes active by writing to Lovelace. He no longer trusts in the ability of Clarissa's "unequalled perfection" to hold Lovelace in check and admonishes Lovelace "that in this lady's situation the trial is not a fair trial" (2: 158). In his second letter Belford argues no longer in terms of Lovelace's family interests and Clarissa's reputation but in moral terms: "Be honest, and marry. . . . If thou dost not, thou wilt be the worst of men; and wilt be condemned in this world and the next: as I am sure thou oughtest, and shouldst too, wert thou to be judged by one who never before was so much touched in a woman's favour" (2: 244).

The precipitant of this drastic change in Belford's position from lobbying for Lovelace's uncle, Lord M., to arguing in terms of general virtue and morality is his encounter with Clarissa. He has been radically affected by the conversation and sight of the novel's heroine: "I have done nothing but talk of this lady ever since I saw her. There is something *so awful*, and yet *so sweet*, in her aspect, that were I to have the virtues and the graces all drawn in one piece, they should be all taken, every one of them, from different airs and attitudes in her. She was born to adorn the age she was given to, and would be an ornament to the first dignity. What a piercing, yet gentle eye." Belford is deeply affected by his encounter with Clarissa, by her presence, which goes beyond her looks: "She is at the age of bloom, and an admirable creature; a perfect beauty: but this *poorer* praise, a man, who has been honoured with her conversation, can hardly descend to give." It is Clarissa's "mind," her particular relation to language, that induces Belford's total admiration and that transforms her into an angel, a being beyond the mortality of the flesh: "I am ready to regret such an angel of a woman should even marry. She is in my eye all mind. . . . Why should such an angel be plunged so low as into the vulgar offices of domestic life? Were she mine, I should hardly wish to see her a mother, unless there were a kind of moral certainty that minds like hers could be propagated. For why, in short, should not the work of bodies be left to *mere* bodies?" (2: 243–44)

Clarissa's "mind" or gaze has direct access to truth; since it is not refracted by the materiality of language, it shows itself as virtue and purity of the heart. Thus Lovelace describes her effect on a rakish conversation: "She is above the affectation of not seeming to understand you. She shows by her displeasure, and a fierceness not natural to her eye, that she judges of an impure heart by an impure mouth, and darts dead at once even the embryo hopes of an encroaching lover, however distantly insinuated, before the meaning hint can draw into *double entendre*" (2: 399). Whereas Lovelace escapes Clarissa's gaze in his witty writing, Belford is utterly transformed by his first encounter. Initially he, like all the other rakes, had attempted to impress the young and beautiful woman with witty and flirtatious conversation. Then her gaze and her speech force him to alter his attitude toward language altogether: "But when, as I said, I heard her speak, which she did not till she had fathomed us all; when I heard her sentiments on two or three subjects, and took notice of that searching eye, darting into the very inmost cells of our frothy brains, by my faith, it made me look about me; and I began to recollect and be ashamed of all I had said before" (2: 484). The subject of Clarissa's conversation that brings about

Belford's conversion is wit. Instead of being an end in itself, the enjoyment of mastery over language, true wit has to be joined to the service of virtue. In rejecting wit and performance-oriented rhetorical theatricality, Belford also rejects the physicality of the body and sensual pleasure; instead, he is inserted into Clarissa's representational aesthetics of mental sight and purity of heart and soul when he ends his letter with these words: "I conclude with recommending to your serious consideration all I have written, as proceeding from the heart and soul of Your assured friend" (2: 490).

Once Belford's conversion has been achieved and his reform is under way, Clarissa accepts him as a friend at the point when she is about to leave all worldly things behind. After reading some representative letters from Lovelace to Belford, she asks him within the framework of representational aesthetics to become the executor of her will and protector of her memory as the editor of her correspondence: "I request it [the protection of her memory] of the only person possessed of materials that will enable him to do my character justice. . . . It will be an honour to my memory, with all those who shall know, that I was so well satisfied of my innocence that, having not time to write my own story, I could entrust it to the relation which the destroyer of my fame and fortune has given of it" (4: 78–79). Lovelace's letters to Belford serve a double function for Clarissa. They provide her with "unquestionable" justification for her decision never to marry. Thus they promote her transformation into the angelic, ideal Woman that Belford sees in her when he expresses the hope that such a pure mind as hers should never be enmired in the work of "mere bodies." But not only do those letters strengthen her resolve, they also become part of her transfiguration after death as documents of her innocence and proof that purity of the heart wins over witty conceits. By making Belford the editor of her correspondence, she removes Lovelace's letters from the context of a rake's performance for his friend and confidant and places them into the hands of an editor. There they will be part of the archival material put together and read for its representational contents and subjected to the eye of discerning justice and truth: "And if all his strangely communicative narrations are equally decent, nothing will be rendered criminally odious by them. But the vile heart that could mediate such contrivances as were much stronger evidences of his inhumanity than of his wit" (4: 77). Beyond those letters' theatrical achievements, they will testify against their author's intention.

Clarissa also hopes that assigning Belford this editorial role will strengthen his reform. She describes this in terms of Belford rereading Lovelace's letters in the light of her death and under the gaze of the transfigured angel.[15] Thus Belford will become *Clarissa*'s first reader: "And who knows, but that Mr. Belford, who already, from a principle of humanity, is touched at my misfortunes, when he comes to revolve the whole story, placed before him in one strong light, and when he shall have the catastrophe likewise before him; and shall become in a manner interested in it: who knows but that, from a still higher principle, he may so regulate his future actions as to find his own reward in the everlasting welfare which is wished him by his obliged servant, Clarissa Harlowe?" (4: 79) When Belford writes Lovelace about his new role, he elaborates on the aesthetic pleasure he expects from his editorship. He praises Clarissa's epistolary technique as perfect illusionism capable of evoking a presence and immediacy that transcends the mortality of the body.

You cannot imagine how proud I am of this trust. I am afraid I shall too soon come into the execution of it. As she is always writing, what a melancholy pleasure will the perusal and disposition of her papers afford me! Such sweetness of temper, so much patience and resignation, as she seems to be mistress of; yet writing of and in the midst of *present* distress! How *much more* lively and affecting, for that reason, must her style be, her mind tortured by the pangs of uncertainty (the events then hidden in the womb of fate), *than* the dry narrative, unanimated style of a person relating difficulties and dangers surmounted, the relater perfectly at ease; and if himself unmoved by his own story, not likely greatly to affect the reader. (4: 81)

In this description Belford characterizes the transformation and transfiguration of Clarissa into *Clarissa*, the work of art.

From the time Belford assumes his editorship, he and Clarissa collaborate in the construction of this documentary work of art. Clarissa, for instance, gives her sister a second chance at writing her a kind response in order to allow her to be vindicated in the eyes of posterity (see 4: 81). Clarissa's death, too, becomes in its elaborate and exhaustively documented preparations part of the composition, as she announces in her prison cell: "Let my ruin, said she, lifting up her eyes, be LARGE! Let it be COMPLETE, in this life! For a composition, let it be COMPLETE" (3: 441). Consciously involved in the construction of *Clarissa*, Belford deliberately contrasts Clarissa's preparations for her death with the rake Belton's and the whore Sinclair's deaths.[16] Since Lovelace has been able to close his eyes to Clarissa's gaze, Belford makes a last attempt to give Lovelace a chance to convert by conjuring up the spectacle of torture. He begins by stating the letter's purpose: "I have a scene to paint in relation to the wretched Sinclair, that, if I do it justice, will make thee seriously ponder and reflect, or nothing can" (4: 379). Thereupon he depicts Sinclair in bed with

Fig. 6. *Illustration for Richardson,* Clarissa, *the dying Sinclair. This illustration
by Daniel Nicolas Chodowiecki (1726–1801), dated 1796, is clearly influenced by
Gravelot's illustrations for* Julie.

a broken leg as a horrible sight of filth, decay, and pain. After relating the shock, horror, and self-condemnation this scene induces in Sinclair's "partners," he describes the surgeons' decision to amputate her leg for the mere sake of profit and torture: "And so the poor wretch was to be lanced and quartered, as I may say, for an experiment only! And, without any hope of benefit for the operation, was to pay the surgeons for tormenting her!" (4: 385) This letter, however, like all of Belford's efforts at reforming Lovelace, has to fail; Lovelace would have to be a hallucinatory reader to be at all affected by reading this description.[17]

Belford becomes Clarissa's accomplice in her ultimate defeat of Lovelace. When she writes her famous allegorical letter, she counts on Lovelace's inability to read in terms of "mental sight." "I am setting out with all diligence for my father's house. I am bid to hope that he will receive his poor penitent with a goodness peculiar to himself; for I am overjoyed with the assurance of a thorough reconciliation, through the interposition of a dear, blessed friend whom I always loved and honoured" (4: 157). Although this is how Clarissa finally protects herself from Lovelace's intrusions, she manages to trick him without having to lie. Her letter becomes utterly true since her body is taken to Harlowe Place and her soul goes home to the Father. All the elements of her letter can be deciphered in terms of their literal (historical) and their spiritual (allegorical) meaning. She writes that the reconciliation is brought about by the "interposition" of a "dear" friend. In a religious sense, this "friend" is Christ, who brought about the reconciliation with the Father and who, as the incarnation of the Word, provides the prerequisite for religious allegory, the truth of the four senses of Scripture. In the historical sense, the reunion of Clarissa with the Harlowes is mediated by her cousin Morden and her friend and editor Belford. Yet, as opposed to Christian allegory, based on the Word that became flesh, in *Clarissa* the flesh and body of Clarissa become the word that then comes to life in a hallucinatory, visualizing reading.

Thus Belford, the reformed rake and Clarissa's editor, presents the exemplary reading—the reading of the disciplined subject—in his response to cousin Morden's long and minutely detailed record of Clarissa's return to her father's house: "I once had thought to go down privately, in order, disguised, to see the last solemnity performed. But there was no need to give myself this melancholy trouble, since your last letter so naturally describes all that passed, that I have every scene before my eyes" (4: 411). Morden's epistolary documentation allows Belford to participate in the funeral without having to join the physical world of appearances and disguise. Reading and seeing are joined within the presence of Belford's mental cinema and immediately recorded in his response to Morden.

You crowd me, sir, me thinks, into the silent slow procession—now with the sacred bier do I enter the awful porch: now measure I, with solemn paces, the venerable aisle: now, ambitious of a relationship to her, placed in a near pew to the eye-attracting coffin, do I listen to the moving eulogy: now, through the buzz of gaping, eye-swollen crowds, do I descend into the clammy vault, as a true executor, to see that part of her will performed with my own eyes. . . .

Nor do your affecting descriptions permit me here to stop: but, ascended, I mingle my tears and my praises with those of the numerous spectators. I accompany the afflicted mourners back to their uncomfortable mansion; and make one in the general concert of unavailing woe; till retiring, as I imagine, as they retire, like them, in reality, I give up to new scenes of solitary and sleepless grief; reflecting upon the perfections I have seen the end of.   (4: 411)

In this letter, the reader of *Clarissa* is presented with the paradigm for the proper attitude toward the realm of language. This letter can also function as a concluding summary of *Clarissa* as a paradigm of a new genre as well as of a new kind of subjectivity within the program of Anschaulichkeit. Here reading, seeing, and writing have become one, shortcircuiting the treacherous distractions of the materiality of sign vehicles and the physicality of the body. Spectatordom and theatricality have been replaced by the interiority of the solitary silent reader's visualizations. And just as there is no material opacity in this transparent representation, there is also no temporal gap or absence in the written mediation. The reader's identificatory involvement creates a perfect synchronicity between an event, its recording, the reading of the document, and the documentation of the response.

Clarissa achieves its disciplinary aims not simply through the pedagogical agency of Clarissa as a female character. Rather, the pedagogical intervention of this epistolary novel is situated at the threshold of representation, at the level that effects the illusionary reading of a vast collection of individual letters as one organized whole. In other words, it is situated exactly at the level that turns the character Clarissa into the novel *Clarissa* as it exists within the immaterial, ideational realm of pure representation.

Drame Sérieux and *Bürgerliches Trauerspiel*

The second part of this chapter presents the generic innovations of the *drame sérieux* and the *bürgerliche Trauerspiel* as a response to the epistolary novel.[18] In fact, the theory and practice of the bourgeois tragedy may be characterized as a radicalization of the semiotic constellation of Richardson's fiction. This radicalization takes its departure with a shift in the medium from the book to the theater. Richardson's anti-theatrical impulse is shaped into a new kind of writing "to the moment," subjecting writers and readers alike to documentary evidence and aiming at perfect transparency by negating the specificity of the novelistic medium in a visualizing reading. Diderot and Lessing pursue similar aims for the drama, and they equally negate their specific medium, the theater. This can best be analyzed by looking first at how Diderot sets the stage for the *drame sérieux* with his framing narrative introduction to *Fils naturel*. I then focus on pity and illusion, the terms in which Lessing defines the particular affective and moral dimension of the *bürgerliches Trauerspiel*. This programmatic positioning of the new drama is followed by a close reading of Lessing's first bourgeois tragedy, *Miß Sara Sampson*.

Framing the Anti-theatrical Drama

Diderot radically opposes the drame sérieux to a culture of spectacle when he programatically introduces his *Fils naturel* (1757) as a familial "docu-drama."[19] In presenting this dramatic text, he uses framing conventions similar to those of a typical editor-author of an eighteenth-century epistolary novel.[20] Thus Diderot narrates that after the publication of the sixth volume of the *Encyclopédie*, he withdrew to the countryside in a state of melancholia. In this separation from urban culture, he meets Dorval, a young man who sacrificed his love and fortune to a friend. When he hears from Dorval the story of his life, Diderot remarks that it would be the ideal subject for a drama. It turns out that this drama has already been composed at the suggestion of Dorval's father.

"The point here is not to draw up treatises, but to preserve the memory of an event that touches us, and to render this event as it happened... We are going to renew it ourselves, each year, in this house, in this living room. The things we have said, we shall all say again. Your children shall do the same, and so will theirs and their descendants. And I am going to outlast my existence, and thus I am going to converse from age to age with all of my nephews... Dorval, don't you think that a work that would transmit for them our very ideas, our true sentiments, the discourse from the most crucial events of our lives, don't you think that this work would not be worth much more than family portraits which merely show of us a momentary facial expression?"

"You mean to tell me that I should paint your soul, mine, the one of Constance, of Claireville, and of Rosalie." (p. 16)

Quoting this conversation with his father, Dorval explains the genesis of the familial docu-drama.[21] After the death of his father, the family had discontinued the play's annual performance, but they are planning to revive it soon. Dorval understands Diderot's wish to attend this commemorative service and smuggles him into the family room as an invisible spectator in order not to embarrass the actor-characters.[22]

This introductory narrative, which negates the fictional status of the work, makes clear that the drame sérieux requires a new acting style. Actor and character must become identical. In "De la poésie dramatique" (1758), Diderot explains how this can be achieved through the anti-theatrical establishment of a fourth wall.

I observed that the actor played badly all that which the poet had composed for the spectator; and if the audience had participated in this, it would have said to the actor: "To whom do you address yourself? I don't exist. Would I get involved in your business? Go home." And if the author would have attended to his business, he would have come forth behind the stage setting and would have responded to the audience: "Sorry, Gentlemen, it is my fault: next time I and he shall do better."
    Whether you compose or act, never think of the spectator's existence. Imagine along the edge of the stage a great wall that separates you from the orchestra. Act as if the curtain would never rise.   (p. 373)

The existence of the audience has to be ignored, but the discourse in the new drama has to be supported by a gestural language that is "natural" as opposed to conventional and stylized histrionic gestures. Diderot calls these gestures *pantomime*, a crucial dramaturgical means that helps to authenticate the play's action and speech: "I have said that pantomime is part of the play; that the author must seriously attend to it; that if it isn't familiar and present to him, he will neither be able to start, to carry out, nor to end his scene convincingly; furthermore, that frequently stage directions have to take the place of dialogue" (p. 409). Pantomime becomes a means for veiling any mediating instances. It renders the play "true" in the sense that it makes it anschaulich. Thus Diderot postulates that it is placed in the service of producing a tableau: "Stage directions have to be such that they produce a tableau; pantomime must give energy and clarity to the discourse. It must connect the dialogue, be characteristic; it has to be delicate and subtle, to take on the function of a response. Stage directions are almost always required at the beginning of a scene" (p. 410).[23]

Having described the function of the pantomime, Diderot examines various theatrical examples and ends with a reference to Richardson's epistolary novels, his source for the ideal of "painting" the movements and emotions of the characters like a "natural" gestural language: "It is the painting of movements that charms us mainly in the sentimental novels. Consider how obligingly the author of *Pamela*, *Grandison*, and *Clarissa* attends to it. Consider how this endows his discourse with force, meaning, and sentiment. I see the character: whether he speaks or whether he is silent, I can see him; and his action affects me more than his speeches" (p. 411). Before pantomime is realized as a particular acting style and technique, it already exists in the author's and recipient's mental cinema; it is for this reason that Diderot can slide so easily from one medium to another.

Pantomime is the product of the author's or recipient's hallucination, the means that allows a nonmediated transmission from the mind of the author to the mind of the recipient: "Pantomime existed in the imagination of the author at the moment he was writing, and he wanted that it would be shown by the scene in each moment when it would be performed. Stage directions are the simplest means by which the audience can learn what it can expect from its actors. The poet tells you: Compare this play with the one of your actors, then judge" (pp. 417–18). Diderot concludes his discussion of pantomime pointing out the contemporary necessity of stage directions: "Meanwhile I admit that if pantomime were carried to such perfection during performances, one could often spare oneself the trouble of writing it down; this might be the reason why the ancients did not need stage directions. But among us I wonder how the reader—and I am talking even of that reader who frequently goes to the theater—how the reader should be able to supply it during his reading since he never can see it during a performance. Should he be more of an actor than the professional?" (p. 417) Professional actors have lost their persuasive gestural language, and hence stage directions have become indispensable for the actors as well as for the hallucinatory engagement of the reader of the drama.

In his dramaturgical writings, Lessing shares many of Diderot's concerns. Their terminology differs, however: what Diderot calls pantomime Lessing calls *mahlerische Gesten* (painterly gestures). Pantomime is for Lessing a derogatory term meaning a stilted, exaggerated, or highly stylized gestural language; it is to be replaced by the more "natural" mahlerische Gesten.

Each movement by which the hand accompanies moral passages must be significant. Often it can extend into the painterly realm; if only pantomime is avoided.... The moral is a general statement abstracted from the particular circumstances of the acting persons; in its generality it becomes somewhat alien to its object, it becomes a digression in which the less attentive or less sharp listener does not realize its relation to the present action. If there are means by which this relationship can be made accessible to the senses, to bring back the symbolic aspect of the moral to the intuitive cognition, and if this means could be particular gestures, the actor must by no means neglect to make them.[24]

It is of special interest that Lessing raises the issue of acting styles when he reflects on the actor's ability to make a morally important passage graphic for the audience. This passage draws our attention to the continuity between Lessing's discussion of the fable's graphic and thereby moral impact and the dramatic contribution to the didactically successful inculcation of morality. Similarly Diderot's discussion of the persuasive force of pantomime in classical antiquity should remind us of Condillac's description of the "langage d'action." Clearly, the poetics of the bourgeois tragedy participates in the project of Anschaulichkeit. Both as a particular acting style and as elaborate stage directions, pantomime becomes an elaborate attempt at veiling and dematerializing the medium of writing or of the stage in order to project the dramatic action immediately on the recipient's mental screen. Through the introductory narrative of *Fils naturel*, Diderot's reader-spectator encounters the text not within a theatrical context but in the intimacy of a familial setting in which the dramatis personae and the actors are identical. The introductory narrative invites the reader of *Fils naturel* to assume Diderot's position as an invisible spectator. The family tableau is to unfold in the reader's mental cinema. The drama is detheatricalized, taken out of its spectacular context; the actors are only themselves. There is no audience, and the stage is part of an imaginary domestic space. The drama becomes the occasion for an identificatory experience. Up to this point, it seems to require a type of reception similar to Belford's reading of Morden's description of Clarissa's funeral.

However, *Fils naturel* is not an epistolary novel, and it does not aim at the evidential effect of a minutely detailed written account. Not only the medium of the theater but also the medium of writing is negated. Having presented the text of *Fils naturel*, Diderot begins the "Entretiens sur le fils naturel" with an explanation of how he obtained the written version of the play. He missed the last act of Dorval's performance because of the entrance of the only actor not impersonating himself. At the entrance of an old friend representing Lysimond, the dead father, all the characters were so deeply moved that they broke out in tears, and the performance could not be continued. Thus Diderot was to know the last act only from reading the script. The spontaneous response of Dorval and the other characters-actors authenticates the drama's truth and prevents the spectator-Diderot from taking it as a mere fiction: "The representation was so true that in several instances I forgot that I was a spectator, an ignored spectator, and I was about to leave my hiding place and to add a real character to the scene" (p. 83). In the same context Diderot quotes Dorval's response to his request to read the text: "A piece of theater is less there to be read than to be represented" (p. 84). And finally, Diderot recounts how he experienced the truth of Dorval's statement when he tries to present to his own readers his conversation with Dorval about Dorval's drama: "But what a difference between that which Dorval told me and that which I wrote down!... These might be the same ideas, but the genius of the man does no longer exist... . . . I am alone among the dust of books and in the shadow of a room... and I write weak, sad, and cold lines" (p. 84). The framing narrative of *Fils naturel* lays out the basic characteristics of the *drame bourgeois*. The weakness, coldness, and dryness of a written text, as well as the spectacular conventions of the stage, are rejected. The play is to be seen or read *as if* it were part of a lived experience. As Lysimond describes to Dorval the representational nature of the drame sérieux, it can be seen neither as the mere words of a treatise nor as the fixing of exterior and accidental qualities of a pictorial portrait. Rather, as becomes clear from Dorval's response, the drama has to become a representation of the characters' souls. In brief, it must achieve what Diderot in the *Lettre sur les sourds et muets* ascribes to the emblem or hieroglyph, the semiotic ideal that mirrors the *tableau mouvant* of the soul.[25]

This understanding of the representational status of the drame sérieux is based on a postulated liberation from the concrete medium of representation and amounts to a certain idealization. In that sense it raises important questions about the difference between the representation and its "real counterpart." If Diderot introduces *Fils naturel* as a familial docu-drama aimed at the intense identifcatory participation of the audience-reader, we are nevertheless dealing with dramatic illusion and conventions diametrically opposed to those of modern street theater or documentary film. Of course, the bourgeois tragedy aims to a certain degree at the negation of the difference between lived experience and a representation of it; yet it also enhances this difference. In fact, the genre's fundamental impact on the affective economy and moral constitution of the recipient hinges exactly on the illusionary and idealizing effects of the representation. The best exposition of this issue can be found in Lessing's epistolary exchange with Mendelssohn and Nicolai.

Illusion and Pity

For Lessing, as for Diderot, the bourgeois tragedy must produce a perfect illusion, whether the drama is actually performed or merely read.[26] According to Diderot, the aesthetic illusion depends mostly on the veiling of any mediation, thereby producing the imaginative and identificatory engagement of the recipient. Lessing's notion of the perfect illusion addresses the role of affects in an even more radical fashion: "Since the imitation can be called perfect only if one is tempted to mistake it for the thing itself, nothing can be true of imitated passions that does not apply equally to real passions" (*Briefwechsel*, p. 107). Lessing searches for that kind of affective involvement that makes the audience forget the drama's status as a mere representation and guarantees its efficacy beyond the duration of the performance.[27] Not only is the affective involvement of the audience crucial for the "authenticity" or "truth" of the drama, but it also constitutes the moral purpose of tragedy.[28] The *Briefwechsel*, the collected letters of Lessing, Moses Mendelssohn, and Friedrich Nicolai on tragedy, begins with a discussion of Nicolai's *Abhandlung vom Trauerspiele*, in which Nicolai defines the purpose of tragedy as moral improvement through agitation of the passions. Mendelssohn specifies the passions that are to be produced in the service of virtue as admiration and pity. Lessing contradicts his two friends and postulates that only pity can positively further the purpose of moral improvement. In the following I demonstrate how, in Lessing's theory of bourgeois tragedy, the notion of illusion and pity are inseparably connected. I begin by tracing Lessing's rejection of admiration.

We can read Lessing's opposition to his correspondents' position that admiration contributes to the tragedy's moral efficacy as an anti-theatrical argument.[29] He rejects admiration because ultimately admiration foregrounds the tragedy as a mere representation. This passion obstructs an immediate appeal to the audience's emotional receptivity and intuitive cognition. Lessing grants that admiration can be part of the emulation of virtue, originating in intuitive cognition: "I am not going to deprecate the validity of the affect of admiration, but I demand that you do not reduce virtue to a mere daughter of admiration. It is true that virtue very often is the daughter of emulation, and emulation is a natural consequence of the intuitive cognition of a virtuous quality" (p. 64). Lessing concedes that admiration—understood in a more general sense as a recognition of good qualities leading to an impulse of emulation—does not have to be rejected. However, he introjects, those qualities of tragic characters that generally call for admiration are not good qualities; nor should they be emulated. If anything, they reduce the audience's affective receptivity: "I want to exclude only those great qualities that we subsume under the general term of heroism. For each of those qualities is connected with a certain insensitivity, and insensitivity in the object of pity weakens my own capacity to feel pity" (p. 64). Pity and admiration are mutually exclusive because they engage the audience's faculties in diametrically opposed fashions.

Although we might intuitively recognize the virtue of a certain dramatic character and feel an impulse to emulate him, we cannot just reproduce his behavior from the stage: "As part of the general faculty of understanding, admiration amounts to a particular delight in a rare perfection. Admiration leads to moral improvement by way of emulation, and emulation presupposes a distinct cognition of the perfection I want to emulate. How many people have this distinct cognition? And without it, does admiration not remain sterile? Pity, however, leads to moral improvement immediately. We do not have to make any effort; pity improves the man of understanding as well as the fool" (p. 66). Admiration could achieve its moral efficacy only if it induces the spectator to abstract from the particularity of the individual exemplary action in order to recognize its exceptional perfection and then—should life provide an opportunity—to decode this insight in order to apply it. Since admiration in the service of virtue involves such a highly developed faculty of moral reflection and experience, its potential benefits are limited to an educated elite. But more important, in its complex detour through symbolic understanding, admiration removes the immediate appeal of virtuous examples to the intuitive cognition, turning them into more or less abstract moral maxims. Heroic action aiming at admiration obstructs tragedy's moral efficacy in a fashion similar to that of an allegorical fable, which necessarily misses its goal by engaging the distancing, symbolic understanding.[30] But Lessing's notion of the moral efficacy of the bourgeois tragedy also differs decisively from his theory of the fable. Whereas the fable has to rule out any emotional engagement of the recipient, the moral impact of the bourgeois tragedy is to be found precisely in the recipient's affective relation to the dramatic performance. The fable aims merely at the constitution of a new kind of sign, at becoming a quasi-naturalized sign that enables an immediate access to our intuitive cognition, or Anschaulichkeit; by producing "graphic" tableaux, the aesthetic effect of the bourgeois tragedy also reorganizes the recipient's subjectivity by using the affect of pity.

Lessing states quite early in the *Briefwechsel* that tragedy must be defined exclusively in terms of pity: "The purpose of tragedy is to enlarge our ability to feel pity. . . . The most empathetic man is the best man, best disposed for all kinds of social virtues, most inclined to all kinds of generosity" (p. 55). Of course, his correspondents did not deprecate the value of pity. By that time, pity, sympathy, and benevolence had become generally accepted in the catalogue of virtues. Nicolai and Mendelssohn merely argue that pity should not be the exclusive aim of tragedy; this leads the correspondents into the dispute over admiration and produces

Lessing's argument about the mutual exclusivity of these two passions. For Nicolai and Mendelsohn pity is just one of many virtuous sentiments; for Lessing pity has a very specific structure that sets it apart from any other affect. Although Lessing initially writes that tragedy should not produce any affect other than pity, toward the end of the correspondence, he argues more sharply that tragedy cannot produce any "true" passion but pity.

It is only in Lessing's letter of February 2, 1757, that his full theory of pity is developed. This letter is a response to Mendelsohn's theses "Von der Herrschaft über die Neigungen" (On the control of the inclinations), which were included in a joint letter from Mendelssohn and Nicolai. Lessing's friends had reopened the discussion of Lessing's claims for the exclusivity of pity by restating their position in a more radical manner. The genre of tragedy should not be restricted to pity. In the name of mimesis, all passions should be admitted. Aesthetic pleasure can, but need not always, be subsumed under a moral purpose. In his theses, Mendelssohn explains in terms of rationalist psychology and semiotics what constitutes aesthetic pleasure and how an aesthetic construct can lead to moral insights and improvement. Although Lessing's response is relatively short, it contains his central argument about the bourgeois tragedy. In this letter Lessing combines his theory of illusion with an explication of the structure of pity, and from this conjunction of illusion and pity results his poetics of genre. In a way, one must read this letter as one would read a story. Since the force of the argument lies in the stringing together of various examples, I pay particular attention to how Lessing manages the transition from one example to the next.

Lessing begins with a critique of Mendelssohn's conclusions about the nature of illusion and aesthetic pleasure. In order to establish some common ground, he provides a basic definition of the passions. In this definition Lessing describes the passions in terms of the subject's relation to an object.

Dearest friend, I suppose both of us agree that any passion is either a strong desire or an abhorrence. But also: that each strong desire or abhorrence heightens the awareness of our own reality, and that thus this heightened awareness can only be pleasant. As a result all passions, even the most unpleasant ones, are as passions pleasant. I don't have to tell you that we can lose sight of that pleasure which is related to a strengthening of our faculty since it can be infinitely surpassed by the displeasure that we experience toward the objects that initially define our faculty. (p. 101)

Passion is defined in the most general terms as desire or abhorrence. Both affects are induced by something other than the subject. The intensity of the affect enhances the subject's sense of reality. Lessing seems to evoke in this description a narcissistic scenario in which the subject gains pleasure from the faculty of desiring or abjecting an other—defining oneself as subject exactly in that affective space of love/hatred where the object comes into being.[31] Thus the affect (desire/abhorrence) seems to have two dimensions or directions: on the one hand it points to the other (an object of desire or abhorrence); on the other hand to an auto-reflexive moment. Since Lessing develops all his further arguments from this initial statement, it is important to note that neither the subject nor the object are defined in any stable manner. Not only does the subject's sense of reality depend on the affective force by which an object is desired or abjected, but also, as we shall see in the following examples, the object-to-be can be anything from a concrete physical object to a representation or an idea. In other words, Lessing explores the affects at the threshold where an other is becoming a representation.

From this initial statement about the nature of the passions, Lessing hopes to overturn his correspondents' position on the role of the affects and the nature of aesthetic illusion. He singles out Mendelssohn's explanation of aesthetic pleasure: "If we suddenly look at a painted snake, we tend to take more pleasure in the painting if we are initially frightened. Aristotle thinks we are delighted because we see ourselves freed from the supposed danger. But how unnatural is this explanation! I would rather think the brief moment of anxiety proves to us intuitively that the representation matches the original" (p. 100). Lessing does not agree with this explanation, which defines aesthetic pleasure as the delight in the technical perfection, in comparing the representation with the original. On the basis of his definition of the passions, Lessing explains the pleasure we experience once we recognize the trompe l'oeil differently: the original of the snake (or the trompe l'oeil as long as we do not recognize it as such) poses a real threat to the subject. The affect is one of such strong abhorrence that it cancels the auto-reflexive pleasure. Once we have recognized the trompe l'oeil as such, once we perceive the snake as a mere representation, the annihilating danger of the material object vanishes, and we are left with the sheer auto-reflexive pleasure. Whereas for Mendelssohn aesthetic pleasure derives from a comparison of the representation with the original, Lessing locates the source of aesthetic pleasure purely in an affective dimension: in the auto-reflexive affect affirming the subject's sense of reality. Lessing's interpretation displaces the issue of artistic technique. Rather than focusing on mimetic perfection, he seems to emphasize the degree of material reality attributed to the object of the passionate response. It is the other, perceived as physical threat to the subject, that can cancel the auto-reflexive pleasure of the affect.

And indeed, this issue of the object's material reality motivates the transition to the following example.

> Over there in the distance I perceive the most beautiful, most charming woman, who seems to be waving to me with her hand in a mysterious way. I get into affect, desire, love, admiration, whatever you want to call it. In this case the pleasure at the object = 10 can be added to the pleasant sensation of the affect = 1, and the effect of both is = 11. Now I approach it. Heavens! It is only a painting, a sculpture! According to your explanation, my dearest friend, my pleasure should be even greater, for the affect has intuitively convinced me of the perfection of the imitation. But this is against all we know from experience; rather, I get morose. And why do I get morose? The pleasure at the perfect object vanishes, and merely the pleasant sensation of the affect remains.   (p. 102)

Faced with the absence of the object of desire—that is, with the immateriality of the object of desire—the observer no longer receives pleasure from the illusionistic representation and is left merely with the resonance of the auto-reflexive affect. For the initial affect, the question of whether it is induced by a "real" object or by a trompe l'oeil does not matter at all. It seems to be important, however, whether what induces the affect is clear and distinct as an actual material other for the subject or merely a vague stimulus for the subject's emotional faculties. In other words, the medium of the representation seems to matter, since the remaining affect will depend on the denouement of the trompe l'oeil. If only the observer could not have approached the beautiful woman, if she had been kept in the distance, mysteriously waving, he would not have had to become morose. Pleasure is maximized within distance, a distance that could also be called the imaginary, since it produces a misrecognition, a mistaken identification, of signifier and signified. Lessing's two examples from the visual arts pay particular attention to the discrepancy between the trompe l'oeil, which has all the power of the real material object, and the representation as such, which in its own materiality draws attention to the missing object. Both examples from the visual arts provide only a minimum of auto-reflexive pleasure.

Maybe the aesthetic pleasure is diminished by the materiality of the artifact? This seems to be the direction of Lessing's argument, as he adds another example. He leaves the media of painting and sculpture, which tend to foreground the difference between the materiality of the representation and the material object being represented, and shifts to the nonrepresentational medium of music: "The unpleasant affects in an imitation are pleasant because they produce *similar* affects in us, which are directed toward *no specific object*. The musician makes me sad; and this sadness is pleasant for me, because I sense it merely as affect, and any affect is pleasant. For if you suppose I really thought of something sad during this musical sadness, the pleasant side of it would disappear" (p. 102; my italics). With this shift in media something that would have been impossible within the realm of painting becomes suddenly possible. An unpleasant affect can be experienced as pleasant before its occasion has been made explicit as a mere semblance. The snake could not initially have been pleasant. The medium of music establishes and maintains a pleasurable distance from concrete objects, and the moment of horror and abjection vanishes in favor of a structural "similarity" when the occasion of the primary affect loses its material concreteness. The imaginary is organized in a different way. The source of pleasure is some generalized signifier of sadness. Displeasure would enter this scene not from an outside threat but from within, if I supplied a concrete memory. The example from music further introduces a new temporal structure of aesthetic pleasure. Whereas in painting aesthetic pleasure was an aftereffect, music allows for the continuing existence of the pleasure as long as I am absorbed in my experience of listening. During the whole time I as subject am relieved from having to affirm my boundaries vis-à-vis a concrete other, and in this narcissistic scenario I am able to enjoy my affective faculties per se. Both desire and abhorrence are left behind.

The musical example leads Lessing into the physical example that becomes crucial for his definition of *Mitleid* (pity). He distinguishes between two strings: one vibrates when touched, and the other resonates sympathetically with the first, without being touched. If the vibration of the strings stands for the agitation of the passions, one can distinguish two aspects of this movement. On the one hand, there is the mere resonance that Lessing calls *Bebung* and defines as an exclusively pleasurable experience, an experience that describes the auto-reflexive affect. On the other hand, there is the contact, or *Berührung*, that causes the initial vibration of the first string, or the affect as it is provoked by an other, which might very well be unpleasant, for example, the affect at the sight of a snake. Lessing applies this "physical" example directly to the passions of the tragedy.

The first string, which vibrates on contact, can have a painful sensation; however, the other string, regardless of the similarity of the vibration, has a pleasant sensation, because it has not been touched (at least not in such an immediate manner). The same applies to tragedy. The acting person gets involved in an unpleasant affect, and I am involved too. But why is this affect pleasant for me? Because

I am not the acting person who is immediately affected by the unpleasant idea, because I sense the affect as a mere affect without having to think of a particular unpleasant object.   (p. 103)

It is important that Lessing immediately erases the difference between actor and impersonated character in his term *spielende Person* (acting person), to whom he attributes the affect produced by the actual contact with the other. With this description we are already in the closed realm of illusion. As in Diderot's introduction to *Fils naturel*, the difference between actors and the dramatis personae is canceled. The spectator, however, experiences the passions of the acting person merely vicariously in terms of a Bebung; for him the affect is limited to its auto-reflexive dimension as a pure source of pleasure.

But here Lessing intervenes in a decisive way. The vicarious nature of the spectator's passions is sufficient to explain the pleasure obtainable from a dramatic performance; however, it is insufficient as a program for the type of drama he wants to promote. Indeed, Lessing rejects those emotions of a vicarious sentimentality when he describes them as merely secondary affects as opposed to the "originary" affect of Mitleid: "Such *secondary* affects, however, that arise at the sight of such affects in others, hardly deserve the name of affects; this is why in one of my first letters I have already stated that tragedy excites no other affect in us but *pity*. For this affect is not only felt by the acting persons, and we do not only feel it because they do, but it originates in us from the effects of the objects on us; it is not a secondary and communicated affect" (p. 103). Pity is the only primary affect that can be stirred in the spectator of a tragedy, and since it originates in the spectator of a tragedy himself, it includes both aspects of the movement: the vibration on contact (Berührung) and the resonance (Bebung). It would be wrong to read Lessing's explication of the structure of pity merely as the self-indulgent sentimental voyeurism of the Bebung.[32] However, the other causing the Berührung is not of a material reality that would lead to an actual physical threat to the subject, as in the case of the snake. The experience of pity is removed from the sensation of physical pain. The subject can suffer in an original way without being reminded of his or her own body.

In order to understand fully the structure of Lessing's notion of pity, one must not forget the context that precedes his explication of the affect—the discussion of illusionist aesthetics and the specific examples from various media. Pity cannot be produced by all artistic media. The pictorial representation loses its primary affective force in the denouement, and music can cause the pleasure of the auto-reflexive affect only as long as we do not supplement the sensation with an affective involvement from our own experience. With those media the affect depends on whether its occasion is perceived as originating from a sign/representation and therefore mediated or as originating from a real object/event and therefore immediate. The dramatic tableau, however, produces a mediated immediacy. On the one hand, pity, like any primary affect caused by a "real" other, is immediate; on the other hand, it is mediated in the sense that it sustains the subject's narcissistic pleasure in his affective capacity. The other, from whom our affect originates, is safely integrated into the subject's mental cinema. Far from any possible corporeal or material contact, the other is unable to threaten the demarcations of the subject. Therefore, the object of pity will never be an object of desire or abhorrence.

The bourgeois tragedy establishes a semiotic constellation in which the subject is constituted vis-à-vis a representation in a particular affective dimension. It is an affective dimension that excludes all physical sensation of the subject as well as the materiality of the representation as "mere" sign vehicle. The object of pity is an other that does not disintegrate into the difference between representation and original—as in the case of painting in which the two moments of the affect, contact and vibration, are at odds with each other—nor can it be located in the imaginary involvement of the music listener, which beyond any representational specificity merely stimulates the listener's affective resonance like an echo. Lessing has managed to preserve the advantages of both painting and music in the dramatic genre: sustaining it in the distance of a musical vagueness, he can preserve the "other" from painting without the physical threat or the disruptive denouement.

Due to the specific nature of the drama's illusionistic representation (its mediated immediacy), the nature of the passions—originally defined by Lessing as a strong desire or abhorrence—has been modified or purified; one might even call this transformation a catharsis.[33] Since the object of pity, the other, is perceived as another subject, the subject of pity is affected neither by desire nor by abhorrence but constitutes his relation to the other in terms of a relation of similarity.[34] Pity, according to Lessing, leads to the subject's moral improvement to the extent that it both affirms the subject's identity and his sociability. In order to induce this relation of similarity, however, the other, which is to become the object of pity, must not differ too much from the subject feeling pity. For if the other appears to be involved in circumstances that cannot be perceived as a meaningful whole, it will become an object of horror and disgust. Another subject involved in an apparently unpredictable, meaningless accident threatens the sense of my subjectivity; it disturbs the peaceful solution of the narcissistic scenario and obliges me to abject what is beyond my means of interpretation. This is why Lessing rejects unpredictable catastrophes as well as superhuman heroes and postulates the *Mittelcharacter*, the new nonheroic hero of the bourgeois tragedy (pp. 82–83). Pity is both removed from the carnal passions (desire and abhorrence) and from the alienation of admiration. For admiration of heroic characters can take the detour through the symbolic understanding and thereby negate the concrete subjectivity of the hero; or, in another form, as the enthusiasm and imitiation of an acrobat, admiration can cancel the autonomy of the admiring subject (pp. 79–81).

Lessing's explication of the structure of pity highlights the idealizing tendency that supports the moral efficacy of the bourgeois tragedy. The new genre aims at the constitution of subjectivity as an affective inner psychical space. This interiority is constituted in a certain relation to representations that lies apart both from the realm of any material mediation and from the carnal passions. Nevertheless, the narcissistic scenario organizing the subjectivity of pity has also its dark side. The relation of similarity can be established only by rejecting that which is asserting an otherness, by rejecting that which escapes assimilation into the nonmaterial realm of a mediated immediacy. Pity itself has an abhorrence of the carnal passions, the body, the material of representation, extravagant heroism, and catastrophes. For only after anything that is disruptive, chaotic, or undifferentiated has been rejected can we enter the peaceful realm of "similarity." This is my focus when I turn to Lessing's first bourgeois tragedy, *Miß Sara Sampson*, and analyze the process of subject formation postulated by the new genre. In this reading of *Miß Sara Sampson*, I pay particular attention to how Sara becomes the innerfictional subject of pity and the audience's object of pity, to how she is shaped into a relation of similarity toward others through a process of abjecting Marwood as the primary object of desire and abhorrence.

Miß Sara Sampson and Her Ideal Father

Miß Sara Sampson is interesting in the context of this study not only because it is Lessing's first and programmatic bourgeois tragedy but also because it responds in detail to the epistolary novel, in particular to *Clarissa*. The conflict at the outset of the play echoes Clarissa's situation on her way to London: the female protagonist stays at a hotel with a man who is in love with her. She is distressed at having to live under the same roof with a young man who is not her husband. However, unlike Clarissa, Miss Sara left her father's house willingly, and she is in love with the former rake, Mellefont. Whereas Clarissa spends the rest of her life yearning for a reconciliation with her family and a return to her father's house, Sara's family situation is altogether different. Her mother died in childbirth. She is an only child and has grown up in the loving care of her father, Sir William, and his servant Waitwell. Clarissa models her ideal of communication on the preverbal mother-child dyad; Sara sees in the death of her mother a prerequisite for falling in love with Mellefont: "You are looking at me so tenderly, Mellefont? You are right; a mother might only have tyrannized me with her love, and I would not belong to Mellefont. But then why should I desire what a wiser destiny has mercifully denied me? His foresight is always the best. Let's make good use of his gifts: a father who has never made me sigh for a mother" (IV, 1; p. 215).

In absence of the "tyrannical" maternal love, Sara is extremely attached to her father, whose love is very different from the mother's possessive love. The love of the father, unlike the love of the mother, can be transferred to another.[35] Thus Sara, as opposed to Clarissa, is no longer caught in a dyadic ideal of communication. Her father occupies a tertiary position within the symbolic realm of exchange. However, it is still not easy for Sara to come to terms with her father's position. She claims that he can make up for the loss of her mother in a positive sense. Once this order of exchange is admitted, he too can be replaced according to its logic. When Sara falls in love, however, she substitutes carnal passion for a non-sexual familial love and fundamentally threatens the order of the family. Her father's loving care and gentle understanding are precisely those qualities that define his authority and make Sara his educational product. Thus the conflict that the bourgeois tragedy must negotiate can be formulated as the following question: How and at what cost can the decarnalized, non-passionate love of an ideal father and educator be preserved? How can Sara be reintegrated into the order of the family?

Sir William is only too willing to be understanding and to forgive his daughter for eloping with Mellefont.

Without me Sara would never have met this dangerous man. Out of some sense of obligation, I granted him an all-too-free access to my house. It was only natural that my thankful attention to him attracted my daughter's respect for him. And it was equally natural, that a man of his kind of mind would be tempted to transform this respect into something higher. He had been cunning enough to

Fig. 7. Rousseau, Julie (1761), plate 6, "La force Paternelle." The father forces the daughter to comply with his wishes by kneeling before her, thus displaying weakness rather than paternal strength and authority. He assumes a posture more appropriate to a child or lover.

transform it into love before I noticed anything and before I had the time to inquire into his general conduct. The misfortune happened, and I would have done well if only I had forgiven them everything immediately.   (III, 1; p. 198)

Note how Sir William formulates this transference of love: his "thankful attention" ("dankbare Aufmerksamkeit") to Mellefont translates into Sara's "respect" ("Achtung") for this man. Then Mellefont's "cunning" ("Geschicklichkeit") transforms Sara's "respect" into "love." As long as Sara feels no sexual attraction to Mellefont, as long as all the affects in question can be subsumed under "respect," Sir William can allow the exchange since he is included in Sara's love for Mellefont. In contrast to Clarissa's father, Sir William follows his daughter to the hotel in order to achieve a reconciliation. But this desired reconciliation is not unconditional. Sir William can forgive Sara and even allow her to marry Mellefont only if her attachment to her lover can be subsumed under her attachment to her father and ego ideal. The father fears that carnal passion may have determined her to elope with Mellefont; if so, Sara has become alienated from him and is no longer his daughter.

When Sir William and Waitwell arrive at the hotel, the father does not immediately try to see his daughter, but sends Waitwell to Sara with a letter in the hope of investigating her psychic disposition. By way of the letter, he hopes to assure the permanence of her filial love: "That shortly removed from virtue she cannot yet have learned the art of disguise to which habitual vice takes its refuge. You will read all of her soul in her face. Don't let any trait escape you, particularly none that could indicate indifference toward me, a disdain for her father" (III, 1; pp. 198–99). It is noteworthy that Sir William uses the epistolary medium in order to deny his daughter's sexuality. Invoking Richardsonian reading conventions, he hopes that the letter can circumvent any possible "disguise," that by "reading" her read, his servant Waitwell will see Sara's true emotions. Sir William is afraid to lose Sara's love. Now, he has to forgive her and turn her escape with Mellefont into a mere "absence," because he cannot face his old age without her. "I can no longer do without her; she is the support of my old age, and if she doesn't help to sweeten the sad rest of my life, who else should do it? If she still loves me, her fault will be forgotten. It was the mistake of a tender girl, and her flight was the result of her remorse" (I, 1: p. 170). Here we have a definite departure from the central conflict in *Clarissa*. Whereas in Richardson's epistolary novel the father's hard-heartedness drives the daughter to elope with Lovelace and prevents Clarissa's reconciliation with the family, in Lessing's play the father is all-understanding and sympathizes with his daughter's "mistake" ("Fehler eines zärtlichen Mädchens").

Despite the father's willingness to forgive Sara, the play ends tragically. In fact, Sir William's strategy of denial helps precipitate this ending, which is foreshadowed by Sara's nightmare. She sees herself following Mellefont along the edge of an abyss when she suddenly hears the voice of her father telling her to stand still. At the moment she turns around to see him, her foot slips. However, she is saved from the fall(!) by a person similar to herself. When she begins to express her profuse thanks, that person takes out a dagger and stabs her. The dream predicts what will happen to Sara. Marwood, a woman similar to Sara and equally in love with Mellefont, has given her father the address of their hotel in the hope of separating the lovers. When she learns of Sir William's willingness to forgive them and to adopt Mellefont as his son-in-law, she tries to separate the lovers by telling Sara about Mellefont's past and his illegitimate child. When this plan fails and Sara refuses to empathize with her situation, Marwood poisons the girl.

The dream directs our attention to the obstacle that stands between Sara and her father, the obstacle that both saves and kills her. We are forced to ask not only what makes Sara similar to Marwood but also what in Sara obstructs the happy reunion with her father, because at the time of the dream Sara does not even know of Marwood's existence. What is it *in* Sara that prevents this union? We can find some clues to the nature of this obstacle in Sara's reaction to her father's letter. When Waitwell brings her the letter, her first reaction is shock. She immediately assumes that Sir William is dead, and she accuses herself of having shortened his life. When she learns that he is still alive, she hopes that he has forgotten his daughter. She cannot face the idea of his mourning for her. When Waitwell tells her that his letter is all loving and forgiving, she does not want to read it. She is appalled to hear he would be willing to let her marry Mellefont: "And that is exactly what I fear. To trouble a father like him, I had the courage. But to see him moved by this very sadness, by his love, which I renounced, moved to a point where he would tolerate anything I, driven by an unhappy passion, would do: this, Waitwell, I would not be able to stand this" (III, 3; p. 202). She could face his anger, but she cannot bear to see her father weak, to see him accepting even her running away with a lover. She could accept his forgiveness only if she were able to renounce her love of Mellefont: "If at that moment when he would allow me everything I could sacrifice everything for him, things would be altogether different," (III, 3, p. 202). Her erotic attraction to Mellefont makes her return to her father impossible. She can no longer be everything for her father since her father is no longer everything for her.

Finally Waitwell tricks her into reading her father's letter, but this does not end her resistance to the reconciliation. And she is at pains to find the appropriate response. All she can do is start a letter in which she depicts her fault in the most horrible way. It seems she must abject that part of her that is Mellefont's lover as an object of horror, that part of her that made her run away from her father, before the reconciliation with the father becomes possible. Thus at the end of Act III, the tragic course of events is well under way.[36]

The dream has already mapped out Sara's relation to her father, and she now works out that relationship by way of her highly ambiguous relation to a person similar to herself, Marwood, alias Lady Solmes. In the choice of names for this character Lessing refers to the two literary ancestors for his bourgeois tragedy: we can hear in Marwood an allusion to Lillo's *George Barnwell*, whose femme fatale is called Milwood; and Solmes is the name of the objectionable suitor whom Clarissa's parents try to force her to marry. Clarissa's martyrdom began with her repugnance toward her suitor Solmes, which led her into a lifelong struggle to affirm the purity of her heart against her family's accusations and Lovelace's intrigues. To the extent that the rejection of Solmes in *Clarissa* constitutes the crucial issue for defining the protagonist's identity and integrity in her relation to her parents (that is, she flees with Lovelace in order to escape this marriage and then is tortured by her inability to communicate to her parents that this act did not imply an erotic attraction to Lovelace), Lessing's choice of Marwood's pseudonym becomes very suggestive. For both Richardson and Lessing, Solmes is the name of the object whose rejection defines the subjectivity of the protagonist in relation to parental authority. Yet, in Lessing's play this rejection is more complex: the person similar to Sara both saves and kills her. In fact, Sara's subjectivity is reorganized through the ways in which she comes to articulate her difference and similarity vis-à-vis Marwood.

Marwood is anything but a pious daughter. She is a worldly femme fatale who knows how to manipulate intersubjective codes and conventions to her own purposes. But she is also a passionate woman whose self-control can suddenly disintegrate. As opposed to Sara, whose soul can be read in her face, Marwood is introduced as an experienced actress. Nevertheless, her attractions have little effect on Mellefont: "Marwood, you are talking perfectly in line with your ugly character. I have never really got to know this ugliness until the association with a virtuous friend has taught me to distinguish love from lust" (I, 3; p. 186). Mellefont rejects Marwood's ugly character; now that he has met Sara, he can differentiate lust and love—a distinction Sara in turn has learned from her father. Marwood's love is possessive, like the tyrannical maternal love Sara was spared by being raised by her father. Marwood tries to win Mellefont back by all available means. As their conflict becomes more violent, he calls her the shame of her sex, an impure animal, and a wanton, egotistical, dangerous courtesan. When Mellefont informs her of his intentions to marry Sara, Marwood loses her self-control, threatens to become a new Medea, and to revenge herself by torturing their child, Arabella. Finally, she tries to attack him with a dagger. But Mellefont disarms her and decides to separate her forever from her child. He threatens to accuse her of murder unless she disappears to London. Marwood agrees to go to London only if he lets her meet Sara just once. She is then subsequently introduced to Sara as Mellefont's relative Lady Solmes.

Once Marwood is alone with Sara, she slowly begins to unpack the gory details of Mellefont's past. She claims to criticize Mellefont as an advocate of the female sex. But Sara refuses to join Lady Solmes in female solidarity. In the name of love, she defends Mellefont's decision to leave Marwood, whereupon Lady Solmes tells her the story of Marwood. However movingly Lady Solmes describes Marwood's unfortunate fate, emphasizing her virtuous generosity as the explanation for her decade-long liaison with Mellefont, Sara nevertheless refuses to empathize with Marwood and to give up her claims on Mellefont. Instead, Sara insists on the absolute difference between the hardened courtesan and herself, who is plagued by remorse and a bad conscience because of her own sexuality.[37]

Lady, if you only knew what kind of remorse, what pangs of conscience, anxiety, this error has cost me. My error [*Irrtum*], I say; for why should I continue to be more cruel to myself and consider it a crime? Heaven itself discontinues to see it as such; he takes the punishment away from me and gives my father back to me— . . . Let me, Lady, let me supplicate—(*prostrating herself*). For your friendship, Lady,—And if I can't obtain the latter, at least for your justice not to place me and Marwood in the same rank. (IV, 8, p. 232)

At the moment she expresses what differentiates herself from Marwood, she suddenly is able to accept her father's pardon. Her decision to follow her lover—her sexual attraction to Mellefont—which had previously stood between her happy union with her father, has now been rejected by being declared an error. Once she has abjected that part of herself that is similar to Marwood, she has regained her access to the order of the fathers and can see herself pardoned even by God.[38] At the same moment

Lady Solmes reveals her true identity, and Sara sees in her the murderous, false savior figure of her dream and cries out for help from Mellefont and her father: "You Marwood?—Ha! Now I recognize her—now I can recognize the murderous savior, whose daggers were revealed to me in a warning dream. It is her! Fly, unhappy Sara! Save me, Mellefont; save your beloved! And you, sweet voice of my beloved father, resound! Where does it resound? where shall I hurry?—here?—there?" (IV, 8; p. 232)

As Sara recovers from her fainting spell and begins to feel the first pangs of the deadly poison, she sees a happy union in the friendship of herself, Mellefont, Arabella, and her father. And while Mellefont is cursing Marwood, yearning for revenge, Sara's attitude toward Marwood turns to mildness, and she wishes he would not even read Marwood's note: "Do not let me hear of revenge. Revenge is not ours!—You still break it open?—Ah Mellefont, why are we less disposed to virtue if our body is healthy and aware of its physical strength, than when our body is sick and weak. How sour are gentleness and meekness for you, and how unnatural appears to me the impatient heat of the affect!—Keep the contents to yourself" (V, 5; pp. 238–39). Now Sara can feel pity for Marwood, plead for forgiveness, and condemn the violent passion of revenge. But Mellefont cannot discipline his hatred of his former lover and reads the note: "But what kind of spirit forces me to disobey you? I opened it against my will—against my will I have to read it." Mellefont is still caught up in the realm of love and hatred that surfaced when he and Marwood were arguing. Although Mellefont claims that he has learned the difference between "love and lust," he is not entirely free from "the impatient heat of the affect." Sara comments on how Mellefont is split between his will and his passions: "How cleverly man knows to separate himself from his passions and turn them into another being, which he can blame for all that which he rationally cannot approve of—" (V, 5; p. 239). Sara's statement is meant to address Mellefont's question "What kind of a spirit forces me to disobey you?" Through this question he excuses his undisciplined spirit of revenge and his disobedience to Sara's request for mercy for Marwood; however, Sara's phrase can also be read in the larger context of the play. In this pronouncement Sara unintentionally sums up the function and fate of the femme fatale, at whose expense the bourgeois tragedy achieves the construction of virtuous subjects: reformed rakes and virtuous daughters.

The reconciliation with the father is preceded by a process of rejecting a threatening other and of splitting off those parts in the self that obstruct the peaceful realm of familial love, empathy, and pity. Only by the end can the other be perceived as similar without being threatening to the self.

The names of this abject/reject are femme fatale, female sexuality, the body. For only after Sara has abjected Marwood in her conversation with Lady Solmes and rejected her own sexuality as "error," only after she has renounced her corporeality, only after Marwood is exiled and Sara accepts her own death as merely the death of her body ("I am sick, very sick; but suppose the utmost, that I would die: would I really be lost?"; V, 6; p. 240), only then can she respond to her father's letter. At this point she asks Wait-well to reiterate all he had to say about her father's love and pardon. And finally she hears her father's voice, as in her dream. When he enters, she is reconciled with him in the face of death. She forgives Marwood and pro-tects her from the worldly law by destroying the note that could be used as evidence against her. Then she bequeaths her father's love to Mellefont and Arabella and dies. At last even Mellefont overcomes his inability to accept Sir William's love and paternal embrace, but he does so only after he has chosen his own death, after he has stabbed himself with Marwood's dagger in a guilty gesture of self-punishment.

The transformations of Sara's relationship to Marwood are set at the core of Lessing's definition of the bourgeois tragedy. The sole purpose of this type of drama is the excitation of pity, and it is in this affective dimen-sion that the moral efficacy of the genre is situated. The subject of pity is affected neither by desire nor by abhorrence, but constitutes his/her rela-tion to the other in terms of similarity. Pity, according to Lessing, leads to the subject's moral improvement, for it affirms both the subject's identity and sociability. Subjectivity is formed and stabilized at the threshold of representation through a process of abjecting undifferentiated otherness and affective ambiguity. Only when the other is freed of any reminder of the concrete material of the body, and thereby integrated into the realm of illusion, can this other become the object of pity. Thus only after Sara has overcome the carnal passions by rejecting the corporeality of the body, female sexuality, and a tyrannical maternal love can she become both a subject of pity and the object of the audience's pity.

Written before Lessing's theory of the bourgeois tragedy, Diderot's introduction to *Fils naturel* stresses the importance of the domestic space for the drame bourgeois. The family setting is part of the genre's anti-theatricality; it is opposed to the exteriorized, rigidly codified conventions of *le monde*, which would disrupt the drama's illusion. In terms of the drama's moral efficacy and affective impact on the audience, the charac-ters' primary definition as family members favors the identificatory in-volvement of the audience and offers definitions that transcend class- and status-bound specifications.[39] Neither of the predominant explanations for the importance of familial relations as the site of conflicts in the bourgeois tragedy is satisfactory. One suggests that the family constitutes a "mere" dramaturgical strategy, which allows the representation of "universal," human conflicts.[40] The other interprets the familial setting as an implicit critique of the dominant social-political situation, that is, in terms of an opposition of private and public spheres.[41] I find the latter more convincing, but it remains too vague, for it does not explain what differentiates the bourgeois tragedy from the epistolary novel, for instance. Those explanations reach an impasse in that "universal Human conflicts" or the "rise of the bourgeoisie" cannot account for the absence of the mother in the new genre.

For both Diderot and Lessing, the crucial familial relation is the one between child and father. The issue of the family as a specific bourgeois problem can become clearer only if this is recognized. What is at stake in these plays is the specific asset of that social class: the child as the result of a particular education, as the cultural product of an ideal gentle father.[42] Only if we take into account the theory of pity and illusion and its constitution of a particular subject vis-à-vis representations can we understand how this subject is structurally similar to the subject of the gentle education: aesthetic illusion requires a veiling of mediation; the gentle formation of subjectivity a veiling of the educator's authorial power. The subject of pity has to affirm itself in an abjection of material concreteness, just as the virtuous subject has to reject her body and the reformed rake his erotic imagination. The anti-theatrical bourgeois tragedy formulates an education in relation to an ideal father, and an "autonomous," morally responsible subject produced by excluding the mother. However, such a scenario of subject formation will last only as long as this *citoyen* of a general humanity is thought to inhabit a sphere apart from the state.[43] Rousseau will be the one to give up the anti-theatrical fiction of the drama together with the primacy of the ideal father, which will yield to the ideal wife and mother in the service of the new state. In order to trace these transformations, the following chapter returns to the genre of the epistolary novel, to Rousseau's *Julie ou la Nouvelle Héloïse*.

3

'Julie ou la Nouvelle Héloïse': The Mother and the State

Chapter 1 outlined Rousseau's political and pedagogical investment in constructing the image of the ideal Woman as the only locus for the containment of masculine desire. The ideal Woman is a privileged semiotic constellation that can install and secure the authority of the law and public morality. Rejecting theatricality for its frivolous display of a shifting signifying praxis and for its undermining of authority, Rousseau's programmatic statements call for new literary genres that produce this semiotic constellation. Although the *Lettre à d'Alembert* mentions Richardson's epistolary fiction favorably, Rousseau's own epistolary novel, *Julie ou La Nouvelle Héloïse* (1761) departs from the Richardsonian paradigm in significant ways.

The framing of this epistolary novel is quite exceptional. In a way the novel has three titles: *Julie*, a title like *Clarissa*, taken from the name of the heroine; *la Nouvelle Héloïse*, designating the text as an actualization of the famous medieval paradigm; and the subtitle *Lettres des deux amants habitants d'une petite ville au pied des Alpes*. Under the subtitle we find the Petrarchan epigraph: "Non la connobe il mondo, mentre l'ebbe: Connobill' io ch'a pianger qui rimasi" ("The world did not know her while it had her; I knew her who remain here to weep"). In these two lines Petrarch refers to his lost beloved in words freely borrowed from John the Evangelist's reference to the divine logos. Furthermore, the novel has two "prefaces" (Rousseau's term): one at the beginning, the other at the end.

Despite the variety of literary allusions on the title page, the first preface warns the reader not to expect the kind of sophisticated literary entertainment common among people of *le monde*: "This book was not at all fashioned to circulate among society and suits very few readers. The style will discourage people of taste; the matter will alarm the austere; all the sentiments will be outside of nature for those who do not believe in virtue. It must displease the devout, the libertines, the philosophers; it is bound to shock gallant ladies, and scandalize honest women" (p. 3). And since *le monde* is divided into a multitude of social styles, each tied to its preferences, interests, and biases, and since virtue is a matter of belief or disbelief, the style and subject matter of the *Lettres de deux amants* will not satisfy any worldly norms and expectations. The collection of letters claims to be radically different.[1] The reader of this novel has to discard the norms by which he usually judges a piece of writing: "Whoever wishes to be resolved to read these letters must arm himself with patience on account of the faults of language, the flat and bombastic style, the common thoughts rendered in high-flown terms; he must tell himself beforehand that those who wrote them are not French, wits, academicians, philosophers; but provincials, strangers, solitary people, young people, nearly children, who in their novelistic imaginations, take for philosophy the honest deliriums of their heads" (p. 3). One might have expected the argument that these correspondents do not comply with the literary norms of educated and corrupt Parisian society, but it is exactly the naiveté of these letters that makes them true and valid. The letters are, however, not presented in the guise of the naive stranger who provides a critique of contemporary society, as, for instance, Montesquieu's *Lettres Persanes*. The argument takes another direction altogether: although the epistolary style of the two lovers is not distorted by the conventions of a specific social group and although the correspondents are almost children and as provincials least alienated from nature, their letters offer no particular insights into the contemporary situation or human nature. The editor calls the letters a mere delirium of the writers' imaginations, however "honnête" they might be. With this statement the letters can no longer be placed within the frame of a representational aesthetics; rather, they are located within an aesthetics of expression, which valorizes the authenticity and intensity of the passion producing the text, not the documentary transparency of the text vis-à-vis an objective content.[2]

A closer look at the title page in the context of the first preface highlights some aspects in which this novel departs from some by then customary framing devices. Thus the title page and the first preface do not quite resemble those eighteenth-century novels that present a piece of fiction as if it were an objet trouvé the author in the role of an editor offers to readers in order to make the story into a "history."[3] The editor of the first preface departs from this convention in a decisive way. He does not claim for these letters, which do not comply with aesthetic conventions, an extra-textual validity in terms of "historical truth." The question of the fictionality of these letters is suspended. Their referentiality is an issue of their illusionary effect. Furthermore, the preface at the beginning of the novel refers to the letters without naming the collection. Only the second preface is called the "Préface de Julie ou Entretien sur les romans." The first preface appears without title, but the second preface refers back to the first as "Préface aux Lettres des deux amants." The two prefaces make it clear that the novel can be called *Julie* only after it has been read. For only once the aesthetic illusion has produced its effect does the collection of letters form a totality that can be called *Julie*. As opposed to *Clarissa or the History of a Young Lady*, *Julie ou la Nouvelle Héloïse* posits *Julie* as the name of a *lecture* and a specific aesthetic illusion, not as the name of an extra-textual signified. *Julie* is not so much the protagonist of a narrative as the name of a passion and the focus of a reading experience that undergoes certain transformations, or, to be more precise, a reading experience and a passion that are classified as an actualization of the literary and cultural paradigm of Héloïse and Abelard.

Although the editor does not claim that his collection provides sophisticated entertainment or that it contains philosophical or historical truths, he still ascribes to it a special value for his contemporary readers.

Spectacles are necessary in large cities and novels among corrupt people. I have seen the mores of my time, and I have published these letters. That I did not live in an age where I ought to throw them in the fire!

Although I bear only the title of editor here, I have myself worked on this book, and I do not hide it. Have I done everything, and is the whole correspondence a fiction? People of the world, what does it matter to you? For you it is surely a fiction. (p. 3)

The love letters are supposed to address the contemporary corrupt world. The worldly audience will certainly take the book for a mere fiction, since their experiential background cannot validate the novel for them. But the novel will also be a necessary fiction for them, for—as we know from *Emile* and the *Lettre à M. d'Alembert*—in a corrupt society only certain illusions can improve people's moral conduct. The list of those readers to whom the book will not be convenient not only preempts inappropriate criticisms but also manages to make the book more interesting. The editor's promise in the first preface that the book will flout all literary conventions excites the reader's curiosity. His warning that any innocent girl who reads the first pages will be lost gives the book a certain titillating touch. He concludes the first preface with the declaration that he sympathizes with any austere man who, after perusing the first parts, throws the book into a corner; however, he cannot understand the reader who can condemn the book after reading it in its entirety. Thus the first preface sets the stage for the book as an alluring antidote to a corrupt world, as a promise of a seduction to virtue. Even though the editor acknowledges the possibility of the text's fictionality, of its illusionary quality (to the extent that all language produces illusions), he nevertheless claims that the text produces a superior illusion, an illusion with redemptive effects.

The second preface, the "Préface de Julie ou Entretien sur les romans," also claims that the novel will produce a special reading experience. This preface is presented as a dialogue between the novel's "editor," R., and its first reader, N. In an introductory statement the editor informs us that he decided to defer this dialogue, which offers "some useful insights on the object of these kinds of writings" to the end of the book, waiting "until the book has achieved its effect" (p. 571). He thereby implies that reading *Julie* will have an impact so powerful that it will change the reader's notions about the status and function of that collection of letters—in other words, a reading with the force of a deferred action. Not only the two prefaces but also the title page mark the temporal structure of Rousseau's novel in a way that calls attention to its *Nachträglichkeit*, the Freudian term that describes psychic temporality and causality as deferred action.[4] The alternative titles provide the juncture of the textualized experience (i.e., the correspondents' experience, mainly their love story) and the experience of the text (i.e., our reading of *Julie*). As the fictional love story actualizes and transforms the Héloïse/Abelard paradigm—as Saint-Preux learns to love virtue through his attachment to Julie d'Etange, the fallen girl who is transformed into the virtuous and chaste Julie de Wolmar—the reader moves from being involved in a romantic love story to being affected by the image of the lost object of love, the emblem of virtue, and a new social order.

Richardson offered his epistolary novel as an example and occasion of moral improvement. *Clarissa or the History of a Young Lady* is placed in the service of virtue within an aesthetics of representation. My reading of the novel shows how subjectivity is reorganized vis-à-vis an exhaustively detailed written documentation. "Writing to the moment" is by itself the condition for truth and virtue. The letters function as mirrors of the soul. In that capacity they are able to work as instruments of reflection, of a critical self-examination in the gaze of the Other, the authority seeing beyond any ruse or disguise. Belford's model of moral improvement is one of conversion, if we define conversion as the reorganization of the subject through the application of the truth of scripture to the subject's own life. Belford subjects himself to the truth of the letter. He is reformed at that moment when reading, writing, and seeing have become shortcircuited, when he gains access to that ideal of transparency that defines the status of the letters throughout *Clarissa*, and when that becomes "graphic" in Clarissa's martyrdom and decarnalization. Rousseau's model for moral improvement is altogether different. Instead of history and conversion—a linear temporal development and a seizure of this history's truth that produces the subject's reinscription in this history—we find a continuous process of repetitions and returns, whose effects unfold in terms of deferred action. Rousseau does not rely on the letter as mirror. For him writing does not produce this smooth surface of reflection. Writing and reading produce only illusions and desire, and the way to moral reform is through these necessary illusions. *Julie* has to create those illusions that focus desire and tame the imagination.

If *Julie* can be described as a specific semiotic constellation that constitutes the disciplinary programming of a young man, it is reminiscent of the tutor's strategy as he is about to introduce Emile to Parisian society. The tutor paints for Emile an imaginary beloved in order to protect him from the false illusions of *le monde*. *Julie* is this illusion in the service of virtue that Rousseau postulates in *Emile*. And according to Rousseau, as I show in the last sections of Chapter 1, the relationship of women to representation is altogether different from that of men. Consequently in *Julie* only the female protagonist undergoes a conversion, since she—like Sophie—is subjected to paternal authority and can thus be subjected to the gaze of the Other. The male protagonist undergoes a continuous process of being conditioned as a subject in his relation to the image of his beloved. Saint-Preux—like Emile—is disciplined through love. Yet the construction of Julie as the ideal woman is far more complicated than that of Sophie. In *Emile* the authority of the tutor and his evocative speech are sufficient to create such a powerful image of an imaginary beloved that Emile is turned away from all the seductions of Parisian society. Whereas *Emile* only formulates the principles for educating the average young man, *Julie* becomes the book about the education of the educator. A tutor of an old order is reprogrammed to become the educator of the subjects of a new social order. In *Julie* the education of the educator is accomplished without the paternal authority of a tutor. His education starts from point zero and works solely through the affects and passions of the protagonist, gradually taming and shaping his imagination, forming and focusing his desire.

My reading of the novel analyzes *Julie* as a specific semiotic constellation that constitutes the disciplinary programming of a young man. The expression "disciplinary programming" may sound crude, but I think it captures the fact that Saint-Preux's education is a radical—though gentle and gradual—reorganization of his subjectivity, a process that excludes all external force or violence, that works exclusively through love. In the following sections, I show how Saint-Preux's passion for Julie is an intervention in his psyche at exactly that threshold where the subject comes into being: the threshold that defines for him referentiality in language through the organization of his affects.

In terms of formal organization, the novel is divided into two parts, and each part into three books. Part I spans the time from the lovers' discovery of their fateful attraction to Julie d'Etange's forced marriage to Wolmar. Book 1 develops the love story as the lovers meet in the house of Julie's father. Then, in Book 2, Saint-Preux is exiled to Paris. Book 3 culminates in Julie's conversion during her marriage ceremony and her vow to be a chaste and faithful wife and mother. Part II spans the time from Wolmar's invitation of Saint-Preux to Julie's death. In Book 4, the former lovers are reunited, and Saint-Preux introduced to the new social order, the utopian household of Clarens. In Book 5, Saint-Preux leaves to accompany his friend Edouard to Italy. Book 6 focuses on Julie's death. A closer look at this structure shows that the two parts of the novel are symmetrical; the books in Parts I and II are related in terms of repetition, reversal, and contrast.[5]

	Part I *la maison paternelle* (*old order*)	*Part II* *Clarens* (*new order*)
1. Union of the lovers	love consummated (Bk 1)	chaste love (Bk 4)
2. Separation of the lovers	Saint-Preux in Paris (Bk 2)	Saint-Preux on the way to Italy (Bk 5)
3. Transformation of Julie	conversion (Bk 3)	death (Bk 6)

The education of Saint-Preux takes place within two scenarios. First, the house of Julie's father, which is part of the traditional social order. Saint-Preux is Julie's tutor, defined and restricted by his social class. Monsieur d'Etange is a fallible, brutal, loving, and incompetent father. The lovers presume that they can be united in an anarchic dyad, that they can take control over their conduct on their own behalf, excluding any disciplinary tertiary agency. Second, Wolmar's household at Clarens, which anticipates a perfectly regulated, peaceful social utopia. Wolmar is a competent and invisible policing agent. Saint-Preux is judged not in terms of his social class, but in terms of his ability to control himself. Julie has become wife and mother. The former lovers can no longer assume an exclusive relationship. The main objective in Saint-Preux's education consists in his transfer from the one order to the other. This transfer is negotiated through Julie's conversion during the marriage ceremony.[6] Although both the end of Part I and the end of Part II focus on Julie, her conversion and her transfiguration, the first two books of both parts are centered on Saint-Preux's relation to his beloved. Books 1 and 2 stage various semiotic constellations that organize his desire and imagination in relation to Julie d'Etange, first in her presence and then in her absence, when he is left with "mere" representations. Books 4 and 5 repeat those constellations in relation to Julie de Wolmar, the new Julie, who has become part of the order at Clarens. Based on the model of the novel's composition and structure sketched above, the next five sections focus on those passages concerned with the organization of Saint-Preux's subjectivity and with the construction of the image of the ideal Woman.

Virtuous Julie Versus Eroticized Image: "Les transports aveugles" (Book 1)

The novel begins in medias res with a sequence of letters from Julie's tutor to his student. Except for his status as a private tutor who has fallen desperately in love and who knows that class barriers and social conventions define his attraction as a transgression, we learn no exterior data about this writer. We are not even informed of his name. Not until the second part of the novel is he called Saint-Preux. In this respect the nameless lover resembles the nameless, vague, and shifting speaker N. of the second preface, the novel's first reader, who defines himself in the dialogue with R. exclusively in terms of his relation to *Julie*. In other words, Julie's tutor must be understood as a subject in process, a subject that is constituted vis-à-vis Julie. Book 1 focuses on the first stage of this construction, when the lovers are for the most part united in the house of Julie's father. It examines how self-control and discipline are possible under those conditions, and what secures and threatens the stability of Saint-Preux's subjectivity.

Already in the first letter, when the tutor voices his passion and asserts the impossibility of reconciling this situation with the standards of good behavior and politeness, he expresses his inability to act according to reason. He knows he should leave, but he is unable to act on his decision. Julie, finally, urges him to stay. The male subject is to be educated gently: he is to find the way to virtue not through prohibition and the renunciation of passion but through love, through the disciplining of desire. Urging him to stay and confessing her own love, Julie assigns to him the responsibility of protecting the chastity of their love. He gladly accepts this task but quickly recognizes its problems. Despite his virtuous intentions and efforts, he cannot gain control over his fantasies. In order to subjugate his passionate impulses, he strictly separates the actual Julie from his erotic imaginings: "Your glances, your voice, convey to the heart, with love, the touching charm of innocence; it is a divine charm that one would regret to destroy. If I do dare to form extreme desires, it is only in your absence; my desires, not daring to go as far as you, address themselves to your image, and it is on that that I avenge myself for the respect that I am constrained to bear for you" (p. 26). Saint-Preux describes himself as split between imaginary gratification and an external perception that demands the deferral of gratification. It is noteworthy that already at this stage all the previous instances of control—namely, social restrictions that are part of an intersubjective constellation beyond the lovers' dyadic unity—have been put aside. Saint-Preux safeguards his discipline by separating image and referent. But this virtue amounts to nothing more than mere self-control in her presence; in her absence, his imagination runs wild.

Yet this form of self-discipline is canceled by a single transgression. His precarious self-control and tranquillity end quickly with the kiss in the grove, offered to him in the guise of innocent familiarity: "Alas! I was reveling in an apparent tranquillity; submissive to your supreme desires, I no longer murmured about a fate over which you deigned to preside; I had tamed the impetuous fits of a reckless imagination, I had covered my glances with a veil and set a shackle to my heart, my desires dared to loose themselves no more than halfway; I was as content as I could be" (p. 34). The veil that separated the sight of Julie from the image of his erotic fantasies has been lifted. The actual Julie has become indistinguishable from the Julie of his erotic imagination. Image and referent have been fused, and Saint-Preux's subjectivity has been reorganized in this removal of the veil. This canceling of any mediation or difference places him in the realm of illusion and allows him to unify his split subjectivity. With this possibility of sliding between the sight of Julie and her image, chastity or the deferral of gratification can no longer be guaranteed. And despite Julie's last and desperate attempt to preserve her virtue by sending him away after the kiss, she will lose her innocence. For it is exactly this slide from image to referent, the fusing of an internal image with the perception of an other, that leads Saint-Preux to write the letter from Meillerie that persuades Julie to consent to a nocturnal encounter.

In the letter from Meillerie, Saint-Preux describes his melancholia, as he wanders around the autumnal landscape on the other side of the lake. Removed from his object of love, he has lost the reference point for both his perceptions of an exterior world and his own imaginings. He sees in himself as well as outside himself only a horrible disintegrating chaos (see p. 54). Finally, when he discovers a spot from which Julie's village can be seen, he finds a focus for his errant desire. He borrows a telescope from the village pastor in order to discern her house. From then on he passes all his days at that spot.

It is there, my Julie, that your unfortunate lover finishes enjoying the last pleasures that he will perhaps taste in this world. It is from there through the air and walls he dares in secret penetrate even to your room. Your charming features wound him still; your tender looks revive his dying heart; he hears the sound of your sweet voice; once more he dares seek in your arms that delirium he felt in the grove. Vain phantom of an agitated soul that he loses himself in his desires! Shortly forced to return to myself, I at least contemplate you in the circumstances of your innocent life. . . . I even dare to see you busy yourself about me; I see your tender eyes run over one of my letters, I read in their sweet languor that it is to your fortunate lover the lines you trace are addressed. I see that it is of him you speak to your cousin with such a tender emotion. O Julie! O Julie! and we would not be united? . . . No, that this frightful idea would never present itself to my mind! In one instant it changes all my tenderness into fury, rage makes me run from haunt to haunt. (p. 55)

The telescope allows the frustrated lover to reenact the semiotic constellation of the kiss. Through it he can project his memory image of Julie to the other side of the lake, fusing this image with a referent. He constitutes his own unity in her image. Through this apparatus he can "see" her reading and "read" in this sight while he himself is writing to her. This letter from Meillerie creates a shortcircuiting of reading, writing, and visual perception culminating in a hallucinatory presence and transparency similar to that enacted by Belford's funeral letter. But although Belford's hallucinatory reading and writing were devoid of sensual fantasies, Julie's lover writes out of libidinal frustration and only after his imagination has been fused with the pleasure received from the actual Julie. In Richardson's novel the reform of the rake became possible through Belford's decorporealized sight of Clarissa, but the letter from Meillerie is far from affirming a moral conversion; its specularity is eroticized and transgressive, and it

Fig. 8. Rousseau, Julie *(1761), plate 1, "Le premier baiser de l'amour."*

constitutes the decisive step toward the lovers' fall. Although this specular moment does not lead to the sublimation of Saint-Preux's libidinal impulses, it does momentarily focus and stabilize his errant desire, but only as long as the optical apparatus can produce Julie's imaginary presence. Any reminder of their separation throws him back into a raving disintegration. He ends by urging her to let him come back as quickly as possible. He also threatens suicide in an attempt to blackmail her, describing his frustration in the most lively colors.

And indeed, this letter induces their nocturnal encounter. Julie describes to Claire how she lost her innocence:

A hundred times my eyes were witness to his struggles and his victory; his eyes flashed with the fire of his desires, he launched toward me in the impetuousness of a blind rapture, he stopped suddenly; an insurmountable barrier seemed to have surrounded me, and never did his love, impetuous but honest, break it. I dared too much to contemplate this dangerous spectacle. I felt myself unsettled by his raptures, his sighs oppressed my heart; I shared his torments by merely thinking to pity them. I saw him, in convulsive shakings, ready to faint at my feet. O my cousin, perhaps only love would have saved me! It is pity that has lost me.   (p. 59)

Obviously, his blackmail has been successful; he has managed to move Julie's pity. Julie phrases the sight of her frustrated lover in terms of his being held back from a "transport aveugle" by a "barrière insurmountable." She uses an image that goes back to Saint-Preux's letter describing his self-control before the removal of the veil. What she describes to her friend as a sight, this "dangereux spectacle," is in fact a fusion of hallucinations, taken from her memories of the time before she sent him away and from his letter from Meillerie (see pp. 26, 56). Julie is also caught in a realm of illusion. Although for Julie specularity is not eroticized, she is nevertheless caught in an imaginary union similar to that Saint-Preux had produced through the telescope. For their union appears to her in the image of their souls mirroring each other, a congruence that manifests itself in a communication transcending any separation through the correspondence of their hearts: "Our souls were so to speak touching at all points, and throughout we felt the same coherence. . . . Fate may well separate us, but not disunite us. We will only have the same pleasures and the same pains; and like those lovers of whom you were speaking to me, who feel, it is said, the same emotions in different places, we will feel the same things at the two antipodes of the world" (p. 27). Only this imaginary union with her lover allows the "dangereux spectacle" of his tormenting frustration to affect her with pity.

Although *pitié* is, in Rousseau's anthropology, a natural disposition toward compassion for one's fellow beings preceding any social institution and regulation, it is nevertheless an aesthetic category as well, to the extent that it refers to an act of the imagination, an illusionary identification with an other: "In effect, how do we allow ourselves to be moved by pity, if it is not by transporting ourselves outside of ourselves and by identifying with the suffering animal by leaving, so to speak, our being to assume his? We only suffer as much as we judge he suffers; it is not within ourselves, it is within him that we suffer. Thus no one becomes compassionate until his imagination animates itself and begins to transport him outside of himself" (*Emile*, p. 289). Pity in this description has the same structure as love: we are transported outside ourselves, we lose ourselves in order to reconstitute ourselves in the other. And, like love, pity depends on an aesthetics of illusion, an illusion that allows the fusion of image and referent. More precisely, it is grounded in an aesthetics of illusion that obliterates the materiality of the signifying praxis. In her account to Claire, Julie is totally captivated by this aesthetics of illusion, since she does not mention that her sight of the "dangereux spectacle" has been mediated by Saint-Preux's letters from Meillerie. Not until after her conversion does she cease to repress the letters from Meillerie: "Sadness and love were consuming my heart; I fell into a despondency of which my letters felt the effects. Those you wrote me from Meillerie saw the lowest depth; to my own sorrows was joined the sentiment of your despair" (p. 252).

From the moment of Saint-Preux's return from Meillerie, virtue is conceived differently. In the beginning, virtue was defined in terms of the lovers' chastity, the deferral of gratification, and the separation of the actual Julie from the Julie of Saint-Preux's imagination. Henceforth virtue will be defined as fidelity to the beloved. To some extent Saint-Preux's errant desire and his wild imagination have indeed been curbed, since they have been focused on one object. But since this channeling of desire accompanied the removal of the veil between the chaste Julie and the object of his erotic imagination, his object of love runs the risk of being submerged in the undifferentiation of sexual pleasure. Julie would then no longer be the Woman but only a woman; his desire would again become errant, and he would lose himself in promiscuity.[7]

Julie addresses this danger in a letter in which she reprimands her lover for the excessive drinking that caused him to use obscene language in her presence. She insists that her complaint is not so much about this particular instance but about the state of his heart, which revealed itself in his loose talk. His love must be purified of sensual imagination, otherwise he will fall prey to the "préjugées du monde."

True love is the most chaste of all bonds. It is that, it is its divine fire, which knows how to purify our natural proclivities, by concentrating them in a single object; it is that which steals us away from our temptations, and which allows that except for that unique object the one sex is no longer anything for the other. For a common woman every man is always a man; but for her whose heart loves, there is no man but her lover. What do I say? Is not a lover a man? Ah! he is a being so much more sublime! There is no man at all for her who loves: her lover is more; all others are less; she and he are the only ones of their kind. They do not desire; they love. The heart does not follow the senses a bit, it guides them; it covers their wild aberrations with a delightful veil.   (pp. 90–91)

Julie introduces anew the veil as that which covers the wild aberrations ("les égarements") of the senses in order to preserve the uniqueness and individuality of the beloved. His response adopts her metaphor but shifts its function.

A single one of your looks would have restrained my mouth and purified my heart. Love would have covered my desires swept away by the charms of your modesty; it would have conquered without abusing; and in the sweet union of our souls, only their ecstasy would have produced the errors of the senses. I appeal here to your own testimony. Say whether, in all the furors of a passion without measure, I have ever ceased to respect the charming object. . . . When for an instant an indiscreet rapture tears away the veil that covers them [the charms], does not kind shame at once substitute itself there? Would this sacred vestment abandon you one moment when you did not have another? Incorruptible like your honest soul, have all the fires of mine ever deviated from this? Does not this so touching and tender union suffice for our happiness?   (p. 92)

The function of the veil that in Julie's letter was to control his "egarements des sens" is in his letter assigned to her gaze. He need not control his sensual imagination, and thus his letter slides to a memory of their "douce union." When he comes to discuss the veil as guarantee of her uniqueness, it covers her naked body. A psychoanalytic interpretation might read this passage as Saint-Preux's attempt to protect himself against the threat of lack and castration posed by the naked female body.

Saint-Preux does not comply with Julie's demand that he protect the uniqueness of his beloved by purifying his imagination of its sensual aspects. Rather, Julie is unique for him because she is the site/sight of the fulfillment of all his desires. He thinks himself beyond any possible infidelity since she can provide him with all possible happiness in this world. Thus he takes their imaginary dyad as a guarantee of his virtue. He concludes his letter with a vow to abstain from wine forever, swearing by her image: "If I break this solemn vow, Love, crush me with the punishment I deserve: at that instant may the image of my Julie leave my heart forever, and abandon it to indifference and despair" (p. 93). Yet, as we read in Book 2, once Saint-Preux is away from Julie, the vow will be broken: he will lose himself in drunkenness and in the arms of a prostitute. Nevertheless, for the time being he is entirely captivated by the plenitude of their imaginary union. His very next letter provides another clue for the function he has assigned to the veil. In the previous letter the veil covered her naked body. The subsequent letter is written in her closet while he is fingering her clothes, which had covered her naked body; now the veil has been turned into a fetish and serves as a screen for the hallucination of her body: "All the parts of your scattered clothing present to my ardent imagination those parts of yourself that they conceal; this delicate headgear that adorns the long blond hair it feigns to cover, this happy fichu against which..." (p. 97). And his aroused imagination flows directly into his pen: "What happiness to have found ink and paper! I express what I feel in order to temper the excess; I hoodwink my raptures by describing them" (p. 97).

Whereas in his previous letter the veil was used metaphorically for a protective device that prevents the exposure of the naked female body, this "pornographic" letter materializes the veil in her underwear, which reveals her body's sensual attractions. However, at the beginning of the letter the metaphorical veil recurs: "Charming room, fortunate room, which once saw so many tender looks to restrain, so many burning sighs to stifle; you who saw grow and nourish my first fires, for the second time you will see them crowned; witness to my immortal constancy, be the witness to my happiness, and veil forever the pleasures of the most faithful and happiest of men" (pp. 96–97). Julie's room is to veil the sight of their nocturnal encounter in order to protect the secret of their "douce union" from the intrusion of an other—Julie's "barbare père." But the room is also to witness his "constance immortelle" and his "bonheur." Veiling the possibility of lack and the gaze of the other will, in turn, guarantee his "immortal constancy"; thus the room/veil comes to stand for the perfect self-sufficiency of the two lovers. Yet the next time Saint-Preux enters this room—in Book 3—this veil will be torn, the imaginary unity of the two lovers will be disrupted. By that point Mme d'Etange has read their letters and has died; Julie has been confronted with her father's will and is lying ill with smallpox in a delirious fever precisely in this room. Her lover is admitted to see her under the pseudonym Saint-Preux (see pp. 243, 311).[8] He receives this name and social identity only after all hopes of returning to the earlier state of bliss and plenitude have been eradicated, after he has been confronted with lack and separation.

When toward the end of Book 1 Julie dissuades her lover from a duel with Edouard, masculine desire has been disciplined through love. Since Saint-Preux has come to define himself exclusively in relation to Julie, he can renounce the mondaine definitions of honor and the practice of dueling.[9] Nevertheless, Saint-Preux's self-discipline depends on Julie's presence and active intervention. Book 1 traces this focusing of masculine desire on one particular object that promises the fulfillment of all desires. This is achieved in a fusion of Saint-Preux's imagination with his perception of Julie. I have analyzed how this fusion is established through an optical apparatus, a hallucinatory, illusionary presence, culminating in his letter from Meillerie and Julie's "sympathetic" response. Negating the materiality of the signifier and ignoring all problems of representation, the two lovers perceive their correspondence as that of two souls speaking to each other the pure language of the heart. They conceive of their love as a self-sufficient dyad, a union that preserves its promise of plenitude by excluding the world, any intrusive other, which would introduce lack and absence into their relationship. Whereas Emile's love for his imaginary Sophie allows him to overcome all the temptations of a corrupt Parisian society, Book 2 of *Julie* questions the efficacy of the image of the beloved once the lovers are separated. What happens to Saint-Preux's discipline once he is unable to find himself in her mirroring soul, once he is without a fixed reference for the projection of his imagination? Can he maintain the image of his beloved against a world of chaotic perceptions and representations?

The Image of the Woman in the Realm of Representations
(Book 2)

After Saint-Preux has overcome his initial desperation over his separation from Julie, he decides to live in knightly fashion for the honor of his lady: "That immortal image that I carry with me will serve as an aegis to me, and will render my soul invulnerable to the blows of fortune. Have I not lived enough for my happiness? It is now for her glory that I must live" (p. 155). But instead of having to master glorious tasks, he finds himself lost in the big city of Paris: "With a secret horror I enter into this vast desert of society. This chaos offers me only an awful solitude where a gloomy silence reigns. Among the throng my soul expands to spread itself, and finds itself everywhere constricted. . . . In a crowd I am only alone, where I can belong neither to you, nor others. My heart would like to speak, it senses that it is not heard; it would like to reply, nothing is said to it that can reach it. I do not understand the language of this country a bit, and no one here understands mine" (p. 163). His first impression of Paris recalls his situation in Meillerie. In Meillerie his "horreur" was due to the disintegration of his wild imagination and the loss of the stable reference point for his perception and his imagination. Paris confronts him with a similar horror. But he perceives the problem in another light. Chaos confronts him as a multitude of unintelligible languages, rendering him mute and lonely. His disorientation shows itself now as a lack of a stable reference point within language as a social construct; language no longer produces the transparency of the correspondence of hearts.

Writing to Julie, he tries to cope with his disorientation. He attempts to describe his first impressions of Paris: the discrepancy between the Parisian manner of talking and acting, the emptiness of their sentiments, and the ever-changing show of appearances. Lacking any point of reference to study and write about the "véritable état de choses," he mimics the theatricality and inauthenticity of Paris in a satirical fashion. Julie reprimands him for this letter, for it shows ingratitude toward his hosts. Even worse, by imitating their discourse, he seems to alienate himself from her.

Tell me, I pray you, my dear friend, in what language or rather in what jargon is the narration of your last letter? This would not by any chance be wit? If you have the intention to serve yourself of it often with me, you had better send me a dictionary. . . . Instead of taking as others do souls in the colors of houses, would you not like to have taken for your mind the hue of the country? Take care, my love, I am afraid that it will not go well upon this foundation.   (p. 168)

Did wit ever have the time to show itself in our private talks, and if the charm of a passionate conversation dispelled it and prevented it from appearing, how then can letters that absence always fills with a bit of bitterness, and in which the heart speaks with more tenderness, how can they endure it? . . . I do not wish for all that that love be always sad; but I do wish that its gaiety be simple, without ornament, without art, bare as it is; that it shine of its own graces, and not with the finery of pretty wit.   (p. 169)

His response acknowledges her criticism; however, he rephrases Julie's opposition between wit ("bel esprit") and the language of true love. The distinction between the two types of speech is not that only "bel esprit" has recourse to figurative language. It is not the use of figurative language per se that is blameworthy, but the manner in which these metaphors are employed. "For the little that one has of passion in the mind, one needs metaphors and figurative language in order to make oneself understood. Your letters themselves are full of them without your dreaming of it, and I maintain that it is only a geometer and a fool that can speak without figures" (p. 170). Although figurative language is inevitable, one has to make a distinction between false or merely ornamental metaphors and figurative language that goes beyond the level of mere representations, a language that creates a full presence. Opposed to the opaque discourse of Parisian society, Julie's language can produce this presence. Thus he acknowledges that a letter he receives while writing affects him as if she were there: "What other Julie ever loved, thought, spoke, acted, wrote as she! Do not then be surprised if your letters, which portray you so well, sometimes have the same effect upon your idolatrous lover as your presence" (p. 173). But her letters have an effect only for the time he is reading them. Once he has finished reading a letter, he finds himself left with a piece of paper that testifies only to her absence. The contents of the letter relate to the past and make him aware of his ignorance of Julie's present situation: "I received your letter with the same raptures that your presence would have caused me; and, in the transport of my joy, a trifling letter held me instead of you. One of the greatest ills of absence, and the only one for which reason can do nothing, is the anxiety one feels over the actual state of that which one loves" (p. 170). He is confronted with the epistolary medium and the materiality of the signifier. The letter disrupts the transparent communication of their hearts, and, even worse, it documents the nonexistence of this immediacy.

The question arises how and whether Saint-Preux can achieve some stability among the fleeting show of appearances and the bewildering play of representations. How can the image of Julie be of any help to him? The opening paragraph of his next letter contrasts the noise and the fleeting appearances of Paris with his focus on her: "I spend my entire day among society. I lend my eyes and ears to everything that strikes them; and perceiving nothing resembling you, I gather myself in the midst of the noise and converse in secret with you" (p. 174). By the end of this letter, however, he remarks that even Julie is about to lose her ability to lend any focus to his perception; her image is about to vanish into the undifferentiated noise of *le monde*.

However, I begin to feel the intoxication into which this agitated and tumultuous life plunges those who partake of it, and I fall into a stupefaction like that of a man upon the eyes of whom are made to pass rapidly a multitude of objects. None of those that strike me bind my heart, but all together by disturbing and suspending the affections to the point of forgetting in some instances who I am and to whom I belong. . . . Thus forced to change the order of my moral affections, forced to give a value to chimeras, and to impose a silence on nature and reason, I see thus disfigured that divine model I carry within me that served at once as the object of my desires and as the rule to my actions; I waver from whim to whim; and my tastes being subjugated without cease to opinion, I cannot be sure for a single day of what I would care for the next.   (p. 181)

As Saint-Preux is continuously exposed to the frivolous talk and pleasures of Paris, he sees himself in danger of being corrupted, of losing the focus for his desire and his inner guidance. Comparing the opening and the concluding paragraph of this letter—his initial trust in the force of the image of his beloved that by the end of the letter turns into the fear of being corrupted—one might ask what brings about this change of his position. What happens in between those two paragraphs? The main part of this letter, between these two paragraphs appealing to Julie's power to focus his perception and desire, is a criticism of the theater in Paris. His discussion of the theater follows his initial description of his problems in observing Paris with his own eyes: the objects of his observation change too frequently and quickly and leave him merely with an undifferentiated mass of minute visual impressions. And when he enters social circles, all he hears is mere talk, a language void of true sentiment or serious reflection.

This dilemma of the observer recalls Condillac's discussion of constituting a synthetic unity out of a multitude of sense perceptions. For Condillac the problem is solved by the focusing ability of our faculty of attention, which he illustrates with the example of the illusion of the theater, the tableau, and silent reading. Thus Saint-Preux, faced with his inability to constitute a synthetic unity out of the multitude of perceptions, also turns to the theater, but for him the theater fails to produce the hoped-for effect of framing and stabilizing his perceptions. The theater can say nothing significant about contemporary society; nor does it produce true sentiments or show significant actions. The theater produces a discourse as empty and theatrical as the rest of Parisian society. The inefficacy of the theater lies in its failure to produce an illusion.

All this comes from the fact that the French do not at all seek the natural and the art of illusion on the stage and that they only want wit and maxims there; they value pleasantness and not imitation, and do not worry about being seduced provided that it amuses them. No one goes to the spectacle for the pleasure of the spectacle, but in order to see the audience, in order to be seen by them, in order to pick up food for gossip after the play; and no one thinks about what they see except in order to know what they will say about it. *The actor for them is always the actor, never the character he represents.*   (p. 181; my italics)

Saint-Preux's critique of Paris and the theater seems to echo Rousseau's *Lettre à M. d'Alembert*. In the *Lettre* Rousseau rejects the "false" illusion of the theater with its unfounded representations and substitutes the "true" illusion of the ideal woman. Equally Saint-Preux seeks in Julie his salvation from the false and chaotic Parisian theatricality. But he fears that his memory of her will lose its power. What can be done to make the "illusion of love" more forceful than all the other illusions? Particularly in the absence of the beloved, there is the danger that her image will become a mere representation, like all the other illusions.

Julie, "la belle prêcheuse," seems to have consulted the *Lettre à M. d'Alembert* before composing her response to Saint-Preux's critique of the Parisian theater. Faithful to Rousseau's advice that male mores can be improved and maintained only with the collaboration of women, she assumes a pedagogical role toward Saint-Preux. And like the *Lettre*, which suggests a double strategy for the intervention of women in the disciplining of male desire (in terms of female chastity and modesty as wives and mothers, and in terms of a modesty that emphasizes their erotic attractiveness), Julie comes up with two complementary solutions for Saint-Preux's precarious situation in Paris. On the one hand, she wants to counterbalance his impression of the corruption of Parisian society by drawing his attention to those who do not indulge in the city's frivolous pleasures. She assigns her lover the task of describing Parisian women, hoping to hear something about serious wives and mothers. On the other hand, she promises him a present, which she describes to him as a magical object that will have a special effect on him. It is her portrait, which is to become his talisman. Julie's attempt, however, to preserve her lover from the seductions of Parisian society has to fail. She has planned his rescue without fully considering the problems and dangers of this "éternelle représentation." Assigning him a topic to write about does not provide Saint-Preux with the ability to observe and to represent his observations truthfully in his own language. Her assignment takes for granted both an objective perspective on the part of the observer and a transparent language of description. Her hopes for the portrait ignore the fact that the illusionary presence created in a pictorial representation, the trompe l'oeil, quickly fades. The representation will disintegrate into the material artifact, and the absence of the represented object will become apparent.

Indeed, Saint-Preux's reactions to the portrait mirror and anticipate his final disintegration in the realm of unstable and deceptive representations. Initially the portrait produces its hallucinatory effect, but only as long as he believes in the illusion. Just after writing Claire about the opera, he begins to express his dissatisfaction with the picture. This letter about the opera must be read in its contrast to the letter about the theater. Whereas he criticized the theater for its inability to produce a true illusion, he remarks that the opera is the only institution in Paris capable of creating a powerful illusion. But, he points out, it is a ridiculous illusion that captivates the Parisian audience and makes them believe in all kinds of frivolous nonsense. Thus his letter to Claire attempts to destroy the operatic illusion by focusing his description on the production of this illusion. He writes a very funny letter debunking the operatic gods and heroes and looking at the machinery that produces them (pp. 201–8, esp. pp. 202–4). In the letter about the theater Saint-Preux sought a salutary solution to confusion and chaos by making illusion effective, but his analysis of operatic illusion alerts him to the fact that illusion itself is merely the product of a machine. Within a discourse on aesthetics, Saint-Preux shifts his focus from an aesthetics of reception to one of production. The glance at the hidden machinery alters Saint-Preux's perception of the talisman portrait. After his letter to Claire, its magic begins to wear off. Now he can see in the portrait the material artifact rather than the referent it is supposed to evoke. He begins to examine the portrait as an imitation and to criticize the artistic technique. And the more he concentrates on the shortcomings of the artist who tried to portray Julie, the further removed he becomes from the referent of the picture; instead of getting closer to the referent, he gets more and more involved in the realm of representations.

At first Saint-Preux criticizes the artist for idealizing Julie. Thus he hires another artist to make a copy of his copy in order to create a portrait closer to the original by adding those individualizing imperfections omitted by the painter of the original. But since those additions of "realistic" details fail to evoke Julie's presence, Saint-Preux then concentrates on what should have been omitted from the representation in order to leave some space for the imagination of the beholder. He suddenly accuses Julie of having chosen the wrong clothes for the sitting and the artist of having painted too much.

In regard to the bust, it is peculiar that a lover be more severe than a father, but in effect I do not find you clothed there with enough care. The portrait of Julie should be as modest as she is. Love! these secrets belong only to you. You say that the painter took everything from his imagination. I believe it, I believe it; Ah! if he had perceived the least of your veiled charms, his eyes would have devoured them, but his hand would not have tried to paint them. Why did his bold art have to try to imagine them? It is not only a lack of decorum; I maintain that it is even a lack of taste. Yes, your face is too chaste to sustain the disorder of your bosom; one sees that one of these two objects must prevent the other from appearing; it is only the delirium of love that can reconcile them, and when his ardent hand dares to unveil that which modesty covers, the intoxication and the agitation of your eyes speaks at a time when you forget it, and not when you expose it.   (p. 210)

As his gaze wanders downward, he pretends to have to veil her *charmes* in order to protect them from the gaze of the painter; however, in doing so he identifies with the erotic imagination of the painter. At this moment the portrait is far removed from Julie; like her clothes in the closet, the material artifact of the portrait has become a screen for the projection of a male fantasy. Furthermore, his looking at the portrait does not produce as strong an illusion of the presence of his beloved as was the case, for instance, with the telescope. The gaze is no longer contained within the transparent dyad of the lovers, but includes the gaze of others, namely those of the father and the painter. It is the gaze of a man looking with the eyes of other men at a nude female body.

By concentrating on the portrait as a material object, he loses sight of Julie, whom the portrait is supposed to represent. The image loses its reference to Julie. And indeed, in the subsequent letter Saint-Preux confesses how he came to break his oath, sworn by her image, that he would abstain from excessive drinking. He went to dinner in the company of some officers, the dinner turned out to be given at a brothel, he was drinking and did not notice that what he took for water was white wine.[10] Initially the immodesty of the prostitutes' obvious attempts at seduction repels him, but after banning Julie's image, he gives himself over to the general confusion of the senses.

I reproached myself for the charming memories as so many crimes that pursued me in spite of myself... In what places dared I think of her... Alas! not being able to break from my heart a too dear image, I forced myself to veil it.
   The noise, the remarks that I heard, the objects which struck my eyes, roused me insensibly. . . . The intoxication did not delay in snatching from me the little discernment that remained to me. I was surprised, upon coming back to myself, to find myself in a remote closet, between the arms of one of those creatures, and at the same instant I had the despair of feeling as guilty as I could be.   (p. 213)

Julie's response points out that his fall was predictable from his description of the Parisian women. Instead of attempting to represent them as wives and mothers, he delivered himself of mere clichés, received opinion; his discourse came not from himself but from others. Just as he let his discourse be dictated by others, he let his behavior be determined by others when he was in the company of the officers. However, Julie's critique does not acknowledge that her magic portrait, the image of the beloved as she is hallucinated as an imaginary erotic presence, also failed to prevent his fall.

Book 2 seems to contradict *Emile*'s postulate that the image of the beloved suffices to discipline the young man's desires once he is exposed to the corrupt discourse of urban society. Saint-Preux cannot confront the confusions of Paris at this stage since he lacks any stable point of reference apart from his imaginary ties to Julie. Analysis of the subsequent four books shows that both the beloved woman and her image have to be transformed before this image can serve virtue.

Transformations of the Woman (Book 3)

Book 3 begins with the disruption of the imaginary, self-sufficient unity of the two lovers. Their letters have been discovered, and Julie's mother dies. Saint-Preux writes to Claire: "Finally the veil is torn; that long illusion has vanished; that hope so sweet has been extinguished" (p. 232). The two lovers are confronted with loss and separation. The veil protecting their unity and providing a screen for their illusion is, however, not torn as Saint-Preux expected when he appealed to it to keep their secret from Julie's "barbare père." Monsieur d'Etange does not confront Julie's lover directly as the Other in the figure of the brutal father protecting his property and name. Saint-Preux's confrontation with law and order is always mediated through female figures. Julie's mother does not reveal the correspondence to her husband. Her prohibition on seeing Julie is announced through Claire, who assures Saint-Preux of Mme d'Etange's sympathy. Monsieur d'Etange's command that he renounce Julie and leave her to be married to another is mediated by a letter and accompanied by a note from Julie. Milord Edouard's command, that Saint-Preux should go out into the world and become a man, can be obeyed only once he has learned of Julie's maternity.

Books 1 and 2 center on the issue of disciplining male desire through a focus on the image of the beloved woman and on the ultimate failure of this project in the disintegration of this image; Book 3 concerns Julie and the introduction of an Other beyond the lovers' illusion. Not only is the lovers' unity disrupted, but the Woman undergoes a radical transformation that finalizes this separation. No recuperation of the primary imaginary dyad is possible. Julie is to be reintegrated into the order of the family and to pass from the family of generation into the family of procreation. She has to renounce her lover in order to become part of a larger social order. This transformation of Julie from lover to wife and mother proceeds in three stages: the loss of Julie's mother; the demand of Julie's father; Julie's epiphany in the church during her wedding.

The death of Mme d'Etange suddenly substitutes an economy of want and absence for an economy of plenitude as it was thought to exist in the lovers' self-sufficient unity. As long as Mme d'Etange was alive, Julie could hope she would intercede with the father on behalf of the lovers' reunion. With her death all hopes vanish. In a despairing letter to Saint-Preux, Julie describes the effect of her mother's death: "The memory of my dying mother effaced yours." (p. 256).

Julie's love for Saint-Preux returns, however, when her father demands that she marry M. de Wolmar. She is unwilling to replace her lover with a husband given to her by her father, and as long as M. d'Etange uses his authority, she resists him.

He saw that I had taken my position and that he would gain nothing over me by authority. For an instant, I thought myself delivered from his persecutions. But what do I divine when suddenly at my feet I see the most austere of fathers softening and moved to tears? Without allowing me to raise myself, he clung to my knees, and fixing his moistened eyes upon mine, he said to me in a touching voice that I still hear within me: "My daughter, respect the white hair of your unfortunate father; do not make him descend into the grave in grief as she whom you bear within your breast. Ah! Do you wish to bestow death upon the entire family?" (p. 256)

In this scenario of a weeping father kneeling before his daughter, Julie confronts the threat of a total collapse of paternal authority. He makes her responsible for her mother's death and threatens that unless she gives up her resistance he will follow his wife into the grave. Julie becomes the object that will make up for the threat of loss. Only if she accedes to her father's demand will her father be able to keep his promise to the man to whom he owes his life. She interiorizes his want, his touching voice that commands in a display of weakness. In an effort to prop up paternal authority, she reintegrates herself into the patriarchal order as an object of exchange. She lets her father give her to M. de Wolmar.

Although compassion for her father makes her agree to the marriage with Wolmar, she has not yet entirely renounced her lover. Monsieur d'Etange has broken Julie's resistance to the marriage, but he has not changed the state of her affections. Julie is torn between filial duty and longing for her lover, she falls sick and is ready to die. Even on her way to the marriage ceremony, she entertains adulterous fantasies until the marriage ritual itself suddenly transforms her.

Already in Book 2 of the novel a wedding is mentioned. Julie begins her letter responding to her lover's description of the Parisian theater by telling him about Claire's marriage to Monsieur d'Orbe: "My dear friend, I have just enjoyed one of the sweetest spectacles that can ever charm my eyes" (p. 182). Opposed to the theatricality of Parisian society, the "doux spectacle" of Claire's wedding has truly placed their friend "into a new order of things" (p. 183), which makes it impossible for Claire to continue to be their confidante in their illicit love affair. As a social ritual, Claire's wedding has the power to prevent her from collaborating with the subversion of authority.

Julie's wedding is described in much greater detail; all the conditions that distinguish this spectacle as a true ritual from a mere theatrical show are elaborated. The narrative does not present the wedding as a social event, nor does it render many exterior details of the ceremony. The whole spectacle is represented exclusively in terms of its effect on Julie, as an interior drama. She enters the church and is struck by its august solemnity. Everything she sees fills her with terror, the terror of committing a perjury. While the minister is giving his sermon, she sees in him "l'organe de la Providence" and hears in the liturgy "la voix de Dieu." And as she perceives the Other behind the minister's performance, she suddenly undergoes an inner revolution: "All at once an unknown power seemed to correct the disorder of my affections and to reestablish them according to the law of duty and of nature. The eternal eye that sees all, I was saying within myself, now reads to the bottom of my heart; he compares my hidden will to the response of my mouth: heaven and earth are witnesses to the pledge that I am taking" (pp. 261–62). From being a spectator, she suddenly becomes the spectacle for the divine eye, a gaze that would cancel any possibility of a mental reservation. Under His gaze, she sees Monsieur and Mme d'Orbe looking at her, an exchange of looks that affects her so deeply that she cannot but attempt to emulate this exemplary tableau of marital fidelity: "I envisaged the holy knot that I was going to form as a new state that should purify my soul and render it fit for all its duties. When the minister asked me if I promised perfect obedience and fidelity to him whom I took as spouse, my mouth and my heart promised it" (p. 261). After this exchange of looks under the gaze of the Other, she tests how her conversion has transformed her. She imagines the image of her former lover: "I could not conceive by what miracle your [Saint-Preux's] unyielding image could have left me so long in peace with so many subjects to remind me of it; I would have distrusted this indifference and oblivion, as though of a delusive state that was too little natural for me to be endurable. This illusion was scarcely to be feared; I felt that I loved you as much and more perhaps than I had ever done, but I felt it without blushing. I saw that I had no need to think of you to forget that I was the wife of another" (p. 261). The test confirms her conversion: she is no longer part of a dyadic unity with her lover, no longer his "mirror soul." She can conceive of herself as belonging to another, as part of a system of exchange regulated by a third party.

A more detailed analysis of Julie's belief and her image of god makes it quite clear that her conversion has little to do with Christianity and the personal God of the New Testament.[11] This conversion integrates her not into a religious history of salvation but into a new social order; it subjects her to a law and an authority beyond the sensations of her heart. When she reports her conversion to Saint-Preux, she describes her placement in a different order of perception and representation, her subjection to a symbolic order that combines the law of "duty" with the law of "nature." Her conversion makes her reflect back on her previous life and recognize even in all her aberrations a guiding and protective principle. She evokes it in a line that echoes the psalmodic appeal to God as the protective shepherd: "The succouring hand that leads me through the shadows. . . . Eternal Providence, which makes the insect crawl and the skies roll, you keep watch over the least of your works" (p. 262). And this image of the omnipotent, omnipresent, protective shepherd, caring for each of his creatures, makes her pray: "I want, I tell Him, the good that you want, and of which you alone are the source. I want to love the spouse you gave me" (p. 262). God in this prayer replaces her father, a father who in his absence was unable to survey her conduct and who showed himself feeble and mortal.

This Other to whom she addresses her prayer is, however, not quite the God of the Old Testament. As her subsequent reflections show, rather than an external lawgiver and authority, he is merely a postulate, a function, and a "principe intérieur" that guarantees the stability of a social order and the subjection of the individual to the law. In an attempt to illustrate to her former lover the necessity of this postulated Other, she ventriloquizes a variety of philosophical, theological, and moral discourses: "It is He who gives an end to justice, a foundation to virtue, a value to this short life employed to please Him; it is He who never ceases in crying to the guilty that their secret crimes have been seen, and who knows how to tell the forgotten righteous one: 'Your virtues have a witness'" (p. 264). God is the principle of perfect surveillance that guarantees justice, an all-seeing eye. Furthermore, God is the principle of truth and the condition for our ability to distinguish essence and appearance. "It is He, it is His unalterable substance, that is the true model of perfections, of which we all carry an image within ourselves. In vain our passions disfigure it; all its traits bound to infinite essence, they present themselves always in the manner of reason and serve Him to reestablish what imposture and error have denigrated. These distinctions seem easy to me; common sense suffices to make them. Everything that cannot be separated from the idea of this essence is God: all the rest is the work of man" (p. 264). Despite its Neoplatonic overtones, all this pseudo-philosophical speculation amounts to is that God is what makes common sense true. He is a corrective principle providing a stable reference point beyond the reach of human artifacts. He is a protection against error, imposture, and the distortions of the passions. In fact, this god need not even exist: "It is upon contemplation of this divine model that the soul purifies and elevates itself, that it learns to scorn its base inclinations and to surmount its vile proclivities . . . the charm of meditation wrests it from earthly desires: and if the immense Being to which it attends were not to exist, it would still be good if it were to engage itself in it without cease in order to be more the master of itself, stronger, happier, and wiser" (p. 264). In contrast to the Christian God who became flesh, this god surely has no body. And his place—empty or not—is a focus for contemplation and meditation that can purify human desire of its sensual and material attachments. In some vague sense this god is a paternal principle, "le père commun des hommes" who understands human weakness. He can forgive, and through him alone can we overcome weakness (see p. 267).

To sum up, this Other is a system of perfect surveillance, a recording of each individual life, a guarantee of truth in the public and in common sense; it has an invisible, immaterial body and the ability to create social order by focusing and purifying the desires of each individual and channeling them toward higher aims. This "god" provides Julie a unified self. From the moment of conversion in the church, she is able to narrate all of her previous life in a coherent, developmental history. Whereas before she conceived of herself as split between the demands of her heart and the requirements of reason and family, she is now able to construct her self in a larger social realm. She has found an Archimedean point from which she can distinguish truth from error and can criticize even her sentiments.[12]

But this "god" is not merely Julie's private principle of psychic stability. Although for Julie he has some characteristics of the pastoral god of the Old Testament, the king as shepherd, he is also a very modern and worldly agency. Her letter describes him as both a principle that governs the "soul" and a principle for the "government of the world." Some critics have complained of the naive utilitarian moralism in Julie's "religious" discourse; I would argue that her reflections on god and the public sphere, in terms of his power to erect a stable and just society by ensuring the happiness of each individual, are not quite as naive as they sound.[13] Rather, her "theology" is the foundation for the articulation of the modern state as opposed to traditional theories of the state. God is a perfect ruler because he does not rule by violence but by love. He does not rule over a territory; rather, his rulership extends over the soul and life of each individual subject. Briefly, his order is based on the perfect surveillance of each individual by a well-organized police force and administrative apparatus that ensures the happiness and discipline of each subject.[14]

In this sense, Julie's conversion is the condition for the possibility of the social utopia, the modern state of Clarens.[15] Her subjection to this Other will be materialized in her life with Wolmar. Indeed, the very next letter describes her marital bliss in terms of her integration into a beautiful new social order.

The order that he [M. de Wolmar] has set in his house is the image of the one that reigns in his innermost soul and seems to imitate in its small household the order established within the government of the world. One sees here neither that inflexible regularity which causes more difficulty than advantage, and which is tolerable only to the one who imposes it, nor that poorly understood confusion which for too long had taken away the purpose of the whole. One always recognizes there the hand of the master and one never feels it; he has ordered the first preparations so well that at present everything goes entirely by itself, and one enjoys at the same time rule and liberty.   (p. 274)

The "government" of Wolmar's estate seems to mirror the divine order.[16] The sine qua non of the social utopia at Clarens is Wolmar's total surveillance of everybody and everything. To quote only one of the numerous examples: "His workmen have surveyors who motivate and observe them. These surveyors are people of lowly birth, who themselves work, and who are interested in the others' work by means of a small interest that is granted them, beyond their wages, for everything that they gather through their cares. Moreover, M. de Wolmar visits them personally every day, often several times a day, and his wife loves to accompany him on these walks" (p. 331).

Wolmar likes to describe himself as "un oeil vivant" (a living eye; p. 368) who can read people's hearts. He even appears to be informed about Julie's romance: "Monsieur de Wolmar's greatest taste is to observe. He likes to judge men's characters and the actions that he sees accomplished. . . . I do not know how he heard you spoke of, but he has spoken to me of you several times with much esteem, and I know him incapable of disguise. Sometimes I thought to have remarked that he was observing me during these conversations, but there is a great appearance that this alleged remark is only the secret reproach of a troubled conscience" (p. 273). Julie is plagued by the uncertainty of how much Wolmar might know of her past. She is tempted to confess everything to him, but Saint-Preux urges her to remain silent, and she finds her own reasons for not confiding in him.

Thus I risk through an indiscreet confidence to afflict him, for pure loss, without taking any other advantage from my sincerity than to unload my heart of a fatal secret that weighs cruelly upon me. I will be tranquil, I sense, after having declared it to him, but he, perhaps he will be less so, and it would be better to mend my wrongs poorly than to prefer my peace to his.

What then should I do in the doubt that I am in? While waiting for heaven to better illuminate for me my duties, I will follow the counsel of your friendship; I will keep silent, I will not mention my faults to my spouse, and I will try to efface them by a conduct that one day can merit pardon.   (p. 277)

This uncertainty of what the "all-seeing" eye knows and thinks of her makes her invest all her energy in an effort to compensate for her youthful aberrations. Here, Wolmar's function could be compared to the Other of Calvinism, who holds his subjects in constant fright and uncertainty about their state of grace, forcing them to relentless efforts in order to confirm their salvation. This is how Julie becomes the perfect wife and mother, assisting Wolmar in the government at Clarens, adding her maternal love to his surveillance (see, e.g., p. 332).

Only years later, when Saint-Preux is being integrated into their household, is Wolmar's quasi-magical psychological insight demystified: his reading in their hearts turns out to have been a reading of their love letters (pp. 373–74). Wolmar can devise his manipulative schemes by consulting the detailed record of Julie's and Saint-Preux's inner lives. The administrative bureaucracy can control individual subjects through its files, which contain individual psychic histories.

In *La Nouvelle Héloïse*, the lovers' transgressive union is not disrupted by the brutal authority of a castrating uncle Fulbert. The agency of law and the establishment of a new order appear in the more gentle guise of the pastoral care of an omniscient and omnipotent father, god, and husband who sets up a well-regulated and peaceful society through a system of perfect surveillance that excludes the possibility of misrepresentations and secrecy.

Julie de Wolmar as the Emblem of Virtue (Books 4 and 5)

In Book 4, after the transformed Julie has become a constitutive part of Clarens as mother and wife, Saint-Preux's education can be resumed. He too can be introduced into the new order, where he is to become the educator of Wolmar's sons. He has traveled around the world and seen many sights, but he has never lost his focus on his former lover, he still wears the medallion bearing her portrait. Unlike Julie, whose father coerced her into marriage and thus into the new order, Saint-Preux is not forced into this order but only too gladly accepts the invitation from Claire, Wolmar, and Julie. Saint-Preux is lured to Clarens by the image of his former lover only to find out gradually that the original of the portrait no longer exists, that his image is without referent.

Instead of his former lover, Julie d'Etange, he finds Julie de Wolmar, the chaste mother and wife. In order to prevent Saint-Preux from confounding the image of the beloved with the new Julie, he is subjected to Wolmar's gaze: "Our friendship begins here; here is the tender bond, which should be indissoluble. Embrace your sister and your friend; treat her always as such; the more familiar you become with her, the better I will think of you. But behave in private conversations with her as though I were present, or before me as though I were not there; that is all that I ask of you" (p. 317). When Saint-Preux, after this initial introduction to Clarens, leaves to visit Claire, it turns out that the prohibitive gaze has not yet affected his image of Julie. Wolmar's control is effective only in the presence of Julie de Wolmar; in her absence Saint-Preux still clings to his talisman-portrait. Claire reports this to Julie: "He pushed his temper and his obstinancy as far as swearing that he would rather consent to not seeing you any more than to relinquish your portrait. Finally, in a transport of indignation, making me touch it fastened over his heart: 'There it is,' he told me in a tone so moved that he was breathing with difficulty, 'there is the portrait, the only good that remains to me, and it is still wanted from me! Rest assured that it will never be torn from me except with my life'" (pp. 326–27). Although Saint-Preux respects and admires the virtuous Julie de Wolmar, his love remains tied to the image of Julie d'Etange. And if we compare this situation with the situation before the kiss in the grove (Book 1), we can recognize in both the distinction between a virtuous, chaste Julie and an eroticized, dangerous image. What makes the two situations different is that in the beginning of Book 1 Saint-Preux believed he was able to control himself, to keep image and referent separate; now this separation is reinforced by a third person: M. de Wolmar.

Saint-Preux's moral trial up to this point has shown the impossibility of his being directed by any notion of virtue that exists apart from his imaginary idol. As long as virtue exists for him as a mere prohibition, moral maxims merely as prescriptions, mere words, he will be unable to control himself independently of the discursive conventions of his environment; that is, he will be unable to control an ever-erratic and unstable desire determined by the discourse of *le monde*. This was the lesson of the dinner at the brothel in the company of the officers at the end of Book 2. Consequently virtue itself must be grounded in the imaginary; it must be fused with the hallucinatory effects of his object of love. Virtue must become "anschaulich"; it must go beyond the mere level of representations. And these are exactly the pedagogical steps M. de Wolmar will take with Saint-Preux. Wolmar goes with Julie and Saint-Preux for a walk in Julie's bower, the Elysée. Behind every aspect of this exquisitely hidden, fertile oasis, which *seems* to be a miracle of nature and a second paradise, Saint-Preux learns to see the work of Julie. As Wolmar's conversation opens Saint-Preux's eyes to all the details of this beautifully planned and attended garden that "illustrate" Julie's care and guidance, Saint-Preux begins to recognize an extremely patient care that combines an utmost attention to the natural disposition of the fauna and flora of Clarens with protection from external destructive influences. Wolmar explains to him the well-hidden manipulation in the overall layout and in the sophisticated irrigation system.[17] Like Julie, who learned to "read" Wolmar's household at Clarens in the light of her conversion as an illustration of divine providence, Saint-Preux is taught by Wolmar to "read" Julie's garden allegorically: behind the visible objects, he is made to discover the totality of a well-ordered system.[18]

The following morning Saint-Preux returns alone to the Elysée in order to immerse himself in Julie's presence. Suddenly he remembers M. de Wolmar's words from the previous day. When he asked why they built this garden when they already had a charming orchard, Wolmar admonished him not to confound the place of pleasure with the one of virtue. At this instant Saint-Preux's perceptions change.

I thought I saw the image of virtue where I was searching for that of pleasure; *this image was confounded in my mind with the traits of Mme de Wolmar*; and for the first time since my return, *I saw Julie in her absence*, not such as she was for me and as I still love to present her to myself, but such as she shows herself to my eyes every day. Milord, I thought I saw this woman so charming, so chaste, and so virtuous, in the midst of the same cortege that surrounded her yesterday. I saw around her her lovely children, honorable and precious pledge of conjugal union and tender friendship, giving her and receiving from her a thousand touching caresses. I saw at their sides the grave Wolmar, that spouse so dear, so happy, so worthy of being hers. *I thought I saw his penetrating and judicious eye pierce to the bottom of my heart, and it makes me blush still; I thought I heard leave his mouth reproaches too well merited and lessons too poorly listened to.* . . . With what indignation I had stifled the vile raptures of a criminal and ill-extinguished passion and also that I would be deluded to sully with a single sigh *such a ravishing tableau of innocence and uprightness*. In my memory I was rehearsing again the conversations that she had held with me upon leaving, then ascending with her into a future that she contemplates with so many charms, I was seeing that tender mother wipe away the sweat from her children's brows, kiss their ruddy cheeks, and devote that heart made for love to the sweetest sentiment of nature. *Finally there was the name Elysium that corrected in me the departures of the imagination and carried into my soul a calm preferable to the unsettledness of the most seductive of passions. In some way it painted for me the interior of her who had found it*; I was thinking that with a troubled conscience one would never chose that name. I told myself: "Peace reigns at the bottom of her heart as in the sanctuary that she has named." (p. 365; my italics)

For the first time Saint-Preux can represent to himself Julie de Wolmar. Within the enclosure of her bower, he hallucinates her presence no longer as his lover but as mother. The emblem of virtue is the Mother. In her image the attractions of her tender caresses can coexist with the prohibitive gaze of the father. And as a truly virtuous mother, her bliss seems otherworldly; she seems beyond the realm of the senses.[19]

The subsequent steps Wolmar undertakes in the programming of Saint-Preux are predictable from their analogy to the first part of the novel. Once Saint-Preux carries within himself a tableau of Julie de Wolmar, once he has an image, this image is to be taken back to its referent, to be grounded in a sensory experience. Thus Wolmar takes his wife and Saint-Preux to the orchard that was the scene of their first kiss and asks them to kiss again. Once this image of virtue has been fused with a sensory experience, Wolmar can leave the two former lovers alone. For in the second embrace in the orchard, under the eyes of Wolmar, Saint-Preux has clasped Julie as Mother, his beloved woman as the Woman, who belongs forever to another. And indeed Wolmar's gaze remains with them in his absence. However, confronted with the sites of his past longing on their outing to Meillerie (the sight of an eroticized specularity from Book 1) and on the dangerous waters of the lake, he has to struggle to overcome "cette horrible tentation," that is, the temptation to throw himself together with Julie into the lake.[20]

Virtue, the presence of Julie de Wolmar, makes him realize the loss of his former object of love. He is tempted to revolt against the deferral of gratification, although its consummation is associated with death. And it is only Julie's example that makes him overcome the temptation: "This adventure has convinced me more than all the arguments about man's liberty and about the merit of virtue. How many people succumb if slightly tempted? But as concerns Julie, my eyes saw it and my heart felt it: on that day she undertook the greatest fight that a human soul could undertake; however, she conquered. But what have I done to remain so far from her?" (p. 392) By the end of Book 4, Saint-Preux has found in Julie de Wolmar the graphic example of virtue. He can love in the image of Julie de Wolmar virtue itself, and this image can even motivate him to emulate virtue. Yet behind this image of virtue, there is still his image of the former lover, on which the emblem of virtue is grafted. Therefore, if Julie de Wolmar is not present to hold him back, the portrait of Julie d'Etange, an image that represents for him his lost state of happiness, still threatens a relapse.

In order to guarantee Saint-Preux's virtue and the permanence of the order at Clarens, not only Wolmar but also Julie hope to marry him to the now widowed Claire. They seem to believe that only if Saint-Preux's image of the beloved Woman is tied to another referent will his memory of his former lover no longer be a danger for him. This solution, however, will not be possible. Books 5 and 6 lead to an alternative solution, a solution beyond the ending of a happy marriage.[21]

As it turns out, the Wolmars' worries about Saint-Preux are justified. On his way to Italy with Milord Edouard, he stays overnight in the same room where he had spent a night on his way to Sion when he could still hope to be united with Julie d'Etange. There he suddenly makes the dangerous discovery Wolmar had hoped to conceal from him: "If one were to reveal to him the true state of his heart, one would confront him with the death of what he loves" (p. 383). He realizes that his former love is forever lost to him. Had she died, he could at least mourn her, but she lives as the wife of another: "She lives, but not for me; she lives for my despair. I am a hundred times farther away from her than if she no longer existed" (p. 466). After these thoughts, he falls asleep and is haunted by a recurring nightmare.

I thought I saw the worthy mother of your friend expiring upon her bed, and her daughter on her knees before her, filled with tears, kissing her hands and harboring her last sighs. *Again I saw that scene that you had depicted for me on another occasion and that will never leave my memory.* "O my mother," Julie was saying in a tone to wound my soul, "she who owes you the daylight snatches it from you! Ah!

Fig. 9. Rousseau, Julie (1761), plate 10, "Où veux-tu fuir? le fantome est dans
ton coeur."

take back your kindness! Without you it is only a fatal gift to me." "My child," replied her tender mother, "it is necessary to fulfill one's fate... God is just... you will be a mother in your turn..." She could not finish. I wanted to raise my eyes to her; I saw her no more. *I saw Julie in her place, I saw her, I recognized her, although her face was covered with a veil.* I gave a cry, I launched myself to tear away the veil, I could not reach it; I extended my arms, I was tormented and touched nothing. "Friend, calm yourself," she told me in a weak voice, "*the forbidding veil covers me, no hand can tear it.*" At this word I stirred myself and made a new effort: this effort awakens me; I find myself in a bed oppressed with fatigue and drenched in sweat and tears.

Shortly my terror dissipates, exhaustion puts me to sleep again; the same dream gives me the same anxieties; I awake, and fall asleep again a third time. *Always this lugubrious spectacle, always the same trappings of death, always the same impenetrable veil escapes from my hands, and steals from my eyes the expiring object that it covers.* (p. 466; my italics)

Saint-Preux is utterly disturbed by this nightmare and finally tells his friend Edouard about it. At first Edouard tries to turn Saint-Preux's anxiety into a joke; then he reproaches him for his unmanly behavior. But Saint-Preux insists: "Ah! I tell him, it is too true. All that I had of goodness came to me from her: I will never see her again; I am nothing anymore" (p. 467). In this statement Saint-Preux equates the loss of his object of love with Julie's loss of her mother.

Realizing that he cannot dispel Saint-Preux's nightmare, Edouard lets their carriage return to Clarens. At the entrance to the estate he sends Saint-Preux off on his own to reassure himself of Julie's presence: "Do not come back until you have torn away this fatal veil woven in your head" (p. 467). As Saint-Preux approaches the house, he feels ashamed of his boyish fears: "With what effrontery would I go to state my ridiculous terrors and to endure the scornful look of generous Wolmar?" (p. 468) In this state of ambivalence, he approaches the Elysée. He stops at the hedge veiling the interior of Julie's garden and hears the two women: "And, without my being able to distinguish a single word, I found in the sound of your voice some kind of languor and tenderness that moved me, and in hers a sweet and affectionate accent as usual, but peaceful and serene, which cured me upon the instant and was the real awakening from my dream" (p. 468). He can hear merely the intonation of their voices; the words are no longer representations but are reduced to a purely affective medium. Until then Saint-Preux's predominant perceptual mode had always been the sense of sight and the effect of a representation in terms of visual hallucinations; here, certainty is grounded in the emotional effect of auditory perception. Before the hedge of the Elysée, the veiled emblem of Julie de Wolmar,

Saint-Preux is satisfied with the pure affect produced by the voices of the two women, a tender languor and an assuring, serene presence.

Saint-Preux's nightmare was based on his hallucinatory reading of Claire's letter announcing Mme d'Etange's death and the irreparable dissolution of the lovers' imaginary unity. The dream indicates the end of specularity in the economy of loss; one dying woman is being replaced by another dying woman. Finally it focuses on the diaphanous but unremovable veil as an "appareil de mort." Beyond expressing Saint-Preux's unconscious wish for Julie's death, as Wolmar interprets the dream (p. 470), the dream focuses on the loss of visual certainty. But also, as if to compensate for this loss, Saint-Preux's hallucination of Mme d'Etange's death goes beyond Claire's script: he can *hear* Julie's and her mother's voices. And when Julie takes her mother's place, he *sees* her, although the veil covers her face and he again can *hear* her voice. Only after he has tried in vain to remove this veil does he call it "impénétrable." His attempt at removing the veil between his image and the referent makes the veil opaque and turns it into an "appareil de mort." The scene before the Elysée takes up the perceptual configuration of the nightmare but effaces Saint-Preux's desire to tear the veil, assuaging him with the sound of the two invisible mothers' voices. In his letter to Claire, Saint-Preux prides himself on having resisted the scopic drive: "Claire, I swear it to you, not only did I not see her at all, but I also returned proud of not having seen her, of not having been weak and credulous to the very end, and proud for having at least rendered that honor to my friend Edouard of setting him above a dream" (p. 468). Belatedly he has found the assurance and certainty Edouard had tried to give him on the night of his bad dream. However, he cannot tell Edouard that his words of rational assurance have become true not through a visual experience but only through the maternal voices: "When he asked me if the veil had been raised, I affirmed it without hesitation, and we did not speak of it any more. Yes, cousin, it is raised forever, this veil by which my reason was for so long obscured. All my unsettled raptures are extinguished. *I see all my duties, and I love them.* Both of you are dearer to me than ever, but my heart can no longer distinguish one from the other and does not at all separate the inseparables" (p. 468; my italics). Saint-Preux's education has been almost completed: he can "see" his duties clearly, and he loves them. He can function as Edouard's guide, and he is ready to teach Wolmar's sons. Virtue has become anschaulich for him in the emblem of the Elysée as part of the order of Clarens and as the image of the beloved woman. In his claim that the two woman friends have become inseparable for him, Julie has been integrated into a series of mothers, which together form the image of the Mother. This maternal presence is not accessible to a transgressive specularity, but it appears in the disembodied maternal voice.[22]

However, when Julie suggests that Saint-Preux should marry Claire, he refuses. Ultimately he still clings to his vivid memories of his former love. The carnal image of Julie provides a memory that he claims would obstruct marital intimacy with Claire. Although all the basic terms for the constitution of the disciplined subject of the new order at Clarens are worked out, there still remains the question of the permanence and reproduction of this order. Julie's conversion proved the importance of postulating the divine Other, the Other that enabled Julie's transition from the family of generation to the family of procreation, an Other that also stands behind Wolmar's household as a legitimizing principle. As Julie integrates herself into Wolmar's Clarens and assumes in it the role of chaste wife and mother, however, she discovers that there is no Other behind this Other; she is confronted with Wolmar's agnosticism. As she is plagued by this absence, her own religious concerns intensify. Saint-Preux expresses his worries over her preoccupation in the same letter in which he declares his inability to marry Claire. The ultimate question of the foundation and reproduction of the new order thereby is linked to these religious issues.

Since Julie cannot force Saint-Preux into a marriage that would guard the stability of Clarens against human weakness, another safeguard has to be found. There is no brutal and weak archaic father, as in Julie's case, who could force Saint-Preux into a marriage ceremony that then would produce a conversion through the gaze of the Other. Nobody at Clarens shares Julie's religious devotion: Saint-Preux believes in a watered-down, rationalist Christianity; Wolmar is a skeptic. Therefore, the crucial issue that remains to be settled is that of stabilizing the order of representations, of preserving the new order of Clarens, of lending it the ultimate principle of authority and legitimacy that it had only at the time of Julie's conversion and only so long as she assumed the existence of the Other behind Wolmar.

The Veil as Protection from Disfiguration (Book 6)

Marrying Saint-Preux to Claire would probably be insufficient to secure the permanence of the order at Clarens, for stability and happiness themselves can become a source of misery and disorder. The regulated bliss at Clarens only apparently assuages all desires; in fact desire itself without any object or aim can reemerge from the boredom of satisfaction. As Julie writes to Saint-Preux:

That is what I feel in part since my marriage and since your return. Everywhere I see only subjects of contentment, and I am not content; a secret languor insinuates itself into the bottom of my heart; I feel it empty and consumed, just as you were speaking of yours at another time; the attachment that I have for everything that is dear to me does not suffice to engage it; there remains in it a useless force with which it knows not what to do. This pain is strange, I agree; but it is no less real. My friend, I am too happy; happiness wearies me. (p. 528)

Julie claims that religious devotion alone can support, direct, and channel this desire arising from the void in her soul. Furthermore, religious devotion leads her soul into another existence, beyond the passions of the body (p. 529). Yet she shares Saint-Preux's suspicion of an exclusive and exaggerated mysticism and rejects religious literature that would stimulate the erotic imagination (p. 531). There is a strange contradiction in Julie's explanation of religious devotion. She introduces the subject with regard to her conversion, describing religious zeal as the only effective moral guidance in sublimating her desire. Then she suddenly complains about the void and boredom she has felt since her marriage and since Saint-Preux's return, only to come back to the necessity of religious devotion. She ends her letter with her plan to awaken religious sensibility in Wolmar.

What causes this feeling of a void? Julie's integration into the order at Clarens became possible only through the equation of God's eye with Wolmar's surveillance and of the divine order with the household at Clarens. Once part of that order, however, she is confronted with Wolmar's agnosticism: Wolmar's surveillance is not the divine eye; it is merely psychological insight gained by reading the letters. And when she is alone with Saint-Preux, Wolmar's gaze is not quite sufficient to protect their tête-à-tête from transgressions; she supplements the disciplinary power of Wolmar's gaze by turning the conversation to religious topics (p. 449). If Wolmar himself is not religious, Julie's religious certainty is endangered. If the Other is not behind Wolmar, how can she still see Clarens as an illustration of the divine order as she did after her conversion? And if Wolmar cannot see God, "God himself has veiled his face" (p. 532).

It is in order to fill this gap, to compensate for the lack of an ultimate authority and point of reference, that Julie decides to turn herself into an example of religious devotion that will move even Wolmar.

At the expense of my life I would like to see him for once convinced; if it is not for the sake of his happiness in the other world, it is for the sake of his happiness in this one. For from how many pleasures is he not deprived! What sentiment can console him in his pains? What value can he expect from his virtue? . . . There remains to me one resort to pull him from this [horrible state], and I consecrate the rest of my life to that; it is no longer to persuade him, but to touch him; it is to show him an example that can guide him and to make religion so amiable to him that he cannot resist it. Ah! my friend, what greater argument against the unbeliever than the life of a true Christian! . . . Wolmar is cold, but he is not insensitive. What a tableau we can offer to his heart, when his friends, his children, his wife, will all converge to instruct him by edifying him! When, without preaching God to him in their conversations, they will show Him to him in the actions that H/he inspires, in the virtues of which H/he is the author, in the charm that is found in pleasing H/him! when H/he will see rendered brilliant the image of heaven in his house! When a hundred times a day he will be forced to say to himself: "No, man is not thus by himself; something more than human reigns here!"   (pp. 533–34)

The third-person singular pronoun in the last few sentences shifts back and forth between God and Wolmar in an ambiguous fashion. Whereas Julie's religiosity at the time of her conversion was a way of integrating herself into the new order as chaste wife and mother, her revived religious zeal has to be seen as an attempt to legitimize this order, to turn it from an artful construct into an illustration of the divine order.[23] If God has veiled His face, it will be up to her to compensate for the *deus absconditus*, to become a tableau that will consolidate the new order at Clarens. She will have to become an *image sensible* for God and virtue, a project that can be accomplished only in the face of the Other, in her facing death.

Both the minister and Wolmar are surprised at Julie's manner of approaching death. Instead of praying and turning her mind toward religious questions, she is most exquisitely what she has always been: an attentive hostess, an attractive woman, and a loving friend, wife and mother. She explains to the minister and the surprised Wolmar that she need not make any special preparation for death, that her entire life was led under God's eye and was her preparation for death. She has nothing to fear or to regret; she has only to accept her fate with patience. The evening before her death she professes her faith in an afterlife. As in her conversion during her wedding, her religiosity is far from the Christian belief in redemption and resurrection. If anything, it is opposed to the doctrine of the resurrection of the body: "Following the thread of her ideas on what of her could remain with us, she spoke to us of her old reflections on the state of souls separated from bodies" (p. 554). The souls of the dead will come back to be with the living; they will perceive the living and communicate with them in a way that is beyond sense perception.

A soul free from the body, which once lived upon the earth, can still return there, wander, perhaps dwell among those that were dear to it . . . in order to know what we think and what we feel by way of a transparent communication, similar to that by which God reads our thoughts during this life, and by which we will in turn read His in the other, until we will see Him face to face. For at last, she added while looking at the minister, for what would the senses serve when they no longer have anything to do? The eternal Being does not see itself nor hear itself; it makes itself felt; it speaks neither to the eyes nor to the ears, but to the heart.   (p. 554)

During her conversion, Julie was subjected to the divine gaze that creates the perfect congruence of words, actions, and belief; here, Julie transposes herself, her immaterial soul, into the place of the Other for the others. Christian love (in the Pauline interpretation of agape) is being replaced by maternal love. Both kinds of decarnalized love provide an immediate communication and understanding, independent of material mediation, an identity of reading and seeing. Rousseau even underlines and attempts to stress Julie's notion of perfect understanding and a transparent communication in a footnote: "This seems to me very well put; for what is it to see God face to face, if not to read within the supreme intelligence" (p. 554). And when the minister mildly protests, reminding her of Christian doctrine, Julie insists on her opinion that the eye of the Other reading our hearts is the eye of a deceased beloved: " 'A hundred times,' she was saying, 'I have taken more pleasure in doing some good work by imagining my mother reading in the heart of her daughter and applauding her. There is something so consoling to still live under the eyes of one who was dear to us! It allows that for us only half of him dies' " (p. 555). What her dead mother was for her, she will be for those that love her. Thus we are taken back to the announcement of her death in Saint-Preux's nightmare. She will die, and her dead face will be veiled only to be with those that love her in a perfectly immediate communion. If the Christian God hid until He revealed Himself through His love in His son, if God's love makes possible our return to Him to see Him "face to face" (1 Corinthians 13.12), the god of the new order at Clarens, the Other of the social contract and the State, is mediated through maternal love.

The analogy between Christ's and Julie's deaths is emphasized in the symbolism of her "last supper." She declines to eat any chicken but takes some fish and bread, and everybody drinks wine. Faced with the despair and false hopes of the people at Clarens, she whispers her last words into Wolmar's ear: "I have been made to drink even to the lees the sweet and bitter cup of sensibility" (p. 558). But the analogy to Christ is not a complete one. Julie is not an incarnation of the divine logos. Yet representations obtain their truth from her, and the order of Clarens its Other. Finally, through Julie's death and transfiguration a symbolic order can be grounded in the imaginary without the risk of a transgressive, eroticized specularity. As in the scene before the Elysée, in which her words were transformed from representations into the mere sound of her voice, the scene after her death dissociates her soul from the carnal aspects of her body. Her body is not incorruptible like that of so many martyrs.[24] Indeed, in order to cathect Saint-Preux's love, to be the perfect lover and mother, Julie had to have a body. After her death, however, this body and source of pleasure decomposes, and it is her decomposing and disfigured face that Wolmar makes Claire cover with the veil: "Cursed be the unworthy hand that ever raises this veil! Cursed be the impious eye that ever sees this disfigured face!" (p. 562) Only the veil that covers the sight of horror, in which the flesh is no longer the source of pleasure but the site of putrefaction, can ultimately prevent any transgressive specularity. Only this veil can prevent Saint-Preux from ever returning to his erotic fantasies; only this veil can provide everybody with a screen on which to project the image of Julie de Wolmar, the emblem of virtue. And although this emblem has no material referent, it has a voice. Again, like the hedge of the Elysée, this veil is permeable to her voice: Julie has written a last letter to Saint-Preux, which Wolmar and her lover will read after her death, her disappearance behind the veil.

This reading of *Julie* has traced in detail the disciplining of desire, the taming of the masculine imagination, through the construction of the ideal Woman in the epistolary novel. An initially carnal passion is transformed into maternal love as a constitutive part of the new order and finally becomes its principle of legitimation, stability, and reproduction. Saint-Preux's subjection to the new order and his education as educator of the new subjects had to pass through the various stages of his love for Julie. Only through Julie's mediation is he bound to law and order. Only through her does he learn the meaning of loss and renunciation. Only through her is he subjected to the surveillance of the state. Julie teaches him to love the new order and become its "civil servant," the educator of Wolmar's children. It is in this sense that *Julie* can be considered the counterpart to the *Contrat social*: the illustration and *conditio sine qua non* of the social utopia.[25]

Fig. 10. Rousseau, Julie *(1761), plate 12. The death of Julie. Rousseau chose not to entitle this illustration.*

The Second Preface: "Entretien sur les Romans"

The first preface to *Julie* merely dissociates the text from the conventional aesthetic norms of *le monde* by placing it in the frame of an aesthetics of expression and by postulating the authenticity of the letters not as nonfiction but as the "raw material" of desire. The second preface is attached to the end of the novel and raises the question of the text's totality and truth value. I conclude this reading of *Julie* with a brief outline of the movements of this dialogue between *Julie*'s first reader, N., and the editor, R. By retracing on this meta-narrative level N.'s questions, statements, and changing positions vis-à-vis *Julie*/Julie, I hope to support the preceding analysis of the novel and show how this epistolary novel not only is supposed to be produced by desire, but also cathects and channels the desire that arises from the correspondence.

The second preface introduces the question of the text's relation to truth in N.'s question "Is this correspondence real, or is it is a fiction?" and in N.'s suggestion that it must be either a "portrait" or a "tableau" (p. 571). This is reminiscent of Lessing's theory of the fable, in which the peculiar Anschaulichkeit and Wirklichkeit of this genre derive from its position between the referential specificity of the historical anecdote and the universal validity of the parable. The case of *Julie* seems similar to the extent that this text refuses to be easily subsumed under either of the two categories. But there is also a decisive difference. In the discussion of the bourgeois tragedy, Anschaulichkeit, with its specific effect on intuitive cognition, gets more and more enmeshed with the subject's affective economy, a tendency that also holds for Rousseau's epistolary novel. For N. interrupts R.'s attempt to explain the status of the work with the exclamation "Oh, if she had existed!" (p. 572) Suddenly N. no longer refers to *Julie* as a text but shifts his poetological discussion to the register of desire, referring to Julie as a woman he wishes had existed. Voicing his longing for an extra-textual referent, N. testifies to the impact reading the novel had on him.[26]

After this lapse N. checks himself and quickly returns to poetological issues, classifying *Julie* as a bad tableau: "But surely it is only a fiction." The characters are too perfect to be real and seem from another world. R. responds to this normative judgment by inquiring how N. is able to outline so precisely the limits of human nature, considering its broad social and historical spectrum.

R.:   I agree, provided that one also knows how to discern what constitutes the varieties of what is essential to the species. What would you say of those who only recognize us in a French outfit?
N.:   What would you say of he who, without expressing either traits or height, wished to portray a human figure with a veil for clothing? Would one not have the right to ask him where is the man?   (p. 572)

Here N. introduces in a derogatory way Rousseau's crucial aesthetic term: the veil of illusion. N. wants to accuse R. of leaving out all the necessary details required for a recognizable portrait of a human being; R. counters by enumerating specific traits of the novelistic characters in order to show that they are not void of specific features. Interrupting him, N. points out what he considers an extraordinary absurdity in terms of plot: a husband lodges the former lover of his wife. Thereupon R. refers him to the caption of the novel's seventh illustration. But N. is not convinced by this reference; he quotes it and dismisses it: "*Les belles âmes*!... Le beau mot!" (p. 573) For N. this caption is merely a beautiful phrase. The illustration, the text as a whole, nothing seems to make the "beautiful souls" graphic to him. What would ultimately give Anschaulichkeit to the text, make it into more than mere words? What would hold together the portrait that has a specific extra-textual referent, the tableau that has universal validity, the veil as a screen for the projection of the reader, the image as the illustration of the text and the words on the page?

And what about the book's moral position? Who bears responsibility for it? N. focuses on Julie's extraordinary conversion, her strange ties to some Other that cannot be grasped in traditional Christian terms. The issue, however, is not settled in theological terms but is sidestepped in a return to the poetological debate. R. tells N. that his text is not a traditional novel with ordinary characters and extraordinary events, but the reverse: the characters turn out to be quite uncommon, and the text is not a novel but a collection of letters. At this point N. severely criticizes the stilted, elevated rhetorical style of the letters, which seems quite inappropriate to the characters' trivial observations. But R. reverses this argument in the manner of the first preface; rhetorical imperfection is proof of the text's authenticity. Yet, in the context of the second preface, another dimension is added to the issue. Whereas the first preface insists on passion as the source of the illusions in the text, in the second preface it is the text that produces desire that then can be cathected and transformed as N. works out his relation to that *Julie*/Julie he wishes to have really existed. Whenever N. slides from the text to the postulate of an extra-textual referent,

Fig. 11. Rousseau, Julie *(1761), plate 7, "La confiance des belles ames." Saint-Preux is welcomed to Clarens by the husband of his former lover; Wolmar's gaze controls their future relationship of frankness and sincerity.*

he gets involved in ethical concerns. Thus N. constructs an argument in which he refers to Julie as an "excellente prêcheuse" and points out the discrepancy between Julie as a woman moralist and what he assumes to be Rousseau's position in the letter to d'Alembert. Here, N. implicitly postulates the author as unifying principle of that author's oeuvre: if the author of the *Letter to M. d'Alembert* states the opinion that women should never be made the preceptors of men, the author of *Julie* cannot make his heroine a public pedagogue. N. does not realize the difference between the role of actual women—they are indeed banned from any public function in Rousseau's political and social theory—and the Woman as an ideal with a crucial ideological function.

Is R. an author or merely an editor? As the dialogue proceeds, N. attempts to find more contradictions and problems in Rousseau's moral pronouncements. If Julie is not an actual female preceptor but an object of desire and a product of the imagination, R. should have censored those dangerously inflamed and inflaming passages like the kiss in the orchard and the scene in Julie's closet. Yet R. does not object to those passages; he is even willing to sign his name on the title page of the book and assume full editorial responsibility. This leads N. again to press the question of authorship. N. believes he can easily recognize R. as the author of some but not all of the letters. What makes the issue so difficult for N. is the fact that the styles of the individual writers seem to flow into each other. An author who constructed those letters by himself would have avoided this blurring of individual styles. This seems to be an indication of the authenticity of those letters: "I observe that in a very intimate society styles approach one another so that the characters and the friends, confound their souls, confound their ways of thinking too, of feeling and of speaking. This Julie, such as she is, must be an enchanting creature; everything that can approach her must resemble her; all her friends must only have a single tone; but these things are experienced and not imagined" (p. 585).

By this point N. has made a full circle back to his initial questions, doubts, and point of criticism of the novel. He has, however, been completely won over by *Julie*/Julie. In the passage quoted above, he takes the converted, ideal Julie de Wolmar, who initially had seemed to him too perfect to be real, for granted, since she so strongly affects her friends' way of thinking, feeling, and speaking. He adopts R.'s argument that stylistic imperfection authenticates a letter, although previously the issue was related to Julie's and Saint-Preux's passion whereas here it is seen in the context of Julie's omnipresent beneficial influence. Julie's magic charm has made him forget or has purified the inflammatory passages he criticized earlier. The correspondence has for him the status of a portrait; it posits an actual referent. At the same time he accepts the idealized tableau of human nature, in which the representation goes beyond the mere particular, concrete individual character. And as in the beginning, he voices his desire, only this time extending it to Claire: "But say that these two women existed, and I will reread this collection every year until the end of my life" (p. 585).

Up to the end of the dialogue, R. refuses to give a clear answer with regard to his problematic authorship. All he says is that to declare himself the author would be a lie, and since the two women are dead, their representations can no longer have a referent. Julie and Claire come to represent the lost object of desire. Since their idealized image also implicates the author in the register of desire and in the figurative language of love and, as N. himself admits, since the other has an effect on our discourse, how could R. claim authorship for the entire work? It is for these reasons that R. insists on the Petrarchan epigraph that refuses to settle the question. Although the words are quoted from Petrarch, there is no way of telling whether R. found them attached to these letters or whether he added them. And whoever added the epigraph might have had many possible intentions. The epigraph does, however, express a longing for a lost object of love. Whether this beloved woman will be made present depends entirely on the engagement of the reader's affects and imagination; otherwise the novel exists only as words on the page. However, the reader's engagement in this epistolary novel is altogether different from that required by Richardson's fiction. The hallucination and the evocation of a specular presence is contained in the longing for an unretrievable past: visual hallucination and the identificatory urge to merge with the image of the Woman are transformed into the hallucination of the maternal voice that always and already contains the prohibition of the father.

4

The Project of Bildung in German Classicism and Neo-humanism

Toward the end of the eighteenth century the "project of Anschaulichkeit" is superseded by what might be termed the "project of *Bildung*." These transformations and shifts of emphasis in the conjunction of semiotic, aesthetic, and pedagogical concerns occur primarily in the German context of an expanding state bureaucracy and of major reforms in institutions of higher learning. In the most general terms, in the field of semiotics, the arbitrary nature of the sign is rejected; in the field of aesthetics, sculpture replaces the tableau as the privileged medium; in the discussions of sensory perception, hearing and touch are placed above the sense of sight; and in the context of pedagogy and anthropology, a stress on freedom and autonomy as the markers of humanity is substituted for the former valorization of sensibility and pity. All these transformations were to have a strong impact, mainly through Schiller and Goethe, on the literary production of the period that became known as Weimar Classicism. Thus, the anti-theatrical genres of the epistolary novel and the bourgeois tragedy, which tended to veil the artificiality of the aesthetic object, were relegated to "trivial literature." Art was proclaimed an autonomous institution in a revalorization of aesthetic distance and the spectacle.[1] One new literary genre that breaks away from the previous culture of immediacy and sensibility is the Classical German Tragedy; another is the bildungsroman.

These transformations constitute a new stage in the organization of subjectivity, a subjectivity closely linked with the term *Bildung*. This word cannot easily be translated into English. Derived from the verb *bilden* (to form, shape, mold, constitute, educate, cultivate, civilize, train, organize, establish, construct, found, create, to name only a few of the many possible translations), it carries a suffix denoting both a state and a process. Both significations are audible in the wide spectrum of possible translations: formation, growth, foundation, constitution, organization, form, shape, physiognomy, structure, forming, development, training, education, learning, schooling, culture, higher education, accomplishments, refinements, polish, and good breeding. The term gains weight in the last decades of the eighteenth century at the time when both language and the subject are invested with an organic depth and an individual history in terms of an entelechial development. At that time Bildung comes to replace—increasingly with a polemical edge—the term *Erziehung* (education in the more external and technical sense). Bildung is used in the description of artifacts, mainly sculptures, as well as in the description of humans; in the case of humans, Bildung refers to the body and face as well as the mind, with the first two terms frequently acquiring a diaphanous quality with regard to the latter. The term is applied in the arts to the creative activity of the sculptor and poet and denotes the shaping *poesis* of a self-sufficient beautiful construct. Finally, Bildung was to become throughout the nineteenth century and even up till today an extremely loaded term related to German educational theories and ideologies and their state institutions. In this context it became the name and ideology of middle-class professionals and bureaucrats, those products of the Bildungs-apparatus, that formed the *Bildungsbürgertum* (educated middle class). Within that history the main repository of Bildung was the liberal arts curriculum of the neo-humanist Gymnasium, which through its specific adherence to the cultivation of classical antiquity and the classic authors of German literature interpellated the subjects of Bildung.[2]

As in my discussion of Anschaulichkeit, I shall examine the project of Bildung from the point of view of the period's semiotics and aesthetics as the emergence of a new type of "interface," or suture, between subjectivity and representations. The model established by this approach allows for an understanding of both the rise of two new literary genres, German Classical drama and the bildungsroman, and a new layer in the genealogy of the modern disciplined subject, the subject of Bildung. That subject can be described as modeled on a very particular ideal of sublimation, which, in my view, can be interpreted as a type of narcissism (as opposed to the various oedipal constellations analyzed in regard to the epistolary novel and the bourgeois tragedy). This argument is developed across readings of various texts written in Germany between 1770 and 1800. Using Johann Gottfried Herder's prize-winning essay, *The Origin of Language* (1772) and his writings on sculpture, which were produced between 1769 and 1778, I trace the formation of a new subjectivity in the context of a semiotic discussion and with regard to the establishment of a new hierarchy of sensory perceptions. I treat some essays on similar topics by Karl Philipp Moritz from the mid-1780's more explicitly within the field of aesthetics. Finally, I conclude the discussion of classicist aesthetics within the project of Bildung with an analysis of Schiller's response to the French Revolution and the Reign of Terror in his *Letters on the Aesthetic Education of Man* from the mid-1790's.

Language as the Mark of the Soul: Herder's Narcissistic Subject

Herder's "Abhandlung über den Ursprung der Sprache" was selected as the prize essay by the Königliche Academie der Wissenschaften in Berlin on a question announced in 1769: "If men are left to their natural faculties, are they capable of inventing language? We demand a hypothesis that elucidates the issue clearly and that answers all the difficult questions it raises in a satisfactory manner. Submit to Mr. Formerey, the permanent secretary, by January 1, 1771. The decision will be taken by May 31, 1771."[3] The treatise was part of a continuing debate among members of the Berlin Academy over the origins—divine or human—of language. On the one hand, Herder rejects Johann Peter Süßmilch's position that human language, because of its high degree of logical perfection, must be a divine gift.[4] On the other hand, he opposes those theories of language that locate the beginnings of human language in a gradual departure from animal or natural language. On that front, Herder combats Rousseau's notion of language arising from a "cri de nature" and Condillac's theory of semiosis. German literary history has celebrated Herder's essay as the foundation of a philosophy of history, hermeneutics, and "modern" theories of language, but, as Hans Aarsleff has painstakingly elaborated, Herder's treatise owes much to other eighteenth-century theories of language, especially to that of Condillac.[5] Although Herder is important with regard to the emergence of nationalism, history, and hermeneutics, my concern in this chapter is his elaboration of a humanist anthropology that breaks with the classical episteme.

Let us recall the major tenets of the rationalist conceptualizations of language as they concerned us in the context of the project of Anschaulichkeit, mainly with regard to Condillac's semiotics. For Condillac or Locke, a theory about the origin of language is part of an epistemological investigation, which means that, for the classical episteme, to know language provides a privileged access to knowledge. True knowledge and scientific progress depend on the development of man's analytic faculties. Human language, as a tool of analysis, is a repertoire of arbitrary signs. Only after language has become this repertoire of arbitrary signs and a tool of analysis does it also become a means to exercise that control over the operations of the soul Condillac calls reflection (i.e., the controlled use of the attention, imagination, and memory). For initially man's response to the environment was the same as that of the animal, but man is not overwhelmed by a flood of undifferentiated sensory data because his faculty of attention, directed by survival needs, singles out relevant data and conditions his response. As long as man remained bound to the presence of a given situational context he relied merely on natural signs or gestural language. However, man gradually emancipated himself from this situation through the development of arbitrary signs, signs that are conventional and freely chosen and that therefore can be dissociated from the ideas they evoke.

Herder's theory of language is a clear break from the classical episteme. His departure is indicated by the fact that his treatise does not address epistemological questions at all. For him, knowing language no longer provides a privileged access to knowledge and truth; rather, language and man are objects of study endowed with their own history and depth.[6] His break with the classical episteme is situated in the reconceptualization of the transition between natural language and human language; this new theory implies an altogether different notion of the emergence of the faculty of reflection and its function. Although Herder develops the notion of a natural language common to man and beast alike, he rules out any gradual transition between this natural language and human language. As opposed to Condillac's natural signs, which can become arbitrary signs, Herder's sounds and sighs of nature do not represent anything; they have merely an index value. For him natural language is a matter of a sheer vital expressivity (Rousseau's "cri de nature," which means any creaturely urge to express a sensation or emotion). Herder's sounds of nature will never achieve the status of a proper human language since they are extremely undifferentiated and rely on a very limited repertoire of sounds. Nevertheless, this natural language of the sighs and sounds of passion provides the raw material and vitality of human language (*Abhandlung*, pp. 9, 13).

Whereas for Condillac the human faculty of reflection emerges by taking hold of natural and gestural language as representations, which then are employed as signs and dissociated from their original contexts, for Herder "reflection" has an altogether different meaning.[7] In Herder's anthropology, man does not have to free himself gradually from an instinctual response to his environment; rather, by definition he is free of any instincts. In the animal realm each species is defined by its proper sphere of activity, its milieu or ecological niche. The lower the species, the more restricted is this sphere of activity. Thus Herder points out that the spider's art of constructing a web is conditioned by an extremely limited world. Since the spider's world is so small, the spider has clearly defined, strong, and sharp sensory perceptions, a very limited set of stimuli, to which it automatically responds in terms of its instinctually channeled vital activities. Species with a higher degree of development have a wider sphere of activity; consequently their sensory perceptions are less focused and more diffused, and their responses to the environment are less strictly defined. Finally, the human creature exists without any limitations to its sphere of activity, and therefore it is without focus. Its sensory perception is totally diffused and weakened, its desires errant, and its attention unfocused. Besides the ability to express pleasure or pain, humans have no naturally endowed language or art. The infant is mute, incapable of expressing its undefined wants.

However, since nature is not unjust but regulated by a well-balanced economy, it has provided man with an ability to satisfy his constitutional openness. Not being limited to a predefined sphere of activity, man can seek out his own sphere of activity, just as he also must organize his diffuse faculties and find his own center. Herder formulates man's instinctual lack by opposing the human organization of the faculties to the automatic and infallible but blind and machinelike constitution of the animal.

Since he [man] does not blindly fall onto one single spot and remain there blindly, he stands freely in the open, *he can seek for himself a sphere of mirroring, can mirror himself in himself* [my italics]. No longer an infallible machine in the hands of nature, he becomes the purpose and telos of his own work.

Call this entire disposition of his faculties as you like, *understanding, reason, reflection*, etc. As long as one does not take those names for isolated faculties or mere gradations of animal faculties, I will not care. It is the *total organization of all human faculties; the entire economy of his perceptual and cognitive, his cognitive and willing, nature*; or rather it is *the only positive force of thinking*, which related to a certain *organization of the body* is called *reason* in man as it becomes *craft* in animals, which is called *freedom* in man and becomes *instinct* in the animals. (p. 26; Herder's italics)

I have translated Herder's terms so that their literal force—the reference to the mirror—is preserved. Are we justified in seeing in this mirror the indication of a narcissistic dynamic? Can Herder's theory of the origin of language be articulated with a psychoanalytic theory of narcissism? I think it can. Consider the basic similarities between the two theories: both concern the question of the lack of instincts and a theory of sublimation, and both recognize language as the structure that allows for the first narcissistic identity. Theories of primary narcissism postulate this stage at a point when the infant's drives are being focused and differentiated, in terms of libidinal (sexual) energy, which can be bound to objects, and in terms of those drives that are directed at and bound to the ego (the organized part of the id), which then will function as a reservoir for object investment and disinvestment. In that context, primary narcissism occurs at the earliest formative stage of the ego, which establishes the ego's boundaries against external and internal stimuli because of the tendency to minimize tension.[8] Against the background of psychoanalytic models of narcissism, Herder's radical reconceptualization of subjectivity and language can be viewed as emerging from this postulate of lack of instincts.

In the passage quoted above, Herder vehemently rejects traditional theories of the mental faculties. He wants to speak only of one "positive force of thinking," which is not part of a hierarchy of faculties but is the entirety of their organization. Man does not differ from the animal in the sense that some human faculties are more highly developed; rather, the totality of his organization differs from that of the animal. An animal is determined by instinct in the sense that the organization of its faculties is predetermined; man is free in the sense that the organization of his faculties is his own work: he has to construct himself as subject just as he has to construct the objects of his world. Man's primarily narcissistic approach to the world forms the center of Herder's anthropology. Man finds his own gravitational center as well as his sphere of activity, his inside and outside, through a mirror relation. Whereas the animal is defined with regard to specific points of reference in an outside world, which as a set constitute its sphere of activity, and whereas the animal's faculties are organized in relation to this set of external definitions, man's faculties are organized and structured only with regard to themselves. In a self-reflective manner, he constitutes the totality of his otherwise diffused and disorganized faculties. He has to find a mirror relation to any number of outside references that will become a set in the process of being selected and assembled through his collective faculties. In other words, man becomes a subject at the same time he relates to the things in the world as objects.[9]

The biped becomes human in the mirror stage through an act of reflexion/reflection and identification, the gathering of his otherwise dispersed faculties into the collective force of his soul. Therefore, according to Herder, reflection (*Besinnung, Reflexion*) is no longer, as for Condillac, a gradually developed faculty, but a primary force and activity of the human soul. Simultaneously with the power of reflection, man also has language.

The invention of language is as natural to him as he is human! Let us now develop the two notions: reflection and language [*Reflexion und Sprache*].

Man demonstrates reflection when the force of his soul becomes freely active in such a manner that it isolates in the whole ocean of sensations rushing through all the senses a *single* wave, if I may say so, when it arrests this wave, directs its attention to it and is conscious of its attending to it. He proves his reflection when he gathers himself into a moment of awakening out of the whole floating dream of images that passes his senses, if he freely rests on *a single* image, takes it into calmer observation and isolates for himself those marks that make it this and no other object. He also proves reflection, when he not only has a vivid or clear cognition of all qualities but in addition is able to *apperceive* one or several distinguishing qualities for himself: the first act of this apperception produces a distinct notion; it is the first judgment of the soul—and—

How did this apperception come about? Through a mark which he had to isolate and which as a mark of reflection distinctly fell into him. Well! let us hail him with ευρηκα! This *first mark of reflection was the word of the soul! With it human language has been invented!* (p. 32)

The first word is not a representation of something, nor does it communicate anything. In its origin, language is not a symbolic order. Rather, language arises as the soul's defense mechanism against the flood of sensory data. The first word of the soul, the mark, is an act of positioning, of choosing and of finding difference. This act is one of isolation and identification. It establishes the soul as a unity and an interiority and marks the point where inside and outside can be negotiated. It is located between activity and passivity. Whereas Herder's initial examples stress the soul's active mobilization of defense mechanisms against undifferentiated sensory data, in the last phrase the soul is a receptacle into which one isolated mark "falls" as distinct.[10]

With this conception of language, Herder rejects both a mimetic notion of language and the notion that language consists of a repertoire of arbitrary signs, constituted in social commerce and regulated through conventions. "There is no mimetic principle in the soul; the potential imitation of nature is only a means to the one and only purpose, which I am about to explain. Least of all is it based on agreement, an arbitrary social convention; savage man, the lonely man in the woods, would have had to invent language for himself, even if he had never spoken this language. It [language] was the agreement of the soul with itself" (p. 35). Thus Herder strips language of its external qualities. Although he does develop a phonocentric notion of language, he refers primarily not to the spoken word but to the inner language, the voice or sound through which the soul becomes present to itself.

In order to illustrate the invention of language, the activity of reflection in the choice of the mark, the point where the *infans* finds its sphere of mirrors, Herder tells a little narrative.

Let that lamb, as an image, pass his [man's] eyes: the man reacts like no other animal. Not like the hungry, sniffing wolf! Not like the bloodlicking lion. Their minds already anticipate scent and taste! Sensuality has overwhelmed them! Instinct throws them onto it! Nor like the male sheep in rut, who can only feel it as an object of his pleasure, whom again sensuality overwhelms and instinct drives to attack. Nor like any other animal that is indifferent toward the sheep, that therefore lets it pass in chiaroscuro, because its instinct directs it toward something else. No, man is altogether different! As soon as he feels the need to get to know the sheep, no instinct disturbs him, no sense drives him too closely toward it or too far away from it: it stands there in its entirety as it expresses itself to his senses. White, soft, woolly—his contemplating soul seeks a mark—the sheep *bleats*! It has found a mark. The inner sense is active. This bleating that made the strongest impression on the soul, that tore itself away from all the other qualities of sight and touch, that stood out, that penetrated most deeply, remains with it. The sheep comes again. White, soft, woolly—the soul sees, touches, reflects, searches for a mark—it bleats, and now [the soul] recognizes it! "Ha, you are the bleating one!" The soul inwardly feels that it has recognized the lamb in a human manner, for it recognizes and names the lamb distinctly with the aid of one mark. More darkly? In that case it would not have perceived anything, because no senses, no instinct for the sheep, would have substituted the lack of distinctness by a more vivid clarity. Distinctly in an immediate manner, without mark? No sensual creature can perceive its external world in such a manner, for it always has to repress other feelings, to extinguish them and to recognize the difference between two [objects] via a third term. Then, in terms of one mark? And what else was this mark but *an internal mark of recognition [ein innerliches Merkwort]*? The *sound* of bleating, perceived by a human soul as the distinctive mark of the sheep, became due to this reflection the name of the sheep, even if no tongue ever would have tried to stutter it. He recognized the sheep in the bleating: it was a chosen sign in which the soul distinctly contemplated itself in an idea—what else is it but a word? (pp. 32–33)

The first section of this narrative describes the specifically human faculty of reflection (*Besinnung*) as contemplation. The second part narrates the various stages of man's reflective activity in terms of the mediation of external stimuli and the soul's response. Man's contemplative state is distinguished from animalistic brutality. Although the animal is not disoriented by a flood of undifferentiated external stimuli as is man prior to language and reflection, sensuality overwhelms the animal with an onslaught of internal stimulation, such as hunger, rut, and anticipated satisfaction. The object, the female sheep, thereby is reduced to a partial object that corresponds to the animalistic drive. Man, on the contrary, is not determined by drives but constitutes his soul in its wholeness and self-sufficiency as the sheep becomes a total object: "white, soft, woolly." Compared to Herder's previous references to the animal realm, the moral tonality, the insistence on the violence of the animalistic drives, is quite striking. I would argue that in this passage Herder displaces to the animal realm all those demands and desires that in other theories of language lead to the human invention of language. From Augustine to Condillac, the first word is the infant's expression of a want. In Rousseau, some of the social, communicative aspects of language emerge in human courtship. For Herder things are altogether different. Since man lacks everything, he is already beyond particular needs, wants, and desires: the sheep appears to man as a white, soft, and woolly entity. Once Herder has displaced the libidinal drive's dependence on an external object to the realm of the animals, man's lack of instincts can be formulated in positive terms as contemplation, as a calm and distanced attitude of beholding an object: "he feels the need to get to know the sheep." The sheep's bleating then fixes this state through a memory trace that allows man to take this external object into himself, reproduce it in a hallucinatory manner, and affirm in this reproduction the self-sufficiency and unity of his soul.

One might read this tender approach to the sheep in psychoanalytic terms: the infans asserts its independence from the partial object, the maternal breast (with its not altogether controllable ability to satisfy all demands) through the hallucination of the total object, the mother as object of tenderness and as object of an aim-inhibited drive: "white, soft, woolly."[11] In any case, this passage suggests that for Herder the human faculty of contemplation implies aim-inhibition and thereby sublimation, the mechanism by which the soul's integrity and autonomy are established and maintained.

Now to the active side of Besinnung. How does man hold on to his self-sufficiency and wholeness, how does he preserve the hallucinated total object? Herder's answer is that man preserves his humanity through language. He internalizes the sound of the voice of the total object, which then becomes his inner language and the medium in which his soul is present to itself. Although Herder still attempts to integrate into his narrative some relics of rationalist discourse (such as the differentiation of obscure, clear, and distinct cognition), he has left the semiotics of the Age of Reason behind. His attention has shifted to the soul-shaping function of language, its negotiation of inside and outside. The terms *dark*, *clear*, and *distinct* become building blocks in his edifice of a hierarchy of sense perception. Sound and the sense of hearing provide the ideal means for negotiating and organizing the soul's interior space and its exterior sphere. Sounds are external givens that function as a minimal difference or mark, and they can resonate in the internal space.[12]

What are the implications of this model of man's primarily narcissistic, reflexive/reflective disposition? In his attempts to account for man as a social being and language in its social and historical dimension, Herder again takes up the opposition between instinctual drives and man's sociability, which can only partly be explained in terms of a constitutional weakness. It is not conjugal love that Herder opposes to the mating instinct but parental love. Whereas in his *Second Discourse* Rousseau describes maternal love in terms of *pitié*, Herder's parents love in their baby the product of their educational efforts.

Why is this weak and ignorant infant hanging on the breasts of his mother, on the knees of his father? In order to develop a desire for instruction and to learn language. He is weak that his species may become strong. With language the whole soul, the whole way of thinking of his progenitors, will be imparted to him, *but they will impart it to him with pleasure, because they communicate what they themselves have felt and invented. The infant* who stammers his first words *repeats in his stammer his parents' feelings* and swears with each stammer, *after which his tongue and soul form themselves*, to preserve these feelings forever, as true as he calls them his father- or mother tongue. (p. 98; my italics)

Man's constitutional openness makes him the product and the producer of Bildung. The aim of learning is not the acquisition of certain skills, nor does education mean the disciplining of the little creature. Rather, the infant's reflection or sphere of mirrors, his soul and language, is formed through his parents' narcissistic love for "his Majesty the Baby."[13] Therefore the infant relates to its environment in primarily narcissistic terms. Bildung provides the means of establishing and preserving the totality and harmony of the psychic apparatus against internal and external stimuli.

In Herder's version of the child's acquisition of language, the question of language as a symbolic order, related to law and authority, does not arise. Rousseau negotiates the disciplining of the student in terms of an attachment to an ideal woman, and in *Julie* maternal love provides the scenario for a gentle discipline. Herder provides a scenario in which the prohibiting or punishing agency is even less visible than in the case of Rousseau. The law reproduces itself automatically in the successive Bildung of generations, through what he calls a *Familiensprache* (family language).

Those first impressions of his childhood, those images from the soul and the heart of his parents, will live and be effective for the duration of his entire life; the entire feeling that used to flow through his soul with abundance shall return with the word, all associations that used to be present to him in the early morning perspective on the realm of creation shall return with the idea of the word—they shall return and be more powerful than the pure, main idea itself. And that shall be the family way of thinking and thereby a *family language* [Herder's italics]. And there we see the cold philosopher [Rousseau] posing the question: "Through which law could men possibly have managed to force their arbitrarily invented language on others and how might they have induced the other party to accept the law?" . . .

Isn't there enough law and eternity in this family tradition of language? Woman, in nature so much the weaker part, doesn't she have to accept the law from the experienced, providing, and language-forming man? Why should one call law what is merely a gentle benefit of instruction? *The weak child, who is called the infant in the true sense of the word, does he not have to accept language since with it he can enjoy the milk of his mother and the spirit of his father?* [my italics] And if anything should be perpetuated, would it not have to be this language? Oh, the laws of nature are more powerful than all conventions that are formed by clever politics and that the sage philosopher attempts to enumerate! (pp. 98–99)

Herder rejects the notion that tradition and social conventions have to be enforced, and he expresses his dislike for the term "law," which seems to remind him of an external force or a threat of violence. Rather, he wants to conceive of the process of socialization in an even more gentle and interiorized manner than does Rousseau: the infant's sphere of mirrors and the perspective on the world provided by the parents' narcissistic love for their child become the exclusive model of socialization. The force of this socialization lies in the infant's learning of language, which makes him independent of an immediate parental presence and which embodies plenitude, the land where milk and honey flow. As the child acquires language, he takes the "maternal milk and paternal spirit" into himself and thereby identifies with his parents. What is decisive in this passage is its emphasis on a retrospective point of view: it is childhood as it appears in the adult memory that evokes the golden age that knows neither want nor desire.

From a psychoanalytic perspective, the exclusion of sexuality in this model of socialization is striking. Herder's story transforms any potential libidinal object investment into a desexualized narcissistic investment. As such, it is a master narrative of sublimation and a repression of the oedipal drama. The child's acquisition of language allows for a libidinal disinvestment of the object through the introjection of the object ("maternal milk and paternal spirit") and its narcissistic investment ("the entire feeling that used to flow through his soul with abundance"); the child replaces an object investment with an object identification ("those images from the soul and the heart of his parents will live and be effective for the duration of his entire life"). Demanding the renunciation of the object (the mother), the father of the oedipal scenario becomes an object of ambivalent feelings. He is repressed and internalized as the ideal-ego, which draws its force from the ego-ideal of childhood, that retrospective account of a primary object identification of the child with an omnipotent father. In Herder's account of the child's acquisition of language, the prohibition of the father against being like him, part of the castration threat of the oedipal scenario, is supplemented and repressed in the construction of the father as an ego-ideal, which not only entails the demand not to be like him, but also its opposite: to be like him.[14] In brief, the child's acquisition of language becomes the site of the ideal ego, the supposedly self-sufficient entity one used to be. Law and morality need no external enforcement since it is on this site, on the ideal ego, that the ego-ideal, the self-sufficient entity one wants to be in the future, can be grafted.[15]

It is also interesting that Herder postulates, in passing, a naturally given difference between men and women in regard to access to language. Although his theory about language arising from man's constitutional openness would not require any gendered difference, he asserts that only the male biped has the language-forming (*sprachbildende*) ability and thereby the power to establish the law. For Rousseau, the gendered access to representations has to be regulated through a public/private split in which woman must be restricted to the private sphere while at the same time she is situated on the level of appearance, representations, and *paraître* (dictated by public opinion). Herder "naturalizes" gender and excludes woman from the fundamental human faculty of reflection, of finding her sphere of mirrors.

To conclude my analysis of Herder's humanist anthropology, I turn to the phonocentric aspects of this narcissistic subjectivity. Just as he rejects the division of man's cognitive ability into a hierarchy of faculties, Herder also opposes his contemporaries' analysis of sensory perception in that he substitutes an emphasis on hearing for the rationalist emphasis on sight. Herder claims that the medium of sound provides the most distinct marks, because individual sounds are presented in a temporal order. The world speaks to man in terms of its natural languages, each creature's "cri de nature."

Faced with the question how man comes to name things that do not produce a sound and unwilling to admit arbitrariness into human language, Herder has to develop a theory of sensory perception. He asserts that all kinds of sensory data, whether optic, acoustic, or haptic, can be translated into each other; they are not incomparable but parts of one synesthetic continuum. Herder does not attempt to differentiate sensory data by media (light, sound, or the shape, density, and texture of matter). Instead, he considers them from the perspective of how they structure the soul's self-reflective unity. The synesthetic continuum accordingly is set between the poles confused/diffuse, inside/outside, dark/clear, and intense/cold. Between these poles the soul has to find its structure and set up its internal and external boundaries. Within this model of the senses, Herder then argues that the sense of hearing is the privileged, mediating sense in the soul's effort to establish its unity and center through an inner language. The sense of touch lacks a sufficiently externalized reference point and tends to be confused; the sense of sight provides the soul with data that are too diffuse and too far removed from it. Even in terms of the soul's temporal structuration, hearing is the mediating sense, since touch overwhelms the soul in a strong and discontinuous manner and sight disorients the soul by confronting it with synchronous data. Only through hearing does the soul receive a continuous, temporal flow of impressions. Since all the senses are nothing but modes of representation (*Vorstellungsarten*), the soul has to stabilize itself through that kind of representation that provides it with a maximum of stability, balance, vividness, and independence—in Herder's words, with a distinct representation. Finally, hearing is also the mediating and therefore privileged sense in that it is most immediately tied to the expressive side of language. Only the objects of hearing can and must be pronounced; they are already speech. And even in terms of man's phylo- and ontogenetic development, hearing is the sense that guarantees the progressive evolution of humankind. Speech provides the subject with depth and a creative productivity that constitute the continuity of the species' tradition.

In Herder's description the subject of Bildung is organized through the spoken and heard word. Oral language circumscribes the subject like a layer of skin that protects against disintegration from within as well as overstimulation from without; it functions as a porous membrane that organizes the chaotic inner world of affects and selects significant marks from the outer world through the double movement of introjection and projection. As a result, this narcissistic subject becomes a self-regulating mechanism whose productivity can be stimulated by mobilizing its defense mechanisms. In the next two sections, I turn to the discussions of ancient Greek sculpture in Herder's and Moritz's aesthetic writings, to those art objects in which the narcissistic subject finds its ideal mirror image, its objects of a secondary narcissism.

Pygmalion's Dream in Herder's Aesthetics

While Herder was working on his treatise on the origin of language, he started to elaborate a theory of sculpture, of which he published a final version in 1778 under the title "Einige Wahrnehmungen über Form und Gestalt aus Pygmalions bildendem Traume" (Some observations about form and gestalt from Pygmalion's formative dream). In the context of the classical episteme, aesthetics and pedagogy developed the project of Anschaulichkeit in an effort to re-naturalize the arbitrary sign. Diderot's aesthetics in particular, as well as Lessing's *Laokoon*, revolves around the *image sensible*, the hallucinated sight modeled on the pictorial tableau that mirrors the *tableau mouvant* of the soul. With Herder these aesthetic ideals of illusion come to an end. In a way, one can read his writings about sculpture as the rewriting in haptic terms of Diderot's *Lettre sur les aveugles* and *Lettre sur les sourds et muets*. The place and function of the tableau are to be assumed by sculpture, and the predominance of the sense of sight is to be replaced by the sense of touch. Furthermore, Herder wants to revise Lessing's theory of the arts, which rests on the opposition of figures and colors in a spatial order to articulated sounds in a temporal order. Sculpture, according to Herder, is an artistic medium in its own right. It is wrong to subordinate it to painting, whose flat surface is accessible only to the sense of sight. Instead of the sight versus sound opposition, Herder proposes a tripartite system for the various arts:

painting	music	sculpture
surface	sound	body
sight	hearing	feeling
coexistence	succession	coexistence and succession
space	time	force

In his treatise on the origin of language, Herder makes the ear the privileged organ and describes the sense of touch as conveying initially confused sensations. However, the sense of touch in that essay differs from the one in his writings about sculpture. In a way, it is not even correct to speak of tactile sensations with regard to the latter. "Feeling" ("Gefühl") in Herder's essay on sculpture is not localized in fingertips tracing the texture of a surface ("Tastsinn"). In fact, in regard to Greek sculptures, "Feeling" must not be confused with the tactile mapping of a surface; rather, it means the total comprehension of the spatial form, of the body's organization in space, the *Körpergefühl* (body feeling) that provides the beholder with a comprehensive notion of an organized totality, with a *Begriff*.[16] Feeling in that sense is exactly the apprehension of an object that goes beyond its mere surface to its structure and depth. In that sense feeling means a special access to truth: "Im Gesicht ist Traum, im Gefühl Wahrheit" ("In the sense of sight there is dream, in feeling truth"; p. 9).[17]

As the synthesized comprehension of a gestalt, feeling is far removed from actual sensory perception: rather, it is a certain spatial hallucination of an ideal object. Furthermore, we must not forget that whereas the *Ursprung* essay deals with sensory perceptions per se, the aesthetic writings on sculpture discuss perceptions vis-à-vis representations. In the earlier essay, the primary issue of the subject's constitution involved a defense against overstimulation; the artistic media in the sculpture essays have already mastered this obstacle. In Herder's terms, once man has been faced with aesthetic objects, once he is in the realm of representations, he has already found his sphere of mirrors, his reflection. Of course, Herder's choice of Greek sculpture as the privileged form of aesthetic representation has to be understood within the context of a broader project of a cultural critique. Herder is not concerned with these art objects in terms of an art historical inquiry. Rather, the sculpture provides him with a heuristic device for describing an ideal type of representation. In his writings on sculpture, Herder's interest in artistic products is directed toward their ability to shape subjectivity.

But what qualities of Greek sculpture allow it to become the paradigm of the aesthetic object? They can be summarized in these lapidary terms: Greek sculpture is the spatially isolated representation of a beautiful and vigorous nude human body, preferably in polished marble and certainly without the use of colors. As a spatial representation, sculpture provides an image of the body in its totality and accessibility to the senses of sight and feeling. As an isolated entity, the sculpture asserts a certain independence from its environment. A sculpture has to have its own center of gravity without becoming frozen; it can thereby combine calmness and movement, displaying its autonomy and force. The Greeks chose to represent only those human bodies that were free of imperfection, neither diseased nor old, but young athletic men and beautiful women. The perfection of the human body can be represented only if the body is not restrained or hidden by clothes, for only then can the harmony of all its parts be exhibited. It is here that the Greek style proves its superiority over other styles. For the Greeks had the good taste to avoid color or exaggerated details in terms of body hair or protruding veins, details that would foreground in a disturbing manner the materiality and mortality of the body.

Many finer things than color and cowhide have to be kept away from statues, for they resist the feeling, for they are not a continuous beautiful form for the feeling of touch. These veins at the hands, these knuckles on the fingers, this cartilage on the knees, has to be treated with caution and clothed by the fullness of the whole; else the veins are crawling worms, the gristles protruding growths for the silent sense of touch in the dark. No longer fullness of *One* body, but separations, isolated pieces of the body, which predict its destruction, and should be already removed for this very reason. (p. 27)

Who has not seen how in the first plaster cast of a face *each individual* hair sticks out in such an obstinate and ungentle manner, like any pockmark or fatal unevenness and separation from the human face. The individual hairs make us shudder, it is like a dent in a knife, only something that opposes the form and does not belong to it. Therefore the Greek artist only *suggests*. (p. 29)

Like Lacan's infant of the mirror stage, the beholder of the Greek statue appreciates in this representation, via a certain imaginary identification, the wholeness and health of his own body, a protection against fragmentation and disintegration.[18] This imaginary identification presupposes a specific degree of stylization, the sculptor's restraint with regard to those details that would disorganize the representation of a totality and recall in the beholder his own, very material bodily details.[19] The representation is not to be judged in terms of a proximity to nature; mimesis is not at issue. Instead of referring the beholder to a concrete human body of hair, fat, cartilage, veins, the sculpture is supposed to represent an ideal. Hence, the human body comes to stand for the human soul or for the ego, which cannot be represented and which supports itself on an idealized body image.[20]

But how does the Greek artist allow the beholder to identify himself with an ideal body, how does he *suggest* this immortal body? Sculpture manages to signify this ideal body in a manner that painting cannot. The surface of Greek sculpture functions like a specific screen veiling the material details of the concrete body from the eye, but its three-dimensionality appeals to the hallucinatory body-feeling by which the beholder identifies with the sculpture. Thus the sculpture acquires a certain diaphanous quality, a transparency with regard to this ideal body. Herder analyzes this effect by looking at how the Greeks draped clothes on their statues.

Given that even the Greek had to use clothes, that a law obliged him to hide the beautiful body, which he wanted to form, and which art alone *can* and *must* form, behind rags; was there a means to escape this alien pressure, or to accommodate oneself to it? To clothe without hiding anything? To apply a vestment in such a manner that the body would still retain its growth and beautiful, rounded fullness? What if it were to *shine through*? In the sculpture of somebody like Solido nothing can shine through: this kind of sculpture works for the hand and not for the eye. And look, it was exactly *for the hand* that the Greeks solved the problem. If only the touching finger can be betrayed into perceiving the feeling of clothes and the body simultaneously, the *alien* judge, the eye must *follow*. In brief, it is the Greek's *wet clothes*. (p. 22)

In Herder's aesthetics the veil of illusion serves very different ends compared to its role in Lessing or Rousseau. As explained in Chapter 2, in Lessing's theory of pity and illusion, the bourgeois tragedy is supposed to produce a catharsis that transforms and unifies the violent and mixed affects of desire and abhorrence toward an other. In Lessing's theory of illusion, this aesthetic effect is freed from mimesis, inasmuch as the trompe l'oeil threatens to disintegrate into representation and original object. Lessing explained this effect of disillusionment, of a failed mediated immediacy, in terms of the representation of a beautiful woman. Herder also uses the example of a beautiful woman; however, he does so to utterly different ends.

And generally, the closer we approach an object, the *more vivid* becomes our language, and the more vividly we feel it *in the distance*, the more unbearable the separating space becomes for us, the more we want to approach it. Woe to the lover who can calmly contemplate his beloved from the distance like a flat picture and be satisfied! Woe to the sculptor of Apollo and Hercules, who has never embraced Apollo's form, who has never felt Hercules' chest or back, not even in his dream. From *nothing* truly nothing but *nothing* can originate, and the unfeeling sunray will never become a warm and shaping hand. (pp. 13–14)

In Herder's description of the beholder's attitude toward a beautiful object, there is no question of distance. And quite clearly Herder does not want a relation of similarity toward an other, but a relation of identity toward an object, which then no longer remains an other. In fact, the context of this passage celebrates the enthusiasm of the art lover and artist. The enthusiasm aims at proximity to, even fusion with, the desired object. Herder opposes Pygmalion's dream to the cold and distanced eye of reason. This particular love for the beautiful gestalt is an important aspect of Bildung. The remark that this enthusiasm even enlivens language forges the link with the primary medium of Bildung, with language as the mark of the soul, man's sphere of mirrors and contemplation, his product and what produces his humanity.

Herder elaborates in his essay on sculpture a long and detailed semiotics of the human body. His interest is not to study physiognomy, but to demonstrate how the human body, from head to toe, provides humanity with the germane representation of its soul.[21] The human body is the only natural sign and embodiment of an internal perfection: "The well-shaped human form is not something abstract out of the clouds, not a composition produced according to learned rules or arbitrary agreements; it can be *grasped* and *felt* by everybody, who feels *in himself* or *in an other* the form of life, the expression of force in the vessel of humanity. Only the *signification* of an *internal perfection* is beauty" (p. 56). In the contemplation of Greek sculpture man gains an immediate access to the ideal of beauty and hears the language of nature, which is beyond material signifiers and mere sensory data, for it speaks through his soul: "Again, one must not study letters or clouds, one must merely *be* and *feel*: be human, and sense blindly how the soul operates in each character, in each position and passion *in us*, and then touch. It is the loud language of nature, audible to all peoples, even to the blind and deaf" (p. 58). The sculpture is not so much a sign for something else; rather, its semiotic status seems in this passage to be sliding toward the classical-romantic symbol, which has a necessary internal relation to what it signifies. The process of signification assumes an organic character. Instead of a model of reading, we find the model of osmosis or assimilation. Beholding a sculpture effects a mutual metamorphosis of object and subject: "Each bending and raising of the chest and the knee, and how the body rests and how the soul represents itself in it, permeates us in a silent and incomprehensible manner: such that we are embodied, as it were, through the statue and it is endowed with a soul through us" (p. 60). In the sculpture we do not perceive an other; rather, the soul receives through the sculpture an image of itself. What endows the product of Pygmalion's hands with life is the passionately narcissistic love for this ideal representation of himself.

From here we can link the narcissistic aspect of Pygmalion's dream to the subject's constitution in language, which was traced in the *Ursprung* essay in terms of a primary narcissism. The white, soft, and woolly sheep, the total object of a "disinterested interest," was given its mark by the soul through its sound, allowing the soul to constitute and stabilize itself. In the white, full, and smooth but well-defined and hard body of the sculpture, the soul then can find a representation of itself in terms of a secondary narcissism; its ego-ideal and Bildung will be reflected in the mirror of a humanist idealism.

We approach a sculpture as if we were entering into a sacred darkness, as if we had to feel for ourselves for the first time *the simplest notion* and *meaning of form*, the most noble, beautiful and rich form, the one of a *human* body. The simpler the manner we go about it, and if, as *Hamlet* says, all trivial fond records, all saws of books, are erased from our brain, the more the silent image will speak to us and the sacred, forceful form, coming from the hands of the greatest sculptor and standing there animated by his breath, will enliven itself under the hand, under the fingers of our inner spirit. Breath of the one who created, blow toward me, that I may remain truthful to his work, that I may feel and write authentically. (p. 41)

Whereas Ovid's Pygmalion, disappointed with the love of flesh-and-blood women, made for himself a beautiful ivory girl, who then is endowed with life through his passionate love and finally becomes his wife, Herder's Pygmalion relates to the sculpture in terms of a complex narcissistic structure. The erotic attraction toward an other is replaced by a desire for an ideal self: the statue endows Pygmalion with the form of his own soul. Not only does the beholder of the statue find in it a representation of his ideal body and soul, but he also encounters the creative genius of an Other who commands him to remain truthful to his work. In order to be animated by "his breath," that the "silent image" will speak to us, that it will "enliven itself under the hand, under the fingers of our inner spirit" ("sich unter der Hand, unter dem Finger unsres inneren Geistes beleben"), "all trivial fond records, all saws of books" ("alle Alltags-kopien und das Gemahl- und Gekritsel von Buchstaben"), need to be erased. What does this mean other than to read and write according to the hermeneutic ideal of authorship, that totalizing spirit that prohibits attention to the materiality of the letter, which would disrupt the beautiful autonomy and continuity of the self of Bildung? Thus, the sculpture finally becomes that ideal aesthetic object or "interface," which provides the seam or suture (for it has to stitch up the wounds of lack and mortality) through which man inserts himself into the order of creation, the order of sense and the senses.[22]

Mirroring the Mirror: Moritz's Theory of Suture

Karl Philipp Moritz's aesthetic theory, which he articulated in numerous short essays published in the 1780's, is one of the founding statements of German classicism.[23] To the extent that his aesthetics postulates an autonomous aesthetic realm, it marks the departure from the Enlightenment demands of educating the citizen in the public realm.[24] Moritz shares with Herder the neo-humanist concern with Bildung. Therefore, I shall situate his aesthetic theory in close proximity to Herder's postulates about human language and its implications in terms of soul-making or subject formation and focus my reading of Moritz's essays on his concern with sublimation.

Succinctly, and in agreement with Herder, Moritz describes the impact

Fig. 12. Piranesi, Vedute di Roma *(engravings made between 1748 and 1778), frontispiece (detail). Among the debris from Classical antiquity, note the Medusa's head on Minerva's breastplate.*

and value of humanist studies: "Let us recall in our imagination the life of a people that had once been all that man can become, uniting all his forces, and in doing so we shall gaze into a mirror, which reflects back to us our own image more perfect and truer than our contemporary world" (p. 106). Again Greek art is described in terms of its mirror-like ability to present our ideal ego. As in Herder's essay on sculpture, Moritz develops a notion of aesthetic illusion and mimesis based on the structure of narcissism and a mutual metamorphosis of object and subject. When Moritz examines the ethical validity of aesthetic autonomy in his essay "Über die bildende Nachahmung des Schönen" (On the forming imitation of the Beautiful), however, the stress of his analysis lies more on the productive side of imitation than on the receptive side.[25] He begins with the distinction between three kinds of imitation: the sage man who imitates Socrates as a moral ideal; the actor who parodies the individual and external traits of Socrates, tongue in cheek and merely superficially; and the fool who thinks he discerns in himself a certain proximity to Socrates and thus apes the great man. The sage alone manages to imitate or emulate in the noble, moral sense. Moritz introduces the term "imitation" (*Nachahmung*) as an internal transformation, an internalization and emulation of an ethical ideal rather than mere external copying. Then he explains how the imitation of beauty differs from the imitation of the good and the noble. Both the good and the noble are distinct from the useful in the sense that they have an intrinsic value. The noble does not need external beauty; it is the internal dignity of the soul. The beautiful becomes the surface of the noble, what enables us to perceive externally an internal nobility. Therefore, the imitation of the beautiful must encompass both an inward and an outward movement: the internalization of the moral ideal and the externalization of the beautiful, autonomous composition: "The beautiful, however—to the degree that it distinguishes itself from the noble and, as opposed to the internal, means only external beauty—cannot enter into us through an imitation but has to be formed out of us from the inside, if it is to be imitated" (p. 66). Whereas Herder describes the creation of an organized internal depth through the sculpture's soul-shaping influence, Moritz focuses on the particular productivity that emanates out of this depth.

Like Herder, Moritz values man's freedom and autonomy, his ability to position himself as an organized totality. Whereas, however, Herder's theory of sublimation postulates man's primarily narcissistic approach to the world (as a stage that necessarily complements his constitutional openness), and whereas for Herder the aesthetic object merely reinforces man's contemplative faculty, Moritz's theory of sublimation is—as I shall demonstrate—worked out in more complex and dynamic terms. Herder's theory starts out with aim-inhibition, the hallucination of an organized totality (man's reflection or sphere of mirrors), as already given through human language; for Moritz this sphere of mirrors has to be produced, and art becomes a decisive vehicle in this process. If, however, art is crucial in the constitution of man's humanity, Moritz's postulate of aesthetic autonomy must not be misunderstood as a disregard for art's social function. Indeed, despite Moritz's insistence on aesthetic autonomy, his writings on aesthetics are not restricted to a concern with art objects. On the contrary, they are pervaded by considerations of modern man's alienation, destructiveness, misery, and mortality. Three levels of argumentation can thus be distinguished in his essays: a consideration of the aesthetic in terms of its social function; a consideration of the aesthetic in terms of a psychological theory of production; and a consideration of the aesthetic in allegorical or mythological terms, in Moritz's attempt to describe the ideal work of art. These three levels intersect in a model of sublimation conceived in dynamic terms.

In developing the notion of aesthetic autonomy vis-à-vis man's alienation, Moritz begins by comparing the aesthetic object to the useless object: neither can be subordinated to any extrinsic purpose. In contradistinction to the useless, however, the aesthetic object cannot be subsumed under an extrinsic purpose because it is in itself already perfect. The example Moritz employs to explain his notion of an autonomous totality is interesting: each part of a whole has to have a relation to the whole, but the whole must have no relation to anything external to itself. Hence each citizen has to have a certain relation to the state in order to be useful to the state; the state itself, however, need have no relation to anything external, for it forms a totality in itself and therefore it need not be useful for anything (p. 71). Nonetheless, although the state constitutes an autonomous totality, it is insufficient to explain the notion of an aesthetic totality. Because we can comprehend its totality only in our understanding, the whole that the state is cannot be represented to our imagination or our senses. Moritz uses the example of the state's autonomy as a negative clue and opposes the totality of the state and aesthetic autonomy. The state comes to stand for an experiential and perceptual inaccessibility, that is, a condition of alienation for the subject that can be compensated for only through aesthetic illusion: "Therefore the notion of the beautiful, which we derived from the fact that it need not be useful, does not merely also imply that it has to be an autonomous whole, but rather that it can be perceived by our senses or comprehended by our imagination as an autonomous whole" (p. 72). The aesthetic object has to produce the *illusion* of an autonomous totality, which is precisely what the state cannot provide.

Moritz next focuses on the order of creation in toto and on Man. In nature, as he explains, everything is connected to everything else and its entirety can be comprehended only by the Creator.[26] The aesthetic object, however, produces an illusion of an autonomous whole that allows its beholder to constitute himself equally as an autonomous subject: "For this great connection of things is actually the only, true totality; each individual whole in it is only imagined, because of the indissolvable interconnection of things—but even this imagined totality still has to shape itself in a manner similar to that great totality in our imagination and according to the eternally fixed rules that center it and let it rest on its own existence" (p. 73). Whenever man encounters this beautiful illusion of an autonomous totality, he strives to imitate it. He does not remain a passive beholder but actively reconstitutes this totality out of his interiority: "The sense for the highest beauty in the harmonious construction of the whole, which the human imagination cannot comprehend, lies immediately in the *productive activity* itself. For this productive activity cannot rest before at least one of the representative faculties is brought into proximity with what is dormant in it—it intervenes in the connection of things, and whatever it takes hold of it wants to shape, like nature, into an *autonomously* existing whole" (p. 74). The aesthetic object stimulates man's productive activity by providing an anticipation of a beautiful totality, an anticipation that prompts him to realize and externalize this totality through his own artistic production (pp. 77–80). The passage just quoted displays Moritz's tendency to conceive of the work of art in dynamic terms. The apprehension of beauty stimulates and channels man's productive energy inasmuch as art simulates nature's totality and man's autonomy. In terms of its social function, art compensates for man's alienation in an incomprehensible modern world. It allows man to conceive of himself as an "autonomously existing whole" through a fundamental intervention in the organization of his faculties and his productive activity.

Man not only transforms animal and plant through becoming, growth, and incorporation into his internal being, but at the same time through the most brilliantly polished, *mirroring* surface of his being, he gathers all that is subordinated to his organization into the circumference of his existence, and once his organism has shaped its own perfection, he will represent and externalize it in a more beautiful manner.

When this is not possible, he will have to draw through destruction whatever surrounds him into the circumference of his actual existence, he will have to relate to his environment in a devastating manner, expanding as far as possible; for pure and innocent contemplation will not be able to replace his thirst for an expansive actual existence.   (pp. 82–83)

Moritz describes man's relation to his environment in terms very similar to those of Herder; however, there is a decisive difference. For Herder, man's collective faculties and his reflectivity are identical (the *Ursprung* essay calls them *Besonnenheit* and *Denkkraft*). For Moritz, the substratum of man's collective faculties, or *Thatkraft*, amounts to a sheer vital energy. It is the urge of an organism to assert itself through expansion, through the annihilation, destruction, or incorporation of anything other. In that sense, Thatkaft implies a certain aggressive and destructive urge.[27] To contain this expansive force, another force is needed: "the mirroring surface of his being" is invoked as the power that can transform the aggressive incorporation and destruction of external objects into a more peaceful process of internalization and externalization. The active forces have to be brought into an internal harmony so that they strive toward the constitution of an other as a mirror rather than toward the annihilation or subordination of the other. The function of the "brilliantly polished mirroring surface of his being" consists in establishing a more stable boundary between self and other. At this point the mirror produces a separation between inside and outside by reflecting its structure back to itself and thereby constituting the inside as an organized totality. Once the organism has its "circumference," it no longer has to annihilate or incorporate the other because the other serves to reinforce the organism's boundaries. The previously threatening other is transformed into yet another mirror of the self. In this sense, the mirror of Moritz's image has two faces of reflection. This double mirror transforms the libidinal investment in external objects into a narcissistic investment: that is, it constitutes and preserves those external objects analogously as autonomous entities that mirror the organism's perfection and independence. It is only through this mirror that the vital energy of the Thatkraft is transformed into the *Bildungstrieb* (the drive to shape).

Up to this point, however, the transformative power of this mirroring surface is not quite clear. How is it introduced? What gives it its force? In order to bend the productive activity back toward itself, to transform this vital energy into *Bildungskraft*, yet another faculty is needed, the one Moritz calls *Empfindungskraft* (faculty of feeling), which comes closest to Herder's Besonnenheit (contemplation). This faculty is opposed to the understanding of a totality (Denkkraft) as well as to the shaping of a whole (Bildungskraft) and means the anticipation of a structured totality. It is also the disinterested interest, the contemplation of a totality without the urge to turn this object of contemplation into an object of use or pleasure: "To the extent that the active force *takes into itself* everything that does not fall under the realm of thinking *and brings it forth*, it is called 'Bildungskraft': to the extent that it comprehends that which lies outside the borders of thinking within itself and *leans merely receptively toward the activity of bringing forth*, it is called 'Empfindungskraft' " (p. 82).

How does Empfindungskraft, this contemplative state of receptivity that enjoys the contemplation of an other as a structured totality, compare with Herder's Besonnenheit? Herder's Besonnenheit designates the peaceful state of satisfaction beyond need and desire; Moritz's Empfindungskraft is merely the yearning for that state of bliss. It is the contemplation of a whole carried out with the knowledge that one will never be able to become like it. As a contemplative state of mere receptivity, it transforms object investment into narcissistic investment (like Herder's Besonnenheit); however, the disinvestment of the object also entails a certain renunciation. And it is this aspect of renunciation for the sake of independence from the pleasure obtained from external objects that makes Empfindungskraft the model by which Bildungskraft has to be measured. If Bildungskraft wants to realize and externalize the autonomous totality that it anticipates, it can do so only independently of the pleasure this external object yields.

If the beauty we anticipate in its production retains its attraction in and for itself, and if this attraction is sufficient to motivate our productive activity, then we can give in to our forming drive, because then it is pure and genuine.

If, however, after we have obliterated pleasure and effect, the attraction vanishes—well, then, there is no need to struggle—our internal peace is reconstituted—and the faculty of feeling in its old right opens itself to the purest pleasure of all beauty that is compatible with its nature, it is rewarded for its modest stepping back into its own borders.   (p. 80)

Bildungskraft must not realize itself unless it will reproduce the beautiful totality regardless of the pleasure obtained. For the beautiful must never be subordinated to any extrinsic purpose. And unless the Bildungstrieb has the internal motivation and ability to strive continuously for the perfection of the beautiful for its own sake, it should renounce productive activity and become mere *Empfindungsfähigkeit*, or the recognition of one's insufficiency and lack.[28] Empfindungsfähigkeit ensures the difference between the externalized beautiful object and the self. It preserves the autonomy of the work of art and prevents its being reduced to an object of pleasure; in return, the work of art upholds the illusion of an "autonomously existing whole." In that sense, Empfindungsfähigkeit also denotes a certain vulnerability in the perceiving subject; this lack endows the aesthetic object with the promise of a cure.

From here it becomes clear that Moritz's theory of aesthetic production is sexually overcoded in terms of gender polarization: "In the faculty of feeling there will always be a gap, which can be filled in only through the result of the forming force—the forming force and the faculty of feeling relate to each other like man and woman. For the forming force is in the first emergence of its work, in the moment of greatest pleasure, identical with the faculty of feeling, and it produces, like nature, the imprint of its essence outside of itself" (p. 81). The mere faculty of feeling as sheer receptivity is feminized, but artistic production has both masculine and feminine components. But, as we have noted in a previous passage, both faculties are also related to an economy of pleasure and renunciation: that feeling that realizes itself in terms of pleasures or rewards is a false production, one that has to be ruled out.

According to the model that emerges, there is self-indulgent sensibility, the pleasurable tears and feelings of the literature of the age of sensibility, which now appears as the degraded form of an effeminate mass culture. There is also the sensibility of sheer receptivity, that of the woman, who recognizes her own limits and steps back in modesty. She thus can become the ideal listener, who can fully appreciate that art she will never be able to produce, and as the mother/lover/nature she can even become the source of the artist's creativity. Finally, there is the receptivity and asceticism of a yearning for perfection, which forms a constitutive aspect of a masculine and truly artistic productivity. This true artist produces his art for its own sake, independently of the pleasure or rewards obtained by it: he is the professional of Bildung. This professional is an artist at night, independent of the dictates of the literary market. He makes his living as a scholar, academic, teacher, bureaucrat, or engineer, and he is almost always a civil servant. He is Moritz, Novalis, E. T. A. Hoffmann, Humboldt, or the Schlegels, to name only a few, or a civil servant, like Schiller, the Jena professor of history, who expresses the alienation from an abstract state bureaucracy in the famous sixth letter of the *Aesthetic Education of Man*.

Given Moritz's discussion of productivity and aesthetic sublimation, how does he approach art's social function? By constituting man in his independence and freedom, the aesthetic object exercises a crucial function in human life, which is marked by misery and alienation. In "Bildende Nachahmung," Moritz refers to man's alienation from the state only in terms of a brief example. In his essays "Das Edelste in der Natur" (The most noble in nature) and "Das menschliche Elend" (Human misery), Moritz explores in greater detail the redemptive effects of the beautiful and the aesthetic object. In the first essay, Moritz states that man should never be instrumentalized but always be considered an aim in himself, a noble being, independent from his position within the state organization; one of the greatest evils emerges from the division of men into social classes. The educated class considers itself superior and feels justified in considering the laboring class merely in terms of its utility (p. 17). This division between the educated and the uneducated is to be alleviated through Bildung. The seed of this reform, and the consolation for the present misery, lies in each individual's potential recognition of his autonomy, in the possibility of seeing beyond the concrete individual restrictions and suffering to learn to recognize one's autonomy vis-à-vis the totality of nature. This recognition is initiated through the aesthetic object: art can sweeten the bitter political reality by allowing the individual to think himself beyond the limits of society's class divisions. But art also remains a reminder of the individual's autonomy and thereby provides an implicit critique of the current state of alienation (p. 18).

In his essay on human misery, Moritz further explores how art can intervene in a human condition blighted by destruction and warfare. He does not want to pursue a line of thought that suggests the human condition would improve if only each individual could transcend egotism. Although this would bring destructiveness to a halt, it would stop human productivity altogether. Granting the necessity of egotism as the driving energy, he calls for the containment of this productive activity as artistic creativity. Thus the one cure for human destructiveness and the tendency to oppress others is art's ability to channel and sublimate the vital energy (p. 25). A second aspect under which Moritz considers the aesthetic vis-à-vis human misery focuses on the specific difference between the aesthetic object and the beholder. Besides holding up to man a mirror that reflects the truth of part/whole relations, reminding him of his autonomy, stimulating and channeling his productive activity through a self-reflective containment, art also allows man to distance himself from that which is beyond his control, from the circumstances he encounters accidentally. Here, art provides the possibility of relating to war and destruction, chance and suffering, as a spectacle, of enjoying the majestic grandeur of those events and asserting the strength of one's own independence, turning the horrifying event into a sublime spectacle.

And it is the great that we want; our soul wants to be enlarged; our imagination wants to encompass much.

If only this purpose is achieved, anything, no matter what, may perish; perishing is something so tragic, moving the soul so deeply, that we enjoy the sight of it with pleasure as long as it does not touch us.

At the bottom of our hearts we are all little Neros, who would not at all mind the sight of a burning Rome, the clamor of the refugees, the whimpering of the infants if only it is represented to our gaze as a *spectacle*.

Thus we have achieved our purpose: our thoughts are enlarged; we have become equal to the gods; but our new ideas have been produced not only through *building* but also through *destruction*. Since we could not become creators in order to equal god, we became destroyers; we created in a backward manner, for we were unable to create forwardly. We created for ourselves a world of destruction, and now we enjoy the contemplation of our work in history, tragedy, and poetry. (p. 56)

This valorization of the spectacle and the invigorating power of beholding an aesthetically contained scene of horror and destruction stands at a great distance from the preceding aesthetic theories based on ideals of transparency, immediacy, sensibility, and sympathy. Neo-humanist aesthetics, as it takes part in the project of Bildung, aims at the subject's placement in the order of representation in terms of the construction of both subject and aesthetic object as mutually mirroring autonomous entities. In this conceptualization of the subject's formation through art, the seam or suture between subject and object is stressed as a protection from internal and external overstimulation, a protection against chance, lack, and dependence. The mirror has the power of reflection and separation. It introduces a gap or distance between object and subject while it covers up the fragility and mortality of the subject itself. Hence, in entitling this section "Mirroring the Mirror: Moritz's Theory of Suture," I refer to the aesthetic object's capacity to mirror man's mirroring faculty and to the resulting complex relation between aesthetic object and its beholder, a relation for which I borrow the term "suture" from film semiotics.[29]

Since Moritz's aesthetic theory is less a systematic account and more an assembly of axioms, which focus on the relation between subject and representation constructed as a mirroring movement of integration and separation of man and an other, I conclude this analysis of Moritz's aesthetics by looking at two short essays that in an extremely condensed manner recapitulate the concept of Bildung and sublimation traced thus far. The first essay develops the anthropological dimensions of his notion of suture by exploring the ideal of man's integration into the order of sense and the senses. The second essay attends to the aesthetic object as the site where the strategic deployment of horror (i.e., the sublime) becomes a means of sublimation.

The first essay, entitled "Zufälligkeit und Bildung—Vom Isoliren, in Rücksicht auf die schönen Künste überhaupt" (Chance and Bildung—About isolating, with regard to the fine arts in general), consists of two parts. The first part derives the human faculty of shaping external objects from the anthropological given of man's distinction from his environment. Like Herder's theory of language, it celebrates man's capacity to isolate himself from his environment. Man's exceptionally high degree of internal organization constitutes him as an autonomous entity and distinguishes him from whatever surrounds him. Man's separation from his environment is, however, not established by an external and opaque boundary between the two, but rather by the smooth and transparent human skin, which displays the perfection and harmony of his internal organization toward the outside. Whereas the thick bark of the tree and the fur of the animal hide their internal structure, the human skin lets the organization of the body shine through. And since man is naturally distinct from his environment, he can reproduce his humanity in the activity of isolating.

To isolate, to select out of the mass, this is the eternal occupation of man; as a conqueror, he might draw the boundaries of his territory around oceans and countries—or he might bring forth the inner perfection of a shape from a block of marble.

All the delight of poetry rests on this isolation, this selection from the whole, and in the fact that whatever has been isolated is given a point of gravity of its own, by which it can reconstitute itself as a totality.

Through this isolation the poverty of a shepherd's existence becomes delightful and poetic—since it is thought not within an oppressive relation to a state, but existing in and for itself.

Even the horrible, as soon as it is no longer related to us—as soon as it no longer horrifies us—becomes beautiful in itself, and we look at it with pleasure. (p. 116)

First there is the anthropological fact of man's isolation from his environment, already inscribed on his skin; then there is man's relation to his environment in terms of the isolating activity, which can either be expansive and destructive (the conqueror) or self-reflective (the sculptor). In such cases, the function of art consists in channeling and containing man's productive activity. Furthermore, art can remind man of his autonomy by isolating oppressive circumstances and turning them into an aesthetic spectacle. And finally, art has the ability to protect man from the powers of horror through an apotropaic gesture. Beauty is the ideal representation of the structural relation between man and his environment. Thus the second half of this essay is a page-long description of the beauty of the Greek vase (p. 117). What makes a Greek vase so beautiful is its rim. This rim is not just an opening, not just a mere hole: it is a very particular separation of the object from its environment; for as a containing frame (*Einfassung*), it integrates this object into its surroundings even as it asserts its autonomy.

The second essay is entitled "Minerva." Moritz describes the representation of this mythological figure as emblematic of "poetic representation." Within his aesthetics this figure comes to assume a status similar to that Herder attributes to Greek sculpture: it embodies an ideal "interface," an ideal manner of how man is integrated into the order of representation, the best possible structuration of man's antagonistic and ambiguous drives and thereby a model of sublimation. Mars, the Roman god, is merely the personification of war, but Minerva, the patron goddess of the most educated city, contains and harmoniously balances all antagonistic drives. She is a woman, but not subject to any effeminate tendencies.

> *Minerva* is absolutely *cold* and not tender.—
> This *deterring coldness* is the main character of *Minerva's* features.—
> There is the *petrifying* head of *Medusa* on her chest;
> There is the somber *night bird*, hovering over her head;
> There is the cold reflecting wisdom, which never listens to the voice of passion.
> She was not born of a mother, but emerged from Jupiter's head in full armor, with a breast as cold as the steel that covers it.
> This *coldness* makes her capable of cruel destruction, and of the laborious work of weaving, and of the invention of all peaceful arts.— (p. 118)

Minerva is the ultimate representation of the ideal of Bildung, of a particular sublimation and productivity: not a man born from the orifice of a woman, but a woman born from the head of a man. Minerva represents male productivity as parthenogenesis and omnipotent thought. Just as her birth severs her from the chain of human reproduction and mortality, the icon on her chest repeats and wards off the threat of sexuality. The breast, the seat of passions, is covered by cold armor bearing the image of Medusa's head—the ultimate sight of horror, of decapitation/castration. This armor distinguishes her from the other gods; it protects her from the sheer destructivity of a Mars as well as from the libidinal expenditure that even the virgin goddess Diana is not completely free from. It ensures her supreme wisdom, the cold rationality needed to channel and contain the libidinal drives in war and peace, destruction, and formation. This superwoman is as far from an ideal object of love as she is from an idealization of female power; rather, she comes to represent the ideal of a secondary male narcissism, the ideal of masculine self-cultivation, discipline, and autonomy. And indeed, the fixation of male narcissism on amazon-like female figures becomes an important strain in German classicism: Dorothea, Therese, Nathalie, Elisabeth, Isabeau, and the Jungfrau von Orleans are only a few of those great *Frauengestalten*. (This theme is pursued further in the final chapter on classical tragedy and the bildungsroman.)

Before turning to Schiller's *Letters on the Aesthetic Education of Man*, let me contextualize some of the implications of Bildung and aesthetic autonomy as they emerge from Herder's and Moritz's aesthetics. Despite the claims of these theories of Bildung to locate the aesthetic in an autonomous sphere, it was at this time that Bildung found its place within the state. By the end of the eighteenth century, after the pedagogical reforms and experiments of people like Johann Basedow and Joachim Campe (in which Moritz was involved for some time and in whose spirit he wrote a primer and a handbook on logic for children), the state instituted compulsory school attendance and assumed control over the training of the teachers. Finally, by 1810 a general state exam in the humanities, not only for Gymnasium teachers but also for all higher civil servants, was instituted in order to ensure a common level of Bildung among this social class. To put it clearly: the ideal of Bildung, coupled to the notion of art as an autonomous, fundamentally human, supra-historical, and supra-political engagement in cultural values, is not at all a compensatory or utopian project vis-à-vis the social and political changes of that period; rather, it participated in exactly those transformations in subject formation and the reorganization of discursive fields. The theoretical program of humanizing the biped accompanied practical curricular reforms, such as the displacement of traditional training in rhetoric by a canon of classical (including contemporary) authors who were to be read and experienced within the then-emerging hermeneutic paradigms. Furthermore, Moritz could be considered the father of psychology. As the editor of the *Magazin für Erfahrungsseelenkunde*, the journal Γνωθι Σαυτον [know thyself] ("The magazine for the experiential science of the human soul"), he and his friends collected other people's, criminals', and their own "case" histories, in order to explore the spectrum of normalcy and deviation in the development of the individual's psyche. The health of an individual psyche is determined by its degree of wholeness. Yet, as Moritz's other writings suggest, this psychological norm of the individual's wholeness and autonomy is never given a priori but always the result of the aesthetic negotiation of the individual's relation to representations. Although, however, both Herder and Moritz conceive of the individual's autonomy in opposition to the coercive effects of education and an alienating state apparatus, only in Schiller's *Letters on the Aesthetic Education of Man* do these issues receive primary attention.

The Aesthetic Education of Mankind

In 1795 Schiller began to publish in the *Horen*, his and Goethe's newly founded journal, the series of letters *Über die ästhetische Erziehung des Menschen*. Schiller opens his epistolary treatise with the motto "Si c'est la raison, qui fait l'homme, c'est le sentiment qui le conduit." With this quotation from *Julie* he draws attention to the guiding problem of his essay: How can reason and sentiment be brought into harmony in such a way that man is motivated to act in accord with the laws of reason and morality? Through the reference to Rousseau's novel, Schiller immediately points out that it is not sufficient to be rational and enlightened, to know the good. Man's affective structure has to make him want the good.

For Schiller there is no question as to what reason and the law are. In his first letter he asserts that Kant's categorical imperative may have aroused some debate among professional philosophers, but common understanding can only confirm Kantian ethics. The reason that Kant's second critique remains a philosophical postulate and has not yet become a fact of "the moral instinct" lies in the technical, abstract form of the philosophical system.

But it is just this technical formulation, which reveals [literally, renders visible] the truth to our understanding, that conceals it once again from our feeling; for unfortunately the understanding must first destroy the objects of the inner sense before it can appropriate them. Like the chemist, the philosopher finds combination only through dissolution, and the work of spontaneous Nature only through the torture of Art. In order to seize the fleeting appearance he must bind it in the fetters of rule, dissect its fair body into abstract notions, and preserve its living spirit in a sorry skeleton of words. Is it any wonder if *natural feeling does not recognize itself in such a likeness*, and if truth appears in the analyst's report as a paradox? (Letter 1, pp. 571, 24; my italics)

Schiller shares the fundamental assumptions of Rationalism that the progress of knowledge (progress in disclosing the philosophical truth of man's ethical potential) can be achieved only through rigorous analysis, which means at the cost of perceptual immediacy. Furthermore, the moral law that has lost its persuasive accessibility and appeal is not some arbitrary collection of rules of civil conduct, but the fundamental truth about human nature and freedom elaborated in *The Critique of Practical Reason*. The violent image of the shackled, tortured, and dismembered beautiful body turned into a bare skeleton refers to the living individual human being rigorously analyzed by Kant. The limits of philosophical inquiry are such that, by producing a truthful representation of human ethical potential, it renders that ethical truth inaccessible to the sentiments and sensations of the individual. It becomes impossible for man to recognize himself as in a mirror. The whole project of the "aesthetic education of man," or of Bildung, which Schiller develops in this text, consists in outlining the possibility of how this seeming misrepresentation of man can be remedied, how the skeleton can be turned into a beautiful mirror image with which man will want to identify.[30]

With this first letter Schiller situates his treatise on aesthetics in the context of a pressing, contemporary crisis. This crisis is formulated from two perspectives: man's alienation from his own image and the Reign of Terror, the political chaos resulting from man's failed attempt to free himself from oppression and alienation. As opposed to Moritz and Herder, Schiller constructs his aesthetic theory in the context of a concern with historical progress and man's ability to intervene in his own history. The "aesthetic education" has to negotiate the laws of historical progress with due regard for man's freedom to shape his history. If that is to be made possible, the relentless forward progression of history has to be brought to a halt, a space has to be opened, from which man can bring history and human freedom into accord with each other. Schiller then develops a notion of the aesthetic as exactly this "free space" and "potential turning point in time" that allows man to seize control over his destiny.[31]

According to Schiller, the French Revolution failed because it merely abolished the existing order and thus led to a relapse into a primitive state of disorganization and chaos. But even far-reaching political changes that would indeed establish an ideal state in accord with man's ethical potential would still fail. For this state would necessarily have to be perceived by the individual as totalitarian. Only the individual who has undergone a process of sublimation will no longer perceive the ideal moral state as an oppressive agency: "But two different ways can be thought of, in which Man in time can be made to coincide with Man in idea, and consequently as many in which the State can affirm itself in individuals: either by the pure man suppressing the empirical—the State abrogating the individual—or by becoming State—temporal Man being raised to the dignity of ideal Man" (Letter 4, pp. 577, *31–32*). In this formulation of an alternative, Schiller is concerned neither with the nature of the ideal State nor with its practical, political implementation. Rather, the issue is how the individual *becomes* the state. The following passage reveals the mechanism that, in Schiller's view, would bring about such a transformation. The mechanism operates on the level of representation and psychological identification.

Because the State serves as a representative of pure and objective humanity in the breast of its citizens, it will have to maintain towards those citizens the same relationship in which they stand to each other [or to themselves], and it can respect their subjective humanity only in such degree as this is exalted to objectivity. If the inner man is at one with himself, he will preserve his idiosyncrasy even in the widest universality of his conduct, and the State will be simply the interpreter of his fine [literally: beautiful] instinct, the clearer expression of his inner legislation. (Letter 4, pp. 578, *33*)

Invoking the ideal republican state that represents each individual citizen, Schiller postulates that the state should become that representation of man that man has of himself. Consequently, as long as man sees himself merely as a physical being, driven by need and self-interest, the state must be one of force and repression. Only when man identifies himself with his ego ideal will the moral state not be totalitarian but rather truly reflect the image individual man has of himself.

In both the opening passage on Kant and in these passages about the individual versus the state, the issue of the contemporary crisis and its potential solution is clearly formulated as one of representation rather than one of political criticism and practice. Any potential for reform must be sought in the aesthetic realm, in the relation between subjectivity and representations. In this basic model, Schiller stated the aim of civilization and the telos of mankind's development: the social order is to be based on man's ideal, and each individual man should identify with this ideal. The contemporary situation seems to be far away from this goal, however; contemporary civilization is not constructed as an ideal state, nor does it uphold the ideal image of man.

Somewhere in the history of civilization man's ideal image has been lost. What occasioned this loss? How could man's ideal image be retrieved? In order to answer these questions, Schiller turns to a more detailed analysis of contemporary society, which he opposes to Greek antiquity. In the contemporary situation men are fragmented, divided into a lower class directed by raw drives and a higher class marked by decadence and egotism (see Letter 5, p. 580). No single contemporary man combines in himself the totality of the species as both a sensual and a rational being. Whereas any individual Greek could have represented the whole species, no modern man can stand for the whole of humanity. Modern individuality is based on the fragmentation of the human potential (see Letter 6, p. 582).

What was it that fragmented man and thereby tore apart humanity's internal bond? "It was culture itself that inflicted this wound upon modern humanity" (Letter 6, pp. 583, 39). It was the necessary division of labor, which in the service of the progress of knowledge separated the disciplines, the professions, and the classes and turned the state into an abstract, mechanical clockwork instead of a complex organic whole. This lifeless mechanism tore apart church and state, laws and customs, pleasure and work, means and end, effort and reward. Not only is the individual restricted to the exercise of a very specifically defined type of work, but, in addition, the state supervises and prescribes each individual action. Furthermore, the state jealously controls the individual even beyond his "office," so that he will not define himself in any terms other than those the state has prescribed for its "servant."

But even the meagre fragmentary association, which still links the individual members to the whole, does not depend on forms which present themselves spontaneously (for how could such an artificial and clandestine piece of mechanism be entrusted to their freedom?), but is assigned to them with scrupulous exactness by a formula in which their free intelligence is restricted. The lifeless letter takes the place of the living understanding, and a practised memory is a surer guide than genius and feeling.

If the community makes function ["office" or "department" would be more precise for *Amt*] the measure of a man, when it respects in one of its citizens only memory, in another a tabulating intellect, in a third only mechanical skill; if, indifferent to character, it here lays stress upon knowledge alone, and there pardons the profoundest darkness of the intellect so long as it co-exists with a spirit of order and a law-abiding demeanour—if at the same time it requires these special aptitudes to be exercised with an intensity proportionate to the loss of extension which it permits in the individuals concerned—can we then wonder that the remaining aptitudes of the mind become neglected in order to bestow every attention upon the only one which brings in honour and profit? We know indeed that a vigorous genius does not make the boundaries of its concern the boundaries of its activity; but mediocre talent consumes the whole meagre sum of its strength in the concern that falls to its lot, and it must be no ordinary head that has something left over for private pursuits without prejudice to its vocation. Moreover, it is seldom a good recommendation with the State when powers exceed commissions, or when the higher spiritual requirements of the man of genius furnish a rival to his office. So jealous is the state for the exclusive possession of its servants, that it will more easily bring itself (and who can blame it?) to share its man with a Cytherean than with a Uranian Venus.   (Letter 6, pp. 584–85, *40–41*)

It has become a commonplace to interpret Letter 6 in the perspective of the young Marx as a very early critique of man's alienation in the division of labor. I suggest, however, that although Schiller does allude to the division between manual and mental labor, he is not concerned with relations of production or any other aspect that would easily lend itself to a Marxist critique. Laborers are of little importance to Schiller, and tradespeople are mentioned only in passing. To me it seems better to read these passages as a thorough criticism of the alienation of the middle-class professional, the academic and the bureaucrat, the civil servant of the absolutist state (*Beamte* or *Staatsdiener*). For who else is measured by his "office," restricted to "memory," a "tabulating intellect," divided between "intuitive" and "speculative" understanding, reduced to an "empty subtlety" or "pedantry," and controlled by the "dead letter" of a mere "formula"? (See pp. 583–86.)

If indeed Schiller is concerned mainly with the condition and conditioning of the civil servant, this has far-reaching consequences for the political and social reforms implied in the *Letters on Aesthetic Education*. Schiller's admirer Wilhelm von Humboldt subscribed totally to classicist aesthetics and not only tried to develop a detailed theory of Bildung within its parameters but also later, as director of the Section for Culture and Education of the Prussian Ministry of the Interior, became the architect of the German educational system and invented the *Staatsexamen* for civil servants and the professions, thereby institutionalizing the training of teachers and pedagogues. Humboldt, in other words, mapped out one of the most decisive of the ideological state apparatuses that determined the socialization of middle-class male German subjects throughout the nineteenth and even into the twentieth century. At the time of Schiller's *Aesthetic Education*, Humboldt had just written his famous essay on the necessary limits of the state (*Ideen zu einem Versuch, die Grenzen der Wirksamkeit des Staats zu bestimmen*; 1792), advocating what was later accusingly labeled a mere "Nachtwächterstaat" (a nightwatchman state; a formula that has been attributed to Lasalle), a state that remains in the background and restricts its use of police force and interference in the life of the citizens to a minimum. But his demand that the repressive state apparatuses be restrained is only too compatible with the widening sphere of influence of ideological state apparatuses. Similarly, to admit that Schiller's critique of alienation and contemporary society results not in revolutionary demands but in postulating an autonomous aesthetic realm for the Bildung of the individual subject does not mean that he abandoned the political sphere altogether in order to retreat to the "autonomous institution of bourgeois art." Rather, this postulated autonomous sphere became an integral part of modern society in the disciplining and formation of its male, middle-class subjects.[32] For these reasons, I emphasize that Schiller's famous critique is concerned much less with the division of labor in general and much more with the effects of a modern state bureaucracy.

According to Schiller, this fragmentation of man's potential in the mechanized state apparatus results in the state's overly abstract representation of its subjects and vice versa. The individual has no affective relation to the state but conceives of it in terms of "secondhand" representations; similarly the state cannot know its subjects as individuals but merely in terms of the roles by which the individuals are classified. Therefore the individual has little respect for the law and cannot conceive of common interests.[33] As deplorable as this situation might be, Schiller affirms it as a necessary stage in the progress of mankind. It is the price mankind has to pay for the development of rational discourse. Without analysis, fragmentation, and division of labor, the individual human faculties would not have achieved their current degree of perfection (Letter 6, p. 587). The time for reform has come, however, and the way to improvement lies in the unification of humanity, which can happen only through the unification of the fragmented individual (Letter 7, p. 589). After all these details about the fragmentation of modern man, Schiller appeals to man's courage to realize the human potential that philosophy has laid open to reason. Prejudice and false opinions have been overcome; now is the time to struggle against the "weakness of the heart" and "sluggish sensuality" (Letter 8, pp. 591–92).

What interests me about Schiller's civilization narratives is that they entail both a story of loss and one of gain, one of decline and one of progress. Thus Schiller begins his critique of modern society by contrasting fragmented contemporary society with the Greek polis. Schiller does not, however, attempt to propose a political solution, which would draw its models for reform from the ideals of Greek democracy. Instead, he shifts his attention to that ideal of humanity we can still find in Greek art. This shift constitutes the crucial turning point in the *Aesthetic Education.*

Schiller concedes that the monuments of man's ideal image found in Greek art are products of an epoch when Greek civilization was already declining (Letter 10, p. 599). By pointing out this disjunction between political history and artistic representation, Schiller opposes a model of history as man's subjection to chronological sequence to an entelechial model of man's ideal potential as provided by artistic representation. Whereas in his previous depictions of the contemporary crisis it is mediation and representation that bring about loss, distortion, and alienation, suddenly it is exactly in artistic representation that man finds his wholeness and ideal image. This move entails the revision of representation as mimesis: since Greek art does not reflect a historical status quo nor did it provide the Greeks with moral ideals that would have guided their conduct, art's function must be sought elsewhere. In fact, it is to be found exactly in its transcendence of the particular historical context of its production.

In his tenth letter Schiller takes issue with all those moralists who, in the wake of Plato, want to ban poets and artists from the republic, who fear art's attention to mere representations and the realm of appearance. Schiller does not counter those arguments by claiming that art communicates any specific, morally useful contents. Indeed, he agrees with the opponents of art that the truly aesthetic realm is not concerned with content or reality. However, he attempts to reject the arguments against the supposedly pernicious influence of art in an altogether fundamental way: "Die Schönheit müßte sich als eine notwendige Bedingung der Menschheit aufzeigen lassen" ("Beauty must be exhibited as a necessary condition of humanity"; pp. 600, 60). This transcendental move comprehends the basic tenets of idealist aesthetics, already underlying Moritz's argument: (1) art has a social function; (2) art must be restricted to an autonomous aesthetic realm of mere appearance; and (3) the attention to mere appearance is *the* distinguishing feature of Man. The reconciliation of the seemingly contradictory first and second statements depends on the explanation of the third statement.

Schiller unfolds his basic anthropological assumptions in order to develop a notion of the aesthetic as grounded in the organization of man's psychological forces. First, it is quite remarkable that Schiller bases his theory about the constitution of human subjectivity on an internal split. Man is a priori not unified, but split between his changing being in time—a series of phases determined by his external perceptions and internal sensations (*Zustand*)—and his permanent self (*Person*). On the one hand, there is a permanent structure; on the other hand, the changing attention to concrete objects. The Ego is able to represent itself to itself only asymptotically; that is, it can construct and assert its unity, and thereby realize itself, through the series of its changing representations: "Nur durch die Folge seiner Vorstellungen wird das beharrliche Ich sich selbst zur Erscheinung" ("Only through the succession of its perceptions does the persisting ego come to appear to itself"; Letter 11, pp. 602; 62).

Along this divide of human subjectivity, this fundamental split, Schiller then postulates two antagonistic drives. The living human being is always determined by external sensations, a drive to satisfy its momentary desires; it realizes its drives in specific cases limited by concrete matter and temporal change. This human tendency Schiller calls the sensual drive (*sinnlicher Trieb*). The opposing human drive Schiller derives from man's rational faculties, his drive to preserve the permanence of the *Person* despite temporal changes, to transcend the immediacy of the momentary situation, changing matter, and subjective demands; this drive Schiller calls the drive to form (*Formtrieb*) (Letter 12, pp. 604–6). The drive to form operates in the interest of the ego's stability and boundaries by disinvesting external objects of their libidinal attraction, abstracting them from their concrete qualities, and turning them into formal entities. These two fundamental human drives are utterly antagonistic, and it would be wrong to try to annihilate one of them or to subordinate one to the other. For if man were prematurely to restrict all his passive sensibility and feeling to his reason, he would remain an empty, undetermined, abstract, formal entity. But if he were to give up his active form-giving ability in favor of his passive ties to matter and change, he would likewise lose his human potential. Then he would become mere content without form, which is to say content-less, since without structure and form it does not make sense to speak of content (Letter 13, p. 609).

Since the antagonism of these two forces cannot be resolved by anni-hilating one of them without immediately annihilating the other, a har-monious resolution can come about only through a counterbalancing third drive, a drive that Schiller calls the *Spieltrieb* (the drive to play). The aim of the sinnliche Trieb Schiller calls life (*Leben*): material being and im-mediate presence to the senses. The aim of the Formtrieb he calls *Gestalt*, a notion that comprises all formal qualities of things and all their relations to the faculties of thinking: the abstract representation of a structural rela-tion. The Spieltrieb aims at the harmonious balance of the antagonistic drives, at the *lebende Gestalt*, or beauty in the most general sense.

What does Schiller mean by beauty as the aim of a drive? He explains this concept by citing the figure of Juno Lodovisi as an example of how the Greeks represented this drive.

It is neither charm, nor is it dignity, that speaks to us from the superb counte-nance of a Juno Ludovisi; it is neither of them, because it is both at once. While the womanly god demands our veneration, the godlike woman kindles our love; but while we allow ourselves to melt in the celestial loveliness, the celestial self-sufficiency holds us back in awe. The whole form reposes and dwells within itself, a completely closed creation, and—as though it were beyond space—without yielding, without resistance; there is no force to contend with force, no unpro-tected part where temporality might break in. Irresistibly seized and attracted by the one quality, and held at a distance by the other, we find ourselves at the same time in the condition of utter rest and extreme movement, and the result is that wonderful emotion for which reason has no conception and language no name. (Letter 15, pp. 618, *81*)

Juno Ludovisi represents to man a very particular object of love, not one with which he would seek a unity or fusion, thereby losing him-self, but one that holds him at a distance because of its unapproachable self-sufficiency. And through this particular dynamic of attraction and re-pulsion, this figure holds its viewer in an equally secure position of self-sufficiency, of rest and movement; in the end it represents man to himself in all his human potential and harmoniously negotiates his antagonistic drives. Through the particular tension between fear and love, a space between the object and the subject is opened up. The beauty of the aesthetic object provides man with that gap or void that allows both the sinnlicher Trieb and the Formtrieb to coexist: he can simultaneously attend to all the concrete details of the object and to the structural relations of an organized totality. Since neither of the two drives has to cancel the other, man can overcome his internal split and constitute his unity. The distance between object and subject provides a screen onto which he can project himself, on which he will find the image of his full human potential. If the figure of Juno Ludovisi represents beauty as the object of the Spieltrieb, we can conclude that the Spieltrieb aims at an ideal representation of man as a unified being, as a sensual being, and as an organized totality.

This emblematic representation of beauty in the figure of Juno Ludovisi is reminiscent of the creative narcissism of Herder's Pygmalion. It also celebrates a state of contemplative reflection as that apprehension of a total object of love that gives man to himself in the totality of his faculties. It likewise harkens back to Moritz's admiration for Minerva as the most perfect work of art; indeed Schiller also made the transition to the realm of beauty by introducing Pallas Athene (see Letter 8, pp. 591–92).

Although the example of Juno Ludovisi establishes the basic parameters of aesthetic contemplation, Schiller must still explain how "beauty is a necessary condition of humanity." He has to show that every human being has the rudimentary capacity to experience beauty, as well as how this experience of beauty, in which man is capable of conceiving of himself as a unified and free being, was lost in the course of history. Schiller's argument describing the "aesthetic stage" (*ästhetischer Zustand*) reformulates his theory of human drives and the split self in terms of the origin of human language. Schiller does not make this history explicit, and indeed he is not interested in the emergence and development of verbal language. He is, however, concerned with man's access to representations, his activity of representing the objects of the world and himself to himself. And indeed, with Letters 19 to 26, in which Schiller develops the "aesthetic stage" in great detail, the parallels with Herder's notion of the constitution of the human subject in language become apparent.

Schiller gives two accounts of the aesthetic stage: first in terms of structure with regard to the human faculties, drives, and the origin of self-consciousness; then in terms of a developmental history, or the history of freedom. In the beginning, man is merely passive and determinable, an empty infinity, to be filled with sensory perceptions. However, he can

make sense of external stimuli only through an act of exclusion and negation, coterminous with an act of positing. In this very act of selecting and
giving figure to a specific group of sensory impressions, man's *Person* or
self-consciousness emerges (Letter 19). In this thetic act, in self-consciously
positing a single signifier (Herder's mark of the soul), man experiences
the permanence of the self and its independence from the sensual realm.
Likewise, at the moment man enters the realm of representations, he
is able to represent himself to himself, but he is subject to the rules of
rational discourse. To the extent that he becomes subject to the order of
representation, as a subject in language, he is reduced to a mere signifier; as such he loses the concreteness of his living being. At the moment
man enters language, he is split between sensation (*Empfindung*) and self-
consciousness (*Selbstbewußtsein*). Along with his split self, however, his
antagonistic drives come into existence; neither drive can assert a coercive
necessity over man, and this split opens a space for his will and freedom
(Letter 19, p. 631).

So far Schiller's account of the origins of language recapitulates his
basic anthropological model. Yet the manner in which he integrates this
structural account into a historical narrative reveals that Schiller's notion
of the individual's autonomy is both an effect of and an imperative for
narrativization. In other words, overcoming man's internal split requires
a narrative effort both in Schiller's philosophy of history (cast in terms of
onto- and phylogenetic parallelism) and in each individual subject's search
for autonomy.

The story of human freedom and the history of man's alienation derive
from the fact that man is first a sensual being, then a rational being—this
is the plot of history. The degree of human freedom is determined by how
the transition from the sensual realm to the rational realm is negotiated.
If man progresses linearly from the sensual to the rational stage, he cannot
be free, for he is only replacing his passive determinability by an active
determination dictated by his rational faculties, which make judgments
based on only the material realm as given to them through the senses.
He is able to operate within rational discourse in the same way that a
strategist handles a set of rules. But he will never experience himself as a
total being, who not only operates within a set of seemingly external rules
but also sees itself as a producer of representations in which it can reflect
itself. This limited kind of rational man is unable to conceive of himself
beyond his immediate self-interest and therefore acts merely instrumen-
tally, unable to generalize his self in terms of universal human potential.

He mistakenly rationalizes moral law as a merely arbitrary and oppressive force, restricting his sensual impulses. Such a man would tell himself the story as dictated by chronological sequence.

Only if man retraces the transition from the sensual to the rational stage and persists in the stage of determinability can he gain an altogether different grasp of his own self as well as the law—and this is the imperative to retell the story of history: we must not conceive of the history of civilization or socialization merely as our subjection to the external laws of rational discourse. Instead, we must be brought to retell this history as a story of how our socialization is ultimately in perfect congruence with the unfolding of human potential and thereby constitutes us as free agents. Schiller supplements Kant's categorical imperative with a narrational imperative. It is only through the experience of art, through the act of aesthetic contemplation, that man can obtain experiential access to the "hidden truth" of his own history. It is only in aesthetic contemplation that he can delay the transition from a passive determinability to an active determination and thus, so to speak, relive his entry into the realm of language and representations. Instead of an immediate step forward toward abstraction and instrumental action, he can maintain the state of receptivity and enter the realm of representations only up to the point at which he can contemplate both himself and external objects as autonomous wholes. In the contemplation of a work of art, man can hold on to the moment of positing without an immediate next step toward rational abstraction and instrumental action.

So long as Man in his first physical condition accepts the world of sense merely passively, merely perceives, he is still completely identified with it, and just because he himself is simply world, there is no world yet for him. Not until he sets it outside himself or contemplates it, in his aesthetic status, does his personality become distinct from it, and a world appears to him because he has ceased to identify himself with it.

Contemplation (reflection) is Man's first free relation to the universe which surrounds him. *If desire directly apprehends its object, contemplation thrusts its object into the distance, thereby turning it into its true and inalienable possession and thus securing it from passion.* (Letter 25, pp. 651, *119–20*; my italics)

It is in the state of contemplation that man attends to the production of representations. Schiller conceives of man's representing activity as the structured externalization of a chaotic mass of sensory data that has invaded him. Man separates himself from his immediate environment in this thetic act and becomes for himself a subject at the same time that the world becomes for him an object. Since he produces this object, it no longer has an immediate power over him. If he consciously attends to this aesthetic stage, he can contemplate himself in this representation as both a sensual and a rational being. The aesthetic realm provides him with a mirror of the totality of his human potential and freedom, subject neither to his libidinal investments and the onslaught of random matter nor to the dictates of abstract reason. Aesthetic contemplation sustains him in a balance between the permanence of a structure and the concreteness of the sensual appearance.

Since the power of the aesthetic object emerges only if man attends to the representation as a representation, it is not necessary to define the "content" of aesthetic representations; only their "form" counts. It is absolutely necessary, however, that the aesthetic realm be free of any ties to reality or utility; otherwise, the aesthetic representation would not remain a pure representation. With this argument we have the rationale for aesthetic autonomy. Aesthetic contemplation per se does not make man morally better; however, it provides a possibility of conceiving his human potential as a free and moral being, who can freely choose to act according to the universal law, who recognizes himself in this law, and who therefore no longer perceives it as an arbitrary restrictive force over his sensual impulses.

At this point it is possible to summarize the basic structure and process of Bildung implied in Schiller's aesthetics. Aesthetic education revises and reverses the oppressive effects of education (of subduing the sensual drives to a law perceived to be external and arbitrary) by recasting the formative stage as a narcissist scenario. Aesthetic contemplation allows the subject to conceive of himself as a representative of universal man, the fundamental move required in Kantian ethics. Through the act of aesthetic contemplation, man can identify himself with an ideal ego (a blissful state of independence) that is identical to the ego-ideal (the permanent self, required by rational discourse) and with the state (the order of representation based on Kantian ethics). In a long footnote to Letter 13, Schiller explains his notion of Bildung.

How can we be fair, kindly and humane towards others, let our maxims be as praiseworthy as they may, if we lack the capacity to make strange natures genuinely and truly a part of ourselves, appropriate strange situations, make strange feelings our own: But this capacity, both in the education that we receive and in that which we give ourselves, is stifled in proportion as we seek to break the power of desires and to strengthen the character by means of principles. Because it is difficult to remain true to our principles amidst all the ardour of the feelings, we adopt the more comfortable expedient of making the character more secure by blunting the feelings, for it is certainly infinitely easier to keep calm in the face of an unarmed adversary than *to master a spirited and active foe*. In this operation, then, consists for the most part what we call *the forming of a human being* [Schiller's italics]; and that *in the best sense of the term, as signifying the cultivation of the inner, not merely the outward, man. A man so formed will indeed be secured against being crude Nature, and from appearing as such; but he will at the same time be armed by his principles against every sensation of nature, and humanity from without will be as little accessible to him as humanity from within.* (pp. 610, 71; my italics except as noted)

Man must not be disciplined through moral principles, which attempt to restrict his drives. Rather, the boundaries of his ego have to be stabilized to the extent that he is secure from a disintegration from within as well as from without. The aesthetic contribution to this education lies in allowing man to experience himself in the act of contemplation, an experience that reinforces his primary narcissism and initiates his secondary narcissism.

Thirty years earlier, in the aesthetic and pedagogical theories of sensibility, educational aims were defined with a different emphasis and the arguments took another direction: the realm of illusion was to facilitate a relation to an other in terms of similarity, empathy, and pity. Audience or reader entered the realm of illusion in a decarnalized, hallucinatory, and identificatory way. The status of illusion was one of a quasi reality. The affective relation to an other was molded into the gentle affects of family love, into a simultaneously eroticized and repressed desire. By contrast, classicist aesthetics and its notion of Bildung attend primarily to the stabilization of the subject in terms of the subject's representation of himself. Instead of a valorization of aesthetic illusion, we find a valorization of aesthetic distance. The aesthetic realm is not a quasi reality. In fact, as opposed to the order of reality, it is both mere appearance (representation) and truth (the representation of Humanity's self-reflective potential). The reader's or audience's look of pity is replaced by the controlling gaze.

It is Nature herself that raises Man from reality to appearance, by endowing him with two senses which lead him through appearance alone to a knowledge of the actual. In eye and ear the importunacy of matter is already rolled away from the senses, and the object with which we have direct contact in our animal senses is withdrawn from us. What we see through the eye is different from what we perceive; for the intellect leaps out over the light to the objects. The object of touch is a force which we endure; the object of the eye and the ear is a form which we create. So long as Man is still a savage he enjoys merely with the senses of feeling, to which the senses of appearance are at this stage only subservient. Either he does not rise to seeing, or he is at any rate not satisfied with it. As soon as he begins to enjoy with the eye, and seeing acquires an absolute value for him, he is already aesthetically free also, and the play impulse has developed. (pp. 657, *126*)

With this statement we have come full circle back to Herder: What constitutes man in his Humanity and Freedom is the difference between perception and apperception in the self-reflective act of contemplation, the act by which he produces the objects of the world and his own subjectivity through auditory or visual representations. These representations not only free man from his dependence on objects of the material world but also allow man to attend to himself as this "free" and self-sufficient being.

Each of the three authors considered in this chapter emphasizes and develops different aspects of man's contemplative or self-reflective constitution. Herder's essay on the origin of language marks the basic shift in paradigm from an epistemology of representation to a neo-humanist anthropology, which describes the realm of representations in terms of man's relation to himself. Out of this anthropological postulate, Herder develops a model for the education of the individual as well as for the history of civilization. Within this model, external force to socialize the individual or external laws to impose social order seem equally unnecessary. Tradition maintains itself through its appeal to man's "childhood," as the originary state of independence and protection from external and internal stimuli, a state coexistent with entry into the realm of representations and culture.

In Herder's writings on sculpture and Moritz's essays on aesthetics, the realm of art becomes the order that reactivates man's primarily narcissistic constitution. For Herder the ideal aesthetic object, Greek sculpture, produces an identification with man's ideal image of himself, an immortal, beautiful body. Moritz attributes to the aesthetic object a privileged status within the order of representations in terms of its intransitivity or autonomy. Moritz's theory of how the autonomous aesthetic object reorganizes man's faculties is particularly revealing of the extent to which the sublimation script of Bildung is gendered: true artistic productivity is conceived as male, but whenever the work of art is to master misery, mortality, and aggressiveness, we find the emblem of Medusa's head supporting art's apotropaic function.

Although Moritz introduced the concept of aesthetic autonomy as a necessary illusion, opposed to man's alienation from that other autonomously existing whole, the state, this concept is most explicitly developed in Schiller's *Letters on the Aesthetic Education of Man*. Schiller privileges the aesthetic as the order in which man's representation of himself can be reorganized and brought into congruence with his ideal image; this reorganization then allows man to identify himself with the ideal state, as yet another ideal representation of man. In Schiller's model of autonomy, narrative plays a crucial role. On a structural level, art transforms man's internal split into the locus of self-determination. Once man conceives of himself as no longer merely determined by representations but as the producer of meaning, the experience of heteronomy can be retold as the unfolding of his autonomy.

5

Classical Tragedy and Bildungsroman

The aesthetics of German Classicism allocate a central function in the organization of subjectivity to the "disinterested interest" of aesthetic contemplation. As opposed to an identificatory relation toward representations, crucial to the illusionist aesthetics of sensibility, classicist aesthetics both holds the object at a certain distance, which prevents the identification with an other, and produces an emphatic or enthusiastic identification with an ideal self. In terms of contemporary poetics, this means that theatricality and the spectacle are once again appreciated. In fact, neo-humanist "polis envy" seeks in the theater the place where an alienated modern subject can be reconciled with the invisible powers of the bureaucratic state machinery. Schiller's classical tragedy, *Maria Stuart*, develops this new theatricality in a paradigmatic manner.

The "narrational imperative" to mediate the blissful state of self-sufficiency of a mythical childhood or past for the subject's project of Bildung or self-realization is carried out by the new genre of the bildungsroman. Although Christoph Martin Wieland (1733–1813) belongs to the somewhat lesser known writers of this period and his novel *Agathon* is certainly not as widely read or as famous as Goethe's *Wilhelm Meister*, he nevertheless provides a particularly good example of this literary genre. Wieland's novel makes the wider-ranging cultural significance of the revisionary sublimation script of Bildung especially clear. Although the bildungsroman is a specifically literary genre, it nevertheless has powerful counterparts in everyday life genres, such as the narrativized curriculum vitae (*Lebenslauf*), which still constitutes not only a crucial selection criterion in application procedures but also a primary disciplinary model of self-fashioning for the educated middle class. And it is for this reason—and not solely because the bildungsroman came to be the dominant type of the novel in Germany—that the ways in which its poetics are gendered deserves particular attention.

Schiller's *Maria Stuart*: Medusa and Beautiful Soul

Schiller's *Maria Stuart* (1800) is an extremely carefully crafted artistic construct; indeed, many interpretations of the play have emphasized Schiller's attention to the play's composition, its stylization, and its symmetry.[1] Its symmetrical architecture creates a textbook example for the composition of a five-act classical tragedy. Thus Acts I and V focus on Maria, Acts II and IV on Elisabeth, and Act III on the encounter of the two queens. The characters of the two queens are symmetrically juxtaposed: in Act I Maria is depressed and discouraged, in Act V she returns triumphant; Elisabeth's initial self-assurance in Act II turns into desperation in Act IV. Both women embody fundamental opposites: Catholic versus Protestant, sensuality versus chastity. This opposition is played out in the most basic terms on the axes of appearance and truth and of weakness and strength. Thus Maria's jailor, Paulet, describes her at her first entry in the following terms: "Den Christus in der Hand,/die Hoffart in dem Herzen." ("Christ's image in her hand/Pride, and all worldly lusts within her heart"; I, 1, 142–43; *p.* 9). As the play progresses, however, it is Elisabeth who increasingly produces a false front, covering up for her true intentions and actions.

These formal qualities clearly distinguish this drama from the bourgeois tragedy and situate it in the context of classicist aesthetics: instead of a familiar, intimate setting, we are presented with public personae; the play's formal rhetoric, verse, and stylization produce an aesthetic distance that prevents an identificatory, emotional engagement by the audience. The foregrounding of the play's artistic features, part of the "disinterested interest" of aesthetic contemplation in German Classicism, has led many critics to speculate about its qualities as a spectacle in terms of religious symbolism and ritual. Thus it has been praised as "religiöses Festspiel" and analyzed in terms of its "theatricality."[2] Indeed, the play's qualities as a spectacle deserve detailed analysis. My reading shows how this play about the execution and transfiguration of Maria Stuart is actually a dramatization of the execution and transfiguration of sovereign power, how as a spectacle the play attempts to "make visible" those powers that can structure and anchor the order of representation. I also demonstrate that this spectacle does not operate like the old-style spectacle of tyrannical power, which is displayed through the sovereign's body in the public theater of royal pomp or through public torture and execution. What distinguishes Schiller's *Maria Stuart* from the old-style spectacle is that it is set in an altogether new situation, one in which the sovereign's absolute power has already vanished.

Thus, the two queens never appear in any scenes of public splendor. Mostly they are shown behind closed doors: Maria is incarcerated; Elisabeth is in her "office," surrounded by "advisors" and scribes. Although one might expect that the play would end with Maria's execution, there are five subsequent scenes all centered around the fate of two secretaries. Maria's scribe, Kurl, becomes insane from guilt for having falsely implicated Maria in a plot to assassinate Elisabeth. Elisabeth's scribe, Davison, is condemned to death. He becomes her scapegoat, for she cannot acknowledge the performative power of her signature on Maria's death sentence. And throughout the play the disinterested, cold voice of the *raison d'état*, Burleigh, argues for Maria's clandestine murder for the sake of England's and Elisabeth's safety, not for his own benefit as the old-style intriguing villain (the figure of the Machiavelli) would have argued. Indeed, the setting of the play can be described in words Schiller used to characterize the modern state: "The palace of kings is closed now; the courts of justice have withdrawn themselves from the gates of cities into the interior of the houses; writing has displaced the living word; the sensuous mass of the populus itself—if it does not rule as brute force—has become the state, an abstract term; the gods have returned to the bosom of man."[3] But how then is this situation to be remedied? What does the play qua spectacle have to offer to counter the effects of the abstract, disembodied state? Schiller does not return to the old-style public spectacle in which the scene of the execution itself becomes the spectacle of truth, power, and justice. We are not shown Maria's execution on stage but perceive it mediated through Leicester, who does not see the scene himself but reacts to hearing it. The focus of the spectacle is shifted from the scene of execution to the one preceding it: not a scene of torture and public confession in which the truth is produced through the body of the accused but a scene of the private confession of guilt, absolution, and communion. Schiller himself called this scene the "keystone" of the play.[4] Furthermore, the meaning of the execution is altogether changed, as compared to its traditional function as a public spectacle: for England, Maria's execution is not an act of revenge or retribution but the removal of a politically dangerous object. Not

Maria but Leicester is punished with the execution. For Maria the execution represents the renunciation of her "physical" existence, her sensuality, and her hopes of gaining freedom and being with Leicester—in brief: her sexuality. But before analyzing in further detail the possible redemptive function of these two scenes with regard to an alienated abstract state and the political danger of semantic and social destabilization, I first take a detour beginning with another figure who underwent a transformation, one that consists not of a reformation but of a conversion: Mortimer.

Since Mortimer is not a historical figure but was invented by Schiller, we can assume that this character is quite crucial for understanding the play.[5] Mortimer enters Maria's prison in his uncle Paulet's presence but totally ignores the beautiful queen and pays attention only to his uncle. This apparent rudeness establishes his credibility as Elisabeth's loyal subject and later enables him to see Maria alone. In their first private conversation, he immediately reveals himself as her ardent admirer, who has come from the French Cardinal Guise to free Maria. But before explaining to Maria her imminent fate—Elisabeth's plans to ground her rule in Maria's execution and the Catholic scheme for Maria's rescue—Mortimer narrates in broad detail the history of his conversion. Brought up a Protestant with a strict sense of duty, at the age of twenty he was driven by an ardent desire to leave England for Italy. He was carried along in the stream of pilgrims toward Rome and charmed by the power and magic of the fine arts and music. Exposed to Rome's luxurious display of religious art, music, jewelery, and pomp, he developed a hatred of the "disembodied word" of Protestantism, the "prison" of his own upbringing, which had deprived him of the sensual joys of life.

From Rome he went to Maria's uncle Guise, who became for him the paradigm of masculine power and strength and who sets forth for him the truth of his newly found belief.

> Er zeigte mir, daß grübelnde Vernunft
> Den Menschen ewig in die Irre leitet,
> Daß seine Augen sehen müssen, was
> Das Herz soll glauben, daß ein sichtbar Haupt
> Der Kirche nottut, daß der Geist der Wahrheit
> Geruht hat auf den Sitzungen der Väter.
>
> (He showed me how the glimmering light of reason
> Serves but to lead us to eternal error:
> That what the heart is called to believe
> The eye must see: that he who rules the church

Must needs be visible; and that the spirit
Of truth inspired the councils of the fathers.)

(I, 6, 477–82; *pp. 19–20*)

Mortimer's conversion to and through the senses (the magic charm and palpable splendor of Catholicism) is confirmed and anchored through Guise, who embodies a paternal principle for the young man. Mortimer joins the company of English exiles and Catholics. One day in the bishop's residence, he is struck by the sight of a woman's picture. The bishop tells him that this woman, Maria, is not only the most beautiful of all women but also the most miserable, a true martyr, who instead of being on the English throne is imprisoned by an illegitimate pretender. Upon receiving this knowledge and the news that his uncle Paulet is in charge of Maria, Mortimer decides to rescue her before she is decapitated. He is willing to risk his life for Maria and his own fame.

In the next scene in which Mortimer appears, he is introduced to Elisabeth as her loyal servant, who has come with intelligence from France. Elisabeth tries to recruit him for Maria's clandestine murder; he pretends to agree in order to gain time for her rescue. This private conversation with Elisabeth confirms Mortimer's view of his role vis-à-vis the two queens. He cannot serve this duplicitous queen, head of the abstract state he has learned to hate. Both as woman and as queen, Elisabeth has nothing to promise him. But Mortimer's motives with regard to Maria are not entirely selfless. He wants to free her in order to possess her (see II, 6, 1645–61).

In Mortimer's criticism of abstract, Protestant rule, we can hear an echo of Schiller's own critique of the rigorous moral state of pure law with its administrative apparatus and alienated civil servants articulated in the Letter 6 of the *Aesthetic Education of Man*. But there is a decisive difference: Mortimer's critique is not derived from "man's ideal image"; he is not led to Rome, to his conversion, and to Maria by a "beautiful instinct" or "a drive to play." Consequently Mortimer's conversion cannot be called an aesthetic education in Schiller's sense. Although Mortimer suddenly learns to love beauty, the arts, and the life of sensuality, his conversion to the aesthetic does not result in the formative stage of distanced aesthetic contemplation. He is not rendered calm and reflective by the object of his sensual attraction but rushes to satisfy his desire. When he returns to Maria to rescue her, he is driven by unmitigated hatred and love.

Ja glühend, wie sie hassen, lieb ich dich!
Sie wollen dich enthaupten, diesen Hals,

Den blendenweißen, mit dem Beil durchschneiden.
O weihe du dem Lebensgott der Freuden,
Was du dem Hasse blutig opfern mußt.
Mit diesen Reizen, die nicht dein mehr sind,
Beselige den glücklichen Geliebten.
Die schöne Locke, dieses seidne Haar,
Verfallen schon den finstern Todesmächten,
Gebrauchs, den Sklaven ewig zu umflechten.

(Yes, glowing as their hatred is my love;
They would behead thee, they would wound this neck,
So dazzling white, with the disgraceful axe!
Oh! offer to the living god of joy
What thou must sacrifice to bloody hate!
Inspire thy unhappy lover with those charms
Which are no more thine own. Those golden locks
Are forfeit to the dismal powers of death,
Oh! use them to entwine thy slave forever!)

(III, 6, 2554–63; *p. 81*)

And indeed, he assaults her and would have raped her were he not interrupted by the turmoil over the failed attempt on Elisabeth's life. Finally, after losing all hope of gaining Maria, he commits suicide. Mortimer's aesthetic education fails to the extent that it represents a mere relapse into what Schiller calls the "physical state," the chaotic state of unrestrained sensual drives.

Triggered by the sight of Maria's image in the bishop's house, Mortimer's aesthetic education ends in his idolatrous love for her.[6] But Mortimer is not the only one influenced by a portrait of Maria. Someone much closer to Elisabeth is also affected by Maria's image. Even as Maria rejects Mortimer's proposal to rescue her and insists that only Elisabeth's free will can liberate her, she appears to place her hopes in a private encounter with Elisabeth, "in opening herself to her equal, the woman and sister."[7] In order to achieve this, she pursues a double strategy: through Paulet she sends a letter to Elisabeth, and through Mortimer she sends her portrait to Leicester. It is in this double strategy that the strength and ultimate weakness of the two queens is revealed. Neither woman can rule over the written word. Maria's strength, however, as has already been demonstrated with regard to Mortimer, consists in exerting a powerful influence through her physical appearance as an erotic object captivating the male gaze.

By sending her portrait to Leicester, Maria indicates to him (her former lover, who rejected her in favor of Elisabeth) that she will be his if he frees her. For Leicester this promise comes at an extremely convenient moment: his long period of hoping to marry Elisabeth has come to an end with Elisabeth's engagement to her French suitor. While his ambitions kept him courting Elisabeth, he had been humiliated and kept captive, a toy of her vanity.[8] Leicester is not able to act openly and assert his masculine strength vis-à-vis Elisabeth, as Mortimer urges him to do.[9] He accuses Mortimer of ignoring England's actual situation, which necessitates duplicity and makes any forthright heroic action impossible.

> Wißt Ihr, wie's steht an diesem Hof, wie eng
> Dies Frauenreich die Geister hat gebunden?
> Sucht nach dem Heldengeist, der ehmals wohl
> In diesem Land sich regte—Unterworfen
> Ist alles, unterm Schlüssel eines Weibes,
> Und jedes Mutes Federn abgespannt.

> (Are you acquainted with this court? Know you
> The deeps and shallows of this court? With what
> A potent spell this female scepter binds
> And rules men's spirits round her? 'Tis in vain
> You seek the heroic energy which once
> Was active in this land! it is subdued,
> A woman holds it under lock and key,
> And every spring of courage is relaxed.)
>   (II, 8, 1933–38; *p. 62*)

The only action Leicester undertakes on behalf of Maria is to tease Elisabeth into agreeing to a meeting with her opponent. By appealing to her vanity, he presents this meeting to Elisabeth as an occasion to exhibit not only her sovereign power but also the force of her feminine presence and beauty. Elisabeth lets herself be persuaded, to provide Leicester, as it were, with the spectacle of the two women together. The encounter with Maria does not, however, lead to Elisabeth's victory over her opponent but only reinforces their animosity.

Even before the meeting takes place, it is clear that it will be more than a private face-to-face encounter between the two "sisters"—that the two women will encounter each other within a triangular structure, that their speech and actions will be determined by this scene qua spectacle. For it is not only Elisabeth who arranges their meeting in view of another; Maria too, although it had been her hope to achieve a sisterly understanding and reconciliation with her opponent, makes a spectacle of herself as soon as she learns of Elisabeth's imminent coming. When Elisabeth's advisor

Shrewsbury announces her arrival to Maria, all of Maria's previous hopes of arousing her opponent's pity vanish. She finds herself moved by violent hatred.

> In blutgem Haß gewendet wider sie,
> Ist mir das Herz, es fliehen alle guten
> Gedanken, und die Schlangenhaare schüttelnd
> Umstehen mich die finstern Höllengeister.

> (My heart is turned to direst hate against her;
> All gentle thoughts, all sweet forgiving words,
> Are gone, and round me stand with grisly mien,
> The fiends of hell, and shake their snaky locks.)

(III, 3, 2184–87; p. 70)

Nevertheless, she tries to control her passionate impulses and throws herself at Elisabeth's feet. She does so, however, by pronouncing the "stage directions" for her behavior and words, producing and emphasizing the incongruity between her words and her performance.[10]

> Ich will vergessen, wer ich bin, und was
> Ich litt, ich will vor ihr mich niederwerfen,
> Die mich in diese Schmach herunterstieß.
> (*Sie wendet sich gegen die Königin*)
> Der Himmel hat für Euch entschieden, Schwester!
> Gekrönt vom Sieg ist Euer glücklich Haupt,
> Die *Gottheit* bet ich an, die Euch erhöhte!
> (*Sie fällt vor ihr nieder*)
> Doch seid auch *Ihr* nun edelmütig, Schwester!
> Laßt mich nicht schmachvoll liegen, Eure Hand
> Streckt aus, reicht mir die königliche Rechte,
> Mich zu erheben von dem tiefen Fall.

> (I will forget my dignity, and all
> My sufferings; I will fall before her feet
> Who hath reduced me to this wretchedness.
> (*She turns towards the Queen*)
> The voice of heaven decides for you, my sister.
> Your happy brows are now with triumph crowned,
> I bless the Power Divine which thus hath raised you. (*She kneels*)
> But in your turn be merciful, my sister;
> Let me not lie before you thus disgraced;
> Stretch forth your hand, your royal hand, to raise,
> Your sister from the depths of her distress.)

(III, 4, 2247–56; p. 72)

It is exactly the kind of appeal that will not win Elisabeth's mercy, since Maria makes the fact of Elisabeth's rule an act of God's choice between two alternatives, a divine favor bestowed on Elisabeth rather than an unquestionable right she exercises by virtue of her own power. If Elisabeth raised Maria from the ground, she would recognize her as an equal.

Elisabeth must emphasize the difference and distance between herself and Maria. Therefore she cannot let herself be moved by Maria in terms of sympathy, the identification with an other in terms of a relation of similarity. Ironically, however, driven by hatred and pride, the two women begin to resemble each other more and more. Describing Elisabeth's composure as she approaches her, Maria hails Elisabeth as another Medusa: "Wenn ihr mich anschaut mit dem Eisesblick, / Schließt sich das Herz mir schaudernd zu" ("If you regard me with those icy looks / My shuddering heart contracts itself"; III, 4, 2275–76; *p. 73*). Elisabeth is indeed not moved to pity; instead she accuses Maria of instigating assassination attempts against her. Elisabeth does not want to hear Maria's defense that she was only a victim of fate. Nor does Elisabeth want to listen to Maria's suggestion that the two could peacefully succeed each other in the rulership of England; to her, Maria would always be an instrument of Catholic politics. As their argument heats up, Elisabeth turns her accusations *ad feminam*, calling Maria a whore. At this point Maria's restraint breaks down, and she returns to her initial state of unrestrained passion and open hatred, invoking the basilisk, the reptile with the deadly glance.

> Zum Himmel fliehe leidende Geduld,
> Spreng endlich deine Bande, tritt hervor
> Aus deiner Höhle, langverhaltner Groll—
> Und *du*, der dem gereizten Basilisk
> Den Mordblick gab, leg auf die Zunge mir
> Den giftgen Pfeil—.

>   (farewell
> Lamb-hearted resignation, passive patience,
> Fly to thy native heaven; burst at length
> Thy bonds, come forward from thy dreary cave,
> In all thy fury, long suppressed rancor!
> And thou, who to the angered basilisk
> Impart'st the murderous glance, oh, arm my tongue
> With poisoned darts!)
>   (III, 4, 2438–43; *p. 77*)

Invoking the deadly look of the basilisk, the oriental version of Medusa, Maria unleashes the monster's poisonous words, denying the legitimacy of

Elisabeth's rule by calling her the daughter of a whore, a bastard, and a swindler.

At the moment Elisabeth turns the argument *ad feminam*, she addresses Leicester as the onlooker of the scene. Later, Maria similarly asserts that she was strengthened in their fight by his presence. The two women cannot look at each other without setting themselves in a scene perceived from a male angle. The manner in which they can represent themselves to each other is subjected to the male gaze. It is this gaze that reduces Maria to an erotic object; in Elisabeth's words: "Es kostet nichts die *allgemeine* Schönheit / Zu sein, als die *gemeine* sein für alle" ("She who to all is common, may with ease / Become the common object of applause"; III, 4, 2417–18; *p.* 77). In response, Maria exposes the feminine sex: she insists that although her own history is marked by a guilty sexuality, she at least did not hide this fact. Then she lifts Elisabeth's robe of honor.

> Das Ärgste weiß die Welt von mir und ich
> Kann sagen, ich bin besser als mein Ruf.
> Weh Euch, wenn sie von Euren Taten einst
> Den Ehrenmantel zieht, womit Ihr gleißend
> Die wilde Glut verstohlner Lüste deckt.
> Nicht Ehrbarkeit habt Ihr von Eurer Mutter
> Geerbt, man weiß, um welcher Tugend willen
> Anna von Boleyn das Schafott bestiegen.
>
> (The worst of me is known, and I can say,
> That I am better than the fame I bear.
> Woe to you! when, in time to come, the world
> Shall draw the robe of honor from your deeds,
> With which thy arch-hypocrisy has veiled
> The raging flames of lawless, secret lust.
> Virtue was not your portion from your mother;
> Well know we what it was which brought the head
> Of Anne Boleyn to the fatal block.)

(III, 4, 2425–32; *p.* 77)

The showdown ends in the two antagonists' mutual display of the feminine sex (to put it crudely, the two women end up lifting each other's skirt), which is figured as a sight of violence and horror (Medusa), of the uncontrolled sexuality of an adulterous mother (Anne Boleyn), and of the ultimate destabilization in the realm of representation (the interrupted line of inheritance and the decapitation of the king's wife). Maria reveals Elisabeth's rule as a fraud. From birth on Elisabeth's relation to the realm of representations has been one of compensating for what she has *not*: legitimate birth, masculinity, and control over her sexual desires. Marked by ultimate lack—that is, reduced to a mere woman—Elisabeth is unable to pardon Maria and assert her sovereign presence: a woman cannot exercise the royal prerogative of pardon.

The encounter between the queens in Act III, Scene 4, reenacts the dilemma prefigured in all the preceding scenes, which raise the issues of Elisabeth as sovereign and Maria's executioner. The vicissitudes of the modern abstract state (i.e., its inability to exercise its sovereign power in the open, its false relation to the realm of representation) are figured in terms of Elisabeth's fundamental double bind, her role as woman and her role as monarch. And it is this double bind that connects the subplot of Elisabeth's potential engagement with the French prince with her position vis-à-vis Maria.

In Act I, Scene 8, Burleigh suggests to Paulet that if he were a truly loyal servant of the state, he would not take his role as Maria's jailor too literally; he would make it possible that his captive be secretly murdered and thus spare Elisabeth the duty of having to execute Maria. For if Elisabeth were openly to become Maria's executioner, she would draw the public's ire.

> Das Richterschwert, womit der Mann sich ziert,
> Verhaßt ists in der Frauen Hand. Die Welt
> Glaubt nicht an die Gerechtigkeit des Weibes,
> Sobald ein Weib das Opfer wird. Umsonst,
> Daß wir, die Richter, nach Gewissen sprachen!
> Sie hat der Gnade königliches Recht.
> Sie muß es brauchen, unerträglich ists,
> Wenn sie den strengen Lauf läßt dem Gesetze!
>
> (The sword of justice, which adorns the man,
> Is hateful in a woman's hand; the world
> Will give no credit to a woman's justice
> If woman be the victim. Vain that we,
> The judges, spoke what conscience dictated;
> She has the royal privilege of mercy;
> She must exert it: 'twere not to be borne,
> Should she let justice take its full career.)

                                                    (I, 8, 1018–25; *p. 35*)

Thus Elisabeth is free neither to exercise the male role of judge and executioner nor to pardon Maria. As a woman she has but one choice: she must pity and forgive the other woman. Maria's pardon can never be seen as Elisabeth's assertion of her royal prerogative. She lacks what Burleigh calls the male's "adornment": the phallic sword of the judge.

Elisabeth's reluctance toward the French suitor also illustrates how her double bind as woman and sovereign marks her ultimate weakness. On the occasion of the French courtship, Kent recounts to Davison the allegorical "Ritterspiel" about the siege and attack of the chaste fortress; he seems to be saying that once Elisabeth agrees to the marriage, England will be relieved of the fear of a return to Catholic rule. If Elisabeth produces an heir, Maria can no longer threaten the Protestant succession to the throne; Elisabeth's acquiescence to the engagement would therefore make Maria's pardon possible. Elisabeth's view of the situation, however, is altogether different. For her, the engagement means degradation from sovereign to mere "housewife" ("Bürgersweib").[11] She conceives of her "highest good," her chastity, as the sign of her sovereign freedom, as the compensation for her femininity and lack, a sign she would lose in marriage.[12] Elisabeth acknowledges the "natural" law of woman's subjection to man, but she claims that her relentless work in the service of her country should exempt her from this natural purpose, which "subjects one half of the human race to the other."[13] Thus when the French, after Elisabeth's tentative acceptance of the engagement, plead for Maria, this demand in the name of "Menschlichkeit" (being humane) only reinforces her desire to assert her sovereign power: "Frankreich erfüllt die Freundespflicht, mir wird / Verstattet sein, als Königin zu handeln" ("France has discharged her duties as a friend, / I will fulfill my own as England's queen"; II, 2, 1243–44; *p. 41*).

Elisabeth's resistance to feeling pity for Maria is progressively overcoded as both unnatural and inhuman. Unnatural, in the sense that she attempts to act like a man and does not accept her natural position as woman; inhuman, in the sense that she blocks the human sensibility toward a suffering fellow being. Elisabeth's severance from "nature" is also shown in her relation to writing and reading, which again places her on the side of false appearance and clandestine actions (witness her inability to assume responsibility for her signature).

When Elisabeth reads Maria's letter in the assembly of her advisors, she is moved to tears. However, this letter does not move Elisabeth to feel *Mitleid* à la Lessing; she does not see Maria in terms of similarity. Rather, she reads the letter allegorically and is moved by the instability of human destiny, shocked by the recognition of her own potential weakness.

> —Verzeiht, Mylords, es schneidet mir ins Herz,
> Wehmut ergreift mich und die Seele blutet,
> Daß Irdisches nicht fester steht, das Schicksal

Der Menschheit, das entsetzliche, so nahe
An meinem eignen Haupt vorüberzieht.

(Forgive me, lords, my heart is cleft in twain,
Anguish possesses me, and my soul bleeds
To think that earthly goods are so unstable,
And that the dreadful fate which rules mankind
Should threaten mine own house, and scowl so near me.)

(II, 4, 1538–42; p. 51)

Shrewsbury, the gentle father figure, who could have been borrowed from a bourgeois tragedy, appeals to her feminine duty to exercise her royal prerogative of pardon.

Nicht Strenge legte Gott ins weiche Herz
Des Weibes—Und die Stifter dieses Reichs,
Die auch dem Weib die Herrscherzügel gaben,
Sie zeigten an, daß Strenge nicht die Tugend
Der Könige soll sein in diesem Lande.

(God hath not planted rigor in the frame
Of woman; and the founders of this realm,
Who to the female hand have not denied
The reign of government, intend by this
To show that mercy, not severity,
Is the best virtue to adorn the crown.)

(II, 3, 1343–47; p. 45)

Of course, Shrewsbury's argument has to be ineffective. When he attempts to excite Elisabeth's pity by recounting the circumstances of Maria's upbringing and explains Maria's shortcomings as feminine weaknesses, he only hardens Elisabeth's determination not to identify with the weak sex.

Wo sie, die Schwache, sich umrungen sah
Von heftigdringenden Vasallen, sich
Dem Mutvollstärksten in die Arme warf—
Wer weiß, durch welcher Künste Macht besiegt?
Denn ein gebrechlich Wesen ist das Weib.
ELISABETH. Das Weib ist nicht schwach. Es gibt starke Seelen
In dem Geschlecht—Ich will in meinem Beisein
Nichts von der Schwäche des Geschlechtes hören.

(When she, a woman, helpless and hemmed in
By a rude crowd of rebel vassals, sought
Protection in a powerful chieftain's arms.

> God knows what arts were used to overcome her!
> For woman is a weak and fragile thing.
> ELIZABETH. Woman's not weak; there are heroic souls
> Among the sex; and, in my presence, sir,
> I do forbid to speak of woman's weakness.)

(II, 3, 1369–76; *p. 46*)

Right after this meeting with her advisors, she tries to persuade Mortimer to murder Maria.

Despite Elisabeth's refusal to acknowledge her feminine weakness, the play makes her feminine weakness increasingly obvious. Her lack of control over the realm of representations becomes increasingly apparent through her attachment and dependence on Leicester. It is he who appeals to her *Weiblichkeit* and persuades her to meet Maria. And in Act IV, even after she has discovered Maria's letter to him, Elisabeth cannot maintain her decision to ban Leicester from her presence and to try him for treason; he quickly deceives her by misrepresenting the events. In her soliloquy preceding the signing of the death sentence, she finally acknowledges the end of sovereign power. She cannot exercise the old-style tyrannical power of the monarch, who determines Truth, Right, and Justice; rather, she has to acknowledge her dependence on the opinion of the crowd.

> Die Meinung muß ich ehren, um das Lob
> Der Menge buhlen, einem Pöbel muß ichs
> Recht machen, dem der Gaukler nur gefällt.
> O der ist noch nicht König, der der Welt
> Gefallen muß! Nur der ists, der bei seinem Tun
> Nach keines Menschen Beifall braucht zu fragen.

> (I must respect the people's voice, and strive
> To win the favor of the multitude,
> And please the fancies of a mob, whom naught
> But jugglers' tricks delight. O call not him
> A king who needs must please the world: 'tis he
> Alone, who in his actions does not heed
> The fickle approbation of mankind.)

(IV, 10, 3194–99; *p. 102*)

As a powerless woman, she has no control over representations and public opinion. Ultimately she blames Maria for depriving her of the laboriously constructed front that was supposed to hide her lack of legitimacy and her stained birth, a situation she condenses in the image of her father's incestuous rape:

Ein wehrlos Weib! Mit hohen Tugenden
Muß ich *die Blöße meines Rechts* bedecken,
Den Flecken meiner fürstlichen Geburt,
Wodurch der eigne Vater mich geschändet.
Umsonst bedeck ich ihn—Der Gegener Haß
Hat ihn *entblößt*, und stellt mir diese Stuart,
Ein ewig drohendes Gespenst entgegen.

(A poor defenceless woman: I must seek
To veil the spot in my imperial birth,
By which my father cast disgrace upon me:
In vain with princely virtues would I hide it;
The envious hatred of my enemies
Uncovers it, and places Mary Stuart,
A threatening fiend, before me ever more!)

(IV, 10, 3221–27; *p. 103*; my italics)

She kills Maria (she refers to her as a "specter," a double), who has exposed her sex ("entblößt" means literally: "to strip naked") and her impotence and threatened to take away her lover. Ultimately Elisabeth's execution of Maria becomes—though planned as the final assertion of her sovereign power—an admission of her feminine weakness. Shrewsbury resigns his office, remarking that although he rescued her from the assassination attempt, he has been unable to save her "better half" (V, 15, 4028–29). When she summons Leicester, she learns that he has fled to France. By exposing Elisabeth's rule as ultimately grounded in feminine weakness, Schiller has thoroughly recoded the vicissitudes of sovereign power in terms of gender polarities. And if one considers the powerful mise-en-scène of Maria's execution, it becomes clear that both women work in tandem to assert sovereign power as "true" masculinity. Although in terms of plot the drama appears to be a "conflict" between Maria and Elisabeth, on the discursive level of the text the conflicting parties share a common function. They participate equally in the construction of a specific form of masculine subjectivity.

How does the execution figure with regard to Maria? If Elisabeth is ultimately morally condemned, how does Maria achieve her moral victory? What is the nature of Maria's reformation? Although my reading attributes to the encounter between the queens a crucial function for the play's closure and overall cathartic effect, it certainly does not locate in this scene the origin of Maria's reformation.[14] Instead, I suggest that the main key to her reformation can be found in her incarceration.

This drama about freedom is set in enclosed spaces, and the main char-

Fig. 13. Piranesi, Carceri *(1750), frontispiece. Although contemporary prison architecture was striving for perfect surveillance, Piranesi's nightmarish prisons explore the fantastic.*

acter is detained in prison. Mortimer refers to his English upbringing as "imprisonment," and Leicester describes his relationship to Elisabeth as being held "in chains." It is through Maria's changes, however, that the true meaning of "prison" is established. The traditional function of the prison was to detain the body of the accused until the trial, which would produce the truth of the crime and display this truth in conjunction with the sovereign's power in the spectacle of a public punishment. Traditionally only debtors' prisons held the bodies of the accused after their guilt had been established. During the late eighteenth century, however, the function and architecture of prisons were radically altered. From a place of confinement, the prison became an institution of examination and reform: the individual's isolation was intended to establish the truth of the individual "case" and aid the process of investigation; once this knowledge had been established, the incarceration replaced corporeal punishment as a place where the individual's soul and body were disciplined and reprogrammed.[15]

It is curious that Schiller, in criticizing the abstract modern state in which kings, gods, and courts are no longer visible, produces a play that echoes this critique of an abstract state apparatus but does not revert to the old-style spectacle and instead produces a new spectacle, one that puts on stage the modern penal institution.[16] As early as Act I, we see Maria as somebody who, in her isolation from worldly splendor, has learned to reflect on her history. She internalizes Paulet's reproach that she has seduced too many men (I, 4, 264–67). In her first appearance on stage, on the anniversary of her husband's murder, she utters words of remorse and acknowledges that she is pursued by the specter of this crime. Despite her Catholicism, she seems unable to assuage her guilt by the absolution for her crime she has obtained from the church. Nor is her conscience calmed by her servant Kennedy, who depicts her crime as a sin of her distant youth and suggests that she was seduced by some supernatural power and magic potions. Rejecting all possible excuses, she takes full responsibility for her history and guilt, which she attributes to her feminine weakness alone: "Seine Künste waren keine andre,/ Als seine Männerkraft und meine Schwachheit" ("All the arts he used / Were man's superior strength and woman's weakness"; I, 4, 331–32; *p. 15*).

Although historically Mary's complicity in Darnley's murder has never been established, Schiller's play passes unequivocal judgment on the character.[17] Maria's anamnesis and remorse focus on the murder of her husband, an altogether different crime from the one of treason against Elisabeth of which the court has found her guilty. Thus, the play juxtaposes external and internal guilt, a true and a false crime. At the end of the play, the incarcerated Kurl becomes insane when he learns of Maria's execution. His overwhelming guilt because of his false testimony reinforces the function of the prison as the institution that can produce the truth of the individual. The prison becomes the place for the "construction" of the individual in terms of an inquiry into all the specific circumstances as well as the personal motives that led to the crime, that is, into the particular "case."[18] The findings of the court ("guilty" or "not guilty" of an external crime) are discredited and opposed to the truth-producing power of the prison.

If the modern penal institution and its associated techniques of examination were invoked merely to establish whether the accused committed the crime, the play could be over in the first act. But this is not the focus of the play; as Schiller wrote in a letter to Goethe dated April 26, 1799: "It [the material of Maria Stuart] seems particularly qualified for the Euripidean method, for this method consists of the complete representation of the situation. For I can see the possibility of laying aside the entire court procedure together with all the politics."[19] Since Schiller's interest lies with "the complete representation of the situation," the play, like the prison, has the function of disclosing why and how the crime was committed in the first place: What was behind Maria's murder of Darnley?

In Act I, Scene 4, Maria attributes her crime to female weakness, but only in the confession scene prior to her execution does she formulate her "gravest guilt" in its entirety. Although from the beginning she sees herself as a weak and sensual woman, she still hopes for her release from prison and places her hopes in her physical beauty when she sends her portrait to Leicester. Thus, in the scene just before her encounter with Elisabeth, she finds herself suddenly released from prison to walk in a castle park; she rejoices at the sight of open nature, and a small boat kindles her hope she might be able to bribe the boatsman to take her to France. When her servant, Hannah Kennedy, directs her attention to the hidden guards and warns her not to cherish false hopes, she insists that her freedom is imminent.

> Nein, gute Hanna. Glaub mir, nicht umsonst
> Ist meines Kerkers Tor geöffnet worden.
> Die kleine Gunst ist mir des größern Glücks
> Verkünderin. Ich irre nicht. Es ist
> Der Liebe tätge Hand, der ich sie danke.
> Lord Leicesters mächtgen Arm erkenn ich drin.
> Allmählich will man mein Gefängnis weiten,
> Durch Kleineres zum Größern mich gewöhnen,

Bis ich das Antlitz dessen endlich schaue,
Der mir die Bande löst auf immerdar.

(No, gentle Hannah! Trust me, not in vain
My prison gates are opened. This small grace
Is harbinger of greater happiness.
No! I mistake not; 'tis the active hand
Of love to which I owe this kind indulgence.
I recognize in this the mighty arm
Of Leicester. They will by degrees expand
My prison; will accustom me, through small
To greater liberty, until at last
I shall behold the face of him whose hand
Will dash my fetters off, and that forever.)

(III, 1, 2119–28; *p. 68*)

In spite of hymnic overtones of this passage, the savior she imagines is Leicester, the freedom she anticipates a life with her lover in France.

In the scene immediately after the disillusioning encounter with Elisabeth, however, Mortimer approaches her, not to bring her any message from Leicester, but on his own behalf. He announces that the conspiracy for her rescue is under way and that he is willing to risk his life and even kill his own uncle in order to free her. Maria is shocked and tries to withdraw from this fanatic release of violent impulses. But for Mortimer the violent act of freeing her is intimately linked with his desire to possess her, and at this point he harasses her and attempts to rape her. Maria is saved from her "savior" only because of the turmoil over the assassination attempt on Elisabeth.

This scene forces Maria to recognize that as long as she conceives of her freedom in physical terms, as a release from the incarceration at Fotheringhay, she will remain the erotic object of men, unleashing their violent passions of love and hatred. She cannot be physically free as a sensual, beautiful woman if her alternative is death or rape. She is forced to reinterpret her prison and her freedom. Thus, in the scene before her execution, the transfigured Maria admonishes her weeping attendants:

Was klagt ihr? Warum weint ihr? Freuen solltet
Ihr Euch mit mir, daß meiner Leiden Ziel
Nun endlich naht, daß meine Bande fallen,
Mein Kerker aufgeht, und die frohe Seele sich
Auf Engelsflügeln schwingt zur ewgen Freiheit.

(Why these complaints? Why weep ye? Ye should rather
Rejoice with me, that now at length the end

Of my long woe approaches; that my shackles
Fall off, my prison opens, and my soul
Delighted mounts on seraph's wings, and seeks
The land of everlasting liberty.)

(V, 6, 3479–83; *p. 112*)

In this passage she takes up her previous image of liberation (the loosening of the bonds and the release from prison), except that here she refers no longer to her escape to France with her lover but to her apotheosis. Her true prison is her own body, and the freedom to which she aspires is that of pure spirituality, her beautiful soul released from the prison of her body.[20]

When Melvil administers communion and hears her last confession, she confesses that she has been driven by hatred toward her opponent and that she still feels guilt for the murder of her husband. But her gravest sin she formulates in the following words:

Ach, nicht durch *Haß* allein, durch sündge *Liebe*
Noch mehr hab ich das höchste Gut beleidigt.
Das eitle Herz ward zu dem Mann gezogen,
Der treulos mich verlassen und betrogen!
MELVIL. Bereuest du die Schuld, und hat dein Herz
Vom eitlen Abgott sich zu Gott gewendet?
MARIA. Es war der schwerste Kampf, den ich bestand,
Zerissen ist das letzte irdische Band.

(Ah! not alone through hate; through lawless love
Have I still more abused the sovereign god.
My heart was vainly turned towards the man
Who left me in misfortune, who deceived me.
MELVIL. Repentest thou of the sin? And hast thou turned
Thy heart, from this idolatry, to God?
MARY. It was the hardest trial I have passed;
This last of earthly bonds is torn asunder.)

(V, 7, 3684–91; *p. 118*)

The true transformation of Maria consists in her acknowledgment of her "sinful love," her sexuality as her crime, and in the renunciation of her body. Only once she abandons her body can she be transformed from a beautiful woman, defined in terms of physical appearance, into a beautiful soul. She abandons her idolatrous love of Leicester and turns to God. The transfigured Maria turns away from the gaze of men and subjects herself entirely to the gaze of God.

Leicester, until this moment the fraudulent stand-in for the (male) gaze, is left in despair. He is unable to carry on his deceit; that is, he is unable to attend Maria's execution and thereby free himself from the suspicion of having been her lover. Against the threat of "melting away in womanly compassion" ("in zartem Mitleid weibisch hinzuschmelzen"; V, 10, 3853), he appeals to the reassuring stiffness granted by the sight of horror:

> Verstumme Mitleid, Augen, werdet Stein,
> Ich seh sie fallen, ich will Zeuge sein.
>
> (*Er geht mit entschloßnem Schritt der Türe zu, durch welche Maria gegangen, bleibt auf der Mitte des Weges stehen*)
>
> Umsonst! Umsonst! Mich faßt der Hölle Grauen,
> Ich kann, ich kann das Schreckliche nicht schauen,
> Kann sie nicht sterben sehen—
>
> (Pity be dumb; mine eyes be petrified!
> I'll see—I will be witness of her fall.
>
> (*He advances with resolute steps towards the door through which MARY passed; but stops suddenly half way.*)
>
> No! No! The terrors of all hell possess me.
> I cannot look upon the dreadful deed;
> I cannot see her die!)
>
> (V, 10, 3859–63; *p. 124*)

He is not turned into stone, but his power vanishes and he is unable voluntarily to witness Maria's decapitation. Nevertheless he has to hear the event and hallucinate the scene of horror step by step.[21]

> Nur schluchzen hör ich, und die Weiber weinen—
> Sie wird entkleidet—Horch! Der Schemel wird
> Gerückt—Sie kniet aufs Kissen—legt das Haupt—
>
> (*Nachdem er die letzten Worte mit steigender Angst gesprochen, und eine Weile inne gehalten, sieht man ihn plötzlich mit einer zuckenden Bewegung zusammenfallen, und ohnmächtig niedersinken, zugleich erschallt von unten herauf ein dumpfes Getöse von Stimmen, welches lange forthallt.*)
>
> (And sobs and women's moans are all I hear.
> Now, they undress her; they remove the stool;
> She kneels upon the cushion; lays her head—
>
> [*Having spoken these last words, and paused awhile, he is seen with a convulsive motion suddenly to shrink and faint away; a confused hum of voices is heard at the same moment from below, and continues for some time.*])
>
> (V, 10, 3873–75; *pp. 124–25*)

Castration and decapitation are intimately linked in the perception of the audience: they see Leicester's inability to move to the scene of execution, his "melting away in female pity" and his final collapse on stage, and this collapse is accompanied by the sound track of Maria's decapitation. Leicester, the fraudulent lover and stand-in for the male gaze, is punished with the hallucinated vision of the decapitated woman. The scene of horror, the female sex, which he had already once provoked, this time exercises its annihilating power on him. When "he is seen with a convulsive motion suddenly to shrink and faint away," his castration on stage is substituted for the decapitation of Maria. The hallucinated spectacle of the execution is turned into a powerful image of deterrence.[22]

In terms of the succession of scenes toward the end of the play, between Maria's transfiguration into a beautiful soul, her exit in order to leave the prison of her body, and the play's last four scenes in Elisabeth's office, in which the results of the administrative apparatus reveal their course, the play focuses on Leicester's gaze and collapse. Through the character of Leicester, this scene is connected back to the encounter between the queens.[23] In Act III, Scene 4, the course of history is rendered graphic in terms of the ultimately destabilizing force of female sexuality; in Act V, Scene 10, this "visibility" is recalled as the ultimate threat to the unity and stability of the male ego. The function of the second scene consists in the mobilization of the audience's defense mechanisms. For the audience the sight of horror is both explicitly invoked in all its terror and at the same time kept at a safe distance through the mediation of Leicester. The figure of Medusa is restored to her full ambiguity: terrifying but also reassuring to the extent that it structures anxiety and links it with a perception.[24]

If the genres of the bourgeois tragedy and epistolary novel could be characterized as anti-theatrical rejections of the spectacle in favor of an internalization and an identification with the fictional events in the mental cinema, Classical German Tragedy gives new value and power to the spectacle. This new spectacle is, however, not one of amusement and distraction such as, say, the display of freaks or acrobats in a fair, nor is it one of torture or execution, or of a royal procession, in which an exceptional body displays its power over the undisciplined, anonymous masses. The concrete body of the actor in this new spectacle is of no interest. The spectacle itself addresses not the crowd but each individual member of the audience as a representative of mankind. The new spectacle accomplishes a movement of externalization and internalization that can only come into being once the masses have already been disciplined into individuals.

This analysis of Schiller's *Maria Stuart* as an example of classical tragedy has also addressed the position of the ideal woman with regard to ritual and spectacle and thereby examined those representational strategies that serve to discipline male subjects for the state. In this regard, Weimar Classicism seems to pose a certain paradox: on the one hand, by the last decade of the eighteenth century the ideology of a fundamental gender polarity pervades discourse on language and the arts to an unprecedented degree while, on the other hand, the literature of Weimar Classicism furnishes numerous "strong" female figures (or even amazons) who do not share the virtues of feminine passivity and receptivity celebrated in aesthetic theory.[25] Yet my reading has demonstrated how this seeming contradiction is resolved through the polarized representation of femininity as (1) a threatening corporeality and sexuality (Medusa) and (2) the ideal of a harmonious autonomous appearance (beautiful soul). Both aspects serve to organize male subjectivity vis-à-vis representations: the former prevents identification with the theatrical illusion; the latter provides a model for a unified self.

Love and Formation of the Self in Wieland's *Agathon*

In both *Clarissa* and *Julie*, the virtue of the protagonists is intricately linked to the aesthetics of immediacy and illusion, which in turn determine the parameters of Richardson's and Rousseau's epistolary novel. In *Clarissa* the rake's reform consists in his subjection to a hallucinatory equation of writing, reading, and seeing in the "writing to the moment"; in *Julie* the letters function as vehicles for a seduction to virtue. In both novels, models of identification with an other play the crucial role in the organization of subjectivity, and the decarnalized love of an idealized woman becomes the central force in the stabilization of masculine desire. Bildung, the new model of subject formation, requires a poetics that radically departs from the conventions of the epistolary novel: the "documentary" fiction of the letters is superseded by a narrative rearrangement of an entire repertoire of autobiographical and biographical conventions. Although the first version of Wieland's novel *Agathon* appeared in 1767, only six years after the publication of *Julie*, and although it still partially participates in the discourse of sensibility, in 1774 the German critic Friedrich von Blanckenburg hailed *Agathon* as a new beginning in the genre of the novel and explicitly and polemically opposed this work to Richardson's epistolary novels.[26] In the following I show that particularly the novel's third and final version of 1794 can be situated firmly within the new paradigm for the organization of male subjectivity: that model of sublimation based on an elaboration of male narcissism that Chapter 4 traces in the discourse of neo-humanism and classicism.[27] Whereas in the epistolary novels the disciplining of the male subject centers on the transformations in his love for an other, with Wieland's work the focus shifts to the protagonist's love of himself. In fact, the entire novel is marked by an elaboration of a discourse on self-love.[28]

Why would the bildungsroman, a genre that is part of the classicist, neo-humanist project of Bildung, depart from the narrative conventions of the epistolary novel? Dilthey's classical definition of this much-debated genre still holds an answer to this question.

Yet the bildungsroman differs from older biographical forms in the sense that it consciously and artfully represents in one life what is human in general terms. It is everywhere connected to the new psychology of development, which was founded by Leibniz, to the idea of an education that followed the natural and inner course of the soul, as it originated from Rousseau and influenced all of Germany, and to the ideal of humanity, with which Lessing and Herder inspired their epoch with enthusiasm. A certain lawful development is considered in the individual's life; each stage has a value of its own, while at the same time it forms the basis for a higher stage. The dissonances and conflicts of life appear as necessary transitions in the individual's progression toward maturity and harmony. And the "highest happiness" of the "children of this earth" is "personhood" as the unified and firm form of human existence.[29]

The bildungsroman is an exemplary narrative of an individual vita. What makes it exemplary is that through the narrativization of the course of one life it artfully constructs what is relevant in "universally human" terms. This definition, however, could apply to many novels that claim to depict "human nature." Were it an argument about "psychological realism," it could equally be made about Richardson's *Clarissa*. But this does not seem to be the focus of Dilthey's definition. He is more specific, for he stipulates that this representation of human nature follows a certain inner development of the soul, which is related both to a certain notion of education and to the ideal of "Humanität." Through this specification the bildungsroman is inscribed into an idealist program: what is at stake is the narrativization of the life of an individual in such a manner that each phase engenders the next, a construction that recuperates dissonances and conflicts as necessary stages on the way to maturity and harmony. The aim of this construction is "personhood," which Dilthey defines as the unified and secure form of human existence. And personhood entails a promise of happiness.[30]

Dilthey's definition of the bildungsroman helps to answer the question of why the conventions of the epistolary novel, the aesthetics of immediacy or "writing to the moment," are inappropriate for this new ideal of subjectivity. Personhood can be produced only through the temporalized, mediated, teleological narrative of a vita. Even though it is the story of one life, the bildungsroman also departs from both traditional biography and traditional autobiography. External events and details are relevant only with regard to the protagonist's "inner development." And the product of this "inner development," the ideal of personhood, is the narrative construction as a whole, not the character of the protagonist at any given moment in the story.[31]

Agathon, which I consider the prototype of the bildungsroman,[32] still uses traditional biographical and autobiographical conventions. First-person narratives are mediated and framed by an authorial narrator, who provides long passages of third-person narrative about the protagonist. Although the narrator suggests, however, that Agathon's autobiography (along with Plutarch and other historical sources) provided some of the primary material for his "history of Agathon," the novelistic narrative is by no means identical with this biographical account. In the preface, the editor/narrator establishes a curious tension among his own text, history, and historical documents and sources.[33] In fact, the narrator quotes this biography only a few times and not until the very end of the book. Thus my reading analyzes *Agathon* by focusing on those aspects of the novel through which the narrator constructs the "epochs" of Agathon's soul that finally enable the protagonist at the end of the novel to write his own biography. I argue that whereas the disciplinary function of the epistolary novel is concerned with the transparent relation between subjectivity and representations, the bildungsroman explores the subject's representation of himself as a process.[34]

The novel consists of sixteen books, grouped into three parts. Each part focuses on a particular station of Agathon's life in chronological order. The first part centers on Smyrna and Agathon's love affair with Danae, the second on Syracuse and Agathon's political endeavors, and the third part on Tarent and Agathon's life in the family of Archytas, the ruler of this Sicilian republic. Each part contains first-person narratives that provide a variety of flashbacks. Some of these narratives overlap and gradually call for mutual revisions. Analysis of first-person accounts with regard to their generic affiliations reveals an interesting model. In the first part, some "contemplations" by Agathon draw on the soliloquy conventions of the diary. In the second part, Agathon tells the stories of his childhood and of his political career in Athens; the first narrative contains elements of the romance, the second inclines toward the public apology. In the context in which Agathon tells the two stories to his friend Danae, they resemble a conversion narrative. Danae's autobiographical narrative, her "secret history," which borrows conventions of the confession, parallels Agathon's writing of his own autobiography. Finally, Archytas' narrativized curriculum vitae (or more precisely, his *Bildungsgang*) responds to and corrects Agathon's representation of his own life. In brief, the bildungsroman emerges through a probing of models of self-representation, taken from the available repertoire of autobiographical conventions.[35]

I divide my analysis of *Agathon* into five sections, each of which focuses on a stage in Agathon's construction of himself. The first section introduces the protagonist as a daydreamer and idealist, utterly disoriented in his encounters with the world. The second section traces Agathon's amorous involvement with Danae, his seduction through aesthetic illusion, and his captivation by sensual pleasures. The third section examines Agathon's attempt to reconcile a past and a current self, to fuse a lost object of love with a present one through autobiographical narratives. This attempt, instead of producing coherence and continuity, merely reinforces his mourning for an ideal childhood. The fourth section examines Agathon's political career and his conception of himself as an actor on the public stage. This worldly engagement almost leads him to abandon his childhood idealism as a mistaken form of self-love. Finally, in the concluding section, Archytas as an ideal father figure provides Agathon with a model of self-fashioning that finally allows him to negotiate his otherworldly idealism with worldly responsibilities and activities.

Agathon's Primary Narcissism: Idealism and Happy Dreams

Agathon begins with the protagonist as a homeless, lost wanderer too exhausted to climb a mountain to look for a refuge for the night. Although Agathon, having suddenly become bereft of wealth, friends, and fatherland, could be considered the most miserable of all men, the narrator assures us that our hero does not despair but settles for the night after he has enthusiastically contemplated the sunset and refreshed himself with a drink of water. Thus Agathon falls asleep under the "gently anesthetizing murmur of a spring" and dreams that he "found his beloved Psyche, the loss of whom was the only thing that led him to an occasional sigh" (I, 28).

But this happy dream and sleep are interrupted by a terrible noise. Agathon bravely climbs the mountain to find the cause. The moonlight reveals a bacchanalia: drunken, wild, lascivious, dancing women. At this sight he is appalled and overcome with disgust. When in their intoxication the Thracian women discover our hero, they believe him to be—and at this point the narrator can no longer conceal from the reader Agathon's extraordinary beauty—an incarnation of their god Dionysos. As they approach him, Agathon becomes stiff like a "sculpture." The women become enraged with Agathon's reluctance to comply with their desires, and our hero would have suffered the fate of Pentheus or Orpheus if a sudden interruption of the feast had not rescued him. A band of Sicilian pirates, who happen to have anchored to get fresh water, are also attracted by the noise of the bacchanalia. Agathon is "rescued" by the pirates, who rape the women and take everybody into captivity on their boat. On the ship the orgy continues, and Agathon withdraws into a corner and returns to his dream.

With the first morning light, he awakes and, while everybody else is still asleep, sees a beautiful young man: "their souls simultaneously recognized each other" (I, 37), and they fall into each other's arms. He has found his Psyche, who disguised as a man, has also been captured by the pirates on her voyage to Athens, where she had hoped to find Agathon. Psyche tells him what has happened to her since they were separated. Before they can make plans for their escape, the pirates set out on a new venture. Agathon, "anesthetized by pain and despair" (I, 50), is placed on a different boat to be sold on the slave market, and the lovers are again separated.

At this point, the narrator interrupts and tells us that the chapter to follow, Agathon's "soliloquy," derives from a diary. He quotes Agathon talking to himself about the sudden changes of his fate, which make him confuse reality and dream:

How similar is all of this to a feverish dream, where an exuberant fantasy, without considering order, verisimilitude, time, or place carries away the anesthesized soul from one adventure to another, from the crown to the beggar's cloak, from bliss to despair, from Tartarus to Elysium. And is then life but a dream, a mere dream, so vain, so insignificant, so meaningless like a dream? A fickle play of blind chance, or of invisible spirits, who find a cruel amusement in making us alternately happy and unhappy? (I, 55)

In this curious passage, Agathon describes his fantastic life, its dreamlike quality and the loss of any index for what constitutes a stable reality, by referring to traditional poetic categories: verisimilitude and the unity of time and space.

But Agathon checks his fit of despair over the lack of order and justice by reminding himself of the insignificance of his losses, drawing new hope from the remembrance of his happy and innocent youth at Delphi: "The memory of the happiness I have enjoyed heals the present pain and promises a better future. . . . Come then, O sweet hope of a better future, and captivate my soul with your flattering charms! Calm and Psyche— this is all, you gods!" (I, 58–59) Agathon continues his contemplations during a calm sea voyage, uninterrupted by storms or sirens. After three days, the ship anchors in Smyrna, where he is bathed and dressed and led to the slave market. All these external circumstances happen to him, "and nothing could tear him out of this deep anesthesia, which in some circumstances is the result of a hypersensitivity. Fixated on what was happening in his soul, he seemed neither to see nor hear, because he did not see or hear anything he wished; only the sight of the slave market was capable of shaking him from this waking dream" (I, 60–61). But he is far from awake: "A number of sad representations emerged in dense confusion at this sight; and while his heart was melting away in pity and melancholy, it also burned with angry horror of those men, an anger that only those who love mankind are able to feel. Over those sensations he forgot his own unhappiness" (I, 61). Agathon is sold to a passerby, a transaction that ends the first book of *Agathon*.

The first book performs the expository function in a curious manner. The title of the novel, *Die Geschichte des Agathon*, as well as the preface's reference to historical documents from Plato to Cicero to Plutarch would lead the reader to expect a recourse to biographical conventions to frame the narrative "history of Agathon." However, the narrator neither presents us with the specifics of the protagonist's upbringing nor sets out a descriptive characterization of Agathon that would locate him in a specific time and place.[36] Rather, the novel begins with a great number of episodes and encounters that happen to the protagonist, strung together as events of blind chance and coincidence. Thereby the narrator characterizes Agathon indirectly by reproducing for the reader the hero's disorientation in the external world.

The narrator neither depicts the protagonist as an acting and reflecting agent with definite aims and a purpose nor describes scenes and the sentiments of his protagonist in much detail. Instead, he juxtaposes fragmented and unmotivated events to which Agathon merely reacts, solely by withdrawing from the external situation into a state of anesthesia, or peaceful contemplation, which can be interrupted at any time by another episode. Agathon's dreamy states of contemplation seem to protect him temporarily from the pains of loss as well as from confusion over the rapidly changing external situations. The threat of the external world is disorientation and bodily fragmentation (the Thracian women's revenge). Finally, the pirates who "rescue" him from the "Maenads" ultimately turn him into an object of exchange; he is sold for two talents on the slave market before he even notices what is happening.

Even though we learn few concrete details about Agathon's background and youth, we nevertheless gain a fairly precise picture of this youthful enthusiast. He is in fact entirely defined in terms of his relation to his childhood. Whenever he encounters a painful situation, he withdraws into dreams, which recreate for him the presence of his childhood love, Psyche, and the presence of those works of art in the temple at Delphi, whose contemplation leads him into the spiritual realms of the Orphic religion. Agathon's childhood is a retrospective, compensatory, and hallucinatory product. The two instances through which he evokes a state of self-sufficiency and blissful satisfaction, Psyche and religious representations, contain strikingly little that resembles a memory of parental care, siblings, or family life. And yet, Agathon recounts later, as an orphan growing up in the Delphic temple, the images of the gods as well as his soulmate Psyche come to figure for him exactly that which a happy childhood should be. Psyche and the Orphic religion provide him with a belief in his spiritual existence and render him independent of the contingencies of material needs and physical existence. Agathon's idealist beliefs are firmly tied up with his representation of himself as a self-sufficient being rather than a corporeal and mortal one, as a being in tune with the totality of the life of the spirit. Both of these aspects of his self are grounded in the imaginary.

Agathon seems a toy in the hands of fate. Unable to represent himself to or to act in the external world, he constructs his individuality by projecting himself into the past of a blissful childhood, a state of innocence and peace that he hopes to find back in the future. He is not able to connect the events of his life in terms of a story. He is strangely speechless. Since analytical reasoning or narrative connections are alien to him, his only means of relating to the realm of representations is one in which ideas and images exist in some dreamland outside time. Thus it is not quite possible to conceive of Agathon as a subject. He has a past, but no history.

The past, which for Agathon means his lost childhood, can be recuperated for him only in a hallucinatory manner, as is most elaborately shown in his soliloquy/diary, which functions much as do his compensatory dreams. When he counters the threat of fragmentation posed by his temporal existence by gathering himself into an "in-dividual" through a dreamlike anesthesia, a clinging to childhood images and memories, he attempts to block out external reality. We can observe in Agathon the state of primary narcissism that I analyzed in discussing Herder's sheep narrative: an assertion of independence from the external world and possible pain by hallucinating the state of satisfaction. In Herder's narrative, the human soul is produced through this state of peaceful contemplation, so is Agathon's Psyche. For it is through his lost beloved (the soulmate of his childhood, for whom he had the most tender but innocent love, who does not seem to have a determined sexual identity, who is as beautiful as he is) that he denies the reality of loss. Although her presence and absence in the external world are beyond his control, for his soul she is ever present. In other terms, she is his mirror image and not a libidinally invested external object; she is the total object of a primary narcissism. The conclusion of the exposition shows that these hallucinatory defense mechanisms do not prevent him from becoming a mere object of exchange, a slave, or that subject who is not in possession of himself. Although Agathon is introduced as a young adult, his subjectivity nevertheless still betrays the structure of an almost infantile primary narcissism.

In contrast to the first book's characterization of Agathon as not quite integrated into language and the world, the second book starts with a fairly traditional characterization of Hippias, the Sophist philosopher and current owner of Agathon. This man has made his career and fortune as a rhetorician, training future politicians in the art of ruling over other people's feelings by manipulating the realm of representations. A master in the world of appearance, he is not only well liked and influential in the powerful circles of society but also well versed in the art of making himself agreeable to the beautiful sex. He is a lover of the fine arts and practices a life-style devoted to sensual delights.

Pointing out Hippias' "vanity," the narrator informs us that Agathon is secretly the object of his master's narcissism. For the beautiful and apparently well-educated young man has been bought in order to preserve Hippias' art beyond his death.

He has formed rhetoricians, who knew how through an artful confusion of the true and false and the clever use of certain figures to lend to an evil thing the appearance and effect of a good one; statesmen, who possessed the art among the applause of a seduced crowd to destroy the laws through freedom and freedom through worse morals in order to subject a people that did not want to subject itself to the wholesome discipline of the law to the arbitrary power of their passions; in brief, he has formed people who had statues erected to them for their destruction of their fatherland. But all of this did not yet satisfy his vanity. He also wanted to leave somebody behind who would be able to continue his art. (I, 69–70)

Without knowing it, Agathon is doubly implicated in the order of exchange and representations: as a slave and as future demagogue. In case the reader might doubt the degree of danger Hippias' evil art poses for Agathon's virtue, Wieland points out in a footnote the parallels between the Greek Sophists and "the demagogues who have taken possession of the highest power in France during the last three or four years" (I, 70).

The irony of Agathon's fate is repeated even more forcefully than in the preceding book. The dreamy, otherworldly, and innocent Agathon is destined to become the successor of a master demagogue. Emphasizing this irony is Agathon's official function in Hippias' house: he has been bought because of his good looks and pleasant voice to entertain Hippias and his company by reading to them during meals. At the slave market, Hippias had asked him if he could read Homer. Agathon replied: "I know how to read, and I think I can feel Homer." "Do you know the writings of the philosophers?" "Well enough not to understand anything in them" (I, 62). Distrustful of the uncertain and potentially deceptive philosophical discourse, Agathon can enter the realm of representations only as that reader who feels himself in what he reads. The fallacy or *méconnaissance* grounded in this sentimental equation of reading with feeling oneself is exposed by the fact that Agathon's reading/feeling not only originates from a text of another (Homer) but also serves as a prop for the imagination and sensation of others (the dinnertime entertainment of Hippias and his guests). In the very act by which Agathon means to assert his individuality and identity, he is already utterly alienated as a mere signifier for the sentiments of others. The state of alienation that characterizes Agathon in the house of Hippias is reiterated in the new name he receives from his master: Kallias, the beautiful, a name that describes his outer appearance as perceived by others.

Although he does not understand the principles of Hippias' life-style, he feels uneasy in this world of superficiality. Puzzled by Hippias' fame for his wisdom, overwhelmed with sensuous luxury, and sexually harassed by the seductive and beautiful female slaves, Agathon withdraws to the gardens in his spare time to resume his dreamy contemplations. There Hippias discovers him one night lost in Platonic speculation. They enter a philosophical dispute over the reality of the life of the spirit independent of the body. Although Agathon has only his "feeling" to confirm the reality of the life of the spirit, he does not give in to Hippias' atomistic materialism. They separate after Hippias tells him that Agathon's lack of experience and means makes him substitute the hallucinatory satisfaction of desire for "real" (sensual) pleasure. Agathon remains unmoved by Hippias' arguments and quickly suspects the hidden agenda behind his invitation to breakfast when they are served by a scantily clad, beautiful slave: "The claims of the beautiful Cyane, the artificiality, the cleverness, the lasciviousness, which made her entire person repulsive to him, extinguished whatever was attractive about her to such a degree, and cooled down his senses so much, that one degree more would have been able, like the sight of Medusa, to turn him into stone" (I, 105).

After this failed attempt at integrating Agathon into his household, Hippias concludes that his "pupil's" resistance might be overcome most easily through frank and rigorous philosophical discussion. Agathon, however, is not in the least moved by Hippias' speech. He does not want to debate whether Hippias' materialist philosophy is better than his own idealism; he merely asserts that he is not at all convinced by it, even if Hippias were to show him that the rest of the world agreed with him. Thereupon Hippias calls Agathon a hypocrite. He reminds him of the beautiful Cyane and asks whether he did not desire her. Agathon counters that he might have felt some mechanical, physical attraction, but that his soul did not desire her. The two antagonists' opinions seem irreconcilable. In fact, the narrator points out that although not a complete novice in the world, Agathon nevertheless remains a stranger in it, alien to people like Hippias who constitute the majority. Unfamiliar with the ways of the world, Agathon is "constantly at risk of being surprised by unexpected coincidences and appearances" (I, 176).

Although the narrator is at pains to point out his disapproval of Hippias and his philosophy, he nevertheless seems to agree with Hippias that Agathon has to learn more about the world. Content with hallucinatory satisfactions, Agathon lives according to a pure pleasure principle, unchecked by any external reality. Hippias, who draws his pleasure from the sensual delights of the material world, is forced to engage with this world, and his pleasure principle is mediated by a reality principle. His reality is, however, exclusively interpreted in terms of his materialist and egotistical pleasure principle. He has developed a whole science of the right use of pleasure. And in this dietectics of pleasure the imagination plays a crucial role. For one thing, he wants to protect himself from suffering from "imaginary" evils. To that purpose he must carefully distinguish "real" and merely "hallucinatory" sensations. On the other hand, the imagination, as excited by certain representations, can enhance physical pleasure; here he locates the function of the arts in their ability to prevent boredom. And finally, there is the power of rhetorical figures over the imagination of others; this art is the source of his luxurious life-style and his social position. Laws exist for Hippias as external givens in the realm of representations, which can be manipulated for one's own purposes by the artistic use of rhetoric. Confronted with Agathon's unbreakable resistance, Hippias swears that if he does not succeed in seducing Agathon into accepting his philosophical system, he will renounce materialism and become a hermit.

With this elaboration of the fundamental opposition between Agathon and his master and "teacher," Hippias, the central conflict in this stage of the "history of Agathon" has been laid out. In fact there are two plans for Agathon's future: the narrator wants Agathon to become acquainted with the ways of the world and to become the subject of his own history and no longer a mere toy in the hand of an ever-changing fate. However, the tutor entrusted with Agathon's education is an "evil" rhetorician sworn to seduce the virtuous Agathon to his own corrupt life-style. Although in Hippias' terms the initiation of Agathon would consist in merely changing Agathon's notion of pleasure, for Agathon to give in to Hippias' concept of sensuality would mean the loss of his narcissistic self.[37] The question hovering over Agathon's future is whether he can be initiated into the world without becoming Hippias' replica.

To say that Agathon has not fully entered the realm of representations as a subject means that, although an object of exchange and a signifier for others, Agathon believes he can refuse to enter a symbolic order and can disregard the laws of exchange. His identity is grounded in a remarkable position toward the law and representations, which is most clearly elaborated in terms of his position on incest. When Hippias tries to persuade Agathon of the pleasures and reality of sensual delights, Agathon counters that only by clinging to a desexualized "spiritual" love can he avoid committing a sin like incest. He argues that having once surrendered to physical attractions, he would quickly get tired of the first libidinal object and have to exchange it for another and yet another. The resulting total loss of restraint would make even incest impossible to resist. Agathon pursues a strange logic: in order to maintain the identity of the object of love, in order not to have to exchange this object for another, the drive needs to be arrested before achieving its aim and sublimated into a spiritual love. What is so stunning about this argument is Agathon's implicit denial of the incest prohibition. The incest taboo can also be considered as the command to exchange one primary object of love for another. His desire to cling to the first and only object of love forever is indeed incestuous. Psyche turns out to be his sister, and it becomes clear that it was only through mere chance—the intervention of the sexually threatening priestess—that their love remained innocent.

Agathon's position toward the fine arts and music serves to support his narcissistic integrity. Good painting and music evoke in the soul a state of peaceful contemplation, or, in its more sublime moments, they strengthen the soul's resistance to external threats of fragmentation. Bad or danger-ous art is music or painting that draws attention to its own artfulness, to its material, and to the body. There is, for instance, the sexually arousing dance of the Thracian women or the "artful" dress of a Cyane, which sig-nify female sexuality and threaten his self-sufficiency, a threat averted by turning it into a danger signal: the sight of Medusa, which quickly cools his senses and fortifies his resistance.

Indeed, Agathon's identity is highly fragile, and his resistance could be broken by subjecting him to the powers of his own aesthetics of illu-sion and by substituting another object of love (a woman who would not present herself as sexually threatening but as a prop for his own narcis-sism) for his absent beloved, whom he hallucinates in his dreams. The threat to his narcissistic identity is posed not by pure physical desire but by love. Once his imagination and his "heart" are involved, he loses the ability to spot those danger signals that turn him away from bodily plea-sures. And this is exactly the strategy Hippias pursues by introducing him to his friend Danae: Hippias' "education" of Agathon almost ends in the transformation, if not the total loss, of Agathon's identity. He is seduced by Danae, and they fall in love. He enters a life of sensual pleasure, and "as his soul mingles" with that of Danae, he risks losing Psyche. In this state the ultimate threat to his identity is posed by the arts and by love.

The Song of the Sirens: The Art of Seduction and the Seduction of Art

Agathon's love affair with Danae is framed by two episodes, the perfor-mance of a pantomime by a dancer called Psyche (at his first introduction to Danae) and a dream about the Psyche of his childhood (at the end of the first part of the novel), which follows the performance of another panto-mime. The narrator comments on both of these sections in similar words: "We have learned from our friend Plutarch that very small incidents fre-quently become noteworthy on account of their great consequences, and that very small actions not infrequently let us see deeper into the interior of people than the festive actions, for which one usually is more consciously composed because one is then exposed to public judgment" (I, 209; see also I, 302). The narrator specifies what is constitutive of the "history" of Agathon: it is not the public spectacle or heroic action that leads to decisive change in the hero but a minute shift in his psychic constitution.

Furthermore, by using the identical and highly allegorical name "Psyche" for two distinct characters, the narrator shifts attention from the plot of the individual episodes to the history of Agathon's soul and the minute psychic transformations that condition this history. In that sense, Psyche is to be understood not as an independent, individual character but as an aspect of Agathon's soul itself. This becomes even clearer when, after the pantomime, the narrator adds the following commentary, which draws attention to Agathon's psychic states and distinguishes his fidelity to Psyche from the usual novelistic virtues: "Psyche held possession of his heart, because the mere memories of her that were left to him gave him a higher delight than the sensations other beauties were able to give him; or, because until then he had seen none who suited his heart so well" (I, 210–11). In brief, in these two framing passages the narrator makes quite explicit what I outlined in the previous section as Agathon's primarily narcissistic constitution: Psyche is his soul, his nostalgic projection into a blissful childhood, which anchors his identity by screening out anything that does not respond to his wishes and expectations.

How is Agathon led to replace Psyche by an external object of love? At an evening entertainment at Danae's house, he watches a pantomime of the story of Daphne. The rest of the audience appreciates Psyche's representation of a Daphne who is sexually attracted to her pursuer, but Agathon is not content with the performance because it deviates from his idea of an utterly chaste and innocent Daphne. Whereas the other members of the audience enjoy the physical attraction of the young dancer, Agathon expects her to be a prop for his image of a chaste ideal. After Agathon has voiced his criticisms of the performance, Danae quickly exits and returns in the costume of Psyche/Daphne and repeats the pantomime exactly according to Agathon's idea. By offering herself as a prop for his narcissistic attachment to Psyche, Danae can instantly substitute herself for Psyche and make Agathon fall in love with her as an embodiment of his ideal.[38]

From then on, the seduction is easy. Danae is careful not to awaken his suspicions or stimulate his defenses by displaying a sexual interest in him. Rather, she becomes his constant companion and friend, and he learns to associate her presence with the same state of peace and satisfaction that he used to find in his contemplative reveries tied to memory images. Thus he becomes dependent on the presence of an external object of love. But to transform this spiritual love into physical love, Danae must again employ the arts. Agathon seems visually protected against sexual arousal, but the "magic power of music" utterly confounds his senses and feelings. Danae stages a performance of the competition between the sirens and the muses: the muses appeal to his Platonism, the sirens stimulate his erotic imagination. Finally, Danae (as the head muse) conquers all Agathon's senses by singing of a lost and faithful love that is ultimately rewarded: "The manner of her performance, or rather the impressions she made through it on her lover, superseded everything one can imagine. His senses were all ear while his entire heart melted into the sensations that dominated her song" (I, 249). After the concert, in a semiconscious state, he wanders into a little temple, where he finds the sleeping Danae; the next morning, the little Psyche sees him leave. From then on, the two lovers live a life of sensuous delights apart from the rest of the world. Although initially Danae was Hippias' accomplice in Agathon's seduction, she too falls in love. Not only their bodies but also their souls "begin to mingle." Agathon begins to take on traces of Danae's sensuality and hedonism (she is after all the female equivalent of a Sophist), and Danae begins to enjoy the simple pleasures of an innocent country life.

But this seemingly self-sufficient dyad cannot last. In fact, it only lasts the time it does because Hippias is away. On his return, he quickly figures out what has happened. Although pleased to see the change in Agathon, he also is slightly vexed at this simpleton's transformation of Danae into a sentimental lover. Hippias invites Danae and Agathon to his house for an evening of entertainment. During the meal the formerly prudish and sheepish Agathon displays his newly acquired worldliness and wit. In response, Hippias says: "I am delighted, Kallias . . . that you, as I can see, have become one of *us*. You justify perfectly the good opinion I had of you at first sight; I have always said that a fiery soul like yours lacks only the real objects in order to get away from the chimaeras without pain, those chimaeras that still a few weeks ago you seemed to be clinging to so strongly" (I, 293–94). This praise of Agathon's successful integration into the Sophist society utterly shocks Agathon. He pleads a slight sickness and withdraws only to return after he has convinced himself of his ability to persuade Danae to live with him according to his own principles.

As the revels continue through the night, he occasionally feels debased and blushes for himself. His ultimate crisis is brought about by a pantomimic representation of Leda, whose utter obscenity revolts him. Later he dreams that he is in a meadow with Danae among nymphs and cupids. She offers him a bowl of nectar, which he empties with sensuous pleasure. Everything around him begins to swirl; he joins the dance, and a fog of sweet odors veils the true nature of things. Suddenly all these appearances disappear, and he seems to awaken out of a deep sleep. He raises his eyes and finds himself at the edge of a steep cliff above a wild stream. On the opposite shore he sees Psyche, whose sad eyes pierce his heart. He dives into the river and tries to reach her, but she vanishes like a shadow. He cannot bridge the small distance between them. Her sad gaze remains fixed on him, and her hand points to the Delphic temple in the background. She flees toward a statue of virtue in a ruined temple, embraces the statue, and disappears: "In indescribable anxiety he wanted to follow her, when he suddenly saw himself sunk into deep mud; the efforts he made to work himself out of it were so violent that he woke up" (I, 304).

Agathon repeatedly tries to dispel the effects of this unsettling nightmare by telling himself that his love for Psyche was merely a preparation for his true love of Danae, that it is she who embodies all perfection and real satisfaction, but these efforts are in vain. He is subject to sudden fits of mourning for his lost innocence and can no longer enjoy his life with Danae in the same manner. Danae senses his sadness and finally asks him about it. He asks her whether she still loves him; she emphatically affirms that she does. He assures her that he does not doubt her love but that he must be certain a love like theirs can never end. To acquaint her with the cause of his sadness, he says: "I love you too much, incomparable Danae, and I feel too much that I cannot love you enough in order to hide from you any longer who this Kallias is, whom you, without knowing him, have thought worthy of your heart. I shall tell you the secret of my name and the entire story of my life, as far back as I am able to reconstruct it; and once you know everything—for why should I not be allowed to disclose everything to a soul like yours?—then you will find it natural that the slightest hint that I might lose your love suffices to make me miserable" (I, 317).

With this preface to his life story, the first part of *Agathon* comes to an end as the protagonist is about to reconstruct his former life as a coherent narrative. This biographical narrative is supposed to counter his mourning for his lost childhood love, which he translates into the fear of losing his current lover. Before he fell in love with Danae, Agathon used to counter a situation of unpleasure by withdrawing into daydreams; by the end of Part I he needs to tell a story. What event brought about this change?

The initial impulse comes from Hippias' disruption of the lovers' dyad, his hailing of Agathon as "one of us." Because of this statement, Agathon can no longer conceive of himself as Danae's unique lover but finds himself compared to all the other Sophists. Seeing himself integrated into the discourse of the others, he desperately seeks that part of himself that is not what they say he is, that pre-linguistic part of himself represented by his Psyche. In fact, the precipice of the dream is present in his reaction to Hippias' words: "Ah, it is more than certain that I am no longer myself! . . . These sumptuous paintings—these slippery nymphs—these conversations where everything that should be great and honorable to man is placed into a comical light. . . . At what kind of precipitous declivity do I find myself?—What an abyss below me!" (I, 295) The abyss separating him from his former self is opened by his participation in the unstable Sophist rhetoric. When in the discussion of the performance of Leda he wants to express his disapproval of Sophist taste, he finds his own words turning against his will into a praise of the performance (I, 299). At the moment the others identify him as "one of them," he sees himself split off from his "true" self. The abyss, the splitting of his "false" from his "true" self, can also be read quite emphatically as his constitution as a subject in conformity with the Lacanian algorithm that describes the *I* as the subject in discourse at that point where the signified is barred from the signifier.[39] With this splitting—Agathon's integration into discourse and his subsequent yearning for the part of himself that is lost as soon as he becomes a signifier for others—an important step for Agathon's further development has been reached. This scenario lays the groundwork for Agathon's distantiation from how he is spoken of by the other. This kind of distantiation becomes crucial for his final rejection of the Sophist system in the prison scene in Syracuse. And this splitting is formative for the subject of Bildung, for it motivates the autobiographical narratives by shaping the desire to be loved not for what one appears to be but as one "truly" is.

The dream that follows the evening entertainment at Hippias' house repeats Agathon's inability to reacquire his lost narcissistic identity. And with this loss, he also loses his ability to daydream. This nightmare is not a wish fulfillment, a dream of a peaceful sleep, but a dream about awakening. The narrator locates the dream in the Stoic oneirocritical tradition in order to emphasize its prophetic function. Although the narrator's hint might point out the diagnostic value of the dream for the reader, Agathon himself does not, on awakening from this dream, engage in critical self-examination. Rather, he awakens to the realization that he can no longer find refuge in the compensatory hallucinations that used to screen out unwanted aspects of reality. With this dream, Agathon has lost his illusionist aesthetics based on producing the transparency and immediacy of reading, seeing, feeling, self and other, past and present. Instead, Agathon now seeks refuge in the narrative temporalization of his life, in a coherent story that will produce his identity. Danae is to listen to the "secret of his name," to affirm her love for that man to whom she gave her heart without knowing him.

Agathon's Stories: Gaps and Incomplete Systems

Agathon tells the story of his life in two parts. The first spans the time from his early childhood to his flight from the Delphic temple, which results in the coincidental discovery of his father. The second part encompasses his life in Athens up to his exile, which leads him to finding Danae. Each narrative section culminates in a scenario for autobiographical narrative. The first narrative is addressed to his father, and Agathon skips over his relationship with Psyche, supposedly out of respect for his listener's age. Retrospectively, however, this omission has a significant implication: it prevents Agathon from learning that Psyche is his sister and thereby supports his incestuous idealism. The second section concludes with Agathon telling his entire *Lebenslauf* to the Athenian people to assure them that they will miss him more than he will miss them. This public narrative, from which he quotes the final passage verbatim, is clothed in the form of a defense, comparable to Plato's *Apology*.

Culminating in the discovery of an "origin," the first half of Agathon's life story assumes the form of a romance. He tells about his childhood as a servant at the temple; he did not know to whom he owed his life, but the ideas and ideals represented by the treasures in the rich and museum-like house of worship become the foundation for his belief in the ordered totality of spiritual beings. As a child he works as a tourist guide for the temple; as a young man he becomes the reader for the priestess. His upbringing in Delphi cannot be considered an education in the traditional sense; rather, it is marked by his resistance to various attempts at seduction by his "educators." First the priest, promising the boy an encounter with Apollo, tries to seduce him under the guise of the god. Then the priestess Phytia, a waning beauty whose interest he initially takes for maternal care, makes sexual advances. Although he bravely ignores her, her suggestions that he might learn something about his father through her, that she is a good friend of his father's, might have weakened his resistance had it not been for his innocent and faithful love of Psyche, which was developing at the same time. Nevertheless he finally has to flee the angry priestess, after she discovers his love for her servant Psyche. On this flight he is offered the hospitality of a stranger. At his host's invitation, Agathon tells the story of his life; Stratonikos then reveals himself as Agathon's father. Agathon is the illegitimate offspring of a mésalliance with the virtuous, beautiful but poor Musarion, whom Stratonikos could not marry because of his own father. After Agathon's mother died in childbirth, he was taken to the

Delphic temple, for his father was waiting for the death of his own father in order to take Agathon home.

The second part of Agathon's story has generic affiliations with a public defense or apology and with a conversion narrative. Agathon tells about his quick rise to fame in Athens: from a student of Plato he becomes a public orator, who is nominated the commander of the treasury and of the entire navy of Athens in order to combat an uprising in the Athenian colonial islands. However, Agathon's public-minded resolution of this conflict, his diplomatic skills and avoidance of private profit, his anti-colonialism and understanding for the colonies' complaints, and his policy of not subjecting them but turning them into confederates and allies bring about his downfall: he is accused of treacherously siding with the enemy and is condemned to exile. His arrival at Smyrna and meeting with Danae are phrased in terms of a conversion. As opposed to his previous life, pictured as a series of displacements whenever he encountered the treacherous and materialist world against which he had to uphold his integrity and idealism, he portrays his life with Danae as the crucial turning point and solution to his former state of disorientation. In her he has finally found true happiness and is able to combine spiritual love with physical attraction to this embodiment of all perfection.

Although flattered by his glorification of her, Danae also senses the danger inherent in this idealization. The narrator ventriloquizes Danae's analysis of this phenomenon: Agathon is in love not so much with her as with an ideal of himself. Danae calls Agathon's love a "Wollüstigkeit der Seele." And since she knows that this "lust of the soul" draws its energy from the imagination and that "the energy of the imagination diminishes as the enjoyment of *real* pleasures leaves less of an emptiness in the heart as there is less time to desire something more pleasant than what is present" (II, 152), this experienced woman senses the danger and uses all her art to maintain his attraction for her by deferring gratification. She avoids too much contact, holds him at a slight distance, and thus attempts to keep him as a friend.

Yet, not only for Danae but also for Agathon himself, the story does not produce its intended effect. As soon as Agathon concludes his narrative, the story achieves the opposite of what he had expected. Instead of constructing a continuity between his blissful childhood and his present condition, his innocent love of Psyche and his lover Danae, a continuity that would guarantee the permanence of their love, he wakes up as if out of a dream. As if "a magical mist was falling from his astonished eyes" (II, 154), he begins to see the world around him in a less idealized light. Danae suddenly appears to him to be just another beautiful and accomplished woman. This narrative has accomplished the subsumption of his idealized Danae to his idealized childhood love, an assimilation that, however, emphasizes the difference between the "ideal woman" of the story and the concrete Danae, whose own story he does not know. Exactly at that moment Agathon is overcome by doubt about his relationship with Danae. Although before "he had esteemed his joy equal to the one of the gods, he doubted strongly, whether in this effeminized gestalt in which love had disguised him, he would still deserve the name of *a man* (the German reads "eines *Mannes*," not "eines Menschen"; II, 155; Wieland's italics). As soon as he realizes that he might be in love with a concrete woman who is not identical with his own idealized image, he feels "disguised." Besides the obvious allusion to Circe's magical transformation of men into swine, Danae's magic is interpreted more narrowly and more straightforwardly not merely as a dehumanization but as a demasculinization.

In telling his story, Agathon enters the symbolic order of representation and perceives the rupture between his ideal love and the concrete woman as well as the distance between his ideal self and current state of alienation. Yet ultimately it is again through Hippias, the Sophist master of discourse, that the lovers' happy dyad is disrupted for good. When Danae has to leave her country estate, Hippias visits Agathon and reprimands him for his withdrawal from the world. Hippias suggests that Agathon go out and look at other women while Danae is away. When Agathon rejects this frivolous suggestion by explaining to Hippias the uniqueness of a lover like Danae, insisting that she cannot be replaced by anybody, Hippias reveals to Agathon a part of Danae's past: her life as a courtesan. Agathon refuses to believe him until Hippias discloses that he knows it from his own experience, that he even had seen her "empfindlich" (sensitive; II, 181). Agathon's reaction to this announcement is described as a fatal blow: "During this revelation our hero resembled more a sculpture or a dead person than himself" (II, 178). He almost faints under the onslaught of overpowering and ambivalent feelings but finally unleashes his aggression against Hippias. With this revelation, Hippias repeats his former characterization of Agathon as "one of us," with similar traumatic effects. In fact, this time it precipitates Agathon's ultimate rupture with his lover. The first time Agathon is hailed as a signifier for others, he attempts to withdraw into the "uniqueness" of his and Danae's ideal love. This time even this kind of denial becomes impossible, for with regard to Danae he only "replaces" another who had been there before him.

The narrator points out that after this discovery Agathon's decision to

Fig. 14. Rousseau, Emile (1762), frontispiece to last volume. A curious intersection of illusionary and allegorical representational practices, this engraving by C. Eisen refers to Emile's courtship of Sophie. In passing, the narrator compares Sophie's pride to that of Circe. He reads the transformation of Odysseus' companions into swine as an expression of their deficient self-respect and disfiguring devotion to the whims of the beloved woman.

leave Danae is as sudden as it is "natural" for him, for all Hippias' revelation finally means to Agathon is that he can no longer respect Danae (see II, 195). One might imagine different "solutions" to this oedipal/castration scenario: Agathon could kill Hippias, or he could replace Danae with another lover. What makes Agathon's resolution so "natural" to him is his immediate interpretation of the scenario as a narcissistic injury, which then is worked out in terms of a primary and secondary narcissism, a debate between his ego-ideal and ideal ego. Thus, the outrage against Hippias and Danae is promptly turned into anger against himself.

The idea that he had merely replaced a Hippias, a Hyacinthus, for her made him in his own eyes into a most despicable slave. He felt ashamed before his better self when he thought of the account he would owe to himself about his stay at Smyrna. . . . Displeasure in ourselves is . . . too painful a state for the soul to bear for a long time. The love of the self gathers all its strength to bring relief. . . . Remorse is only useful to give us a deep impression of the ugliness of a stupid or immoral behavior of which we have become guilty. If it lasted, it would sap the strength needed to work ourselves up to a better state. . . . Agathon had all the more reason to listen to the beneficient appeals of his self-love, for his nearly always excessive imagination had shown to him his transgressions in an uglier light than cool reason would have done. . . . He forgave himself for having loved her that much as long as he had believed in the enormity of her soul's beauty, as long as it had been the attractions of her person. But along with the right to his respect, she had also lost all power over his heart.   (II, 191–95)

After telling how Agathon arrives at the decision to separate himself from Danae, the narrator introduces a brief chapter entitled "A Slight Digression" ("Eine kleine Abschweifung"). He proceeds to explain that the "reconstitution of our hero from a state, in which he did not properly deserve that name," his liberation, was owed "neither to his reason nor to his love of virtue" but merely to his "jealousy and injured self-love" (II, 198). In his "slight digression," the narrator foregrounds some of the crucial positions of the "discourse on the love of the self" and with it the departure from the eighteenth-century paradigms of Enlightenment and Sensibility. His statement about the inefficacy of both reason and the love of virtue as opposed to the efficacy of "injured self-love" exemplifies the move to a new paradigm for the constitution of masculine subjectivity: for this new model any kind of love of an other, even the most harmless one, is "poison." In fact the narrator asserts that the harmfulness of love is too obvious for argument. What is needed, according to his assertions, is a recipe for avoiding the dangerous lures of love. The ensnarements of love can best be avoided through the strict separation of spiritual love from the satisfaction of a physical urge. In other words, he recommends the separation of "need" from "desire." Any demand toward an external object has to be construed as need, as a demand that can be satisfied. Desire, which, as Danae so correctly puts it, emerges from the discrepancy between the constructs of the imagination and that which is at hand, must be bound not to an external object but to an internal one if the self is to be stabilized.

But how should this be engineered? The narrator does not expand on this. Nevertheless Part II provides some clues. What occasions the emergence of desire is a perceived lack or gap; these gaps arise whenever Agathon enters the realm of representations, either as represented by others and then perceiving himself as that which is different in himself from what the others say or—and this will become increasingly important with regard to the construction of Agathon's "history"—by the gaps in his own autobiography. Hence Agathon's narrative produces the discrepancy between the actual Danae and his imaginary beloved; once bereft of the illusion of the uniqueness of his love, Agathon is led to leave Danae. But Agathon's integration into discourse has reawakened his yearning for his "lost" or "truer" self, since the illusion of having found that self in Danae has been disrupted. Nevertheless, after having broken with Danae, Agathon has no concrete directions or orientations to connect his past "ideal self" with his current life.

When Agathon is at the harbor, not knowing which ship to take in order to leave Smyrna, he almost returns to Danae. Then he accidentally encounters an old friend, a wealthy merchant and lover of the arts, who invites him to join him on his boat and travel to Syracuse, where great changes are happening: Plato has been invited by the infamous tyrant and now philosophically inclined ruler Dionysos. Happily Agathon seizes this occasion to participate in the political transformation: "Should he not hurry to aid the divine sage [Plato], whose sublime teaching he had started to practice in Athens in such a glorious manner, to complete the glorious work of transforming an unrestrained tyrant into a good ruler and of fortifying the happiness of an entire nation?" (II, 213) Again, mere chance provides Agathon with a means to establish some continuity with his past and to relate that past to the future project of realizing his idealism in the realm of politics. On the voyage, Agathon enthusiastically prepares himself to serve the public good. He dreams not only of reconciling domestic bliss and public service but also of meeting his former lover Psyche. Now she seems to him even more attractive and pure since he is able to contrast her innocence with the dangerous attractions of Danae. In contrast to his public-minded service in Athens, he has become slightly less firm in his idealism: his reason now tells him (and his experience at Smyrna has taught him) that it is not sufficient to cling to lofty ideals, that in fact whether one believes in an unmediated idealism or a sensual materialism seems to be a matter of chance, and that feeling alone seems an unreliable guide.

However, Agathon's skepticism is opposed by his heart, which still clings to the old ideals, and he does not correct or reconcile these contradictions (II, 227–28). His "romance" narrative and Hippias' revelation have produced two contradictory representations of himself. On the one hand, there is his nostalgic clinging to his childhood idealism (the discourse of his heart), and on the other hand, he is fully integrated into a Sophist rationalist discourse. Instead of reflecting on the causes and consequences of his "mistaken" involvement with Danae, he indulges in enthusiastic fantasies of his political future in Syracuse. He thinks he is protected from all possible errors, that he will not fall prey to another Danae, and that he has no other secret passion capable of thwarting his plans. In this sense, Agathon deceives himself by misinterpreting his disillusionment with Danae as a vaccination against all possible error; he reinterprets the end of his love story as a confirmation of his future intellectual omnipotence. The narrator, however, does not share Agathon's optimism and criticizes his intellectual narcissism. The chapter ends with the following comment: Agathon must go to the court at Syracuse in order to learn "that on these slippery heights virtue either has to be sacrificed to wisdom or that the most careful wisdom does not suffice to prevent the fall of the most virtuous man" (II, 230).

Bad Theater, Bad Actors, and Unforeseen Coincidences

In Books 10–12, which deal with Syracuse, the narrator frequently compares the world of politics with the theater. Thus he begins Book 10 by informing the reader that he would like to provide some information about the "scene" (*Schauplatz*), the "audience," and some of the major "players," who then are to act either for or against Agathon. He characterizes the people of Syracuse as highly unstable and their ruler Dionysos as an unlegitimized tyrant who indulges in luxurious excesses. All the courtiers but one are mere parasites; Dion, the brother of Dionysos' stepmother, alone has the courage to criticize the tyrant. Unfortunately Dion lacks the social graces and skills to make effective use of his natural talents. He merely hopes to achieve his nephew's eventual reform by surrounding him with better people. Once, on the occasion of the grape harvest,

Dionysos celebrates a three-month bacchanalia in honor of himself and his divine namesake. This enormous excess leaves him physically repulsed and bored by his empty life of luxury and pleasure. He finally seeks the advice of his uncle, who encourages him to invite Plato to his court. With Plato's arrival, the entire court is suddenly transformed from a place of sensual distractions and wasteful luxury to a sober philosophical academy. But—and the narrator repeatedly assures us of this—all these changes are mere superficial decorations. The philosophical life-style is a kind of court masquerade, and nobody, least of all Dionysos, has undergone any internal transformation: philosophy is a transient fashion. Plato pays little attention to all this humbug and concentrates on the "humanization" of Dionysos, whose imagination he captures with ease. But Plato is deceived and mistakes for a conversion what merely amounts to Dionysos' vanity, his self-representation as a famous, wise, and well-loved ruler. The narrator explains Plato's deception as a narcissistic self-delusion; the seeming conversion of Dionysos corresponds only too well to Plato's hopes; moreover, the philosopher was as usual judging in terms of abstract principles and systems and lacked knowledge of concrete people.

Nevertheless these superficial transformations bring about a few changes that make the lives of some people increasingly uncomfortable. Two former favorites of Dionysos, Filistos and Timokrates, feel threatened by the new style of government and decide to get rid of Dion and Plato. Timokrates stages a feast to celebrate the beginning of spring. He arranges this celebration so cleverly, hiding lust under the guise of virtue, that even Plato is deceived. The high point of the festival is a ballet about "the history of the human soul." Dionysos, who by that time is ready for some fun, immediately falls in love with the dancer, Bacchidion, who performs the role of "Wollust" (lust). Dion makes the mistake of angering Dionysos moralizing about this "relapse." Dionysos exiles him from Syracuse after a mock trial, and Plato leaves in frustration. Although the rigorous phase of Dionysos' philosophical experiment ends with Plato's departure, he still considers himself a patron of the arts and sciences. Additionally, his two advisors, Filistos and Timokrates, convince him that the arts can be used quite cleverly for propagandistic purposes.

On arriving in Syracuse, Agathon is surprised to learn that Plato has left. He does not know whether to stay or leave under these circumstances and decides to let chance decide (see III, 12). He lulls himself to sleep by imagining how he would act if Dionysos invited him to his court: "He imagined many accidental circumstances he might encounter and fixed for himself the rules according to which he would act. A firmer connection between cleverness and righteousness was at the base of these plans. His own advantage was of no importance" (III, 15). Again we see Agathon caught up in his intellectual narcissism, pretending to himself that he is elaborating "realistic" plans that take into account the concrete situation and its strategic requirements while preserving his own integrity. He is obviously not at all aware of the implicit contradictions in this jumble of instrumental action, chance, and the purity of his personal intentions, each of which belongs to very disparate realms. For the strategist the purity of intentions does not matter and only the outcome of an action and its efficient manipulation are important; likewise, strategic planning and chance are mutually exclusive. A good planner attempts to acquire the maximum of information, exactly in order to protect his projects from accidental mishaps. But Agathon believes he has become a sober realist, merely by having reduced his expectations regarding the outcome of his political venture: he wants to be satisfied, if "only so that at the end of the performance [*Schauspiel*], he can step down from the theater with the gratifying thought that he has performed a beautiful role well. With these gently lulling thoughts, he began finally to fall into a slumber" (III, 15). And he is still asleep when Aristipp, his old acquaintance, wakes him up with an invitation to the court.

These opening passages of Part III combine the theater simile with a description of Agathon's mental state of "dreamy anesthesia," a phrase that recalls his primary narcissism. In contrast to the opening scenes of the novel, however, Agathon no longer projects his narcissistic dreams nostalgically backward into his youth, but he seeks his satisfaction in his political "performance." His idealism now depends on an external audience. Since the narrator has already introduced the pitfalls and superficiality of the political "theater" and pointed out that Aristipp is so relatively uncorrupted only because he has remained content with the role of spectator (III, 17), the reader has been sufficiently prepared for yet another failure of our hero.

Agathon quickly becomes Dionysos' favorite through those seductive arts that the narrator has taught us to consider treacherous: music and rhetoric. First, Agathon charms Dionysos with his accomplished playing of the kithara. Then, suddenly asked at an academic debate to deliver a speech on the best form of government, Agathon surpasses all expectations with an extemporized oration extolling the virtues of a just and good monarchy. Dionysos asks him to become his advisor. After some hesitation, Agathon agrees on the condition that he remain free to withdraw as soon as he sees that his services are no longer needed. He also wants to be assured that if anybody accuses him of something, Dionysos will frankly and immediately impart to him those accusations and give him the chance to defend himself. He joins the court, not in any official function, but merely as Dionysos' close friend.

The narrator concludes Book 11 with a chapter comparing his protagonist to the characters of traditional novels. He points out that in his novel, as opposed to "moral novels," the protagonist undergoes changes.

Agathon appeared at different times of his life to be subsequently a Platonic and patriotic enthusiast, a hero, a Stoic, a lecher; and he was none of the above, although he went through all of these classes and took on some of the color of each of them. We have not yet arrived at the end of his course; therefore one can not yet seek in his character that what he really was, that which constitutes his identity through all these gestalten, and finally that which would remain once all that was alien to him was taken away.   (III, 46)

With this statement the narrator encourages the reader to seek a new model of personal identity, to describe the protagonist's character not as something immutable, not as a mere sum of external changes, but as a function of identity *and* change. Character in this new definition is no longer a set of stable qualities but the mark of individual identity, which is achieved through a process of becoming. Thus, with this new definition of character as "personal identity" calling for a reading of internal changes as development, the narrator draws attention to the feature of the novel that then becomes constitutive for the new genre of the bildungsroman.[40]

Book 12 introduces anew the comparisons between the world of politics and the theater. The narrator refers to the frequent blame laid on Shakespeare for mixing tragical with comical elements. He also refers to the *Hanswurst* or fool of German tragedy, the deus ex machina, and those plays that resolve conflicts through marvelous circumstances. He points out that all these instances of incoherence, disorder, and chance are not limited to the world of the theater but form a constitutive component of the real world. And it is in this world that our hero is trying to accommodate himself. He has given up his Platonic idealism and does not have the illusion that he can make Dionysos a good prince. He merely hopes to lessen his evil influence and places all his hopes in the tyrant's indulgence of sensuous pleasures. Agathon hopes to reform the prince gradually by making use of his vice, by sublimating his pleasures and by exposing him to the arts. The narrator comments that in this respect Agathon still views the prince too optimistically, that this vice is a vice by principle and cannot be transformed into virtue. Furthermore, Agathon realizes Dionysos' dependence on his mistress and hopes to stabilize the tyrant by strengthening his relationship with Bacchidion; again, according to the narrator, this is a mistake.

Although for a while Agathon achieves tremendous progress in making Dionysos' rule more just and beneficial to his people, particularly through his good administrative policies, he nevertheless acquires enemies. For instance, Filistos and Timokrates are "neutralized" through Agathon's actions. He manages to have Filistos placed in a public office of high visibility, an office where he is under close scrutiny and surveillance in all his actions, which prevents him from exploiting his political influence for private gain. Likewise, Timokrates becomes his secret enemy after Agathon pacifies the colonies, whose unrest had been advantageous for Timokrates. The women of Syracuse become Agathon's open enemies because their vanity is hurt by his disregard for their attractions. The narrator tells us the "secret" of Agathon's abstinence: Agathon found at his old friend's home a portrait of Psyche he had once given to the merchant in order to enable him to track down his lost love. The woman who is most upset with Agathon's indifference is Filistos' philosophically inclined wife, Kleonissa. She fell instantly in love with Agathon, in whom she sees not only a highly attractive man but also a fellow philosopher. Thus, his resistance to her "charms" wounds her self-love, and she swears revenge. The plot thickens when Dionysos falls in love with Kleonissa. Dionysos' wife and the other women at the court hope that Kleonissa's chastity might have a beneficial influence on Dionysos. When Dionysos complains to Agathon about Kleonissa's resistance to his advances, Agathon makes a great mistake. He tells the prince that Kleonissa is not all that virtuous, whereupon Dionysos feels encouraged in his approaches to Kleonissa. Furthermore, in the role of a "concerned friend" Agathon informs Filistos about his wife's potential involvement with Dionysos. As soon as Kleonissa learns that Agathon has "slandered" her virtue, she cleverly turns it around by suggesting that Agathon spoke badly of her out of resentment at her rejection of him. From this moment, Agathon instantly loses all his influence over Dionysos.

This would have been the moment for Agathon to carry out his plan to leave Syracuse when he is of no further use. But although Aristipp, Agathon's only true friend, advises him to do so, Agathon remains in Syracuse. His injured self-love misinterprets personal resentment and insult as political responsibility. Thus, he claims he must remain in Syracuse in order to protect the people of Syracuse from their tyrannical ruler. Although previously Agathon had shown no interest in the fate of the exiled Dion, he suddenly joins the camp of his supporters and quickly becomes the leader of a conspiracy against Dionysos. Filistos intercepts letters between him and Dion, in which the latter announces his return to Syracuse. Since there is insufficient evidence for Agathon's conspiratorial activities, he is imprisoned under the pretext of having committed mistakes in his administration.

In prison, Agathon begins to see that his hopes have been disappointed, and his political idealism turns into an utter distrust of mankind.

As soon as Agathon had reached the stage where he would begin to think contemptuously of the species to which he belonged, he finally could not but also despair about himself and entertain strong doubts whether it could not be a mere deception of his exaggerated self-love that he had entertained an opinion of his own nature that is higher than what seems to be compatible with human nature. . . . Could the striving for superhuman greatness, strength, and sublimity of the soul not also just be a mere deception and subtle play of a self-aggrandizing egotism? How if even in this point Hippias were finally right, and if this ideal virtue to which you [he, Agathon] have brought already so many sacrifices would itself be the greatest—though admittedly the most beautiful—of all chimaeras? (III, 134–37)

Thus, by the end of his political engagement in Syracuse, Agathon is about to give up the last of those beliefs that had separated him from Hippias. After his stay in Smyrna, he was ready to surrender his belief in overly lofty idealist notions and to arrange himself "realistically" with what was demanded by the particular situation. However, then he still retained the heartfelt conviction that he could trust the purity of his own intentions and goodwill and thus do good in the public. And he also believed in the worthiness of public-minded activities, even if people had their shortcomings. Although he had gone to Syracuse to engage in a humanist realpolitik, after his imprisonment he is ready to abandon his deepest humanist convictions. In the wording of a commentary on Agathon's monologue, the narrator refers back to Agathon's shattering nightmare: "Thus he hovered at the outmost edge of the abyss that separates wisdom and virtue from the system of a Hippias" (III, 137). What finally turns him away from the abyss, this agency that the narrator calls "chance" or "the genius of Agathon's virtue," is again the skeptical rationalist voice of Hippias, who—exactly at the moment when Agathon is about to agree with his philosophy—happens to wander into his prison: "The theory of the Sophist lost in the immediate presence of his hateful appearance all of the glamour that Agathon's morose fantasy had lent it; as soon as he found in the man before him the entire bodily Hippias as he had left him in Smyrna, he also felt in himself anew the entire Agathon" (III, 141–42).

Hippias tells Agathon that his mistake was to abandon many of his own principles without committing himself entirely to those of Hippias. Although Hippias in many ways repeats Agathon's self-critical reflections, once Agathon hears them from Hippias' mouth, he is able to take up a new position. He begins to defend himself and insists on the purity of his own motives; that is, he resumes the position he had held before his engagement at Dionysos' court. The exchange between the two enables Agathon to reflect on both his deeds and the representations of his actions: "Hippias' reproaches awoke in me the full realization that my will had always been honest and my purposes pure, but among my efforts to justify the whole of my life at Syracuse against your accusations my eyes had been opened for the subtle traps of vanity; I was made aware of the oversecure trust in one's own strength and of an exaggerated self-esteem" (III, 169). The determinate negation of what is uttered in discourse structures Aga- thon's representation of himself: the "I am not what you say I am" or the "I am not what I am able to say about myself" describes the movement between the subject of speech and the narcissistic ego that escapes the dis- course of the other. Thus Hippias' comments provoke two reactions in Agathon. On the one hand, he is reminded of the purity of his motives, his idealism, that better part of himself that led to his political engagement. On the other hand, he is confronted with "the subtle traps of vanity," a wrong kind of self-love, one dependent on the approval of others, that is related to the "stage" of politics and to his hopes of gaining satisfaction from his good "performance."

The conversation with Hippias induces Agathon to rearrange the topog- raphy of his psychical apparatus thoroughly and leads him to insights about his "true nature" and "invisible I."

There is an abyss between us, which will separate us as long as each of us is what he is. You see, my experience, my errors, my mistakes themselves, in the end only served to purify my heart, to strengthen my principles, and to give me more and more light over that which is the dignity, nature, and purpose of my existence. I have never felt more intensely than at this very moment that an unswerving and unintentional adherence to what is eternally true, right, and good is the only need and interest of my more noble invisible I to which this visible I with all its needs, inclinations, passions, wishes, and hopes always must be subordinated if things are to be well with me, or, what amounts to the same, if in this great universe, in which we are determined to further the overall purpose with our activity, I wish to be what I should be. Only because I listened to the injured self-love of the visible Agathon, who wanted to take revenge on all mankind out of the anger of seeing his work destroyed by wicked hands, only for that moment my better I sank below itself and forgot that it was its nature to always want the good and to do it, whether it is recognized or not, whether it receives thanks or not, whether it is met with glory or shame, regardless of what it would achieve, how long its achievements might last, and by whom they might be destroyed again. This, Hippias, is what I call virtue, and to this virtue I swear here, in your presence, unbreakable faith. (III, 170)

In Agathon's attempt to outline the abyss that separates him from Hippias, not only does he affirm his adherence to the ideal ego of his childhood (his self-sufficient and therefore independent and "more noble invisible I") and the one he still identified with when he first met Hippias, but he also begins to construct his adherence to his ideal ego in terms of a project for a narrative, when he claims that his errors and mistakes served a higher purpose, that of enlightenment, a purpose anchored in the totality of the "great universe."

Exactly at the moment Agathon firmly rejects Hippias and Sophist philosophy, swears to devote the rest of his life to virtue, rejects Hippias' help in freeing him from prison, and rediscovers his "invisible I," Archytas, an old friend of his father's, comes to his rescue like some deus ex machina. Archytas, the head of the republic of Tarent, threatens Dionysos with war unless Agathon is released from prison. Thus, Agathon's political adventures in Syracuse are brought to a conclusion: once he affirms his ties to his earliest ideals and his ideal ego not merely in terms of hallucinatory dream production but also in terms of constructing his life as a meaningful whole (meaningfully integrated with things at large), a quasi-omnipotent paternal figure comes to his aid and invites him to his home.

Homecoming, the Recovery of the Lost Object, and the Identity of an Idealist

In Book 13 the narrator abandons his previous claims to verisimilitude and historical accuracy and instead foregrounds elements of the marvelous and thereby marks his narrative as a fictional construction.[41] As soon as Agathon enters the home of the wise and widely loved Archytas, who is described as an almost superhuman father figure, and is allowed into the female quarters of the house, he sees Psyche, now married to Archytas' son Kritolaos. However, Agathon's sorrow over the loss of his lover is quickly alleviated when he learns that Psyche is his biological sister.[42] Thus, when Agathon finally finds a home, a father, and the long-sought love of his childhood, he is faced with a definitive separation from his lover, in the sense that she belongs to another man. Yet at the same time he learns that he cannot possess that woman, he also learns that in a way she will always remain his. Thus, Agathon's marvelous recovery of Psyche affirms her function: she will always remain for him not a libidinally invested external object but the total object of his primary narcissism. In this sense the marvelous plot subscribes to Agathon's denial of the castration threat, evading the exchange of the first object of love for an other.

The narrator introduces the marvelous story of Psyche's adventures by telling readers that his restraint to this point in using such extraordinary devices as storms, for instance, now allows him recourse to poetic license. In the same spirit, he suggests to his readers that Psyche's miraculous recovery may herald a sudden return of Danae. And indeed, one day on a hunting excursion, Agathon and Kritolaos are surprised by a storm and seek refuge in a secluded country house. There they find Danae. In depicting this unexpected encounter, the narrator indulges at length in sentimental detail: tears, fainting, tender embraces. From then on Agathon and Danae meet frequently in tender friendship, and Agathon's hopes of confirming Danae's innocence and rejuvenating their love seem promising. But he has not taken into account Danae's "secret story" and the fact that she is no longer the person he left at Smyrna. After Agathon's departure, Danae began to feel remorse for her loose life-style. She secluded herself in the country to devote herself to virtue and chastity under the new name of Chariklea.

Thus, even though the stage is set for a romantic ending, Part III takes an altogether different turn. Danae is allowed two books to tell her "secret" story, and this story neither proves her innocence nor leads to her marriage with Agathon. Rather, her confessional narrative attests to her transformation and proves to Agathon that the woman before him is no longer identical to his former lover. In that sense, Danae's confession is comparable to Julie's post-wedding disclosures. The two stories of the transformation of an ideal woman differ, however. Julie undergoes a quasi-religious conversion that transforms her into a mother in the service of the state; Danae rediscovers her identity as a beautiful soul.

Danae begins with her childhood. From a modest background, she was trained as a dancer. She was called Myris. The fact that she led her life under a variety of different names (Myris, Danae, Aspasia, and finally Chariklea) distances Danae's autobiographical narrative. She talks about those stages in her life as if she were discussing another person. Since she receives all her names except the last one from men who want to fashion her as a particular object of their imagination and give her the name of a woman she supposedly resembles, Danae's perspective on herself always contains the view others have of her. She is the woman who has learned most perfectly to see herself as an object in the gaze of others, as a representation.

However, she has some vague notions of an ideal representation of beauty after which she wants to fashion herself. From her early youth, when she worshipped Venus and the Graces, she has had a certain love and anticipation of a higher beauty. Upon hearing a Pindaric ode celebrating the Graces, this idea of beauty becomes clearer for her and more firmly settled in her mind. Discontented with her fate as a dancer, she cherishes the hope of finding some "higher" vocation. She becomes the model for a painter from whom the famous Alcibiades has ordered a painting of Hebe. This painting turns out to be so beautiful that the young Myris runs the risk of falling in love like Narcissus with this representation of herself (III, 260). Alcibiades likewise falls in love with the painting and demands to meet the model. The painter, however, claims he fashioned it from his imagination alone. Thereupon Alcibiades commissions a painting of Danae, and Myris again provides the model. Alcibiades watches from a hidden cabinet he had installed in the painter's studio for exactly such voyeuristic pleasures. Myris makes such a strong impression on Alcibiades that he comes forth from his hiding place and challenges the painter and the model with the pronouncement that the young woman first has to be formed into a Danae before she can represent her and that he himself will look after her "education" (III, 264). Thus he announces he will introduce her to the famous hetaera Aspasia under the name of Danae.

Aspasia takes her into her luxurious home and treats her as a daughter. She loses no time in warning her new student against the dangerous Alcibiades, who is as charming as he is unfaithful, as accomplished and powerful as he is spoiled and unreliable, and who has broken the hearts of innumerable women. Danae observes Alcibiades' vanity and swears never to fall in love with him. But all unawares, she already has. Aspasia helps Danae improve her skills in dance and pantomime. One day Alcibiades challenges her by suggesting that some subjects, Leda, for instance, do not lend themselves to pantomimic representation without losing the necessary grace of the performance. Thereupon Danae performs the story of Leda, and Alcibiades criticizes the verisimilitude of her performance, for which he blames her lack of experience. Danae flees from him into Aspasia's arms. As Alcibiades tries to seduce Danae by making her jealous, she begins to flirt with another man.

At this point Aspasia delivers a lecture on feminist guerrilla tactics to her student, which Danae remembers and quotes verbatim to Agathon. Women, though by nature in no way inferior to men, have been excluded from legislative processes, subjected to the tyranny of men, and

even mocked by their oppressors, who call them the "weaker sex." Therefore a woman has to try to exert as much influence over men as possible
while keeping her own independence, most important the independence
of her heart. To achieve this, a woman must learn to see men as they
are with all their vanity and weaknesses, she must learn not to admire
them. She should also train herself not to be impressed too much by one
particular object, but should reduce her sensibility and susceptibility by
seeking out manifold distractions. In brief, she must renounce romantic
love. Furthermore, she cannot hope to have influence over a man solely by
means of her beauty; like a siren, she must also use and cultivate her mind.
The image of the sirens in which Aspasia couches her advice about the art
of captivating men by flattering their intellectual aspirations is noteworthy
(III, 311); the allegorical representation of the muses' competition with the
sirens was instrumental in Danae's seduction of Agathon, and Archytas,
in his critique of Agathon's biography, evokes the sirens to illustrate for
Agathon the greatest danger he has had to face.

Danae could have become a second Aspasia, had a certain natural weakness not reduced the efficacy of Aspasia's warnings. After Aspasia's death,
Alcibiades becomes Danae's lover, but the affair soon ends. Danae wants to
leave Athens; the memory of Aspasia becomes too painful, and she wants
to rid herself of her admirers. Her beauty, the admiration she receives from
all sides, and her self-confidence prevent her from falling in love again.[43]
On her voyage to Milet, she is captured by pirates and sold on the slave
market to the harem of the Persian prince. She becomes his exclusive love.
To flatter his vanity, his desire to resemble the famous Pericles, Cyrus calls
her his Aspasia. After Cyrus' death, she moves to Smyrna and builds a
temple for the Graces, but, as she confesses,

the Graces whose priestess she became were not the Graces of a Pindar, nor the
playmates and followers of the celestial Venus; not the chaste goddesses whom
Psyche as virgin, as friend, as wife, and as mother was serving. Danae blushed less
over what she had been than over the thought of wanting to hide from herself or
her friend how far she was from Psyche—even at the height of her triumph and
with regard to the amiability attributed to her at that time. The dancer of Leda
insulted the divinity of the Graces by trying to hide such a character under the
veil of chastity. This is how I feel now; and I know how to justify this feeling,
therefore I do not have to fear to be betrayed by this sensation. But at that time
a pleasant illusion of the imagination and the heart made me think otherwise.
(III, 346)

Her transformation into Chariklea cannot be called a conversion, for she
feels no guilt over any fault, nor does she acknowledge any powerful religious authority in whose light she reinterpreted her life; rather, she is

motivated by a sense of shame. She is concerned about the representation of herself. She blushes at the thought of not living up to her own ideals of chaste beauty, the Pindaric Graces or the "playmates of a celestial Venus," the ideal self she had fashioned for herself in her childhood and the one she sees embodied in Psyche. She abdicated her worldly career as Danae not because she suddenly saw it as a transgression but because it was a deviation from her "true" self.[44] Her transformation into Chariklea is basically a return to the ideals she glimpsed in Pindar's ode, to the ideal ego of her youth, and a disinvestment of all object investments.

As Danae concludes her "secret story," Agathon is more than ever convinced of her ultimate innocence and virtue, and he phrases his image of the virtuous Danae in the image of his nightmare in which he saw himself separated from the virtuous Psyche, who was embracing a statue of virtue: "And is not Danae, who embraces imploringly the statue of virtue, the most glorious triumph of virtue?" (III, 349) Having thus once again fused Danae with Psyche, he begs her to join Archytas' family as his wife. But Danae only repeats that her decision to devote her life to chastity cannot be changed. She could not bear to join this virtuous family; there she, who has so much to regret, would be permanently ill at ease. She reminds him that her liaison with Hippias was not her worst aberration. This finally convinces Agathon that the two cannot marry. He too is seized by the holy fire of the enthusiastic love of virtue and swears he will forever love her, love her as he loves virtue. She leaves, satisfied with the effect of her story and careful not to extend their meeting too long "since she could not yet flatter herself of being regarded by her lover as a mere soul" (III, 357). Once again the pattern is repeated: Agathon can hold on to his lover only at the cost of libidinal disinvestment; only then can she be equated with his Psyche.[45] If he loves her, he will love her as she loves virtue, as a disembodied moral ideal or, rather, as a decarnalized beautiful soul, as the object of his moral narcissism.[46]

The strengthening of Chariklea's and Agathon's ideal ego into an ego-ideal or superego is strongly related to the figure of Archytas. For instance, Danae points out that the idea of seeming better than she is is made particularly unbearable by the proximity of Archytas' family. Similarly, for Agathon, Archytas appears exactly at that moment when he finally and conclusively rejects Hippias and swears adherence to a rigorous ideal of virtue. In that respect it is important to note that the paternal figure of Archytas is not a figure of prohibition, surveillance, or the law. He is not the castrating father who threatens Agathon unless he gives up his object of love. Rather, at the same time that he turns out to be Psyche's father-in-law, who indicates to Agathon that he will never be able to marry her, he also reveals himself as Agathon's father-in-law, as the person who gives Psyche to Agathon as his sister, the object of love he will never lose. Archytas becomes the guarantor of aim-inhibition as the only permissible type of object investment; to the extent that he preserves a desexualized, narcissistic investment, he also becomes the protector of an unperturbed, self-sufficient ego. And it is in this light that we have to understand Archytas' superhuman qualities: he is not the father from the Oedipus complex, but the omnipotent father Freud situates in the pre-oedipal phase and with whom identification is reactivated through the repression of the Oedipus complex.[47] In brief, with Archytas' help, Agathon finally learns to represent himself in perfect congruence with his narcissistic ideals. Archytas helps Agathon anchor his moral narcissism through the denial of a world in which men are driven by conflicting appetites, that is, the denial of object investment, castration, and mortality.

The more Agathon sees in Archytas a second father, the more he desires that Archytas come to know him better.

For merely the fact that he was the housemate of this divine man made him believe that his inner constitution was improving from day to day, but this only strengthened his decision to reveal himself entirely to him and to give him the most detailed account especially of that change in his inner constitution, which happened during his stay in Smyrna. For his heart told him that since that time his inner worth had diminished rather than increased. He neither could nor would leave the gaps that then originated in the system of his uncorrected opinions and beliefs.   (III, 360)

Agathon's decision to give Archytas a precise account of the changes in his moral constitution during his stay in Smyrna—as in the case of Danae's confessional narrative—is motivated not by guilt, the remorse over a transgression, but by shame, the feeling that his inner worth has somehow decreased. This decrease in inner worth indicates that the norm is not provided by a law but that it is relative to a former version of his self. Furthermore, his yearning to reconstitute his better self is articulated as a desire to close the gaps in his system of opinions and convictions. And it is for that purpose that Agathon begins to write his biography. He decides against an oral narrative for fear of being carried away by his imagination.

Yet the written document by itself is only the first step in rationalizing his system of opinions and in retrieving his old self. The decisive contribution comes from Archytas, who immediately lays his finger on the troublesome passage, which deals with Agathon's loss of his youthful enthusiasm when he fell in love with Danae.

It was in the house of the beautiful Danae at Smyrna that without your notice a new kind of charm managed to tune down your heart to the people and objects surrounding you. I think this deception that you were subjected to is very well captured in the image of the competition of the sirens and the muses, which Danae in the first days of a still innocent love gave you to hear and see. You thought you had been placed by the song of a muse into the temple of heavenly Aphrodite; and in fact it was the most dangerous of all sirens who drew you, with fettered eye and ear, without your knowledge into her cliffs.   (III, 368)

What signals to Archytas the degree of this dangerous transformation is not so much Agathon's subsequent actions and life-style but the phrases he uses to describe falling in love with Danae. Archytas is alarmed that in his narrative to Danae Agathon apologized for his previous youthful enthusiasm for the Orphic religion and that he narrated his encounter with Danae as a *conversion* from a beautiful, but empty idealist enthusiasm to the enthusiasm of true love (III, 369). This is highly significant because it indicates to us that the formation of the protagonist, Agathon's Bildung, is to reach its conclusion through a critique of the representation and narrativization of the self.

After reproaching Agathon for misrepresenting his encounter with Danae as a conversion, Archytas reminds Agathon of how he had talked about beauty and value of the Orphic religion before his encounter with Danae. He praises Agathon's rendering of this system of belief by assuring him that neither Pythagoras nor Orpheus could have phrased it better than Agathon, whom he quotes verbatim:

"How welcome is to us at that age a philosophy which combines the advantage of our curiosity with the inclination to the marvelous, which is characteristic of youth, which answers all our questions, explains all riddles, and solves all questions! A philosophy which bans all that is dead from nature, which populates each atom of creation with spiritual beings, which fertilizes each point in time with events that shall ripen for future eternities. A system in which creation is as immeasurable as its originator, which shows to us in the seeming confusion of nature a majestic symmetry, in the government of the moral world an immutable plan, in all classes and generations of beings one single state, in the intricate movement of all things one universal point of rest, in our soul a future god, in the destruction of our body the reinstatement of our original perfection, and in the dark abyss of the future bright prospects of boundless bliss." And of such a philosophy, Agathon, you could say to the beautiful Danae: "Happy experiences—What were they other than those she had provided you with?—had taught you to recognize the enthusiastic and unreliable nature of that philosophy?"   (III, 370).[48]

Affirming the "beauty" of representing the world as a spiritually animated totality is Archytas' first didactic goal in his conversation with Agathon.

Then Archytas leads Agathon to the recognition that he drew the wrong conclusion from his experiences at Smyrna, that the simple change of his sensations, the seduction of his senses by Danae, cannot negate the truth of the Orphic religion. Here Archytas introduces a different notion of truth, one that is not disproved by experiential, sensual knowledge but is founded on an inner feeling, or intuition. And indeed, his pupil proves him right, for his argument makes Agathon remember what his distorting conversion narrative had made him forget, that even when he was most immersed in sensual delights, he still had this deep conviction and feeling "that in those ideas, which appear to the sensual man as nothing better than extravagant dreams, there was nevertheless the genuine stamp of truth— that even in those dreams was more reality, more entertainment and encouragement for our spirit, a source of purer joys, and a firmer ground of being self-content than in all the delights the senses have to offer" (III, 373). Thus, the second step in Archytas' lecture is to lead Agathon to the production of an inner truth, a powerful and coherent system, that alone can be the marvelously "firm ground" for self-contentment.

Upon being questioned by Archytas why he had not taken advantage of this deeply felt intuition and changed his life, Agathon acknowledges that he had been seduced by the power of present sensations over the distant and past ideas and ideals and that Sophist rationalizations had allowed him to fabricate a half-consistent system to justify his hedonism. Agathon points to the limitations of human knowledge, which led him to tell himself that since man's reason is limited, since he does not and cannot know where he comes from and where he shall go, since there is so much that is mysterious and inexplicable in nature, he should be content with what is given to him in the present, what he can enjoy through his senses, what gives him and others happiness. He tells Archytas that only when he had reached this extreme position within the Sophist system and almost come to subscribe to it in its entirety was he finally turned away from it through Hippias' visit in the prison. From that moment on, he felt more than ever "the lack of support that an intense feeling of our connection with the invisible world gives to virtue; my former way of thinking became dubious to me, and although it did not greatly perturb my peace, it was at times quite bothersome, I was not capable of resolving in any satisfactory manner those objections that my reason made against those maxims to which my heart had this particular inclination" (III, 378). It is the resolution of this gap in his system, this lack of an encompassing system of support for his virtue, that he hopes to find with Archytas' help. Archytas is supposed to help him "bring myself into closer agreement with me" (III, 379).[49] In other words, Archytas is to help Agathon close the gaps that arose in his system after he was introduced to Sophist discourse, sexuality, and the unpredictable events of the material world. Agathon demands that Archytas help him formulate his own biography as a coherent whole and integrate the autobiography into a larger narrative, a spiritual or hermeneutic system, that provides a reading of the world beyond skepticism and materialism.

After Agathon utters this wish, the two men arrive at the temple of Apollo and sit down on its steps as the sun sets. Despite the beautiful view, Agathon's vision (as at the very beginning of the novel) is turned inward, and his attention focuses on Archytas' words, who answers his demand by providing the recipe for the good construction of the self: he tells Agathon his own *Lebenslauf* or *Bildungsgang*, interspersed by philosophical and moral asides; in brief, he gives Agathon the formula for the construction of the self that rules the genre of the bildungsroman.

Archytas' formula is based on his interpretation of the "know thyself." He understands this imperative not as a command for self-examination but as an occasion for a particular experience of the self, which results from the limits of knowledge. He agrees with Agathon that knowledge of ultimate beginnings and ends is impossible, yet he insists that we must always know how we are connected with the "great totality," the spirit that opposes the manifold and deceptive material world. According to Archytas, this totality lies within ourselves: "Does not in our inner sense lie uncovered to us an invisible world, the boundaries of which no mortal being has so far explored?" (III, 382) Archytas claims that the contemplation of the unity, harmony, uniformity, and order our inner sense reveals to us exposes one common communal purpose, "which is the visible representation of the ideas of an infinite reason, the eternal effect of an eternal spiritual original force, from which all forces draw their being, a single city of god, ruled according to a uniform law, inhabited by reasonable beings, ruled by justice and wisdom and by the constitution of a communal striving for perfection" (III, 402).

Archytas' statements bear a certain affinity to Lessing's ethical ideal of individual striving for perfection in his "Christentum der Vernunft" (The Christianity of reason; 1784) and to Kant's notion of how the contemplation of the mathematical sublime reveals a spirit of law and order as a moral force and how the limits of our intuitive cognition as they become apparent through the mathematical sublime strengthen our respect for man's reason.[50] And indeed, although we are not dealing with the mathematical or other sublime, the contemplation of "this great, all-encompassing thought" has, like the contemplation of the sublime, an effect on our conception of ourselves. This contemplation "exhausts all the forces of our spirit and satisfies all its drives" (III, 402). Because of this overpowering effect, we can think of nothing "higher, better, or more perfect," and "this is the strongest proof of its truth." When we intuit this proof, we feel that we are more than a "mortal earthly creature, infinitely more than a mere animal man" (III, 402–3). From this instant on, Archytas says, "I feel that the spirit alone can be my true ego, that only his business, his well-being, his happiness are mine," and that "the animal has to be subordinated" and "serve this spirit." "In brief, Agathon, from that moment on, when this great thought has taken possession of my interior and has become the soul of all of my drives, decisions, and actions, all those ideas, desires, and passions that would separate my ego from the totality to which it belongs, that would isolate my advantage, that would subordinate my duty to my use or pleasure, vanish" (III, 405). After Archytas has thus set forth the principles of his belief, Agathon is completely convinced of their truth and can finally establish a harmony between his inwardly felt convictions and his reason; he can reaffirm his childhood belief in the Orphic religion from an adult perspective by reestablishing for himself a systematic totality.

Archytas' authority justifies what initially seemed like mere idealist fantasies as a coherent system of belief.[51] He even addresses the potential objection that this belief could lead to dangerous enthusiasm.

Even the objection that the belief in the connection of our spirit with the invisible world and the general system of things can easily become the cause of one of the most dangerous diseases of the human mind, of religious or superstitious enthusiasm, is of no importance. For it merely depends on us alone to limit our inclination toward the miraculous by reason, not to overestimate the momentary play of fantasy and feelings, and to regard the images, which the ancient poets of the Orient used in order to illustrate their notions of the invisible and of the future, merely for what they are, that is, to regard them as images of supersensory things, things that cannot be represented. . . . These lovely dreams of fantasy are adequate for the childish age of mankind, and the Orientals seem to want to remain, as in all other things, always children. But we, whose intellectual faculties have developed under a temperate climate and under the influence of civic freedom, who are not fettered by hieroglyphs, holy books, and religious doctrines— we, who are permitted to take even the most honorable fables of antiquity just for fables—are obliged to purify our notions more and more, and in general not to want to know more of what lies beyond our senses than what reason teaches us to believe and what is required by our moral need. (III, 410–11)

In this passage Archytas outlines the teleological model by which the history of Agathon is constructed. In "Erziehung des Menschenge-schlechts" (Education of mankind; 1780) Lessing describes a similar paradigm of onto- and phylogenetic progress in his formula "Erziehung ist Offenbarung" ("Education is revelation"). Yet whereas Lessing in the "Education of Mankind" argues against Warburton's *Divine Legation of Moses* that both the Jewish religion and the Christian religion must be understood within the same macro-historical paradigm of the gradual development of man's reason and consequently of his ethical potential, Archytas posits a different perspective on the history of semiosis. For him the Western progress to a stage of rationality beyond the dependence on "hieroglyphs" and "fables" is not, as in Condillac's reading of Warburton, to be understood as part of the history of semiosis. For Archytas the particular signification of the "hieroglyph" and "fable" does not become obsolete. Rather, by being able to read those earlier modes of signification no longer literally but as mere images of what cannot be represented, Western man has acquired the faculty of "reading in the spirit." In Archytas' version, the history of semiosis is reinterpreted as the history of hermeneutics. Lessing justified the history of successive religions within this hermeneutic paradigm by reading the allegorical truths hidden in religious doctrine and describing them within the providential scheme as "primers" for the education of the human race. But even in Lessing's historical construction, the stage of "revealed religion" and mysteries is one that now and henceforth can be left behind. For Archytas, however, it is exactly Western hermeneutics that justifies and necessitates a return to those religious myths and fables. This return is protected from a potential relapse into superstition, since for the adult Westerner those fables illustrate and affirm the order of the supersensible as well as of his own spirituality.

Furthermore, whereas Lessing uses parallels with the development of the individual to illustrate his macro-historical schema, Archytas derives from the macro-historical paradigm the imperative to reinterpret the history of the individual, to lead Agathon back to his childhood idealism, to close the gaps in his system of beliefs and opinions. In Rousseau's pedagogy and in the aesthetics of Diderot, we encountered a return to the fable and the hieroglyph, the "image sensible" lost in the progress of analytical knowledge. However, those cases dealt with an attempt to compensate for this acknowledged loss within the realm of representations through the aesthetics of illusion. In Wieland's *Agathon*, the return is of an altogether different nature: it is not the recuperation of the image sensible within an aesthetics of immediacy. In fact, the return is not within but through the realm of representations. It is not a matter of making something other present to the subject but of making the subject present to itself at the threshold of representation and through a narrative (re)construction of subjectivity vis-à-vis what has been lost.

Finally, whereas Rousseau's Emile was kept in line through his love for an ideal woman, Archytas' disciple is no longer in search of an ideal lover. In refinding both Danae and Psyche, he also rediscovers his childhood love, not as a love of an other but as a love of the self. As opposed to Saint-Preux, who had to learn to love Julie merely "spiritually," Agathon's spiritual love is not a product of enforcement and of strict surveillance against potential transgressions; instead, it is his original love for Psyche. By casting all the love stories into the mold of fraternal love, the novel sidesteps the incest prohibition. By restoring to the protagonist everything he has lost, it denies both human mortality and the cultural violence of castration.

The novel's happy ending is indicated in the last few pages, which merely outline what happened to Agathon after his conversation with Archytas. Until he finally learns to see in Danae exclusively the new Chariklea, who has joined Archytas' household as a second mother of Psyche's children, he travels around the civilized world. He learns to observe the nature of men and concludes that indeed actual men resemble Hippias' notions; however, such observations can no longer make Agathon lose his trust in man's ideal image as Archytas has laid it out to him. Finally he returns to Tarent, and, after Archytas' death, he and Kritolaos continue the just and wise rulership of this republic. The details of Agathon's history after his conversation with Archytas seem irrelevant. Agathon's history reaches its conclusion by the time Archytas concludes his speech, a speech that began as a commentary on or a critique of Agathon's autobiography. Archytas' lecture can be understood as the blueprint of the sublimation script of Bildung, the truth of which Agathon has to intuit in order to fashion himself into that self, which can then become a wise observer of men and peoples, a good citizen, and an executive of a just state. This kind of closure to the bildungsroman indicates that the narrativization of the self from an autobiographical perspective does not by itself produce the self of Bildung; rather, the new subjectivity must be constituted within a hermeneutic paradigm. The norms for the construction of the subject of Bildung do not derive from external laws or principles but are a hermeneutic procedure for making sense, for constructing a continuity of becoming and a totality of meaning.

In calling *Agathon* and the bildungsroman the master script of sublimation, I want to stress two characteristics of this narrative: the fact that finally it is only the narrative itself that can produce the illusion of an autonomously existing whole, an illusion produced, however, through a series of revisions or more precisely denials; and the privileging and exploration of various types of narcissism in the formation of subjectivity. The novel depicts its protagonist vis-à-vis three types of narcissism. There is a corporeal narcissism, as when Agathon mobilizes his defense mechanisms against any object investment and external stimulation that might threaten the integrity and wholeness of his body. All of Agathon's encounters with sexuality belong to this type of narcissism. Coexistent with corporeal narcissism, we find an intellectual narcissism, that is, Agathon's belief in the omnipotence of his thought. His intellectual narcissism begins with the libidinal investment of his "contemplations," for instance, when he thinks that his reflections and memories of Psyche enable him to transcend the concrete situation. It then becomes particularly dominant in his political careers, in which he thinks he can exercise perfect control over his and his adversaries' actions through his clever schemes and plans. Finally, there is the subsumption or integration of the two prior forms of narcissism into a moral narcissism, that is, a radical renunciation of pleasure, the body, indeed any kind of satisfaction, in the name of duty. Here neither the integrity of his body nor the purity of his motives but merely the compatibility of his actions with the overall purpose of serving the general goal of humanity can justify his actions and the manner in which he fashions himself. Agathon's moral narcissism emerges when he sees himself alienated in rationalist discourse, particularly when he sees the "traps of vanity," the dangers of finding satisfaction in his own rationalizations and apologies. It is here that he suddenly feels ashamed of wanting to appear better than he actually is. This "shame" motivates him to write his autobiography for Archytas, who is then to reinterpret and complete his life's story by integrating it into the entirety of an idealist life-philosophy.

If we look at how the novel itself supports the valorization of narcissism as the necessary condition for an idealist, neo-humanist ethics of duty, we can see the narrative construction as a series of denials of object investments and the Oedipus complex. This can be brought into relief if we recall how the protagonist's relation to other characters is constructed: Psyche is portrayed as Agathon's alter ego, a kind of double to whom he feels attached in terms of a desexualized love. Danae is cast in the mold of Agathon's relationship with Psyche, first by Agathon himself but finally by the narrator, in such a manner that neither of the two women has to be given up and both become fused. Agathon's rejection of Hippias parallels his renunciation of bodily pleasures as well as his denial of a world in which the appetites are at constant war. Archytas is portrayed as a quasi-omnipotent and omniscient father figure, who reaffirms, stabilizes, and justifies the attachment to the ideal ego of Agathon's childhood.

However, the novel can be characterized not only in terms of this series of denials but also in terms of its production of a certain kind of nostalgic utopia. Indeed, the denials are the counterpart and the result of Agathon's and the novel's glorification of childhood. It is in this respect that the cultural and historical significance of the bildungsroman can best be understood. My reading of *Agathon* has traced in detail to what extent both Agathon's character and his development are entirely defined in terms of his relation to his childhood. Clearly, this childhood has nothing to do with the concrete details of the early years of his life but is entirely a retrospective nostalgic projection. One could also describe Agathon's childhood as the hallucination of something that was never there, something produced out of lack and absence. The beautiful images in the temple infuse him with a love for the company of spiritual beings. The divine figures of the Orphic religion compensate for the lack of parental love, for his disorientation in the world, but they also become the permanent model for any future object relation and the ancestors of his superego, Archytas. Thus, his childhood contains the germ of his entire future "development," the realization of his "true" self.

In this chapter I have analyzed exemplary texts representative of two new genres, the Classical German Tragedy and the bildungsroman, as they participate in that paradigm of subject formation propagated with the emergence of German idealism, neo-humanism, and hermeneutics. Both genres leave behind the mid-century concern with immediacy and transparency, so typical of the illusionist aesthetics of the epistolary novel and the bourgeois tragedy, in favor of aesthetic distance and the formal aspects of the artifact. The analyses of *Maria Stuart* and *Agathon* have demonstrated that this attention to artistic form can also be described, in the case of the play, as a revalorization of the spectacle, or, in the case of the novel, as a transformation of the conversion narrative. Both the new spectacle and the narrative of the bildungsroman are crucially concerned with the stabilization of male ego-boundaries.

Maria Stuart is a new type of spectacle because its splendor of stately and religious figures is displayed not vis-à-vis a crowd but vis-à-vis the individual spectator. On the one hand, this spectator becomes acquainted with the workings of a bureaucratic apparatus that only seems abstract. On the other hand—while the machinery of the state reveals its flaws and fraudulent character—the spectator is reassured that the order of representation is ultimately grounded in a fundamental gender polarity. The absence of a positive representative of the law is recoded as the lurking castration threat posed by the female body and sexuality.

Agathon, although it has recourse to conversion as the traditional paradigm of autobiographical narration, transforms this pattern radically. Whereas conversion and confession narratives aim at autobiographical inscription into the truth of Scripture, a reading of one formerly transgressive or sinful life into a life of potential redemption, the bildungsroman accomplishes the "redemption" of the individual independently of an external truth. It advocates and constructs a new model of character and personal identity in terms of an entelechial development. The bildungsroman produces a series of scenarios for autobiographical narration, which fabricate both a version of an ideal self of the past (childhood) and of the future; both versions are to be negotiated, interpreted, and rewritten in terms of their inner coherence and completeness. The subject of the bildungsroman is not implicated in guilt or transgression; rather, he has to narrate, live, read, and write his life until he can overcome any state of shame that makes it impossible for him to recover his ideal self in the present and future.

Finally, I have demonstrated how each text is situated within the historical emergence of new institutions. *Maria Stuart* puts on stage the new penal institution, the prison, which is to reshape or rehabilitate the soul of the individual. In *Agathon* we see the formation of a male subject destined for a position within the state bureaucracy through the narrative organization of his striving for perfection in relation to his idealized childhood. The analysis of Schiller's *Aesthetic Education* demonstrated the extent to which this narrational imperative is intimately bound up with the self-fashioning of an upwardly mobile civil servant in an expanding state bureaucracy, behind which lie the institutional reforms of neo-humanist educational policies. Yet, another new institution has to be taken into account, an institution already present in Rousseau's *Emile* and *Julie*: the new bureaucrat is formed in relation to the new mother.[52]

Granted *Agathon*, as opposed to *Wilhelm Meister*, makes little of an ideal, loving, and all-caring mother.[53] In fact, Agathon's mother is barely mentioned. And yet, I would argue that this absence, though utterly different, is as important as the maternal absence in *Miß Sara Sampson*. In the bourgeois tragedy, the mother is absent in order to leave the business of education to the enlightened father. In its revisionary narrative the bildungsroman draws its specific and careful construction of a sublimation script from nostalgia for a happy childhood. For childhood to be experienced and, what is more important, to be remembered as this especially happy phase in one's life, the emotionally charged figure of the mother as primary caretaker is of utter importance. Yet it matters less whether each individual really had such a mother. It suffices that the Mother has become a cultural postulate, a paradigm of how a child should have been provided with happiness and a measure by which the adult can reconstruct his individual story in the light of this childhood.[54] In that sense, it is not so much the presence or the absence of an ideal mother that becomes a cultural force by the turn of the century but the individual's relation to the position of the Mother from which the narcissistic narrative emerges.

Reference Matter

Notes

For complete author's names, titles, and publication data for the works cited here in short form, see the Works Cited, pp. 317–26.

Introduction

1. Goethe, "Zueignung," *Werke*, 1: 149–52.
2. Saint Augustine, *Confessions*, trans., with an introduction, by R. S. Pine-Coffin (Harmondsworth, Eng.: Penguin, 1983), pp. 151, 154, 156. See also John Freccero, *Dante: The Poetics of Conversion* (Cambridge: Harvard University Press, 1986), pp. 9–11.
3. *Letters from Petrarch*, selected and trans. Morris Bishop (Bloomington: Indiana University Press, 1966), p. 49.
4. See Foucault, *Order of Things*, esp. chaps. 3–6.
5. Wellbery, *Lessing's "Laocoon,"* p. 7.
6. See Foucault, *Order of Things*, chaps. 7–10.
7. See ibid., pp. 232–43.
8. Lacan, "The Mirror Stage as Formative of the Function of the *I* as Revealed in Psychoanalytic Experience," in idem, *Ecrits*, p. 2.
9. Wellbery, *Lessing's "Laocoon,"* pp. 230, 229.
10. Ibid., pp. 232, 231.
11. Ibid., p. 238.
12. Ibid., pp. 236–37.

Chapter 1

1. On fables, see Dithmar, *Fabel*, pp. 162–64, 166–69. As Petrat (*Schulunterricht*) points out, Comenius was the first—in 1640—to develop the modern concept of didactics.
2. Dithmar, *Fabel*, p. 41.

3. In 1730 Johann Christoph Gottsched devoted a whole chapter to the fable in his *Critische Dichtkunst*. Rousseau banned the fable from Emile's education. See also Noel, *Theories of the Fable*; Leibfried and Werle, *Texte*; and Hasubek, *Fabelforschung*.

4. Locke, *Education*, p. 114.

5. See Hornbeak, *Richardson's "Familiar Letters,"* for Richardson's labor in expanding and clarifying the morals and reflections of l'Estrange's edition.

6. See Foucault's analysis of the Rennaissance episteme vs. that of Rationalism in *Order of Things* (p. 54): "Resemblance, which had for long been the fundamental category of knowledge—both the form and the content of what we know—became dissociated in an analysis based on terms of identity and difference; moreover, whether indirectly by the intermediary of measurement, or directly and, as it were, on the same footing, comparison became a function of order; and, lastly, comparison ceased to fulfil the function of revealing how the world is ordered, since it was now accomplished according to the order laid down by thought, progressing naturally from the simple to the complex. As a result, the entire *episteme* of Western culture found its fundamental arrangements modified. And, in particular, the empirical domain which sixteenth-century man saw as a complex of kinships, resemblances, and affinities, and in which language and things were endlessly interwoven—this whole vast field was to take a new configuration."

7. "Who would take anything to be mediocre in which the immortal author of *Pamela, Clarissa, Grandison* has been involved? For who would know better than he what is best for the education of the heart, the love of humanity and virtue? Or who knows better than he how much truth can influence the human mind if it deigns to borrow the magic charms of a pleasing fiction?" ("Vorrede zu Richardsons Sittenlehre," in *Lessings sämtliche Schriften*, 7:75).

8. In his essay on the presentation of the fable, Lessing criticizes La Fontaine and his epigones who alienated the fable from its essential brevity and simplicity by adding poetic ornaments. This playfully poetic amplification of the fable has turned a genre that originally belonged to the discourse of philosophy and the regime of truth into a frivolous entertainment (*Abhandlungen*, p. 469).

9. In his own interpretation of the fable, Lessing puts La Fontaine into the position of the owner of the bow: "Of course, La Fontaine and all of his epigones are in the same position as my *Owner of the Bow*; the man wanted his bow to be more than just smooth, he had ornaments carved into it, and the artist knew very well what kind of ornaments would suit a bow; he carved a hunting scene onto it; now the man wants to try out the bow, and it breaks. But was this the fault of the artist? Who told the man to shoot with it as he did before? He should have nicely hung up the carved bow in his armory and delighted himself with its view!" (*Abhandlungen*, p. 471)

10. Lessing introduces this term immediately in his definition of the fable when he rejects La Motte's definition "The fable is an instruction disguised under the allegory of an action" or Richer's definition "The fable is a little poem that contains a prescription hidden under an allegorical image." He vehemently rejects both the idea of allegory, grounded in a system of resemblances, and the notion of masking or hiding the moral truth of the fable; instead, he insists on

its opposite function—not disguise, but revelation, making evident and concrete. See *Abhandlungen*, pp. 420–27, 432–33.

11. Against the reduction of the fable to an image or emblem, Lessing argues that the fable needs an action, a succession of changes, that unifies the representations for one moral purpose: "One or even several changes that merely stand next to each other and do not follow from each other will not suffice for the fable. And I would take it for an unmistakable test that a fable is bad . . . if its intended action can be painted in its entirety. For then it merely contains a picture, and the painter has not provided a fable but an emblem" (*Abhandlungen*, p. 429).

12. Richardson, *Aesop's Fables*, Preface, p. 12.

13. See *Abhandlungen*, p. 478.

14. For a detailed discussion of the disjunction of reading and seeing, see Foucault, *Order of Things*, p. 39.

15. "Über den Beweis des Geistes und der Kraft," in *Lessings Werke: Schriften II*, ed., with an introduction, Karlmann Beyschlag (Frankfurt am Main: Insel, 1967), p. 309.

16. For a detailed discussion of rationalist theories of the faculties and the related aesthetic theories, see the two first chapters of Wellbery, *Lessing's "Laocoon*," esp. pp. 22, 53, 59–84.

17. In this argument about the animal actors, Lessing refutes Johann Breitinger, who thinks that the animals give the fable the attractions of the marvelous and of novelty. Lessing's insistence on the conventionality of the animal characters contradicts Breitinger's argument about the marvelous and dismisses his implied concept of imitation. See *Abhandlungen*, pp. 447–50.

18. For a detailed study of the centrality of Condillac's *Essai* in eighteenth-century semiotics, see Aarsleff, "The Tradition of Condillac: The Problem of the Origin of Language in the Eighteenth Century and the Debate in the Berlin Academy Before Herder," in his *From Locke to Saussure*, pp. 146–209.

19. Warburton's theory of hieroglyphs was translated and widely disseminated in France by 1744 as *Essai sur les hiéroglyphes des Égyptiens*. See V.-David, *Débat*, pp. 93–103.

20. *Traité des sensations*, in *Oeuvres philosophiques de Condillac*, 1: 22.

21. For a detailed analysis of Diderot's letters as a response to Condillac's *Essai*, see Baudiffier, "Diderot et Condillac." Baudiffier's study concentrates on Diderot's concern with synesthesia and Diderot's position between Locke and Condillac, a position that brings out those nuances that both philosophers omitted.

22. James Creech reads the *Lettre sur les aveugles* in terms of the strategic metaphor of blindness, which he characterizes in the following terms: "In the *Lettre sur les aveugles*, blindness is the metaphor for the representational space that both differentiates object and image and poses the very question of their identity and conformity" (*Diderot*, p. 120).

23. In his "[Additions] à la lettre sur les aveugles" (1782), Diderot takes back this statement and describes at length Sophie Volland's niece, Mademoiselle Mélanie de Salignac, who in spite of her blindness was full of sympathy and consideration for others as well as extremely decorous in her own behavior; see *Oeuvres complètes de Diderot*, 4: 98–107.

24. For a summary of the arguments on inversion, see Creech, *Diderot*, pp. 124–25.

25. This is *the* crucial issue for the new mid-eighteenth-century discipline of aesthetics. Alexander Gottlieb Baumgarten, the father of German aesthetics, writes that the aesthetic experience engages all the *Triebfedern* (driving springs, motives) of the soul.

26. James Doolittle, who analyzed Diderot's notion of the emblem and hiero- glyph in the *Lettre sur les sourds et muets* and compared it with seventeenth-century emblematics, concluded: "And not the least significant phenomenon of the huge rebirth is the disappearance of the emblem from the printed page to be re-created in the imagination of the reader.... Diderot removes the emblem as such from the printed page, leaving there only hieroglyphic suggestions; these his poet presents to the hearer so that the latter may form his own emblems out of the fusion of the poet's suggestions with the totality of his own imaginative existence. What is implicit here is the displacement of reason, and with reason the forms, the rules, and the "taste" that it has made and consecrated, from their hitherto dominant role in artistic creation and criticism" ("Hieroglyph and Emblem," pp. 160–61).

27. Michael Fried shows in his thorough analysis of Diderot's writing and its relevance to the transformations of mid-eighteenth-century art how the status of the painting was to change from an exterior object that had to be seen and in- terpreted by a beholder to "a supreme fiction" that aimed at the negation of the beholder's existence: "In Diderot's writings on painting and drama the object– beholder relationship as such, the very condition of spectatordom, stands indicted as theatrical, a medium of dislocation and estrangement rather than of absorption, sympathy, self-transcendence; and the success of both arts, in fact their continued functioning as major expressions of the human spirit, are held to depend upon whether or not painter and dramatist are able to undo that state of affairs, to *de- theatricalize beholding*, and so to make it once again a mode of access to truth and conviction, albeit a truth and a conviction that cannot be entirely equated with any known or experienced before" (*Absorption and Theatricality*, p. 104).

28. See Wellbery, *Lessing's "Laocoon,"* chap. 3. With Lessing's *Laokoon*, the positions of painting and poetry have been reversed. Whereas Diderot in the *Let- tre sur les sourds et muets* postulates the superiority of painting over the other arts for its ability to achieve a more immediate representation, Lessing valorizes this as the "idea of painting." The actual, material painting is inferior to poetry because its physical aspects limit the recipient's imaginative freedom. See esp. ibid., pp. 236–37.

29. Rousseau chooses this fable as an example of an unfortunately limited re- striction of its appended moral application, since La Fontaine emphasizes the class- and status-bound situation of the subject. And the four verses of this fable that according to Rousseau should have been omitted embody *in nuce* all he re- jects: the association of a social order guaranteed by a class structure and the foregrounding of the moral rule: "Le monde est plein de gens qui ne sont pas plus sages: Tout Bourgeois veut bâtir comme les grands Seigneurs, Tout petit Prince a des Ambassadeurs, Tout Marquis veut avoir des Pages" ("The world is full of people who are not any wiser: Every Bourgeois wants to battle like the great Lords, Every little Prince has ambassadors, Every Marquis wants to have pages";

"La Grenouille qui se veut faire aussi grosse que le boeuf," in La Fontaine, *Fables*, p. 53).

30. Another crucial aspect of this moral training is Emile's training in an imaginary empathy. The role of *pitié* as imaginary empathy in the individual's as well as in mankind's socialization is described in *Emile* as well as in the *Discours sur l'origine de l'inégalité*.

31. See Michel Foucault's analysis of the implications of the penal reforms advocated by the *idéologues* as the first step toward the construction of the modern disciplined subject in *Discipline and Punish*, esp. "Generalized Punishment," pp. 73–103.

32. Only in the natural state is man without language and therefore without desire: "His desires do not exceed his physical needs" and "His imagination does not paint anything for him; his heart does not demand anything from him" ("Discours sur l'origine et les fondements de l'inégalité parmi les hommes," in Rousseau, *Discours*, pp. 182–83).

33. For the imagery of the sirens, see *Emile*, p. 427.

34. For a discussion of the dangers of mimetic desire, see ibid., pp. 442–44.

35. Human females as opposed to female animals are not restricted by seasonal sexual instincts: "Female animals are without this sense of shame, but what of that? Are their desires as boundless as those of women, which are curbed by this shame?" (ibid., pp. 467, 322) "The woman should be strong and active; the man should be weak and passive; the one must have both the power and the will; it is enough that the other should offer little resistance. When this principle is admitted, it follows that woman is specially made for man's delight. If man in his turn ought to be pleasing in her eyes, the necessity is less urgent; his virtue is in his strength, he pleases because he is strong" (ibid., pp. 466, 322).

36. See Starobinski's distinction of *être/paraître* as a guiding binarism in Rousseau's works in his *Rousseau*.

37. "Show the sense of the tasks you set your little girls, but keep them busy.... They must be trained to bear the yoke from the first, so that they may not feel it, to master their own caprices and to submit themselves to the will of others. If they were always eager to be at work, they should sometimes be compelled to do nothing. ... Do not deprive them of mirth, laughter, noise, and romping games, but do not let them tire of one game and go off to another; do not leave them for a moment without restraint. Train them to break off their games and return to their other occupations without a murmur.... This habitual restraint produces a docility that woman requires all her life long, for she will always be in subjection to a man, or to man's judgment, and she will never be free to set her own opinion above his" (*Emile*, pp. 482–83, 332–33).

38. "A woman's thoughts, beyond the range of her immediate duties, should be directed to the study of men, or the acquirement of that agreeable learning whose sole end is the formation of taste; for the works of genius are beyond her reach, and she has neither the accuracy nor the attention for success in the exact sciences; as for the physical sciences, to decide the relations between living creatures and the laws of nature is the task of that sex which is more active and enterprising, which sees more things, that sex which is possessed of greater strength and is more accustomed to the exercise of that strength. Woman, weak

as she is and limited in her range of observation, perceives and judges the forces at her disposal to supplement her weakness, and those forces are the passions of man. . . . She must find a way to make us desire what she cannot achieve unaided and what she considers necessary or pleasing; therefore she must have a thorough knowledge of man's mind; not an abstract knowledge of the mind of man in general, but the mind of those men who are about her, the mind of those men who have authority over her either by law or custom" (ibid., pp. 507, *349–50*).

39. He confesses in a footnote toward the end of the letter: "The truth is that I am charmed by Racine and that I have never voluntarily missed a performance by Molière" (Rousseau, *Lettre à M. D'Alembert*, p. 242).

40. For a definition of the ideological state apparatus, see Louis Althusser's essay "Ideology and Ideological State Apparatuses," in his *Lenin and Philosophy*, esp. pp. 142–48 and 162–77.

41. Rousseau sees the two institutions, the theater and the Consistory and the Chamber of the Reformation, as incompatible: "For it is easy to foresee that these two institutions will not long exist side by side, and that the drama will turn the censors to ridicule or the censors will drive out the actors" (*Lettre*, pp. 156, 75).

42. David Marshall's essay on the letter to d'Alembert, though focusing on different passages, comes to the same conclusion about the totalitarian nature of Rousseau's anti-theatricality, particularly when Marshall compares the utopian *fête de champêtre* to the ball for nubile sons and daughters, which is subjected to a detailed protocol and perfect surveillance ("Rousseau and the State of Theater," p. 84).

43. "I have over and over read Théophraste, la Bruyère and Molière. . . . I can find there all one has to do and all one must not say. Thus when I read the *Miser* I tell myself: Be stingy if you want, but do not talk like a stingy person. When I read *Tartuffe* I tell myself: Be a hypocrite if you want, but do not talk like a hypocrite. Keep the vices that are useful to you but not the tone and the appearances that would make you ridiculous" (Diderot, *Le neveu de Rameau*, p. 90).

Chapter 2

1. Richardson's text is constructed as a commentary around the legal "indenture," the contract between master and apprentice. Whereas the text of the indenture seems to consider visits to taverns and playhouses equally detrimental to the apprentice's good conduct ("He shall not haunt Taverns or Playhouses"; p. 7), Richardson spends ten times as many pages on the dangers of playhouses.

2. Jonas Barish, *The Antitheatrical Prejudice*, pp. 236–38.

3. For the masquerade in eighteenth-century culture as the locus of semantic destablization, see Castle, "Carnivalization," p. 904.

4. For this argument, see Castle, "The Recarnivalization of Pamela: Richardson's *Pamela*, Part 2," in idem, *Masquerade and Civilization*, pp. 130–76.

5. Marivaux, *La vie de Marianne*, p. 83 (my trans.). Nancy Miller also emphasizes the difference between Marianne and Pamela (*The Heroine's Text*, pp. 38, 50). For an analysis of Marianne's presentation of self, see my article "From the Vicarious to the Voyeuristic," *Constructions* 1 (1984): 38.

6. See Wellbery's discussion of bourgeois aesthetics as opposed to the older aristocratic model of performance in *Lessing's "Laocoon,"* p. 45.

7. For the backstage/onstage distinction, see Goffman, *Presentation*; for the material reality of the "Eye of Power," see Foucault, *Power/Knowledge*, p. 146.

8. See also Grandison's reaction when he discovers that the father-confessor of the Poretta family is eavesdropping on his conversation with Clementina: "Allow me, my dear Sir, to say (It is to Father Marescotti) that the man, who, in the greater actions of his life, thinks himself under the All-seeing Eye, will not be afraid of a fellow-creature's ear" (pt. II, vol. 5, p. 578).

9. See Castle, "Interrupting Miss Clary," in idem, *Clarissa's Ciphers*, pp. 57–80.

10. For an exposition of the subject's position in speech and the dialectics of desire, see Lacan, "The Subversion of the Subject and the Dialectic of Desire in the Freudian Unconscious," in idem, *Ecrits*, esp. pp. 304–5 on the Other, and p. 321 on the image of the ideal father.

11. See also Braudy's "Penetration and Impenetrability in *Clarissa*." Braudy also sees in *Clarissa* the breaking away from an allegorical and rhetorical literature: "Whereas Lovelace uses writing as disguise, Clarissa uses it as an inward stay—another re-enactment of the competition between the belief that the self is enriched through role-playing and stylization and the belief that the truly strong self is purified and sincere" (pp. 202–3).

12. See Margaret Doody's study *A Natural Passion* for Lovelace's use of the conventions of Restoration drama.

13. William Warner's reading of *Clarissa* seems to go along with Lovelace's supposed position of power, his misrecognition of language as a mere code and a play of signifiers over which he can assert his control and subvert Clarissa's moralism, when he celebrates Lovelace as a Nietzschean proto-deconstructionist (see *Reading "Clarissa"*).

14. For further discussion, see Foucault's "Body of the Condemned" in his *Discipline and Punish*, esp. pp. 8–9, 28–31.

15. Nancy Miller also describes Clarissa's rejection of her body and her sexuality, culminating in her angelic death, as the prerequisite for becoming an exemplary female character. However, Miller's plot-oriented study neglects the semiotic and aesthetic issues connected with Clarissa's rejection of the body; i.e., how Clarissa's particular relation to the gaze of the Other authenticates her writing within the project of Anschaulichkeit. My reading tries to complicate—but not reject—Miller's reading of Clarissa's exemplary virtue as an instance of patriarchal oppression. See *The Heroine's Text*, pp. 83–95.

16. For scenes of dying and contemporary guidebooks on preparing for death, see Doody, *A Natural Passion*, pp. 151–187 (chap. 7 "Holy and Unholy Dying").

17. For the theatricalization and humanization of the execution in conjunction with an early notion of "deterrence" in the penal reforms of the *ideologues*, see Foucault's *Discipline and Punish*, pp. 93–95.

18. Peter Weber's *Das Menschenbild* analyzes *Miß Sara Sampson* as a programmatic drama that rejects the earlier rationalistic and court-oriented enlightenment of Gottsched's poetics in favor of Richardson's novels, mainly *Clarissa*, as mediated through Christian Gellert and his friends. Although Weber is one of the few critics who takes Richardson's fiction into account, he does not consider the affinity between the two different genres, the epistolary novel and the bourgeois tragedy. Lothar Pikulik's *"Bürgerliches Trauerspiel"* rejects any simplified explanation of the bourgeois tragedy as the expression of a new bourgeois class consciousness. He

sees the bourgeois tragedy as a continuation of the development of the sentimental comedy, mainly Gellert's plays, and as a rejection of the heroic tragedy in favor of a humanization of the tragic character. Although he offers a detailed account of the development of sentimental tendencies and values in early eighteenth century German comedy up to Lessing's *Miß Sara Sampson*, he tends to lose sight of the sociological dimension and the historical specificity of sentimentality. As a study of the theory of bourgeois tragedy and its reception of Aristotle's theory of tragedy, Peter Szondi's *Theorie* remains unsurpassed. Szondi avoids both a crude reduction of the bourgeois tragedy in sociological terms (the expression of the bourgeois class consciousness) and its reduction to an expression of mere sentimentality. He examines Lillo's *George Barnwell* in the context of the historical situation of the English merchant class and the theoretical framework of Weber's *Protestant Ethic* as an interiorization of the familial conflict in the innerworldly asceticism of its heroine, Maria. He sees in Diderot's *drame bourgeois* an attempt to create a utopia of familial intimacy as opposed to the English model in which the bourgeois class is actively integrated into the political sphere as an economic force. Lessing becomes the turning point before Louis Mercier's theory in which the stage is used for explicit political agitation.

19. Jay Caplan also describes the *Fils naturel* as a ritual and "docu-drama" (*Framed Narratives*, p. 32).

20. For Richardson's influence on Diderot's beholder, see Pucci, "Art."

21. The paradigmatic presentation of the *Fils naturel*, Dorval's narrative, serves Friedrich Kittler as starting point for his study of the bourgeois tragedy as part of a semio-technology instituting an epochal life form: the nuclear family. His brilliant essay " 'Erziehung ist Offenbarung': Zur Struktur der Familie in Lessings Dramen" examines Lessing's plays in terms of the new ideal of education in which the father becomes the primary agent of a gentle education operating through interiorized expectations.

22. James Creech begins his highly interesting reading of the *Fils naturel* with the identity of actor and character postulated in the introduction. He sees in the play, in Dorval's and Rosalie's incestuous love, a love originating from a narcissistic relation of identity, an early formulation of what Diderot's later aesthetic theory comes to call the "modèle idéal." His reading emphasizes that virtue is a sublimation of this ideal as opposed to an oedipal scenario in which the father would be an agent of prohibition. Creech's reading is more persuasive than Mehlman's blunt statement about the *Fils naturel*: "The message that is transmitted in Dorval's annual ritual is thus the prohibition of incest." With regard to the "Entretiens," Creech emphasizes the differential aspect of this text, counterbalancing the drama's ideal of transparency, its "greasy" moralism, and narcissistic undifferentiation. It seems to me that his emphasis on the differential moment is too much directed by his desire to create a continuity between the Diderot of the *Fils naturel* and the one of the *Paradoxe sur le comédien*. See Creech, *Diderot*, chap. 7, " 'Who Will Save Me from Myself?': *Le fils naturel*," p. 82; and Mehlman, *Cataract*, p. 35.

23. Godden (" 'Une painture parlante' ") presents a detailed account of the rhetorical tradition and contemporary context of the graphic vividness Diderot postulates for his dramatic tableau. She locates the dominating influence on Diderot's notion of the tableau in the Jesuit theater. She also searches for more specific references between mid-eighteenth-century painting and drama.

24. *Hamburgische Dramaturgie* (4. Stück). For a detailed study of Lessing's position in the mid-eighteenth-century debate on acting styles, methods, and techniques marked by the two opposing positions of Rémond de Sainte Albine and Francesco Riccoboni and of Lessing's experiment with acting styles in *Miß Sara Sampson*, see Ziolkowski, "Language."

25. In the "Entretiens," the term *tableau* acquires more dramaturgical precision when Dorval opposes it to the coup de théâtre: "A *coup de théâtre* is an unforeseen event in the action that suddenly changes the situation of the characters. A tableau is the arrangement of the characters in the scene in such a natural and truthful manner that if rendered by a painter with fidelity it would please me on the canvas" (p. 92). See also Peter Szondi's essay *"Tableau* und *coup de théâtre."* Szondi analyzes Diderot's notion of tableau in terms of its postulated truth, as representing the emotional authenticity of the patriarchal nuclear family. He sees in it the nobilization of a bourgeois ethos as well as the utopia of private happiness as opposed to the pitfalls of exterior intrigue and chance of the coup de théâtre. This essay, which works out the parallels between Diderot's concepts of the tableau and the conditions and Lessing's concept of *Mitleid*, achieves a subtle combination of a social-historical and a poetological approach. Jay Caplan in *Framed Narratives* analyzes the tableau in psychoanalytic terms as fetish and emphasizes the sacrificial structure of the tableau-beholder relation. His study characterizes the drame bourgeois of *Fils naturel* as an attempt to recover the lacuna in the family: "As representation, the tableau displays a loss in the family, but this loss is ideally recovered at the level of dialogue by the beholder. Indeed the tableau entails both the loss of the Father (origin, Author) and his ideal recovery by his children, while simultaneously recognizing that his recovery is only ideal (that no one will ever satisfactorily occupy the position of the Father)" (p. 37).

26. "Even without performance and actors the tragedy has to maintain its strength" (Lessing et al., *Briefwechsel*, p. 85).

27. Whereas Rousseau in his *Lèttre à M. d'Alembert* doubts the moral efficacy of a theatrical performance because of the moment of disillusion after the performance ("People say that tragedy leads to pity through fear; this might be true, but what is this pity? A passing and vain emotion that does not outlast the illusion that has produced it; a remnant of a natural sentiment, quickly suffocated by the passions. This pity is sterile, satisfied with a few tears; it has never produced the least humanitarian act"; p. 78), Lessing searches exactly for that angle from which the recipient's reaction toward a theatrical performance and a situation in "real" life become indistinguishable.

28. To a certain extent, the emotional involvement of the drama's audience can be understood in the context of early eighteenth-century comedy, mainly the English Restoration drama and the German *Rührstück*. For a discussion of Diderot's and Lessing's dramatic influences, see the works of Peter Szondi cited in the bibliography. For Lessing's affinity to elements of the contemporary comedy, see Pikulik, *"Bürgerliches Trauerspiel"*; and Schenkel, *Lessings Poetik*, esp. pp. 59, 128–36. Schenkel analyzes Lessing's use and transformation of the contemporary sentimental comedy in *Miß Sara Sampson*. However, in Lessing's postulate that the bourgeois tragedy's exclusive means and end can be seen in its ability to produce pity, an affect indistinguishable from its occurrence in everyday life, we confront a degree of anti-theatricality that can no longer be sufficiently ex-

plained in terms of dramatic conventions. Rather, we must consider the drama's status as a representation, i.e., its specific relation to a theory of illusion that attempts to formulate the constitution of a representation and a subject within an affective domain: Lessing's theory of pity cannot be separated from his theory of illusion. Hans Jürgen Schings (*Der mitleidigste Mensch*) does not really deal with the "poetics" of *Mitleid*. Against the prohibition of "pity" by Brecht and critical theory, Schings attempts to rehabilitate pity's revolutionary moral impulse. He places the *Briefwechsel* in the context of Mendelssohn's and Lessing's dispute over Rousseau's second discourse. Mendelssohn, the professional philosopher with his attachment to rationalism, cannot approve of Rousseau's and Lessing's radical valorization of the lower faculties and the intrinsic virtue of pity without rational mediation. Schings's analysis of pity insists on Lessing's and Rousseau's notion of pity as an anthropological category that subsumes the aesthetic affect; thus Schings can omit a more detailed discussion of the interrelationship between pity and illusion. See esp. chap. 2, "Positionen der Aufklärung: Mandeville und Rousseau"; and chap. 3, "Mitleid und bürgerliches Trauerspiel: Der Disput zwischen Lessing und Mendelssohn," pp. 22–45.

29. It is interesting that Lessing emphasizes and dislikes the frequency of an association of admiration with exterior qualities and the body; see *Briefwechsel*, p. 81.

30. It is not surprising that Lessing refers the affect of admiration to another genre, to heroic poetry, which is dependent on the mediating persona of the narrator (*Briefwechsel*, pp. 66, 77). Heidsieck's "Der Disput" provides a close reading of Lessing's valorization of the lower faculties as it parallels Francis Hutcheson's moral philosophy. He points out that Hutcheson used "pity" as evidence of universal benevolence. In that light he reads the dispute between Lessing and Mendelssohn as an argument about the degree of influence to be given to intuitive cognition.

31. See Julia Kristeva's psychoanalytic approach to this "subject in process," her analysis of primary narcissism as the abjection of the undifferentiated, and the concomitant identification with an ego-ideal before the entry into the symbolic, in her "L'abjet d'amour." All the interpretations of the *Briefwechsel* and Lessing's theory of pity that have come to my attention presuppose a stable subject. If they interpret the structure of Lessing's notion of pity, they rarely correlate pity with his theory of illusion. I have found no explication that pays sufficient attention to the way in which Lessing introduces his topic by discussing representations from various media. Generally, the discussion of Lessing's notion of pity starts out with an interpretation of his "physical example" of the strings. Even Jochen Schulte-Sasse in his excellent appendix to his edition of the *Briefwechsel* and in his "Poetik" and Martin Schenkel in *Lessings Poetik*—although they establish the proximity of Lessing's theory of pity and his theory of illusion—do not consider how this new notion of illusion collaborates with the socializing and disciplinary effect of pity, intervening at a moment when the subject affected by the representation is precisely in the process of stabilizing itself.

32. See, e.g., Pikulik, "*Bürgerliches Trauerspiel*," pp. 78–79.

33. Of course, Lessing does not bring up the issue of catharsis until he raises the notion of pity purifying itself, which he elaborates in the *Hamburgische Dra-*

maturgie. Nevertheless, a comparative glance at Rousseau might support my point about Lessing's implicit transformation of catharsis and its disciplinary relevance. When Emile has become an adolescent and runs the risk of being corrupted by his carnal desires, his tutor trains his imagination and his ability to feel pity. In this context Rousseau praises the suggestion of an experienced soldier to confront the adolescent with the sight of death and disease, particularly venereal disease, in order to discourage any erotic interests (*Emile*, pp. 300–301).

34. The faculty to perceive the similarity of an other as a primary social virtue is close to Rousseau's definition of this sole natural social virtue that is opposed to our sense of self-preservation: "I was able to distinguish two principles anterior to reason: the one makes us ardently interested in our well-being and our self-preservation; the other inspires us with a natural repugnance to seeing perish or suffer any sensible being that in principle is similar to us" (*Discours sur l'origine de l'inégalité*, p. 153).

35. This becomes the crucial focus for Friedrich Kittler's reading of Lessing's plays; see his "Erziehung," p. 119.

36. Although most interpreters of *Miß Sara Sampson* note that at the end of Act III the happy ending seems to be almost achieved, but, as the play continues, it becomes apparent that the catastrophe was well on its way, they tend to overlook that in fact the letter scene does not reconcile father and daughter but only highlights the obstacles that stand in the way. See, e.g., Schenkel, *Lessings Poetik*, pp. 122–23; and P. Weber, *Das Menschenbild*, p. 54.

37. Claudia Albert's interpretation of *Miß Sara* also highlights Sara's "double morality," i.e., Sara's taking her tormenting self-criticism as a sign of superiority over Marwood (*Der melancholische Bürger*, p. 89).

38. In terms of the centrality and function of the recognition scene between Sara and Marwood, my reading is similar to Manfred Durzak's interpretation. However, whereas Durzak ("Äußere") sees in that scene a condition for Sara's realizing her "guilt" and for her subsequent reconciliation with the divine father, which he sees as the play's implicit critique of the dominant morality in terms of a secularized Christian ethics, I emphasize the moment of abjecting Marwood (the carnal woman, female sexuality, and the "possessive mother") as encompassing the identification with an ego-ideal, which can be both the ideal father and God. Analyzing the apolitical nature of Lessing's ideal of virtue and sensibility Bernhard Spies ("Lessing") provides a reading of Sara's virtue and self-criticism that foregrounds the self-reflective, narcissistic scenario: "Morality means for Lessing not a canon of rules, but a relationship toward one's own interiority [ein Verhältnis, das die Innerlichkeit zu sich selbst eingeht]" (p. 380). "In order to be restored to virtue the painful self-humiliation of a virtuous subject must be entirely the work of an autonomous subject. And the autonomy of this subject must collapse with the self-assurance of being entirely in accord with the internalized norm. Lessing develops the characters of Sara, Mellefont, and Sir William according to this model—it should be noted, however, that he means the image of the dialectic of the scrupulous conscience to be entirely affirmatively. And this less so, as I noted earlier, because he probably shares Sara's morality in terms of its content than because he takes Sara's attempt to reassure herself of her virtue as a positive example for his ideal of a free subjectivity" (p. 382).

39. See, e.g., Dorval's famous statement in the "Entretiens," p. 93: "If only for a moment the mother of Iphigenia were to show herself as queen of Argos and wife of a Greek general, she would seem to me the last of all creatures. The true dignity that strikes and upsets me is the tableau of maternal love in all its truth." See also Peter Szondi's excellent genealogy of the end of social class restrictions for the tragedy from Corneille to Diderot in his *Theorie*, pp. 91–147.

40. See, e.g., Hinrich C. Seeba, "Das Bild," p. 307. Seeba rejects any reflectionist sociohistorical approach to the function of the family in Lessing's plays. Lessing's dramas take the existence of the nuclear family for granted, even if social history would claim that the nuclear family was a product of the industrial revolution. According to Seeba, Lessing's intention was not to present family tableaux— he points out that hardly any of Lessing's families are "complete"—nor are the representations of familial relations to be seen as a withdrawal into a private idyll. Rather, they must be understood as a dramaturgical choice of a common denominator (beyond class specifications) that allows one to represent universally shared human conflicts.

41. For a critical survey of those interpretations in the wake of Koselleck and Habermas, see Spies, "Lessing," pp. 372–76.

42. "Only the bourgeois family whose head is so thoroughly deterritorialized as the merchant Nathan in Lessing's play makes explicit that the entire family is a product and a production site of culture. The bourgeois family functions as a production site not of wares and goods but, at a far more elementary level, of relatives. It produces 'human beings' who claim this fundamental title of bourgeois theory in a strict sense, and it does so in a fashion that not accidentally achieves the rank of a necessity and a science: through education" (Kittler, "'Erziehung,'" p. 121).

43. Spies ("Lessing") provides a brilliant analysis of the apolitical nature of "sensitivity" in Germany as opposed to Rousseau: "Of course, this postulated universality of the 'sentimentally' experienced ['empfindsam' empfundene] virtue represents a perfect idealism. The opposition of this 'sentimentally' experienced idealism of virtue does not merely reject the practical concerns with the absolutist regime as trivial. But this opposition also denies its own political dimension. The same 'sentimental' Frenchman Rousseau who radically dissolved virtue into human nature nevertheless felt obliged to construct the mechanisms of this general fall from virtue and to deduce from those the necessity of a just state power that realizes nothing but the general will thoroughly and against the will of the individual" (p. 387). Spies wants to deny that this particular apolitical critique of absolutism in the name of "general humanity," the construction of virtue as an ideal of a free subjectivity, has anything to do with representations of familial relations (p. 383). I would claim that it is only the construction of those ideal fathers that brings about the new ideal subjectivity and at the same time allows the state as well as the absolutist regime to disappear from sight.

Chapter 3

1. For an explication of the literary allusions in *Julie*, see Hans Robert Jauß, "Der Bruch," pp. 590–96. For a reading of *Julie* and *Clarissa* in the context of

the letter to d'Alembert, see Brooks, "Alceste, Julie, Clarissa." Brooks situates both *La Nouvelle Héloïse* and *Clarissa* in the anti-mondaine tradition of the novel, which finds its strongest programmatic statement in Rousseau's reading of the *Misanthrope* in his letter to d'Alembert.

2. For a general survey of eighteenth-century poetological statements about the epistolary novel, see Ouellet, "La théorie."

3. Starting from the supposedly merely expressive nature of the letters, Carroll ("Morality") provides an excellent analysis of their performative function. According to his interpretation, it is the performative and frequently manipulative aspect even of the most "authentic" piece of writing that generates the moral complexity of the novel. Carrol sees in this Rousseau's growing distrust of language.

4. Jean Laplanche explains *Nachträglichkeit* as follows: "Experiences, impressions and memory traces may be revised at a later date to fit in with fresh experiences or with the attainment of a new stage of development. They may in that event be endowed not only with a new meaning but also with psychical effectiveness" (Laplanche and Pontalis, *Language*, p. 111).

5. For a study of repetition through substitution in *Julie*, see Mercken-Spaas, "*La Nouvelle Héloïse*."

6. Peggy Kamuf's study, *Fictions of Feminine Desire*, which concentrates on eighteenth-century revisions of the medieval love story (the rewriting of "feminine desire") also sees in *Julie* the negotiation of a transition from one symbolic order to another: "Like the Heloise of these twelfth-century letters, Julie is positioned at the juncture of one social order which can no longer sustain its claim to legitimate power and another which must succeed to that claim without violence, that is, legitimately. In *The New Heloise*, this articulation is worked out through Julie's passage from her father's archaic law of aristocratic privilege to the renewed order of an enlightened Wolmar, a passage that marks the intermediate term of her passion for Saint-Preux as disorder. The final moment which sets up the new society of Clarens is also the moment at which Rousseau's heroine converts the unconverted remains of Heloise, who only entered Abelard's new kingdom of the absent phallus on the strength of an "as if" (p. 103). For Kamuf's reading of *Julie* as a transformation and actualization of the Héloïse/Abelard story, see also pp. 100–105. My reading, in contrast to Kamuf's, focuses on Saint-Preux's "education" through his attachment to Julie, on the organization of the subject that will be the educator for the new social order.

7. See also Hall, "Concept of Virtue." Hall describes the notion of virtue in *La Nouvelle Héloïse* as a replacement of exterior heroism by the inner struggle against the self, leading to domestic tranquillity, showing itself in benevolent actions, sincerity, and uprightness. However, Hall's article does not inquire into the strategies used to produce this "interiorization" of virtue. In other words, he does not analyze to what extent Julie's notion of virtue is bound up with the subject's position vis-à-vis language and representations.

8. Kamuf calls Saint-Preux's name "ridiculously oxymoronic," for it "joins the spiritual to the everyday or the useful" (*Fictions*, p. 111).

9. For a more detailed discussion of dueling versus discipline, see the section on Rousseau's letter to d'Alembert in Chapter 1.

10. See Pierre Brunet, "Thème du vin." Brunet's note traces the theme of wine

through the novel and reads its association with sexuality and interdiction from the Valais to Paris to Clarens (the gynécée and the harvest festival), and finally to Julie's death.

11. See, e.g., Mauzi, "La Conversion." My reading of Julie's conversion is diametrically opposed to Mauzi's and his respondents' (except for Starobinski's, who argues for more ambiguity in the religious question). Mauzi interprets the conversion as "truly" religious and the work of divine grace. Gelley ("The Two Julies") offers a far more interesting reading of Julie's conversion. He examines Julie's conversion in the context of her previous love affair and the end of the novel. According to Gelley, the crucial link between love story, conversion, and Julie's death is to be found in the role memory and the imagination play for Julie and Saint-Preux.

12. For a brilliant analysis of the interpellation of the individual as subject subjecting him/herself in a religious ceremony to the divine Subject conceived as a duplicate mirror structure, see Althusser, *Lenin and Philosophy*, esp. pp. 177–83.

13. Paul de Man, for example, is uneasy about Julie's religiosity and moralism: "Virtue is referred to in the most practical terms, yet it is also spoken of in a language of religious awe that had hardly been heard up to this point in the novel and that has led critics to speculate whether or not Julie is supposed to have undergone a religious conversion. Actually, there is nothing in the structure of Julie's relationship to virtue or to what she calls God that does not find its counterpart in her previous and now so rigorously demystified relationship towards Saint-Preux" (*Allegories of Reading*, p. 217). According to de Man, Julie's conversion narrative clarifies the preceding two books but also opens up the path to the allegory of the text's ultimate unreadability: "Thus the text of the pivotal letter that concludes the first part of *Julie*, so clarifying as a recapitulation, bodes little good for the stability of what it proleptically announces. It will be followed by the lengthy description of the political order in the community of Clarens, of which it is difficult to decide whether it is an exemplary model for a state or an ambivalent family romance. When the language of selfhood returns, as in the final letter again centered on the relationship between Julie and Saint-Preux, it is in terms that are not political and not even primarily ethical, but religious. Our reading tries to account for the emergence of the ethical valorization but remains unable to answer the question raised by the interpreters of *Julie* as to the relationship between the political aspects of Clarens and the religious considerations in Julie's last letters" (p. 220).

14. My reading of Julie's conversion to a god with all the qualities of the modern state is based on Michel Foucault's lecture ("Omnes et singulatim") on the genesis of the modern state and the Judeo-Christian concept of pastoral power. The first part of this lecture, which was given at Stanford University in 1979, traces one crucial aspect of the modern state back to the Judeo-Christian concept of power: "those techniques oriented towards individuals and intended to rule them in a continuous and permanent way." Foucault calls this "pastoral power" (p. 227), since the concept is taken from god or the king as the shepherd. "The shepherd wields power over a flock rather than over a land" (p. 128). The shepherd, unlike the Greek king, does not rule over an already existing city, but gathers together dispersed individuals, only "the shepherd's immediate presence and direct attention cause the flock to exist" (p. 129). Unlike the Greek king, who

merely has to protect the city from any danger, for the shepherd it is "not only a matter of saving them all, all together, when danger comes nigh. It's a matter of constant, individualised, and final kindness" (ibid.). In order to be a good shepherd, he has to "know his flock as a whole, and in detail" (p. 230). In order to wield pastoral power, Christianity developed techniques that combine total obedience with self-examination and the confession to another. "All those Christian techniques of examination, confession, guidance, obedience, have an aim: to get individuals to work at their own 'mortification' in this world" (p. 239). The second part of Foucault's lecture concentrates on seventeenth- and eighteenth-century theories of the state and the newly developing science of administration, or *Polizeiwissenschaft*. At that time the notion of "police" was far broader than it is today and included the care of all vital aspects of the lives of individuals: according to Delamare's *Compendium*, the police had to see to "eleven things within the state: (1) religion; (2) morals; (3) health; (4) supplies; (5) roads, highways, town buildings; (6) public safety; (7) the liberal arts (roughly speaking, arts and the sciences); (8) trade; (9) factories; (10) manservants and labourers; (11) the poor" (p. 249). Foucault's study locates the beginning of the modern state at that point where the *Polizeiwissenschaft* develops its knowledge and surveillance of individual lives in the interest of the state's strength and stability, in other words, when pastoral power serves the interest of the state. It is this approach to an analysis of modern state power that leads Foucault to reject those criticisms of state rationality based on the opposition between individual and society: "Just to look at nascent state rationality, just to see what its first policing project was, makes it clear that, right from the start, *the state is both individualising and totalitarian*" (p. 254; my italics).

15. Christie McDonald Vance (*Extravagant Shepherd*) interprets the marriage ceremony in a similar light: "Julie's marriage to Wolmar will be an explicit attempt to rebuild paradise in a social context. Julie, who moves from innocence, to sin, to newfound virtue, personifies the destiny open to man in the path leading from nature to corruption and finally to a new and better society" (p. 125).

16. For a detailed description of the totalitarian aspects of Clarens, see Crocker, "Julie ou la duplicité." My understanding of the totalitarian order of Clarens is very similar to Crocker's. His article provides a very detailed reading of Wolmar's system of surveillance and exploitation. He also links the model of Clarens with Rousseau's political and pedagogical writings. I would, however, argue that Crocker presupposes a notion of a "free" and unified subject against which he reads the "duplicité" in *La Nouvelle Héloïse*. It is that aspect of his reading, especially his reading of the novel's first two sections, that I disagree with. Crocker sees in the passionate love story between Julie and Saint-Preux merely an opposition to the "domesticated" Julie and Saint-Preux. For me, the transgressive love story provides the basis for the conditioning of the two as mother and educator.

17. For an excellent analysis of Julie's bower as emblematic of the transition from the order of Etange to that of Clarens, particularly with regard to the water, see Kamuf, *Fictions*, pp. 113–18.

18. Christie McDonald Vance (*Extravagant Shepherd*) sums up her analysis of Julie's bower in the following words: "The Elysée is the *locus* of virtue, and as such it functions at several levels. The description of this garden can be considered to be the allegorical representation of the 'beautiful soul'" (p. 151).

19. See also Paul de Man's analysis of Julie's garden in his "Rhetoric of Temporality," in *Blindness and Insight*, esp. pp. 200–208. De Man reads Julie's garden as allegory, which is to replace or reject the symbolic mode of an identificatory movement from the Meillerie passage: "Whereas the symbol postulates the possibility of an identity or identification, allegory designates primarily a distance in relation to its own origin, and, renouncing the nostalgia and the desire to coincide, it establishes its language in the void of this temporal difference. In so doing, it prevents the self from an illusionary identification with the non-self, which is now fully, though painfully, recognized as a non-self" (p. 207). Although I fully agree with de Man's claim that the Elysée as an allegory has to replace the identificatory, symbolizing tendency of Meillerie, I attempt to demonstrate that this allegory of virtue, which already contains the prohibition of identification, of an eroticized specularity in the aspects of temporal and spatial distance, can be put to work only if it is grafted on the "image." The allegory gains its stabilizing moment from the image of the mother, combining the image of the beloved woman, the longing for a self-sufficient dyad, with the prohibition of the father/husband Wolmar.

20. Rousseau initially planned to end the novel with Book 4 and have the lovers drown themselves in the lake. See Bernard Guyons's introduction to the Pléiade edition of *La Nouvelle Héloïse*, in *Oeuvres complètes* (Paris, 1964), 2: xliii–xliv, lxi–lxii.

21. My reading of *Julie*'s utopian aspects differs decisively from that of many other interpreters, who read the tragic ending of the novel as proof that ultimately Clarens is flawed and breaks apart because of the unreconcilable conflict between the individual and society, between the virtue and discipline required at Clarens and the passionate love of Julie and Saint-Preux. Thus James F. Jones, Jr. (*"La Nouvelle Héloïse"*), describes the totalitarian aspects of Clarens and ultimately denounces Clarens as "alienation." However, according to his reading, the novel is aware of it. Clarens is multifaceted, and ultimately *Julie* can be read as a novel about the possibility or impossibility of utopias; in that sense it transcends other eighteenth-century utopian models. Lionel Gossman ("Worlds") reads Clarens not as a utopian model but as an escapist fantasy for the contemporary gentry. He proposes a social-historical reading of the novel in which the "world" of Clarens resembles the life of Rousseau's aristocratic friends in the provinces. This life shares some characteristics of the old order, more primitive than the corrupt Parisian society but already marked by progress and change. Gossman sees the novel's guiding conflict as one between the individual (Saint-Preux) and society (see esp. p. 264). According to his reading, the novel still insists on the necessity of the individual's integration into society, though it already foreshadows the escape into subjectivity and fantasy. However, Gossman emphasizes that Rousseau must not be confounded with the Romantics. Peter Uwe Hohendahl (*Roman*) discusses *Julie* in the context of sensibility and moralism: "Julie and Saint-Preux must be understood as examples of a new type of virtue based on a critique of Richardson's notion. The fact that the errors of a passion become the foundation of a virtuous life, that Julie, Saint-Preux's lover, can prove herself as wife and mother, was a message that clearly went beyond Richardson. Familial intimacy and knowledge of the heart replace the rigid moralism. The formal consequences are related to this message: in order to unfold this new morality fully, the action is expanded

in terms of general reflections and digressions" (pp. 54–55). "The price paid for Wolmar's rational and supposedly natural order is the suppression of all those individual forces that do not want to fit into the homogeneity of the planned social structure. In the second part Rousseau had to take back what he had laid out in the first. His counter-image to the mundane world, which he describes in the novel of manners, bridges the rupture between the public and the private domain, but not without restrictions for the individual. This restriction can only be compensated for in the composition of the novelistic closure, when the reader learns that Julie in spite of her exemplary life as wife and mother could not ban Saint-Preux from her heart" (p. 58). Although Hohendahl recognizes that "virtue" in *Julie* is grounded in the transgressive love story, he still insists on the typical opposition between the individual and the new social order at Clarens (see pp. 53–63). My reading stresses the fact that it is precisely the construction of the individual, of sexuality, and its individualized recording, in the love letters of the first two books, that allows Wolmar to construct and control the new order of Clarens. Rather than claiming that "in Saint-Preux we find the beginnings of the modern social misfit [*der moderne soziale Außenseiter*]," (Hohendahl, p. 55), a reading that is influenced by *Werther* as a response to *Julie*, I argue that Saint-Preux is not at all a marginal figure for Clarens, that his subjectivity is that of the new civil servant, technocrat, and educator.

22. The new "professionalized" role of the mother in the construction of the modern subject will be fully institutionally implemented in the pedagogical reforms that occur in the wake of Rousseau. Most crucial is the new semio-technology developed in the phonetic literacy programs, which produce a reader who hallucinates the maternal voice behind the printed page. The pedagogical reforms were closely linked with the education of the new class of civil servants. For an extremely stimulating study of this major cultural transformation in Germany, see Kittler, *Aufschreibesysteme*, pp. 31–75.

23. My reading understands Julie's death as a didactic gesture, a gesture in the service of the new morality and semio-technology. Consequently my interpretation is incompatible with readings based on the individual/society dichotomy, as e.g., Vance's interpretation of Julie's spirituality and death: "Julie's own leap to the spiritual is thus the last stage of the dialogue between man and nature, and her espousal of Christianity marks her rejection of this world. The contradiction between her individual needs and desires, and her social self (a fragment of the collective whole) demands a resolution that the community of Clarens is unable to provide. Indeed, the mere presence of this contradiction within Julie signals the failure of Clarens. . . . Despite Julie's need to transcend the social and natural world, Rousseau meticulously assures us that she does not abnegate her moral allegiance to Clarens" (*Extravagant Shepherd*, p. 173). According to Vance, Clarens is "the response, however complex and paradox-ridden, to the negative criticism of Paris" (p. 174). "Clarens is a society based on *amitié* where there is no room for passion, just as there is no room for desire or the imagination. However, as Rousseau explores the social premises of tranquillity and *bonheur* in Clarens, these premises become more and more untenable as material for his novel. With the cleavage between passionate (individual) man and social (collective) man, the longed-for utopia cannot endure as a viable society. Through Julie's religious

death Rousseau restores the individual both to himself and to passionate love; through death love is reborn, and Julie finds tranquillity in the permanence of death" (p. 178).

24. For instance, St. Cecilia, who was also converted during her wedding and who served Richardson as the model for Clarissa's exquisite cadaver.

25. Jean Starobinski's *Rousseau* is still unsurpassed as an analysis of Rousseau's ideal of immediacy and transparency. Starobinski's reading of *Julie* offers a brilliant study of how this ideal is implemented in the utopian society of Clarens, which he describes as the feminized counterpart of the *Contrat social* (see esp. pp. 107, 116–37). Although my own reading is greatly informed by Starobinski's analysis, I oppose his reading of Julie's conversion and death in the light of Christian theology (see esp. pp. 137–48).

26. Among the numerous studies of Rousseau's reader, I will point out only a few. In an attempt to write a literary history of the reader and on the background of reader response theory, Sieghild Bogumil (*Rousseau*) offers an analysis of inner fictional models for the reader of *Julie*. Claude Labrosse (*Lire au XVIIIe siècle*) analyzes the reading of *La Nouvelle Héloïse* in terms of the text's reproduction in correspondence, periodicals, polemical texts, *l'esprit* (extracts), prefaces, censorship, and illustrations. Robert Darnton ("Readers Respond to Rousseau: The Fabrication of Romantic Sensitivity," in his *Great Cat Massacre*, pp. 215–56) narrates and describes the correspondence of a provincial bourgeois, Jean Ranson, with the Société Typographique de Neuchâtel, an important Swiss publisher in the prerevolutionary period. In those letters Ranson not only orders books but adds news about his family and inquires about his "ami Jean-Jacques." What is particularly interesting about the information in Darnton's essay for my reading of *Julie* is Ranson's large orders of pedagogical and children's literature. Furthermore, Darnton describes a reading primer, of which Ranson had ordered several copies, that was very successful between 1763 and 1830 and advocated the modern, phonetic method of learning to read (see p. 225). For a detailed explication of the cultural implications of the phonetic method, see Kittler, *Aufschreibesysteme*, pp. 48–58.

Chapter 4

1. In 1797, while Schiller was occupied with his tragedy *Wallenstein* and Goethe with his epic poem *Hermann und Dorothea*, they coauthored a short piece "Über epische und dramatische Dichtung," in which they postulated the purity of the two art forms and rejected the blurring of genre distinctions so characteristic of the epistolary novel and the bourgeois tragedy. Anti-theatricality and Anschaulichkeit are not valid for truly artistic endeavors. In a letter dated from December 23, 1797, Goethe wrote to Schiller: "For a hundred times after reading a good novel you might have heard expressed the desire to see it performed in the theater, and how many bad plays have originated from this. In the same way people want to see each interesting situation immediately engraved into copper; in order to leave no activity to their imagination everything is supposed to be realized in a sensuous manner, to be made entirely present and dramatic; and the dramatic is supposed to match actual reality. Now the artist should resist with all of

his might those childish, barbaric, tasteless tendencies; he should isolate one artifact from another through impenetrable magic circles, maintain each in its proper characteristics like the ancients, which has made them such excellent artists until our times; but who can separate his boat from the waves on which it is swimming? Against the stream and wind one can move only very small distances." (Schiller, *Sämtliche Werke*, 5: 1189). Jochen Schulte-Sasse (*Die Kritik*) locates the beginning of the dichotomization of low and high literature and the devalorization of an identificatory enjoyment of art in the "perverted sensibility" of the 1770's and 1780's (p. 41). He discusses as the major polemicists and first critics of "trivial" literature Karl Philipp Moritz, Schiller, and Goethe. Although his study provides a good survey of the emergence of trivial literature in the late eighteenth century both from the perspective of classicist aesthetics and in terms of a broad social and economic background, it does not take into account that the "invention" of this degraded form of mass culture was accompanied by the feminization of the same phenomenon. Andreas Huyssen ("Mass Culture") shows how the female reader/ author becomes the paradigm of trivial literature. However, his main examples are *Madame Bovary* and modernist aesthetics from the nineteenth and twentieth centuries. For a detailed discussion of this phenomenon in the eighteenth century, see Cullens, "Female Difficulties," esp. chap. 1.

2. For an excellent survey of the emergence and transformations of the term *Bildung*, see Vierhaus, "Bildung." For a historical survey of the influence of German classicist and neo-humanist writers (esp. Herder, Schiller, and Humboldt) on the curricular reforms and the origin of the notion of Bildung in German instruction, see Frank, *Geschichte des Deutschunterrichts*, chap. 5, "Bildung durch Dichtung," pp. 218–61.

3. See the "Nachwort" by Hans Dietrich Irmscher in Herder, *Abhandlung*, p. 137.

4. See ibid., pp. 138–40.

5. See Aarsleff, "The Tradition of Condillac: The Problem of the Origin of Language in the Eighteenth Century and the Debate in the Berlin Academy Before Herder," in his *From Locke to Saussure*, pp. 146–209. The main purpose of his study is to show the broader context of Herder's essay, a context in which Condillac holds a central position. Aarsleff argues that Herder basically follows Condillac and that what traditional scholarship attributed to Herder in fact had been developed by Condillac. He argues that Herder's true originality consists in his differentiation between an inner language (the focus of the first half of the essay) and an outer language (the focus of the essay's second part). Although my reading has been greatly informed by Aarsleff's historical contextualization of Herder, it also attempts to show how Herder transforms Condillac's notion of reflection and thereby marks a rupture with the classical episteme.

6. See Foucault, *Order of Things*. Foucault describes the new episteme of the nineteenth century, which he sees beginning with Jacob Grimm and Franz Bopp, as follows: "Language is 'rooted' not in the things perceived, but in the active subject. And perhaps, in that case, it is a product of will and energy, rather than of the memory that duplicates representation. We speak because we act, and not because recognition is a means of cognition. Like action, language expresses a profound will to something. And this has two consequences. The first is paradoxical at first

sight: it is that at the moment when philology is constituted by the dimension of pure grammar, there arises once more the tendency to attribute to language profound powers of expression (Humboldt is not merely Bopp's contemporary; he knew his work, and in detail); whereas in the Classical period the expressive function of language was required only at its point of origin, and in order to explain how a sound could represent a thing, language in the nineteenth century, throughout its development and even in its most complex forms, was to have an irreducible expressive value, for, if language expresses, it does so not in so far as it is an imitation and duplication of things, but in so far as it manifests and translates the fundamental will of those who speak it. The second consequence is that language is no longer linked to civilizations by the level of learning to which they have attained (the delicacy of their representative grid, the multiplicity of the connections it is possible to establish between the elements), but by the mind of the peoples who have given rise to it, animate it, and are recognizable in it" (p. 290). In brief, and with Grimm's words, Foucault concludes: "Language is no longer linked to the knowing of things, but to men's freedom: 'Language is human: it owes its origin and progress to our full freedom; it is our history, our heritage'" (p. 291). I would see Herder's essay as an instance of the emergence of this new episteme. For example, as opposed to Condillac or Warburton (for whom the study of history brings a better understanding of the progress of human knowledge), Herder conceives of historical study as yielding insights into the "spirit" of the speaking subjects and the individuality of the specific peoples. Although Herder does not develop a philological inquiry à la Grimm, I attempt to show in my reading of his essay that for him the primary function of language consists in constituting the "free" human subject. For a different historical contextualization of Herder's essay, see Pross, *Herders Abhandlung*. Pross criticizes Aarsleff for overemphasizing Condillac's influence on Herder and attempts to contextualize the *Abhandlung* more broadly by pointing out Herder's affinity to contemporary and earlier psychological accounts of the origin of language (Bonnet, Mendelssohn), sociocultural and historical accounts (Vico, Montesquieu, Pufendorf), and Bible criticism. In an attempt to reject the methods and findings of Foucault's *Order of Things*, he argues that Herder and his context do not fit into the classical episteme (p. 165). My reading (without, however, rejecting the views of Foucault) agrees with Pross that Herder indeed goes beyond the classical episteme; it also agrees with his assertion that Herder's *Besonnenheit* is different from Condillac's notion of reflection. Nevertheless, I believe that this rupture with the classical episteme can be understood only against the background of the semiotic transformations the *Abhandlung* exemplifies. Pross sees Herder's contribution not in this rupture but in a synthetic effort and in the combination of a sociohistorical perspective with a psychological one. My reading emphasizes the radically new psychological account Herder manages to provide. The innovative character of Herder's psychology, which explains human language as constitutive of human subjectivity, is illustrated by a comparison of Mendelssohn's sheep example with Herder's. See also note 12 below.

7. I translate Herder's term *Besonnenheit*, which he uses alternatively with *Reflexion*, by "reflection." However, "Besonnenheit" also connotes both a state of contemplation and an ethical tonality as a translation of the Greek virtue of *sōphros*

une (moderation, discretion, prudence, good sense). See also Heintel, "Besonnenheit."

8. My brief characterization of psychoanalytic theory as based on an assumption of "lack of instincts" does not mean that Freud does not use the term *Instinkt*. In fact, he talks of both "Instinkt" (instinct) and "Trieb" (drive). Jean Laplanche ("The Order of Life and the Genesis of Human Sexuality," in his *Life and Death*, pp. 8–24) very convincingly argues that "Instinkt" comes to figure as a very general, non-defined vital energy, from which the drive has to be derived. For theories of narcissism, see Freud, "Zur Einführung des Narzissmus," in *Studienausgabe*, 3: 41–68, and "Formulierung über die zwei Prinzipien des psychischen Geschehens," in *Studienausgabe*, 3: 17–24. The central text on narcissism and its relation to sublimation is Freud's "Das Ich und das Es," in *Studienausgabe*, 3: 283–337. See also Laplanche, "The Ego and Narcissism," in *Life and Death*, pp. 66–84.

9. On the relation between self and language in Herder's *Abhandlung*, see Brigitte Schnebli-Schwegler, *Herders Abhandlung*. Schnebli-Schwegler locates Herder's philosophy of language in the context of the anti-rationalist Johann Georg Hamann (1730–88). She emphasizes Herder's seminal influence on German *Sturm und Drang*, Classicism, and Romanticism and points out that the *Abhandlung* anticipates crucial classicist ideas, particularly Herder's notion of "Humanität" as expressed later in his *Ideen* (p. 5). Schnebli-Schwegler shows that Herder in his *Abhandlung* anticipates Schiller's notion of freedom in *Maria Stuart*. See pp. 97–98 on the proximity to Schiller's 25th letter in the *Ästhetische Erziehung*. On the relation to the Romantics, see esp. pp. 106–13; what is relevant for the Romantics (esp. Novalis), according to Schnebli-Schwegler, are Herder's notions of language as constitutive of the soul and of the sensual negotiation of an exterior and interior world. See also Jochen Schütze, *Die Objektivität der Sprache*, esp. pp. 99–131. Schütze attempts to read Herder as an idealist philosopher who conceives of human activity merely as the ideal production of self. He focuses on Herder's anthropology and notion of subjective freedom, which he compares with those of Hegel. The overall purpose of his study is to set into relief those aspects of Herder's writings that combine a specifically bourgeois social criticism with utopian aspects and programs for social reform.

10. In the fourth chapter of "Jenseits des Lustprinzips," Freud describes the emergence of that interface called "consciousness" in terms of the "Reizschutz," the protective shield against overstimulation, which transmits excitation from the outside to the inside and serves as a binding mechanism of free energy. He also compares the "Reizschutz" to feelers, which the organism extends in order to sample the external world and which serve in the formation of signals. See *Studienausgabe*, 3: 234–43.

11. Herder's sheep narrative, which tells the story of both the origin of human consciousness and the unity of the human soul as well as the origin of language, is reminiscent of Freud's narrative of the "Fort-Da" game in "Jenseits des Lustprinzips": the little boy not only rehearses his mother's absence in the game with the reel but also, as a footnote explains, mirrors the mother's absence and his own game by letting his own mirror image appear and disappear in a mirror. See *Studienausgabe*, 3: 224–27. Freud defines aim-inhibition in "Triebe und Triebschicksale" as: "Experience allows us also to speak of 'aim-inhibited' drives in

those situations where the satisfaction of the drive is admitted to a certain degree but then inhibited or distracted. One has to suppose that in these situations we are dealing with a partial satisfaction" (*Studienausgabe*, 3: 86). The notion of aim-inhibited drives is crucial to André Green's theory of narcissism and sublimation. Aim-inhibited drives preserve the object of the drive and renounce the full realization of the drive (satisfaction) and thereby provide an alternative to repression, which demands the substitution of the object of the drive. However, to the extent that aim-inhibited drives rely on the construction of a total object, a hallucinated entity, they ultimately help preserve the narcissistic illusion of independence from an external object. See Green, "Un, autre, neutre: valeurs narcissiques du même," in *Narcissisme*, pp. 31–79, esp. pp. 36, 46.

12. Two recent studies give a more detailed reading of these passages. Karl Grob, *Ursprung und Utopie*, declaring itself a de Manian and Derridian project, centers on the first part of Herder's *Abhandlung*, mainly on the sheep example and the notion of hearing as the mediating sense. Grob points out that the text produces the sheep for the transcendental eye of the reader as if there could be a transparent observer. His commentary on the bleating of the sheep points out that the name is established through a synecdoche. Finally, in his argument about hearing, he shows how for Herder the privileging of sound is produced in the metaphorical interpretation of the metonymy of the sign. Language, which thereby becomes a system of metaphors, will ultimately find its system of analogies in poetry and myth; Herder thereby becomes a pre-Romantic. Unfortunately Grob's study does not consider the contemporary context for Herder's essay and thus is led into some futile speculations, e.g., about the demonstrative pronoun in the phrase "jenes Schaf," which Herder uses when the sheep is introduced for the first time. The intertextual situation, however ("that sheep" is the one referred to in Moses Mendelssohn's "Sendschreiben an den Herrn Magister Lessing"), clears up this puzzle. Furthermore, a comparison with the Mendelssohn passage would have brought out the fundamental difference between Herder and the classical episteme in which Mendelssohn still has to be located. Mendelssohn sees in the bleating of the sheep the origin of its name as a representation; in his "eureka" Herder does not hail the arrival of a signified but the constitution of the unified subject. See Moses Mendelssohn, "Sendschreiben an den Herrn Magister Lessing in Leipzig" (1756), in *Gesammelte Schriften*, pp. 83–109. In this letter to Lessing written after he had completed the translation of Rousseau's *Discourse on Inequality*, Mendelssohn attempts to show that Rousseau's apparent misanthropy harbors a positive attitude toward society, although Rousseau's image of man is distorted to the extent that he praises savage man in all his advantages and sees only the corrupt and degenerate side of civilized man. In the "Nachschrift," Mendelssohn attempts to "correct" Rousseau's view of the origin of language and depict it as a "natural" development of his faculties rather than a mere falling away from his natural state. The sheep is part of a whole set of examples from nature of how man learns to connect images and sounds via associations. In the sense that language arises from an associative memory, Mendelssohn still relies on Condillac and Locke. Friedrich Kittler ("Herder's Sprachanthropologie und der Seufzer Ach," in his *Aufschreibesysteme*, pp. 45–48) situates Herder's sheep narrative in the context of the phonetic reading method, the "professionalization" of

motherhood, and the reforms of the state apparatus. Thus he points out how this narrative achieves a dual purpose of naturalizing the unwritable signified as sound and an oedipal command/prohibition (which is, of course, gendered). Fully acknowledging the importance of the oedipalization of the family and its relevance for the construction of modern subjectivity, my reading of Herder tries to emphasize the addition of another dimension to this oedipal scenario. Kittler's study emphasizes the educational role of the mother, and my Chapter 3 on Rousseau's *Julie* shows how the father steps into the background, leaving the gentle education to a loving mother, who operates in the service of law and order. The prohibitive function of the third agent is complemented and prestructured in the narcissistic construction of the total object, or mother.

13. In "Zur Einführung des Narzissmus," Freud describes parental love as a return to the parents' own infantile narcissism, as a narcissistic object choice: "The most delicate point of the narcissistic system, the reality of the harsh threat to the immortality of the Ego, has been secured in the refuge to the child. The moving, in fact rather childlike, parental love is nothing other than the reborn narcissism of the parents, which in its transformation into the love of an object unmistakably reveals its former identity" (*Studienausgabe*, 3: 57).

14. Freud describes the transformation of object-libido into narcissistic libido as follows: "If the Ego takes on the characteristic traits of the object, it imposes itself, so to speak, onto the Id as an object of love, seeks to make up for the loss of the object by saying: 'Look, you can love me too; I am very similar to the object.' The transformation of object-libido into narcissistic libido, which is taking place here, obviously entails the renunciation of sexual aims, a desexualization, that is, a kind of sublimation" ("Das Ich und das Über-Ich [Ich-Ideal]," *Studienausgabe*, 3: 297). In this move he sees the condition of the possibility of libidinal disinvestment of an object and therefore a crucial mechanism of sublimation. It is also used to explain the repression of the Oedipus complex in the identification with the father and the formation of an ideal-ego, superego, or conscience (see esp. chaps. 3–4 of *Das Ich und das Es*).

15. Lacan's studies of the subject's constitution in language focus mainly on the tertiary structure of an oedipal castration/symbolization scenario. André Green, Julia Kristeva, and others after Lacan have attempted to map in more detail the formation of the ego in the stage that Lacan discusses as the mirror stage. For my reading of Herder, André Green's collection of essays on primary narcissism have been very helpful in suggesting models for conceiving of sublimation in connection with the construction of an ego, particularly chap. 2, "Le narcissisme primaire: structure ou état" (1966–1967), in *Narcissisme*, pp. 80–131. See esp. pp. 102–3 for the difference between aim-inhibition ("an inhibition of the activity of the drive that maintains the object by sacrificing the full realization of the desire for an erotic union, but conserves a form of the attachment that fixes the investment") and repression ("an unrestricted development of the activity of the drive under the sole condition that aims and objects enter into operations of permutation and substitution"). Furthermore, Green's work has been suggestive on how the construction of the total object prestructures the oedipal scenario: "The Oedipus complex evokes relations of both tenderness and hostility. However, those relations of tenderness or hostility are relatively independent from the phallic

organization under which the Oedipus complex is taking its place. The relationship of tenderness toward the parent will be partly related to what belongs to the relation of sensuality, which is censored by the castration threat. Yet, the two are not confused. This is proven by the fact that the tender investment may be the best means by which the castration threat is turned around, like in the situation described in the most prevalent form of degradation in erotic life. If Freud connects the maternal object investments of the Oedipus complex back to those that were in a more primitive state attached to the breast, it might be that we should conceive of aim-inhibition at this level, i.e., at the moment when the loss of the breast object coincides with the perception of a total maternal object" (p. 103).

16. In a study for his essay on sculpture entitled "Philosophie des Wahren Guten und Schönen aus dem Sinne des Gefühls," Herder writes: "1. *Feeling is the first, most profound, and almost the only sense* of men: the source of the majority of our notions and sensations: *the true and first organ of the soul* to gather ideas from the exterior world: *the sense that surrounds the soul in its entirety* and contains in itself the other senses as species, parts, or abbreviations: the measure of our sensuality: the true origin of the true, the good, and the beautiful. 2. The soul makes its way into the world through feeling. *Since its forces are restricted by space and time, it cannot know everything in an immediate manner, only some things, which then become the mirror of the other: that is the body.* Thus the body is formed by the soul through an attraction accessible to feeling; this attraction remains to be figured out in its entirety; moreover, that which can be felt needs to be explained through the formation of the fetus. *Then it will become obvious that the soul forms itself a body through feeling and for the feeling of the exterior, or that it forms itself in the world in a feeling manner!* 3. Development of feeling in the first moments of childhood. How a child attains its first notions in a feeling manner. In which order? *That frequently the most abstract notions are the first ideas of feeling. The first ontology of feeling: of being, being exterior to ourselves, space, time, force, body,* etc." (*Sämtliche Werke*, 8: 104; my italics).

In chap. 2 of *Das Ich und das Es*, Freud describes the importance of the sense of touch and a body feeling in the separation of ego and id: "A person's own body, and above all its surface, is a place from which both external and internal perceptions may spring. It is seen like any other object, but to the touch it yields two kinds of sensations, one of which may be equivalent to an internal perception. . . . The Ego is first and foremost a bodily ego; it is not merely a surface entity, but is itself the projection of a surface. (I.e., the ego is ultimately derived from bodily sensations, chiefly from those springing from the surface of the body. It may thus be regarded as a mental projection of the surface of the body, besides, as we have seen above, representing the superficies of the mental apparatus)" (*Studienausgabe*, 3: 294). This passage first appeared as a footnote in the English translation of 1927, in which it was described as having been authorized by Freud; it does not appear in the German editions.

17. For the position of Herder's writings about sculpture in the development of his aesthetics, see Irmscher, "Mitteilungen."

18. Lacan describes the identificatory movement of the mirror stage as follows: "We have only to understand the mirror stage *as an identification*, in the full sense that analysis gives to the term: namely the transformation that takes place

in the subject when he assumes an image—whose predestination to this phase-effect is sufficiently indicated by the use, in analytic theory, of the ancient term *imago*. This jubilant assumption of his specular image by the child at the *infans* stage, still sunk in his motor incapacity and nursling dependence, would seem to exhibit in an exemplary situation the symbolic matrix in which the *I* is precipitated in a primordial form, before it is objectified in the dialectic of identification with the other, and before language restores to it, in the universal, its function as subject. This form would have to be called the Ideal-I, if we wished to incorporate it into our usual register, in the sense that it will also be the source of secondary identifications, under which term I would place the functions of libidinal normalization. But the important point is that this form situates the agency of the ego, before its social determination, in a fictional direction, which will always remain irreducible for the individual alone, or rather, which will only rejoin the coming-into-being (*le devenir*) of the subject asymptotically, whatever the success of the dialectical syntheses by which he must resolve as *I* his discordance with his own reality" ("The Mirror Stage as Formative of the Function of The I," in Lacan, *Écrits*, p. 2). What is most important in the Lacanian description of the mirror stage is the fact that, since this *imago* is a construct and a fiction, the identification does not produce a simple recognition but a fundamental *méconnaissance*.

19. Hans Dietrich Irmscher ("Grundzüge," p. 17) defends Herder against those interpretations that see him merely as the forerunner of historicism. He explains Herder's sophisticated notion of hermeneutic understanding, which takes into account the limited horizon of understanding as productive for the hermeneutic process. Irmscher points out the relevance of Herder's writings on sculpture and shows how the position of the understanding subject is grounded in his sense of his own body. With regard to the Greek sculpture, he remarks that for Herder this isolated representation of the nude human body comes to signify autonomous individuality (see pp. 31–33). In this attempt to know the individual, as it is developed through the image of the sculpture, Irmscher sees the beginning of morphology and the departure from the classical episteme with its insistence on natural history and the mathesis of the classificatory table (p. 34). Irmscher, however, though insisting on the *Köpergefühl* as constitutive of Herder's hermeneutics, does not consider this feeling to be constructed with the aid of an idealized fiction or to be based on a *méconnaissance*. Dietrich Harth (" Ästhetik," p. 119) sees Herder's concept of "literarische Bildung" as the development of the hermeneutic notion of a divinatory *Verstehen*. Although Harth does not consider the specific role of the ideal body, he acknowledges the idealizing and fictional component in Herder's concept of the soul, which he sees as a compensatory move in idealist aesthetics vis-à-vis modern alienation (see p. 134).

20. See Green "L'angoisse et le narcissisme," in *Narcissisme*, pp. 133–73, esp. p. 139: "The Ego works on representations, it is worked on by representations, it cannot be represented. It can have representations of the object, and this is the only thing it can do. It is through the affect that the Ego gives itself an unrepresentable representation of itself."

21. In "Übers Erkennen und Empfinden in der Menschlichen Seele," Herder writes: "For the soul the body is not a body; it is its realm: an aggregation of many obscure forces of the imagination out of which the soul forms its image, i.e., the

clear thought. They are actually interdependent and made for one another. . . . In brief, the body is symbol, phenomenon of the soul in its relation to the universe" (*Sämtliche Werke*, 8: 250). See also Joe K. Fugate's *Psychological Basis*, which shows how Herder's writings on aesthetics are intimately bound up with Herder's notion of the human soul as a unified totality of man's faculties, perceptions, and creative potential. Fugate's study also points out how Herder's notion of feeling and the body are connected to the soul. Herder's aesthetics thus is presented as a critique of rationalism. In his conclusion Fugate attempts to highlight the difference between Herder's and Schiller's aesthetics; Schiller still seems to be a rationalist and an idealist and dualist, as opposed to Herder, who emphasizes process, natural development, and the unity of the soul. Unfortunately, Fugate pays relatively little attention to Herder's concept of language and the soul's construction in language. More attention to Herder's "Besonnenheit" in relation to Schiller's "ästhetischer Zustand" would have brought those two authors into closer proximity.

22. For another text that celebrates Greek sculpture as an antidote to human mortality, see Friedrich Schiller's, "Brief eines reisenden Dänen" (*Rheinische Thalia* 1: 1785), in *Sämtliche Werke*, 5: 879. Schiller depicts the traveler's reaction to the misery and poverty among pomp and luxury in the following words: "A hollow-eyed, starving figure, which begs from me among the blooming promenades of a ducal amusement garden—a collapsing shingle hovel opposed to a pompous palace—how fast they strike down my soaring pride! My imagination completes the painting. And now I can see the curses of thousands like a ravenous world of worms swarming among this boasting decomposition—the great and delightful is abominable to me—I don't discover anything but a sickly, languishing human body, whose eyes and cheeks burn with a feverish redness and simulate blooming life, while gangrene and putrefaction are raging in the rattling lungs" (p. 879). "Why do all the speaking and painting arts of antiquity aim so much at refinement? Man was able to accomplish something greater than he was, which reminds us of something greater than his species—Could this perhaps prove that he is less than he will be?—then this common tendency toward beautification could save us any further speculation about the permanence of the soul" (p. 883).

23. For a good survey of Moritz's position in the context of German classicist aesthetics, see Schrimpf, "Moritz," esp. pp. 895–904.

24. For the sociohistorical implications of Moritz's notion of aesthetic autonomy, see Woodmansee, "Disinterestedness"; and Bürger, "Autonomie der Kunst als Kategorie der bürgerlichen Gesellschaft: Zur ästhetischen Theorie von Karl Philipp Moritz und Schiller," pp. 119–30. Woodmansee focuses on Moritz's view of the mode of reception appropriate to a work of art and draws a link between quietist pietism and "disinterested pleasure." Comparing Moritz's notion of the function of the artist to the actual historical situation of the artist, she concludes that although literary "entertainment was becoming an industry," Moritz's theology of the autonomous work of art was the response to this situation of the market (p. 39). Bürger understands Moritz's aesthetics against the background of his petit-bourgeois socialization (p. 129) and sees in it a sharp criticism of modern alienation, the exploitation of the lower classes, and the division between manual and mental labor (pp. 123–24). His postulate of a contemplative reception of an autonomous work of art, she interprets as the emergence of the "affirmative" char-

acter of bourgeois art à la Marcuse (p. 126). My reading of Moritz's aesthetics in the context of the project of Bildung acknowledges the sociohistorical background outlined by Bürger, Woodmansee, and others; however, it tries to work out the model of subjectivity and sublimation, which, I would argue, surely does not apply to society as a whole but will become increasingly important for those male subjects who want to be "serious" artists (as opposed to those who write to satisfy the dictates of the market) and who therefore cannot live from their art but have to make their living as scholars, academics, teachers and, almost always and most important, civil servants.

25. See also Todorov, "The Romantic Crisis," in his *Theories*, esp. pp. 148–64. Todorov chooses Moritz (Herder, Vico, Rousseau, or Shaftesbury would have been other "serious candidates") as the representative of the Romanticist and modern notion of the symbol because of his ultimate departure from the traditional notion of imitation. Todorov singles out Moritz's postulates that (1) not the work of art but the artist imitates nature and creation (Prometheus); (2) the work of art is an autonomous whole; (3) the work of art signifies in an intransitive manner ("Signification in art is an interpretation of the signifier and the signified; all distance between the two is abolished"; p. 162). In this sense, Moritz anticipates the notion of the Romantic symbol.

26. See also Saine, *Die Ästhetische Theodizee*. Saine reads Moritz's aesthetics in the context of Leibniz's *Nouveaux essais sur l'entendement humain* (1765). Saine is one of the few critics who attempt to decipher the last passages of the "Bildende Nachahmung." He contrasts Moritz's notion of history, which fuses history and story (Moritz's interpretation of the *Iliad*), to Herder's *Ideen* and Kant's critique of Herder. Since Herder emphasizes both progress and the individuality of certain historical periods, for him human misery is a result of myopia; Kant subsumes all historical individuality under the development of the species; Moritz endows the exemplary historical or fictional individualities with a cathartic capacity to lessen human misery (see pp. 169–73).

27. See also Schrimpf's explanation of Moritz's "Tatkraft" in his *Karl Philipp Moritz*, p. 102.

28. For an analysis of Moritz's distinction between *Empfindungsvermögen* and *Bildungsvermögen* as the beginning of modern "kitsch" theories, see Schulte-Sasse, *Die Kritik*, pp. 63–73.

29. In the most basic terms, "suture," derived from Lacanian psychoanalysis, "names the relation of the subject to the chain of its discourse" (Jacques-Alain Miller, "Suture," p. 25). In an effort to theorize film as discourse and to analyze the positioning of the subject in that discourse, that is, the subject's production at the juncture of the symbolic and the imaginary, contemporary film semiotics has developed various theories of "suture." To the extent that "suture is descriptive of the production of the very possibility of signification" (Heath, "Notes," p. 62), it is, of course, not restricted to the medium of film. What is particularly interesting about the concept of "suture" with regard to Moritz is that it describes how "absence" and "lack" become operative in providing the viewer of a film, or the beholder of an aesthetic object (in Moritz's context), with a desire for closure.

30. See also Düsing, " Ästhetische Form." Düsing traces Schiller's reception of Leibniz and Shaftesbury: "The most perfect of all worlds is no longer objec-

tively given, the subject no longer a mirror of the whole, but—to formulate it poignantly—the opposite is true; the whole becomes a mirror, a representation, of the self" (p. 191). And about the *Kalliasbriefe*, Düring writes: "In the *Kalliasbriefe* the relationship between representation and the representation of self is explicitly formulated as an aesthetic phenomenon. Schiller uses terms such as 'the nature of the thing,' 'the persona of the thing,' he speaks of its 'personality,' its 'individuality,' or its 'self.' The metaphors show that the aesthetic form is understood as the projection of the beholding subjectivity, that the beautiful is not an object like any other object, but rather that it appears as something which leads its beholding subject in the act of contemplation to an encounter with itself. The beautiful object evokes the impression that it is not a thing but a living individuality, as if it possessed a structure analogous to the one of subjectivity" (p. 192).

31. See Letter 2, pp. 572–73. Many interpretations of Schiller's *Aesthetic Education* debate the issue of whether Schiller's notion of autonomous art is a renunciation of politically engaged art, a compensation for the artist's impotence vis-à-vis the sociopolitical circumstances, or a utopian, critical ideal. There is, for instance:

1. The "renunciation" thesis (see Janz, *Autonomie*, p. 66).

2. The "compensatory" thesis (Bolten, *Friedrich Schiller*: "While Schiller in the Augustenburger letters obviously still intended to prove in an empirical and inductive manner that 'the original laws of reason . . . were also the laws of taste,' in his letters *On the Aesthetic Education of Man* he chose the transcendental-deductive method. It is to be shown how this change in method induces, on the one hand, a transition from Kant towards Fichte; on the other hand, it also means the manifestation of a—fundamentally early Romanticist—theory of art, which though it solves the problem of mediation nevertheless also degrades art from an instrument to a substitute for social change"; pp. 213–14).

3. The "utopian, critical" thesis (Berghahn, *Schiller*, who reads Schiller with Marcuse: "In the aesthetic experience alienated man anticipates the experience of his liberation, which ought to prepare the political liberation" [p. 127]. According to Berghahn the aesthetic state aims at a "society beyond the reality principle and beyond any kind of repression, one where the needs and restrictions of life would be canceled: the liberated individual could realize itself in its interactions" [pp. 149–50]).

32. Various interpretations of Schiller's aesthetics and Weimar Classicism have emphasized the degree to which the classicist notion of the total human being and the neo-humanist ideal of Bildung are indebted to Renaissance humanism and the ideal of the courtier. For the most part, these interpretations use this connection in order to understand the elitism and attempts at "nobilization" within the "educated circles" Schiller alludes to. To my knowledge, only one study connects the eighteenth-century education of civil servants and Schiller's aesthetics in the context of humanist Bildung: Ueding, *Schillers Rhetorik*. Ueding reads Schiller's aesthetics and poetics in the tradition of Quintilian's rhetoric and the educational ideals of the courtier and Renaissance humanism. He sees the letters on aesthetic education as a response to Schiller's experience at the Karlsschule: "In the programmatic text from 1771 drafted by Seeger and Professor Jahn for the Duke we can read: 'Upon reflecting on the great and important task of educating youth

with its many advantages for the state . . . we have decided to found a military academy [literally: nursery] on our Solitude, where before our eyes young cavaliers and officer boys will be formed for the future services in the ministry, court and military. . . . The teachers of the Karlsschule, often being asked to do so by the Duke, and the Duke himself have repeatedly presented the methods and the aims of this education: a mixture of Humanism and Enlightenment permeates speeches and curricula. Ambition, performance, and utility are the dominant principles of an education that aims at the smooth integration into society, at practical professional training in order to—as Duke Eugen puts it—'make the human being useful for the whole.' And yet an opposing tendency remains to be felt and even gains ground through neo-humanism: the broadest training in the sciences and arts, the central position of philosophy, the teaching of ancient languages, the reading of classical authors. These aspects run counter to a one-sided education and are often subsumed under the postulate of utility only with great difficulties. . . . It is precisely this aspect that might have had a decisive influence when Schiller later 'reinvented' an educational ideal" (pp. 21–22). Unfortunately, Ueding does not explore in the same critical manner the ideological function of the neo-humanist ideal of Bildung in Schiller's aesthetics with regard to Humboldt and the educational reforms. According to Ueding, the neo-humanist ideals merely serve to camouflage the utilitarian aspects of the Karlsschule, and in Schiller's own educational program they serve as a critical instance vis-à-vis the decadence and instrumental reasoning of the educated bourgeoisie (see pp. 23, 25–33). I would argue that in both instances the neo-humanist ideals function within a fundamental reorganization of subjectivity (the "Veredelung des Charakters" as a model of sublimation) and as a ticket to upward mobility (e.g., for people like Herder, Moritz, Schiller). For the parallels between Schiller's and Humboldt's anthropological assumptions, see Price, "Wilhelm von Humboldt"; and Bürger, *Der Ursprung*, pp. 130–40. For an interesting reading of Schiller's play *Don Carlos* in the context of his experience at the Karlsschule, see Kittler, "Carlos als Karlsschüler."

33. See p. 585: "And so gradually individual life is extinguished, in order that the abstract life of the whole may prolong its sorry existence, and the State remains eternally alien to its citizens because nowhere does feeling discover it" (p. 41). Dieter Borchmeyer (*Tragödie*) reads Schiller's criticism of the modern abstract state through Hegel's aesthetics and Marx's critique of alienation. In Borchmeyer's study alienation is the separation between the general, political sphere and the individual, private sphere, between the *citoyen* and the *bourgeois*. However, Schiller (as opposed to Hegel) does not place the aesthetic state in the unretrievable past but conceives of it as a utopian project: "We can conclude that Schiller's aesthetic theory is determined by the consciousness that man in modern society is situated in the permanent conflict between sensual-individual existence and the existence of mankind as a whole, between human and political life. The attempt to reconcile those two sides marks not only Schiller's aesthetics but also the principles of his poetic activity, the style of his plays since *Wallenstein*. . . . The stage becomes the theater of a beautiful public sphere in its exemplary fusion of the public-political and the individual-human into an institution of aesthetic education" (p. 115). Schiller's aesthetics (and the aesthetics of his time) reject the

class-bound rules of rhetoric and poetics. Similar to Ueding, Borchmeyer points out that Schiller attempts to reconstruct public life by having recourse to aristocratic forms of representation: "In his *Letters on the Aesthetic Education* Schiller attempts to expand that noble prerogative, to let the bourgeois citizen participate in the forms of aristocratic education, which have been transformed and reinterpreted by the spirit of the new aesthetics" (p. 117). Schiller's criticism of abstract rationalism offers as remedy to this dilemma the recourse to rhetoric, the *sensus communis* (see pp. 125–136).

Chapter 5

1. In my reading of *Maria Stuart*, I refer to relatively few of the interpretations of the play, since a fairly recent survey of the major interpretations can be found in Sautermeister's "Maria Stuart."

2. See Wiese, *Friedrich Schiller*, pp. 721, 727–28. For an excellent study of late eighteenth-century relations between Enlightenment rationality, aesthetics, and religion, see Burger "Eine Idee."

3. "Über den Gebrauch des Chors in der Tragödie," preface to *Die Braut von Messina*, in Schiller, *Sämtliche Werke*, 2: 820. Dieter Borchmeyer, ("Die theatralische Sichtbarkeit der Staatsaktion in *Maria Stuart*," in his *Tragödie*, pp. 198–209), sets out from the same problem. He likewise takes Schiller's preface to *Braut von Messina* as the crucial link between the *Aesthetic Education* and Schiller's dramatic praxis.

4. Koopmann, *Friedrich Schiller*, p. 61.

5. Roger Ayrault ("La figure," p. 313) reads Mortimer as representing a mistaken, idolatrous Catholicism, a contrasting foil that Schiller needed to prevent a confounding of Maria's spiritualized, "true" religiosity with Catholicism per se.

6. See Mortimer's response to the meeting of the two queens, which he hallucinates seeing: "Ich hörte alles./Du hast gesiegt! Du tratst sie in den Staub,/Du warst die Königin, sie der Verbrecher./Ich bin entzückt von deinem Mut, ich bete/Dich an, wie eine Göttin groß und herrlich/Erscheinst du mir in diesem Augenblick" (I heard all——/Thine is the palm;—thou trod'st her to the dust!——/Though wast the queen, she was the malefactor;——/I am transported with thy noble courage;——/Yes! I adore thee; like a Deity,/My sense is dazzled by thy heavenly beams"; III, 6, 2469–73, *p.* 79).

7. See Maria's words when she hands Paulet her letter for Elisabeth: "Man hat mich/Vor ein Gericht von Männern vorgefordert,/Die ich als meinesgleichen nicht erkennen,/Zu denen ich kein Herz mir fassen kann./Elisabeth ist meines Stammes, meines/Geschlechts und Ranges—Ihr allein, der Schwester,/Der Königin, der Frau kann ich mich öffnen" ("I have been summoned/Before a court of men, whom I can ne'er/Acknowledge as my peers—of men to whom/My heart denies its confidence. The queen/Is of my family, my rank, my sex;/To her alone—a sister, queen, and woman——/Can I unfold my heart"; I, 2, 170–76; *p. 10*).

8. See II, 8, 1779–93: "Man preist mich glücklich—wüßte man, was es/Für Ketten sind, um die man mich beneidet——/Nachdem ich zehen bittre Jahre lang/Dem Götzen ihrer Eitelkeit geopfert,/Mich jedem Wechsel ihrer Sultans-

launen / Mit Sklavendemut unterwarf, das Spielzeug / Des kleinen grillenhaften Eigensinns, / Geliebkost jetzt von ihrer Zärtlichkeit, / Und jetzt mit sprödem Stolz zurückgestoßen, / Wie ein Gefangener vom Argusblick / Der Eifersucht gehütet, ins Verhör / Genommen wie ein Knabe, wie ein Diener / Gescholten—O die Sprache hat kein Wort / Für diese Hölle!" ("They call me happy! did they only know / What the chains are, for which they envy me! / When I had sacrificed ten bitter years / To the proud idol of her vanity; / Submitted with a slave's humility? To every change of her despotic fancies. / The plaything of each little wayward whim. / At times by seeming tenderness caressed, / As oft repulsed with proud and cold disdain; / Alike tormented by her grace and rigor: / Watched like a prisoner by the Argus eyes / Of jealousy; examined like a schoolboy, / And railed at like a servant. Oh, no tongue / Can paint this hell"; *pp. 58–59*).

9. See II, 8, 1923–30: "Weg mit der Verstellung! Handelt öffentlich! / Verteidigt als ein Ritter die Geliebte, / Kämpft einen edeln Kampf um sie. Ihr seid / Herr der Person der Königin von England, / Sobald Ihr wollt. Lockt sie auf Eure Schlösser, / Sie ist Euch oft dahin gefolgt. Dort zeigt ihr / Den Mann! Sprecht als ihr Gebieter! haltet sie / Verwahrt, bis sie die Stuart freigegeben!" ("Away with feigning—act an open part, / And, like a loyal knight, protect your fair; / Fight a good fight for her! You know you are / Lord over the person of the Queen of England, / Oft hath she thither followed you—then show / That you're a man; then speak as master; keep her / Confined till she release the Queen of Scots"; *p. 62*).

10. Peter Utz ("Auge, Ohr, Herz," pp. 85–86) interprets the dynamics of the gaze as the dichotomy between the look and speech of the encounter of the queens in the following terms: "Because Maria wants to understand her subjection to Elizabeth merely as a political act she prematurely elevates what she sees onto the level of political speech and simultaneously denies that Elisabeth has a 'heart.' . . . Speech becomes a barrier between eye and heart and turns the eye into a cold mirror that merely reflects the public sphere of the court and its moral values. Only the silent spectator can escape this pragmatic paradox. But neither Maria nor Elisabeth is forced to legitimate herself. In the escalation of the 'affect' in the dispute, the gaze is charged with the dominant morality in the same degree as the dispute is shifted from the political to the moral level, where finally the erotic competition of the women erupts" (pp. 85–86).

11. See II, 2, 1207–11: "Hat die Königin doch nichts / Voraus vor dem gemeinen Bürgerweibe! / das gleiche Zeichen weist auf gleiche Pflicht, / Auf gleiche Dienstbarkeit—der Ring macht Ehen, / Und Ringe sinds, die eine Kette machen" ("In this a queen has not / One privilege above all other women. / This common token marks one common duty, / One common servitude; the ring denotes / Marriage, and 'tis of rings a chain is formed"; *p. 40*).

12. See II, 2, 1166–71: "Auch meine jungfäuliche Freiheit soll ich, / Mein höchstes Gut, hingeben für mein Volk, / Und der Gebieter wird mir aufgedrungen. / Er zeigt mir dadurch an, daß ich ihm nur / Ein Weib bin, und ich meinte doch, regiert / Zu haben, wie ein Mann und wie ein König" ("And I must offer up my liberty, my greatest good, / To satisfy my people. Thus they'd force / A lord and master on me.'Tis by this / I see that I am nothing but a woman / In their regard; and yet methought that I / Had governed like a man, and like a king"; *p. 39*). For a study of the historical Elizabeth I, see Montrose, "Elizabethan Subject."

13. The phrasing of these lines is quite interesting if one considers that King Friedrich I of Prussia (r. 1713–40) is famous for referring to himself as the first servant of the state: "Doch eine Königin, die ihre Tage/Nicht ungenützt in müßiger Beschauung/Verbringt, die unverdrossen, unermüdet,/Die schwerste aller Pflichten übt, die sollte/Von dem Naturzweck ausgenommen sein,/Der eine Hälfte des Geschlechts der Menschen/Der andern unterwürfig macht—" ("But yet a queen who hath not spent her days/In fruitless, idle contemplation; who,/Without murmur, indefatigably/Performs the hardest of all duties; she/Should be exempted from that natural law/Which doth ordain one half of human kind/Shall ever be subservient to the other"; II, 2, 1178–84; *pp.* 39–40). See also Vierhaus, "Politisches Bewußtsein": "A remarkable phenomenon: In his two political wills from 1752 and 1768 the Prussian monarch claims to have pursued the 'first' duty of a citizen (*citoyen*) to serve his fatherland (*patrie*) and to be useful to his fellow citizens (*concitoyens*)" (p. 142).

14. Gert Sautermeister ("Maria Stuart") argues that Maria's turning point in becoming a "beautiful soul" lies in the acknowledgment and liberation of her repressed affects: "The liberation from noble morality is here the liberation from self-imposed servitude. In this play Schiller's psychology explodes the classical mean, demystifies the ethics of self-discipline, of the acceptance of suffering and the all-forgiving humanism, and reveals in this a good portion of self-enslavement and self-deception; finally he exposes the dregs of anger and vengefulness that can accumulate behind exaggerated tolerance and heroic love for one's fellow human beings. . . . When Maria finally acknowledges her aggressions, she points at the origin of injustice and suppression and transforms a suffering self-oppression into an active presentation of self" (p. 194).

15. See Foucault, *Discipline and Punish*.

16. For an excellent historical survey of the eighteenth-century homologies between the aesthetic/poetological and juridical arguments about the spectacle of deterrence, see Zelle, "Strafen und Schrecken."

17. See note in *Sämtliche Werke*, p. 1262.

18. See Foucault, *Discipline and Punish*, pp. 225–28.

19. Quoted in *Sämtliche Werke*, p. 1259.

20. See Foucault, *Discipline and Punish*: "If the surplus power possessed by the king gives rise to the duplication of his body, has not the surplus power exercised on the subjected body of the condemned man given rise to another type of duplication? That of a 'non-corporal,' a 'soul,' as Malby called it. The history of this 'micro-physics' of punitive power would then be a genealogy or an element in a genealogy of the modern 'soul.' Rather than seeing this soul as the reactivated remnants of an ideology, one would see it as the present correlative of a certain technology of power over the body. It would be wrong to say that the soul is an illusion, or an ideological effect. On the contrary, it exists, it has a reality, it is produced permanently around, on, within the body by the functioning of a power that is exercised on those punished—and, in a more general way, on those one supervises, trains and corrects, over madmen, children at home and at school, the colonized, over those who are stuck at a machine and supervised for the rest of their lives. This is the historical reality of this soul, which, unlike the soul repre-

sented by Christian theology, is not born in sin and subject to punishment, but is born rather out of methods of punishment, supervision and constraint" (p. 29).

21. Two recent interpretations of *Maria Stuart* also focus on this scene: Benjamin Bennett (*Modern Drama*) sees in Leicester's hallucination of Maria's decapitation the representation of modern consciousness and an instance in which the play becomes self-reflective and appeals to the audience's constructive participation in establishing its "wholeness" and "identity": "The locked room in which he [Leicester] is compelled to experience Mary's execution (V.10) is an example of what I have called phrenographic theater; it represents his entrapment within himself, his inability to undertake any outward-directed action and so escape from the self-conscious circle of his own thoughts. And that it is this scene by which the execution is represented on stage indicates that we are meant to think of Mary's death, at least in one aspect, as an event within Leicester's mind, as the disaster of self-consciousness, as the final collapse into utter despair of a fruitlessly self-preoccupied mental attitude" (p. 200). Peter Utz's interpretation of *Maria Stuart*, "Auge, Ohr und Herz," likewise locates in this scene the cathartic effect and political message for the audience. He claims that the eye is devalorized as the instrument of a cold state rationality and that it is through the ear that finally Leicester's heart is struck (see p. 87). In that sense Leicester's collapse has to be seen in contrast to Elisabeth's composure; it indicates that the realm of political power is always closed to the "heart." For the audience this scene is supposed to bring together the dissociated visual and auditory realms and lead the spectator to a critical weighing of both (p. 84).

22. See Foucault, "Generalized Punishment," in *Discipline and Punish*, pp. 73–103; and for Germany, Gerd Kleinheyer, "Wandlungen."

23. Dieter Borchmeyer ("Die theatralische Sichtbarkeit der Staatsaktion in *Maria Stuart*," in *Trägodie*) concludes that Schiller attempts to render the machinations of the abstract state apparatus "visible" through the psychological analysis of the two women, mainly as their psyches are exposed in the encounter of the two queens: "In the fight of the two queens that Schiller as the 'decisive hour' (line 2176) of the action had placed exactly into the middle of the play the political tension of lengthy historical events is heightened and indistinguishably fused with human conflicts and thus assumes extreme theatrical efficacy. The political contrast is simultaneously revealed as female rivalry, the public is connected with the most intimate sphere. Schiller has succeeded in 'spinning the cold, sterile action of the state out of the human heart and thereby binding it back to the human heart,' as he had set himself the task in the preface to *Fiesco*. In *Maria Stuart* he conjures up a state of the world in which individual passion still entails worldly, historical relevance and the gravest political implications" (p. 206). Although my reading of the play agrees with Borchmeyer's description of the function of the scene, i.e., of "rendering visible" invisible political forces and threats, I do not see Schiller's solution as a flight into a distanced past, in which the "great individual" still could wield power and mark the course of history. Rather, I would read this scene as a topical response to his contemporary situation, a situation of an expanding state apparatus, on the one hand, and the threat of public violence, on the other, which was encoded in terms of the late eighteenth-century gender ideology: a situation

of social peace is portrayed in terms of a blissful domesticity based on gender polarity, one of political upheaval and unrest in terms of women invading the public realm, turning into beasts and assuming the threatening aspects of a castrating Medusa or the Thracian maenads dismembering Orpheus. One example would be Schiller's poem about the French Revolution, "Die Glocke," which refers to the revolutionary violence in the line: "Da werden Weiber werden zu Hyänen / Und treiben mit Entsetzen Scherz, / Noch zuckend, mit des Panthers Zähnen, / Zerreißen sie des Feindes Herz" (And women become hyenas / And jokingly provoke horror, / Still twitching with the panther's teeth / They tear apart the enemy's heart; *Sämtliche Werke*, 1: 440).

24. For a brilliant study of the function of the sight of Medusa in the French Revolution and in 1848, see Neil Hertz, "Medusa's Head."

25. A prime example of this seeming contradiction is Goethe's Dorothea (in the epic *Hermann und Dorothea*), who represents the modern housewife seeking fulfillment in unpaid domestic labor, but who also—otherwise she would not have been worthy of becoming a literary character according to Goethe—committed the heroic (for Wilhelm von Humboldt "appalling") act of killing a soldier in defense of her female companions. For an extensive historical study of late-eighteenth-century gender polarization, see Karin Hausen, "Die Polarisierung." For the role of women in the administrative reforms of an expanding state apparatus in the late eighteenth century with its fundamental changes in the educational system, see Kittler, "Mütterlichkeit und Beamtenschaft," in *Aufschreibesysteme*, pp. 59–75.

26. See Blanckenburg, *Versuch*. Blanckenburg, who contrasts the earlier version of *Agathon* with the Richardsonian novel, argues against a novel based on love and for a novel based on friendship (see pp. 163–68). He opposes *Clarissa*, which is centered on events, to *Agathon*, which is centered on character (pp. 255–56). In a long footnote, he argues that Richardson composed his novel according to dramatic principles, aiming at the reader's sympathy and pity, when he tried to motivate Clarissa's mistake, her involvement with Lovelace (pp. 297–300). Banckenburg's critique of Richardson culminates in the accusation that even the Aesopian fable would be more morally effective than his epistolary novels, for the novels are not able to make the moral message a necessary outcome. He accuses Richardson of a lack of Anschaulichkeit, in the sense that the story does not develop by necessity out of Clarissa's character, that, in fact, Clarissa could be replaced by any other young woman (see pp. 369–70).

27. For Wieland's position within Weimar Classicism, see Jørgensen, "Weimarer Klassik."

28. This concern is indicated, for instance, through the use of names like Narcissus and Hyacinthus, the allusion to the Pygmalion story in the scene with the painter, in Aspasia's discourse on the love of an other versus the love of the self, and in the narrator's deliberations on the topic of admiration and vanity as well as on the dangers of remorse.

29. Dilthey, *Erlebnis*, p. 328.

30. This promise of happiness surfaces in the frequently quoted letter from Wieland to Zimmermann of Jan. 5, 1762: "In spite of all of this I have started a couple of months ago a novel which I call 'Die Geschichte des Agathon.' In it I

describe myself as I imagine I would have been in Agathon's circumstances, and in the end I make myself as happy as I would like to be."

31. For a survey of the discussion of the bildungsroman, see Köhn, "Entwicklungs- und Bildungsroman." See also Sorg, *Gebrochene Teleologie*, pp. 12–55; and Selbmann, *Bildungsroman*. Much of the debate about this genre stems from the attempt to establish a definition that allows for continuity from the beginning of this genre in German Classicism and Romanticism to the twentieth century. Since it is not one of my concerns to turn the bildungsroman into the "Großform des deutschen Romans," I shall not discuss the various positions in this debate.

32. Not all scholars agree that *Agathon* is a bildungsroman; some begin the genealogy of the genre with Goethe's *Wilhelm Meisters Lehrjahre* (1796). For instance, Liisa Saariluoma (*Die Erzählstruktur*, pp. 148–49) (whose notion of the bildungsroman seems to be indebted to Georg Lukács's "bildungsroman" in his history of the novel, *Theorie des Romans*) argues that *Agathon* is not a bildungsroman because the distance between narrator and protagonist is so wide that the problem of the hero cannot simultaneously be explored as a problem of the interpretation of the world at large. For very different reasons, Wolfgang Paulsen (*Wieland*) argues that *Agathon* is not a bildungsroman because the protagonist does not learn anything specific and because the biographical narrative has a cyclical structure—it brings the protagonist back to his beginning. He sees *Agathon* as an autobiographical report shifted into the realm of the paradigmatic. Yet, ironically, Paulsen's humanist, psychological, and autobiographical reading of this novel—his assertion that Wieland searches for the paradigm of his own life in *Agathon*, "such that we must tentatively take *Agathon* to be an analytically operating autobiographical novel in historical disguise" (p. 78)—displays exactly those conventions that were being established with the bildungsroman: "In the last instance the text then is merely a mirror that reflects the poet in all of his humanity. Finally this means then that the psychological relation to literature is of necessity an anthropological and a humanist relation, and this kind of humanism might very well be the only one that is still adequate for our times" (p. 29). Nevertheless, many studies see in *Agathon* one of the first bildungsroman; e.g., Mayer, "Begründung," argues that the two earlier versions of *Agathon* are still an *Entwicklungsroman*, but the last version represents the first true bildungsroman. The most comprehensive account to situate *Agathon* in intellectual history as a bildungsroman is Buddecke, *Wielands Entwicklungsbegriff*. Buddecke points out that Wieland's view of development is indebted to both Leibniz's notions of the prefiguration of the individual and the concept of an entelechial unfolding and to those eighteenth-century theories of how the milieu conditions what individual traits are brought forth. What mediates these two opposing views is the neo-humanist idea that man has to become his own, second creator; this is what Agathon achieves through the course of his development.

33. See Preisendanz, "Die Auseinandersetzung," for comments on the poetological implications of Wieland's preface to *Agathon*. Preisendanz reads Wieland's novels in the context of Johann Christoph Gottsched's and Johann Breitinger's poetics and argues that although superficially the criterion of verisimilitude in Wieland seems to adhere to mid-eighteenth-century poetic norms, Wieland de-

parts from them decisively. For Wieland the issue is no longer historical facticity versus the poetic marvelous; rather, the novel becomes, like Fielding's *Tom Jones*, an exploration of human nature in general. In particular, *Agathon* explores the laws of individual psychology in which the marvelous is no longer a product of poetic fiction but of the individual imagination. Based on Preisendanz's study, Schrader, *Mimesis*, defines the bildungsroman rather too generally and abstractly as the mimesis of poetic productivity.

34. See also Müller, *Autobiographie*: "Wieland did not just transfer his own problems to his novelistic character; he further developed the novel out of the autobiographical form in such a manner that the underlying structure remained visible. This is possible because the history of internal development as the true form of individuality leaves to the external circumstances of life merely a secondary relevance and makes those within their function exchangeable. Thus the problem of autobiography has been reformulated, for under those circumstances it no longer suffices to report the external biographical data. Those have become ambivalent, and they contain no longer the truth of the subject. In *Agathon* the compulsion for interpretation as the condition of the possibility of a higher truth has been objectified in the figure of the narrator who must appear as an editor within the novelistic fiction. Taking a detour over a novelistic representation of autobiographical experience, Wieland has sublated fictional autobiography into fiction. We have here the realization of a representational model, the one of the bildungsroman, that despite all its close connections with autobiography can no longer be realized for autobiography. However, it remains relevant for autobiography because it reformulates the issue of truth and dissociates this issue from the mere authenticity of facts" (p. 106).

35. This could equally be argued for *Wilhelm Meister*. For a survey of eighteenth-century autobiographical conventions, see Niggl, *Geschichte*.

36. For an interesting analysis of the opening passages of *Agathon* as a "quotation" of the Baroque novel, see Saariluoma, *Die Erzählstruktur*, pp. 134–35. She argues that by foregrounding the improbable circumstances the narrator indicates that his category of verisimilitude applies to the inner constitution of his protagonist rather than to the external circumstances.

37. The only study I know of that speaks of Agathon's narcissism is by Campe, *Der programmatische Roman*. Campe also describes Agathon's otherworldly enthusiasm as a form of narcissism. However, he does not analyze this narcissism in any further detail. According to Campe, this narcissism is overcome once Agathon flees from the "homosexual" encounter with the priest. Thus, Campe sees Wieland rejecting narcissism as leading to passivity and perversion.

38. For a commentary on Agathon's seduction through Danae's interpretation of the pantomime of Daphne and Apollo, see Wölfel, "Daphnes Verwandlungen."

39. See Lacan, "The Agency of the Letter in the Unconscious or Reason Since Freud," in *Ecrits*, pp. 146–78.

40. Michael Bakhtin ("The *Bildungsroman*") defines the bildungsroman as the novel that depicts "man in the process of becoming" (p. 19): "As opposed to a static unity, here one finds a dynamic unity in the hero's image. The hero himself, his character, becomes a variable in the formula of this type of novel. Changes in the hero himself acquire *plot* significance, and thus the entire plot of the novel

is reinterpreted and reconstructed. Time is introduced into man, enters into his very image, changing in a fundamental way the significance of all aspects of his destiny and life. This novel can be designated in the most general sense as the novel of human emergence" (p. 21). Bakhtin classifies various types of the bildungsroman on the basis of how "time enters" the novel. He situates Wieland in the genealogy of the bildungsroman among the earlier types that take their lead from biographical conventions. He points out that the decisive difference between Goethe's *Wilhelm Meister* and the later bildungsroman and *Agathon* lies in *Agathon*'s cyclical time, in the fact that historical time does not enter this novel: "If changes did take place in this world, they were peripheral, in no way affecting its foundations. Man emerged, developed, and changed within one epoch. The world, existing and stable in this existence, required that man adapt to it, that he recognize and submit to the existing laws of life. Man emerged, but the world itself did not. On the contrary, the world was an immobile orientation point for developing man. Man's emergence was his private affair, as it were, and the results of this emergence were also private and biographical in nature. And everything in the world itself remained in its place. In and of itself the conception of the world as an experience, as school, was very productive in the *Bildungsroman*: it presented a different side of the world to man, a side that had previously been foreign to the novel. It led to a radical reinterpretation of the elements of the novel's plot and opened up for the novel new and realistically productive points for viewing the world. But the world, as an experience and as a school, remained the same, fundamentally immobile and ready-made, given. It changed for the one studying in it only during the process of study (in most cases that world turned out to be more impoverished and drier than it had seemed in the beginning)" (p. 23).

41. Martin Swales ("An Unreadable Novel?") reads the first version of *Agathon* in terms of how the editor/narrator sets his text apart from conventional novels, particularly in regard to the protagonist's complex character and the problematic, ironical happy ending, by foregrounding the fictionality of the teleology. He argues that this kind of obviously constructed happy ending marks the genre of the bildungsroman and shifts attention from the ending to the process that leads to this ending. Although the ending of *Agathon*'s last version cannot be called ironical, the narrator still emphasizes its constructedness by foregrounding the elements of the marvelous and the romance. Therefore, I would argue that the teleology of the construction of the self as fabricated through the final summary of the protagonist's life as a continuous development and unfolding of all his potential is marked as a narrative and hermeneutic construct, which has the status of an imperative.

42. Paulsen (*Wieland*) also emphasizes Agathon's father fixation: "Agathon's path did not lead him to the woman, for both women become neutralized sisterly figures, rather to the father—more precisely to the father imago" (p. 25).

43. "The more we are in love with ourselves, Aspasia used to say, the less we are able to love something external to ourselves" (III, 334).

44. For an interesting psychoanalytic reading of the difference between shame and guilt, see André Green's introduction to his remarks on Ajax and Oedipus in *Narcissisme*, pp. 178–80.

45. Although Buddecke (*Wielands Entwicklungsbegriff*) emphasizes that Aga-

thon in the end can attain the Bildung of his personality only by subscribing to a Kantian notion of duty through the renunciation of sensuality, he argues that the narrator distances himself in his ironical asides from this rigorous rejection of sensual pleasures. This may make Wieland's philosophy of Bildung more palatable, but I also believe it undercuts the entire concept of Bildung, what has been presented as Agathon's "true" self, i.e., the object of his narcissistic love, which is utterly opposed to any kind of physical love of an other. Buddecke quotes, for instance, the narrator's commentary on Kleonissa: "The beautiful Kleonissa was— a woman. This meant she shared the weaknesses that nature had given to her sex, weaknesses without which the more tender half of the human species would neither be apt for its destiny in this sublunar world nor so amiable as it indeed is" (III, 52). I agree that this quotation supports Buddecke's claim that the narrator does not repudiate Kleonissa for her sensuality but merely for her hypocrisy (see p. 235). However, the quotation brings up another point: since the "destiny" of the "more tender part of humanity" exhausts itself in this world in becoming a wife and mother, woman is indeed allowed to fall in love and succumb to her natural weakness. With men, however, things are fundamentally different. They have to find and shape their destiny, or, as Buddecke formulates it, become their own creator. And in this respect Buddecke is also quite convincing, when he points, despite the many parallels between Danae's and Agathon's history, to the fundamental difference between her as a beautiful soul and him as a subject of Bildung: "As the first part of this study has shown the term [*shöne Seele*] denotes for Wieland as for many thinkers and poets of the eighteenth century a particular type of human being that cannot be changed by external influences and that fulfills even in its highest voluntary functions merely the formula of its creation and that therefore cannot be credited with ethical merit. Agathon who shares so many decisive traits that for the reader their stories can mirror and elucidate each other is consciously never given the predicate of being a beautiful soul. We say 'consciously' for if everything that he accomplishes and achieves were merely due to nature he could never represent a human norm, he could never become an example and encourage emulation" (p. 215). However, what Buddecke calls a "human norm" should be called a "male norm": Bildung is exclusively masculine. Elizabeth Boa ("Sex and Sensibility") situates Wieland's attitude toward sexuality and women in the context of the eighteenth century. She praises him for his "humanity," which combines a liberal attitude toward sexuality with women's spiritual and intellectual aspiration. My reading utterly disagrees with her reading of *Agathon*, which comes to the following conclusion: "*Agathon* so defines virtue that it is compatible with pleasure. Love which is virtuous and pleasurable is the way to true Socratic happiness. But as the twists and turns of the plot and the open ending show such a resolution is not easily achieved." And "had Wieland written a novel called *Psyche* or *Danaë*, his account would not have been much different" (pp. 205, 207).

46. Green (*Narcissisme*) formulates the formation of this moral narcissism in the following terms: "The ideal of the narcissistic Ego is built on the vestiges of the Ego-ideal; i.e., on the idealizing omnipotent power of satisfaction that knows no castrating limitations, one that hence has to do less with the Oedipus complex of the oedipal phase than with the one that denies it" (p. 196).

47. See Freud, *Das Ich und das Es*, chap. 3, "Das Ich und das Über-Ich (Ichideal)," *Studienausgabe*, 3: 298–99.

48. Compare II, 10.

49. Drawing on Freud's discussion of animism in *Totem and Taboo*, Samuel Weber (*Legend*) elaborates the relationship between animism, systematic thinking, and narcissism: "What makes animism not merely a phylogenetic forerunner of systematic thinking, but rather its paradigm, is its tendency 'to grasp the whole universe as a single unity from a single point of view' (S.E. 13, 77), its effort to 'explain the essence of the universe entirely.' . . . The animistic attempt to comprehend the external world in terms of unity and totality correspond to the newly formed unity within the psyche: the narcissistic ego. The single point of view and the all-embracing comprehension it permits thus reflect the composite unity of the ego. . . . If, then, that 'intellectual function' which demands 'unity, connection, and intelligibility,' is able to impose its demands, the energy it requires to do so seems now to have an identifiable source: the libidinally cathected, narcissistic ego. Systematic thought organizes the world in the image of this psychic organization. The intellectual construct we call a 'system' reveals itself to be narcissistic, in its origin no less than in its structure: *speculative*, in the etymological sense, as a mirror-image of the ego, and 'phobosophie' as well. If it is driven to fill in the 'gaps and cracks' in the edifice of the universe, the fissures it fears are much closer to home. The 'expectation of an intelligible whole' described by Freud, the expectation of a coherent meaning, appears thus to denote the reaction of an ego seeking to defend its conflict-ridden cohesion against equally endemic centripetal tendencies. The pursuit of meaning; the activity of construction, synthesis, unification; the incapacity to admit anything irreducibly alien, to leave any residue unexplained—all this indicates the struggle of the ego to establish and to maintain an identity that is all the more precarious and vulnerable to the extent that it depends on what it must exclude. In short, speculative, systematic thinking draws its force from the effort of the ego to appropriate an exteriority of which, as Freud will later put it, it is only the 'organized part' " (pp. 13–14). Herder, whose narcissistic version of the origin of language I outline in Chapter 4, also suggests the close relation between narcissism, animism, and personification: "Since all of nature is producing sounds, there is nothing more natural for the sensuous human being than that nature is living, speaking, acting. That savage man saw the high tree with its gorgeous crown and admired it: the crown roared! that is the weaving deity! the savage falls down and prays! Look there is the history of sensuous man, the dark ribbon, *how verbs become nouns*—and the easiest step toward abstraction! For the savages in North America, for instance, everything is still animated: each thing has its genius, its spirit, and that for the Greeks and Orientals it has been the same proved by their oldest dictionary and grammar—they are like the whole of nature was for the inventor, a pantheon! a realm of animated, acting beings! As man related everything to himself, as everything seemed to talk to him and actually act for or against him, and hence as he participated in or against this, loved or hated, and imagined everything in human terms; *all these traces of humanity are expressed in the first names*! They too speak love or hatred, curse or blessing, gentleness or resistance, and what in particular emerged from this feeling in so many languages were *the articles*! Then everything became human, personified as

woman and man; everywhere gods, goddesses, acting malign or benign beings" (*Abhandlung*, p. 48).

50. In "Das Christentum der Vernunft" (*Sämtliche Werke*, 14: 175–78), Lessing formulates the ethical imperative: "Act according to your individual perfections." For the moral effects of the mathematical sublime, see Kant, *Kritik*, §27.

51. Two studies interpret the philosophical positions of *Agathon*. John McCarthy (*Fantasy and Reality*) reads Agathon as a philosophical novel, in which Wieland works out his idealist philosophy. McCarthy insists on the difference between "Schwärmerei" and "Enthusiasmus." The former means the wrong expectation of finding the marvelous in the phenomenal world; the latter is directed toward the divine, which cannot be found in nature but is discoverable only through the "inner voice." Against the usual overemphasis on the individual psychological aspects of the novel, Horst Thomé ("Menschliche Natur") analyzes the political impact of the philosophical positions by which individual figures in *Agathon* are characterized. Thus he identifies Hippias with an aristocratic and absolutist position, which advocates the materialism, empiricism, and atheism of the French Enlightenment. Agathon is largely identified with bourgeois morality and German Platonism as developed by Leibniz. He traces in the love story of Agathon and Danae, the movement of Danae from an aristocratic life-style to one of bourgeois intimacy. However, Thomé points out that since the happy state to which nature has led Agathon and Danae cannot last within a social context, the novel has reached an aporia, the irreconcilability of man's nature with a social order. His reading overlooks the fact that the narrator, Archytas, and finally Agathon come to see this love story not as a solution between an idealist and a materialist life-philosophy, but as Agathon's "most dangerous" aberration. Therefore, I do not think that one can equate Agathon's idealism with private bourgeois morality, which Reinhart Koselleck (*Kritik und Krise*) describes as the bourgeois critique of absolutism; rather, Agathon's idealism has to be understood within the later neo-humanist and classicist paradigm of Bildung and sublimation, for which there is no opposition between the individual's perfection of himself and the ideal state.

52. See Kittler, "Mütterlichkeit und Beamtenschaft," *Aufschreibesysteme*, pp. 59–75.

53. See Kittler, "Zur Sozialisation Wilhelm Meisters."

54. Here one might think, for instance, of Karl Philipp Moritz's autobiographical novel *Anton Reiser* (1795), which ascribes the protagonist's failures to "parental negligence." The secondary literature on the bildungsroman likes to debate whether this novel is a bildungsroman, a psychological novel (as indeed Moritz calls it in the subtitle), or an anti-bildungsroman. A more interesting approach to this question would compare and contrast the investment of psychological discourse in the position of the mother with the investments of the "successful" sublimation script of the Bildung narrative.

Works Cited

Primary Works

Blanckenburg, Friedrich von. *Versuch über den Roman*. Facsimile reprint of the original edition of 1774. Stuttgart: Metzler, 1965.

Condillac, Etienne Bonnot de. *Essai sur l'origine des connaissances humaines*. Ed., with notes, Charles Porset; preface by Jacques Derrida, "L'archéologie du frivole." Auvers-sur-Oise: Galilée, 1973.

————. *An Essay on the Origins of Human Knowledge*. Trans. Thomas Nugent, with an introduction by Robert G. Weyant. Gainsville, Fla.: Scholar's Facsimiles & Reprints, 1971.

————. *Oeuvres philosophiques de Condillac*. Paris: PUF, 1947. 2 vols.

Diderot, Denis. "De la poésie dramatique." In *Oeuvres complètes de Diderot*, vol. 10, *Le drame bourgeois*, ed., with notes, Jacques Chouillet and Anne-Marie Chouillet, pp. 323–427.

————. *Le fils naturel ou les épreuves de la vértue, comédie en cinq actes, et en prose, avec l'histoire véritable de la pièce*. In *Oeuvres complètes de Diderot*, vol. 10, *Le drame bourgeois*, ed., with notes, Jacques Chouillet and Anne-Marie Chouillet, pp. 13–81.

————. *Lettre sur les aveugles à l'usage de ceux qui voient*. In *Oeuvres complètes de Diderot*, vol. 4, ed. Ivon Belavale, Robert Niklaus, Jacques Chouillet, Raymond Trousson, and John S. Spink, pp. 15–89.

————. *Lettre sur les sourds et muets à l'usage de ceux qui entendent et parlent*. In *Oeuvres complètes de Diderot*, vol. 4, ed. Ivon Belavale, Robert Niklaus, Jacques Chouillet, Raymond Trousson, and John S. Spink, pp. 129–233.

————. *Le neveu de Rameau*. Paris: Garnier-Flammarion, 1983.

————. *Oeuvres complètes de Diderot*. Paris: Hermann, 1975– .

Goethe, Johann Wolfgang von. *Werke*. Hamburg ed. Munich: Deutscher Taschenbuch Verlag, 1982. 12 vols.

Herder, Johann Gottfried. *Abhandlung über den Ursprung der Sprache*. Ed. Hans Dietrich Irmscher. Stuttgart: Reclam, 1966.

————. "Einige Wahrnehmungen über Form und Gestalt aus Pygmalions bildendem Traume." In *Herders sämtliche Werke*, 1: 1–87.

————. *Herders sämtliche Werke*. Ed. Bernhard Suphan. Berlin: Weidmannsche Buchhandlung, 1877–1913. 33 vols.

Kant, Immanuel. *Kritik der Urteilskraft*. Werkausgabe, vol. 10. Ed. Wilhelm Weischedel. Frankfurt am Main: Suhrkamp, 1977.

La Fontaine, Jean de. *Fables*. Paris: Garnier-Flammarion, 1966.

Lessing, Gotthold Ephraim. *Gotthold Ephraim Lessings Fabeln. Drei Bücher. Nebst Abhandlungen mit dieser Dichtungsart verwandten Inhalts*. In *Lessings sämtliche Schriften*, 1: 195–229 (*Fabeln*) and 7: 415–79 (*Abhandlungen*).

————. *Lessings sämtliche Schriften*. Ed. Karl Lachmann; new, enl. ed. by Franz Muncker. Stuttgart: Göschen'sche Verlagsbuchhandlung, 1886. 23 vols.

————. *Miß Sara Sampson*. In *Lessings Werke*, ed. Kurt Wölffel. Frankfurt am Main: Insel, 1967, 3: 167–247.

Lessing, Gotthold Ephraim, Moses Mendelssohn, and Friedrich Nicolai. *Briefwechsel über das Trauerspiel*. Ed., with notes, Jochen Schulte-Sasse. Munich: Winkler, 1972.

Locke, John. *An Essay Concerning Human Understanding*. Ed., with an introduction, Peter H. Nidditch. Oxford: Clarendon Press, 1975.

————. *John Locke on Education*. Ed., with an introduction and notes, Peter Gay. New York: Columbia University, Teachers College, Bureau of Publications, 1964.

Marivaux, Pierre Carlet de Chamblain de. *La vie de Marianne*. Paris: Garnier-Flammarion, 1978.

Mendelssohn, Moses. *Gesammelte Schriften*. Jubilee ed., facsimile reprint of the 1931 Berlin ed. Stuttgart and Bad Canstatt: Friedrich Fromann, 1972– .

Moritz, Karl Philipp. *Anton Reiser: Ein psychologischer Roman*. Frankfurt am Main: Insel, 1979.

————. *Schriften zur Ästhetik und Poetik*. Critical ed. Ed. Hans Joachim Schrimpf. Tübingen: Max Niemeyer Verlag, 1962.

Richardson, Samuel. *Aesop's Fables. With instructive morals and reflections, abstracted from all party considerations, adapted to all capacities; and designed to promote religion, morality, and universal benevolence. Containing two hundred and forty fables, with a cut engraved on copper to each fable. And the life of Aesop prefixed*. London: 1740(?). Facsimile reprint of copy at Harvard University Library. New York: Garland, 1975.

————. *The Apprentice's VADE MECUM*. Ed., with an introduction, Alan Dugal McKillop. Los Angeles: University of California Press, 1975.

————. *Clarissa*. London: Dent & Sons, 1978.

————. *Pamela*. New York: New American Library, 1980.

————. *Pamela*, vol. 2. London: Dent & Sons, 1959.

————. *Sir Charles Grandison*. London: Oxford University Press, 1972.

Rousseau, Jean-Jacques. *Discours sur les sciences et les arts* and *Discours sur l'origine de l'inégalité*. Paris: Garnier-Flammarion, 1971.

————. *Emile*. Trans. Barbara Foxley. London and New York: Everyman's Library, 1974.

————. *Emile ou de l'education*. Paris: Garnier-Flammarion, 1966.

————. *Julie ou la nouvelle Héloïse*. Paris: Garnier-Flammarion, 1967.

———. *Lettre à M. d'Alembert sur son article Genève*. Paris: Garnier-Flammarion, 1967.

———. *Politics and the Arts: Letter to M. d'Alembert on the Theatre*. Trans., with notes and an introduction, Allan Bloom. Ithaca, N.Y.: Cornell University Press, 1986.

Schiller, Friedrich. *Friedrich Schiller on the Aesthetic Education of Man in a Series of Letters*. Trans. Reginald Snell. New York: Ungar, 1980.

———. *Maria Stuart*. In *Historical Dramas by Friedrich Schiller*. Trans. Samuel Taylor Coleridge, E. A. Aytoun, and A. J. Morrison. London, New York, and Chicago: Anthological Society, 1901.

———. *Maria Stuart*. In *Sämtliche Werke*, 2: 549–686.

———. *Sämtliche Werke*. Munich: Hanser, 1984. 5 vols.

———. *Über die ästhetische Erziehung des Menschen in einer Reihe von Briefen*. In *Sämtliche Werke*, 5: 570–669.

Warburton, William. *The Divine Legation of Moses. Demonstrated on the principles of a religious deist, from the omission of the doctrine of a future state of reward and punishment in the Jewish dispensation*. London, 1738, 1741. 2 vols.

Wieland, Christoph Martin. *Geschichte des Agathon*. In *Sämtliche Werke*, vol. 1.

———. *Sämtliche Werke*. Ed. Hamburger Stiftung zur Förderung von Wissenschaft und Kultur in conjunction with the Wieland Archiv, Biberach/Riß, and Dr. Hans Radspieler. Hamburg: Beck, 1984. 16 vols.

Secondary Works

Aarsleff, Hans. *From Locke to Saussure: Essays on the Study of Language and Intellectual History*. Minneapolis: University of Minnesota Press, 1982.

Albert, Claudia. *Der melancholische Bürger: Ausbildung bürgerlicher Deutungsmuster im Trauerspiel Diderots und Lessings*. Frankfurt am Main and Bern: Peter Lang, 1983.

Althusser, Louis. *Lenin and Philosophy*. New York and London: Monthly Review Press, 1971.

Ayrault, Roger. "La figure de Mortimer dans *Marie Stuart* et la conception du drame historique chez Schiller." *Etudes Germaniques* 14 (1959): 313–24.

Bakhtin, Michael. "The *Bildungsroman* and Its Significance in the History of Realism (Towards a Historical Typology of the Novel)." In idem, *Speech Genres and Other Late Essays*. Trans. Vern W. McGee; ed. Caryl Emerson and Michael Holquist. Austin: University of Texas Press, 1986, pp. 10–59.

Barish, Jonas. *The Antitheatrical Prejudice*. Berkeley: University of California Press, 1981.

Baudiffier, Serge. "Diderot et Condillac." In Jean Sgard, ed., *Condillac et les problèmes du language*. Geneva and Paris: Editions Slatkine, 1982, pp. 115–36.

Bender, John. *Imagining the Penitentiary: Fiction and the Architecture of Mind in Eighteenth-Century England*. Chicago: University of Chicago Press, 1987.

Bennett, Benjamin. *Modern Drama and German Classicism: Renaissance from Lessing to Brecht*. Ithaca, N.Y.: Cornell University Press, 1986.

Berghahn, Klaus. *Schiller: Ansichten eines Idealisten*. Frankfurt am Main: Athenäum, 1986.

Boa, Elizabeth. "Sex and Sensibility: Wieland's Portrayal of Relationships Between the Sexes in the *Comische Erzählungen*, *Agathon*, and *Musarion*." *Lessing Yearbook* 12 (1980): 189–218.

Bogumil, Sieghild. *Rousseau und die Erziehung des Lesers*. Bern and Frankfurt am Main: Herbert und Peter Lang, 1974.

Bolten, Jürgen. *Friedrich Schiller: Poesie, Reflexion und gesellschaftliche Selbstdarstellung*. Munich: Fink, 1985.

Borchmeyer, Dieter. *Tragödie und Offentlichkeit: Schillers Dramaturgie im Zusammenhang seiner ästhetisch-politischen Theorie und der rhetorischen Tradition*. Munich: Fink, 1973.

Braudy, Leo. "Penetration and Impenetrability in *Clarissa*." In Philipp Harth, ed., *New Approaches to Eighteenth-Century Literature*. New York: Columbia University Press, 1974, pp. 177–206.

Brooks, Peter. "Alceste, Julie, Clarissa." In idem, *The Novel of Worldliness*. Princeton: Princeton University Press, 1969, pp. 142–71.

Brunet, Pierre. "Le thème du vin dans *La Nouvelle Héloïse*." *Annales Jean-Jacques Rousseau* 38 (1969–71): 273–76.

Buddecke, Wolfram. *C. M. Wielands Entwicklungsbegriff und "Die Geschichte des Agathon."* Göttingen: Vandenhoeck & Ruprecht, 1966.

Bürger, Christa. *Der Ursprung der bürgerlichen Institution Kunst: Literatursoziologische Untersuchungen zum klassischen Goethe*. Frankfurt am Main: Suhrkamp, 1977.

Burger, Heinz-Otto. " 'Eine Idee, die noch in keines Menschen Sinn gekommen ist': Ästhetische Religion in deutscher Klassik und Romantik." In Albert Fuchs and Helmut Motekat, eds., *Stoffe, Formen, Strukturen: Studien zur deutschen Literatur*. Festschrift for Hans Heinrich Borcherdt. Munich: Hueber, 1962, pp. 1–20.

Campe, Joachim. *Der programmatische Roman: Von Wielands "Agathon" zu Jean Pauls "Hesperus."* Bonn: Bouvier, 1979.

Caplan, Jay. *Framed Narratives: Diderot's Genealogy of the Beholder*. Afterword by Jochen Schulte-Sasse. Minneapolis: University of Minnesota Press, 1985.

Carroll, Malcolm Godfrey. "Morality and Letters: *La Nouvelle Héloïse*." *Forum for Modern Language Studies* 13 (1977): 359–67.

Castle, Terry. "The Carnivalization of Eighteenth Century English Narrative." *PMLA* 99 (1984): 903–16.

———. *Clarissa's Cyphers*. Ithaca, N.Y.: Cornell University Press, 1982.

———. *Masquerade and Civilization: The Carnivalesque in Eighteenth-Century English Culture and Fiction*. Stanford: Stanford University Press, 1986.

Creech, James. *Diderot: Thresholds of Representation*. Columbus: Ohio State University Press, 1986.

Crocker, Lester. "Julie ou la duplicité." *Annales de la Société Jean-Jacques Rousseau* 36 (1963–65): 105–52.

Cullens, Chris. "Female Difficulties: English and German Women Writers, 1740–1810." Ph.D. dissertation, Stanford University, 1988.

Darnton, Robert. "Readers Respond to Rousseau: The Fabrication of Romantic Sensitivity." In idem, *The Great Cat Massacre and Other Episodes in French Cultural History*. New York: Random House, 1985, pp. 215–56.

De Man, Paul. *Allegories of Reading: Figural Language in Rousseau, Nietzsche, Rilke, and Proust*. New Haven: Yale University Press, 1979.

Works Cited

————. *Blindness and Insight*. Minneapolis: University of Minnesota Press, 1983.
Dilthey, Wilhelm. *Das Erlebnis und die Dichtung*. Leipzig: Teubner, 1906.
Dithmar, Reinhard. *Die Fabel*. Paderborn: Schöningh, 1971.
Doody, Margaret. *A Natural Passion: A Study of the Novels of Samuel Richardson*. Oxford: Clarendon Press, 1974.
Doolittle, James. "Hieroglyph and Emblem in Diderot's *Lettre sur les sourds et muets*." *Diderot Studies* 2 (1952): 148–67.
Durzak, Manfred. "Äußere und innere Handlung in *Miß Sara Sampson*: Zur ästhetischen Geschlossenheit von Lessings Trauerspiel." In idem, *Poesie und Ratio*. Bad Homburg vor der Höhe: Athenäum, 1970, pp. 44–68.
Düsing, Wolfgang. "Ästhetische Form als Darstellung der Subjektivität: Zur Rezeption Kantischer Begriffe in Schillers Ästhetik." In Jürgen Bolten, ed., *Schillers Briefe über die ästhetische Erziehung*. Frankfurt am Main: Suhrkamp, 1984, pp. 185–228.
Foucault, Michel. *Discipline and Punish: The Birth of the Prison*. Trans. Alan Sheridan. New York: Random House, 1979.
————. *The History of Sexuality*, vol. 1, *An Introduction*. Trans. Robert Hurley. New York: Random House, 1980.
————. "Omnes et singulatim." In Sterling M. McMurrin, ed., *The Tanner Lectures on Human Values, 1981*. Salt Lake City: University of Utah Press, 1981, pp. 226–54.
————. *The Order of Things. An Archaeology of the Human Sciences*. New York: Random House, 1973.
————. *Power/Knowledge: Selected Interviews and Other Writings, 1972–1977*. Ed. and trans. Colin Gordon. New York: Pantheon, 1980.
Frank, Horst Joachim. *Geschichte des Deutschunterrichts*. Munich: Hanser, 1973.
Freud, Sigmund. *Studienausgabe*, vol. 3, *Psychologie des Unbewußten*. Frankfurt am Main: Fischer, 1982.
Fried, Michael. *Absorption and Theatricality: Painting and Beholder in the Age of Diderot*. Berkeley: University of California Press, 1980.
Fugate, Joe K. *The Psychological Basis of Herder's Aesthetic's*. The Hague and Paris: Mouton, 1966.
Gelley, Alexander. "The Two Julies: Conversion and Imagination in *La Nouvelle Héloïse*." *Modern Language Notes* 92 (1977): 749–60.
Godden, Angelica. "'Une painture parlante': The *Tableau* and the *Drame*." *French Studies* 38 (1984): 397–413.
Goffman, Ervin. *The Presentation of Self in Everyday Life*. New York: Doubleday, 1959.
Gossman, Lionel. "The Worlds of the *Nouvelle Héloïse*." *Studies on Voltaire and the Eighteenth Century* 41 (1966): 235–76.
Green, André. *Narcissisme de mort—narcissisme de vie*. Paris: Editions de Minuit, 1983.
Grob, Karl. *Ursprung und Utopie: Aporien des Textes. Versuche zu Herder und Novalis*. Bonn: Bouvier, 1976.
Guyons, Bernard. Introduction to the Pléiade edition of *La Nouvelle Héloïse*. In J.-J. Rousseau, *Oeuvres complètes*, Paris: Gallimard, 1961, 2: xix–lxx.
Hall, H. Gaston. "The Concept of Virtue in *La Nouvelle Héloïse*." *Yale French Studies* 28 (1962): 20–33.

Harth, Dietrich. " Ästhetik der 'Ganzen Seele.' " In Johann Gottfried Maltusch, ed., *Bückeburger Gespräche über Johann Gottfried Herder, 1971.* Rinteln: Bösendahl, 1973, pp. 119–40.

Hasubek, Peter, ed. *Fabelforschung.* Darmstadt: Wissenschaftliche Buchgesellschaft, 1983.

Hausen, Karin. "Die Polarisierung der 'Geschlechtscharaktere': Eine Spiegelung der Dissoziation von Erwerbs- und Familienleben." In Werner Conze, ed., *Sozialgeschichte der Familie in der Neuzeit Europas.* Stuttgart: Klett, 1976, pp. 363–93.

Heath, Stephen. "Notes on Suture." *Screen,* Winter 1977, pp. 48–76.

Heidsieck, Arnold. "Der Disput zwischen Lessing und Mendelssohn über das Trauerspiel." *Lessing Yearbook* 11 (1979): 7–34.

Heintel, E. "Besonnenheit." In Joachim Ritter, ed., *Historisches Wörterbuch der Philosophie.* Basel: Schwabe, 1971, 1: 848–50.

Hertz, Neil. "Medusa's Head: Male Hysteria Under Political Pressure." In idem, *The End of the Line: Essays on Psychoanalysis and the Sublime.* New York: Columbia University Press, 1985, pp. 161–93.

Hohendahl, Peter Uwe. *Der europäische Roman der Empfindsamkeit.* Wiesbaden: Athenaion, 1977.

Hornbeak, Katherine. *Richardson's "Familiar Letters" and the Domestic Conduct Books, Richardson's "Aesop."* Smith College Studies in Modern Languages 19, no. 2 (1938).

Huyssen, Andreas. "Mass Culture as Woman: Modernism's Other." In Tania Modleski, ed., *Studies in Entertainment: Critical Approaches to Mass Culture.* Bloomington and Indianapolis: Indiana University Press, 1986, pp. 188–207.

Irmscher, Hans Dietrich. "Grundzüge der Hermeneutik Herders." In Johann Gottfried Maltusch, ed., *Bückeburger Gespräcke über Johann Gottfried Herder, 1971.* Rinteln: Bösendahl, 1973, pp. 17–57.

———. "Mitteilungen aus Herder's Nachlaß." *Euphorion* 54 (1960): 281–94.

———. "Nachwort" to Johann Gottfried Herder, *Abhandlung über den Ursprung der Sprache,* ed. H. D. Irmscher, Stuttgart: Reclam, 1966, pp. 137–75.

Janz, Rolf-Peter. *Autonomie und soziale Funktion der Kunst: Studien zur Asthetik von Schiller und Novalis.* Stuttgart: Metzler, 1973.

Jauß, Hans Robert. "Der Bruch zwischen Erwartung und Erfahrung in Rousseaus *Nouvelle Héloïse.*" In idem, *Ästhetische Erfahrung und literarische Hermeneutik.* Frankfurt am Main: Suhrkamp, 1984, pp. 589–601.

Jones, James F., Jr. *"La Nouvelle Héloïse": Rousseau and Utopia.* Geneva and Paris: Librairie Droz, 1978.

Jørgensen, Sven-Aage. "Ist eine Weimarer Klassik ohne Wieland denkbar?" In Wilfried Barner, Eberhard Lämmert, and Norbert Oellers, eds., *Unser Commercium: Goethes und Schillers Literaturpolitik.* Stuttgart: Cotta, 1984, pp. 187–97.

Kamuf, Peggy. *Fictions of Feminine Desire: Disclosures of Heloise.* Lincoln: University of Nebraska Press, 1982.

Kittler, Friedrich. *Aufschreibesysteme, 1800/1900.* Munich: Fink, 1985. Trans. Michael Metteer, with Chris Cullens, *Discourse Networks, 1800/1900.* Stanford: Stanford University Press, 1990.

————. "Carlos als Karlsschüler." In Wilfried Barner, Eberhard Lämmert, and Norbert Oellers, eds., *Unser Commercium. Goethes und Schillers Literaurpolitik*. Stuttgart: Cotta, 1984, pp. 241–73.

————. "'Erziehung ist Offenbarung': Zur Struktur der Familie in Lessings Dramen." *Jahrbuch der deutschen Schillergesellschaft* 1977, pp. 111–37.

————. "Zur Sozialisation Wilhelm Meisters." In F. Kittler and G. Kaiser, eds., *Dichtung als Sozialisationsspiel: Studien zu Goethe und Gottfried Keller*. Göttingen: Vandenhoeck & Ruprecht, 1978, pp. 13–124.

Kleinheyer, Gerd. "Wandlungen des Deliquentenbildes in den Strafrechtsordnungen des 18. Jahrhunderts." In Bernhard Fabian, Wilhem Schmidt-Biggemann, and Rudolf Vierhaus, eds., *Deutschlands kulturelle Entfaltung: Die Neubestimmung des Menschen*. Munich: Kraus International Publications, 1980, pp. 227–46.

Köhn, Lothar. "Entwicklungs- und Bildungsroman: Ein Forschungsbericht." *Deutsche Vierteljahrsschrift für Literaturwissenschaft und Geistesgeschichte* 1968, no. 3: 427–73; no. 4: 590–632.

Koopmann, Helmut. *Friedrich Schiller, II: 1794–1805*. Stuttgart: Metzler, 1977.

Koselleck, Reinhart. *Kritik und Krise*. Frankfurt am Main: Suhrkamp, 1973.

Kristeva, Julia. "L'abjet d'amour." *Tel Quel* 91 (Summer 1982): 17–32.

Labrosse, Claude. *Lire au XVIIIe siècle: "La Nouvelle Héloïse" et ses lecteurs*. Lyon: Presses Universitaires de Lyon, 1985.

Lacan, Jacques. *Les complexes familiaux*. Dijon: Navarin Éditeur, Diffusion Seuil, 1984.

————. *Ecrits*. Trans. Alan Sheridan. New York: Norton, 1977.

Laplanche, Jean. *Life and Death in Psychoanalysis*. Trans., with an introduction, Jeffrey Mehlman. Baltimore: Johns Hopkins University Press, 1985.

Laplanche, Jean, and J. B. Pontalis. *The Language of Psychoanalysis*. New York: Norton, 1974.

Leibfried, Erwin, and Josef M. Werle, eds. *Texte zur Theorie der Fabel*. Stuttgart: Metzler, 1978.

Maltusch, Gottfried, ed. *Bückeburger Gespräche über Johann Gottfried Herder, 1975*. Rinteln: Bösendahl, 1976.

Marshall, David. "Rousseau and the State of Theater." *Representations* 13 (Winter 1986): 84–114.

Mauzi, Robert. "La Conversion de Julie dans *La Nouvelle Héloïse*." *Annales de la Société Jean-Jacques Rousseau* 35 (1959–62): 29–47.

Mayer, Gerhart. "Die Begründung des Bildungsromans durch Wieland: Die Wandlung der 'Geschichte des Agathon.'" *Jahrbuch der Raabe-Gesellschaft* 1970, pp. 7–36.

McCarthy, John. *Fantasy and Reality: An Epistemological Approach to Wieland*. Bern and Frankfurt am Main: Peter Lang, 1974.

Mehlman, Jeffrey. *Cataract: A Study in Diderot*. Middletown, Conn.: Wesleyan University Press, 1979.

Mercken-Spaas, Godelieve. "*La Nouvelle Héloïse*: La répétition à la deuxième puissance." In Ronald C. Rosbottom, ed., *Studies in Eighteenth-Century Culture*, vol. 5. Madison: University of Wisconsin Press, 1976, pp. 203–13.

Miller, Jacques-Alain. "Suture." *Screen*, Winter 1977, pp. 25–34.

Works Cited

Miller, Nancy. *The Heroine's Text*. New York: Columbia University Press, 1980.

Montrose, Louis Adrian. "The Elizabethan Subject and the Spenserian Text." In Patricia Parker and David Quint, eds., *Literary Theory/Renaissance Texts*. Baltimore: Johns Hopkins University Press, 1986, pp. 303–40.

Müller, Klaus-Detlev. *Autobiographie und Roman: Studien zur literarischen Autobiographie der Goethezeit*. Tübingen: Max Niemeyer, 1976.

Niggl, Guenther. *Geschichte der deutschen Autobiographie im 18. Jahrhundert*. Stuttgart: Metzler, 1977.

Noel, Thomas. *Theories of the Fable in the 18th Century*. New York: Columbia University Press, 1975.

Nussbaum, Felicity, and Laura Brown, eds. *The New 18th Century*. New York and London: Methuen, 1987.

Ouellet, Réal. "La théorie du roman épistolaire en France au XVIIIe siècle." *Studies on Voltaire and the Eighteenth Century* 89 (1972): 1209–27.

Paulsen, Wolfgang. *Christoph Martin Wieland: Der Mensch und sein Werk in psychologischen Pespektiven*. Munich and Bern: Francke, 1975.

Petrat, Gerhard. *Schulunterricht: Seine Sozialgeschichte in Deutschland, 1750 bis 1850*. Munich: Ehrenwirth, 1979.

Pikulik, Lothar. *"Bürgerliches Trauerspiel" und Empfindsamkeit*. Cologne and Graz: Böhlau, 1966.

Preisendanz, Wolfgang. "Die Auseinandersetzung mit dem Nachahmungsprinzip in Deutschland und die besondere Rolle der Romane Wielands (*Don Sylvio*, *Agathon*)." In Hans Robert Jauß, ed., *Nachahmung und Illusion*. Munich: Eidos, 1964, pp. 72–95.

Price, Cora Lee. "Wilhelm von Humboldt und Schillers 'Briefe über die ästhetische Erziehung des Menschen.'" *Jahrbuch der Deutschen Schillergesellschaft* 11 (1967): 358–73.

Pross, Wolfgang. *Johann Gottfried Herders Abhandlung über den Ursprung der Sprache*. Munich: Hanser, 1980.

Pucci, Suzanne L. "The Art, Nature and Fiction of Diderot's Beholder." *Stanford French Studies* 7 (1984): 273–94.

Saariluoma, Liisa. *Die Erzählstruktur des frühen deutschen Bildungsromans: Wielands "Geschichte des Agathon," Goethes "Wilhelm Meisters Lehrjahre."* Helsinki: Suomalainen Tiedeakatemia, 1985.

Saine, Thomas P. *Die ästhetische Theodizee: Karl Philipp Moritz und die Philosophie des 18. Jahrhunderts*. Munich: Fink, 1971.

Sautermeister, Gert. "Maria Stuart." In Walter Hinderer, ed., *Schillers Dramen: Neue Interpretationen*. Stuttgart: Reclam, 1979, pp. 174–216.

Schenkel, Martin. *Lessings Poetik des Mitleids im bürgerlichen Trauerspiel "Miß Sara Sampson": Poetisch poetologische Reflexionen. Mit Interpretationen zu Pirandello, Brecht und Handke*. Bonn: Bouvier, 1984.

Schings, Hans Jürgen. *Der mitleidigste Mensch ist der beste Mensch: Poetik des Mitleids von Lessing bis Büchner*. Munich: Beck, 1980.

Schnebli-Schwegler, Brigitte. *Johann Gottfried Herders Abhandlung über den Ursprung der Sprache und die Goethe-Zeit*. Winterthur: P. G. Keller, 1965.

Schrader, Monika. *Mimesis und Poiesis: Poetologische Studien zum Bildungsroman*. Berlin and New York: Walter de Gruyter, 1975.

Schrimpf, Hans Joachim. "Karl Philipp Moritz." In Benno von Wiese, ed., *Deutsche Dichter des 18. Jahrhunderts: Ihr Leben und Werk*. Berlin: Erich Schmidt, 1977, pp. 881–910.

——. *Karl Philipp Moritz*. Stuttgart: Metzler, 1980.

Schulte-Sasse, Jochen. "Poetik und Ästhetik Lessings und seiner Zeitgenossen." In Rolf Grimminger, ed., *Deutsche Aufklärung bis zur Französischen Revolution*. Munich and Vienna: Hanser, 1980, pp. 304–26.

——. *Die Kritik an der Trivialliteratur seit der Aufklärung*. Munich: Fink, 1971.

Schütze, Jochen. *Die Objektivität der Sprache: Einige systematische Perspektiven auf das Werk des jungen Herder*. Cologne: Pahl-Rugenstein, 1983.

Seeba, Hinrich C. "Das Bild der Familie bei Lessing: Zur sozialen Integration im bürgerlichen Trauerspiel." *Lessing in heutiger Sicht*. Papers presented at the International Conference on Lessing, Cincinnati, Ohio, 1976. Ed. Edward P. Harris and Richard E. Schade. Bremen and Wolfenbüttel: Jacobi, 1977, pp. 307–18.

Selbmann, Rolf. *Der deutsche Bildungsroman*. Stuttgart: Metzler, 1984.

Sorg, Klaus-Dieter. *Gebrochene Teleologie: Studien zum Bildungsroman von Goethe bis Thomas Mann*. Heidelberg: Winter, 1983.

Spies, Bernhard. "Der 'empfindsame' Lessing—kein bürgerlicher Revolutionär: Denkanstöße zu einer Neuinterpretation von Lessings *Miß Sara Sampson*." *Deutsche Vierteljahresschrift für Literaturwissenschaft und Geistesgeschichte* 58 (1984): 369–90.

Stallybrass, Peter, and Allon White. *The Politics and Poetics of Transgression*. Ithaca, N.Y.: Cornell University Press, 1986.

Starobinski, Jean. *Jean-Jacques Rousseau: La transparence et l'obstacle suivi de Sept essais sur Rousseau*. Paris: Gallimard, 1971.

Swales, Martin. "An Unreadable Novel? Some Observations on Wieland's *Agathon* and the 'Bildungsroman' Tradition." *Publications of the English Goethe Society* 45 (1975): 101–30.

Szondi, Peter. "*Tableau* und *coup de théâtre*." In idem, *Lektüren und Lektionen: Versuche über Literatur, Literaturtheorie und Literatursoziologie*. Frankfurt am Main: Suhrkamp, 1973, pp. 13–42.

——. *Die Theorie des bürgerlichen Trauerspiels im 18. Jahrhundert*. Frankfurt am Main: Suhrkamp, 1973.

Thomé, Horst. "Menschliche Natur und Allegorie sozialer Verhältnisse: Zur politischen Funktion philosophischer Konzeptionen in Wielands *Geschichte des Agathon* (1766/67)." *Jahrbuch der deutschen Schillergesellschaft* 22 (1978): 205–34.

Todorov, Tzvetan. *Theories of the Symbol*. Ithaca, N.Y.: Cornell University Press, 1982.

Ueding, Gert. *Schillers Rhetorik: Idealistische Wirkungsästhetik und rhetorische Tradition*. Tübingen: Niemeyer, 1971.

Utz, Peter. "Auge, Ohr, Herz: Schillers Dramaturgie der Sinne im Jahrhundert der Aufklärung." *Jahrbuch der deutschen Schillergesellschaft* 29 (1985): 62–97.

Vance, Christie McDonald. *The Extravagant Shepherd: A Study of the Pastoral Vision in Rousseau's "Nouvelle Héloïse."* Studies on Voltaire and the Eighteenth Century, vol. 105. 1973.

V.-David, Madeleine. *Le débat sur les écritures et l'hiéroglyphe aux XVIIe et XVIIIe siècles*. Paris: Ecole Pratique des Hautes Etudes, 1965.

Vierhaus, Rudolf. "Bildung." In Otto Brunner, Werner Conze, and Reinhart Koselleck, eds., *Historisches Lexikon zur politisch-sozialen Sprache in Deutschland*. Stuttgart: Klett-Cotta, 1972, 1: 509–51.

————. "Politisches Bewußtsein in Deutschland vor 1789." In Jürgen Bolten, ed., *Schillers Briefe über die ästhetische Erziehung*. Frankfurt am Main: Suhrkamp, 1984, pp. 135–60.

Warner, William. *Reading "Clarissa": The Struggles of Interpretation*. New Haven: Yale University Press, 1979.

Weber, Peter. *Das Menschenbild des bürgerlichen Trauerspiels: Entstehung und Funktion von Lessings "Miß Sara Sampson."* Berlin: Rüttenberg & Löning, 1970.

Weber, Samuel. *The Legend of Freud*. Minneapolis: University of Minnesota Press, 1983.

Wellbery, David. *Lessing's "Laocoon": Semiotics and Aesthetics in the Age of Reason*. London and New York: Cambridge University Press, 1984.

Wiese, Benno von, ed. *Deutsche Dichter des 18. Jahrhunderts: Ihr Leben und Werk*. Berlin: Erich Schmidt, 1977.

————. *Friedrich Schiller*. Stuttgart: Metzler, 1959.

Wölfel, Kurt. "Daphnes Verwandlungen: Zu einem Kapitel in Wielands *Agathon*." *Jahrbuch der deutschen Schillergesellschaft* 8 (1964): 41–56.

Woodmansee, Martha. "The Interest in Disinterestedness: Karl Philipp Moritz and the Emergence of the Theory of Aesthetic Autonomy in Eighteenth-Century Germany." *Modern Language Quarterly* 45 (1984): 22–47.

Zelle, Carsten. "Strafen und Schrecken." *Jahrbuch der deutschen Schillergesellschaft* 28 (1984): 76–103.

Ziolkowski, Theodore. "Language and Mimetic Action in Lessing's *Miss Sara Sampson*." *Germanic Review* 40 (1965): 261–76.

Index

In this index an "f" after a number indicates a separate reference on the next page, and an "ff" indicates separate references on the next two pages. A continuous discussion over two or more pages is indicated by a span of page numbers, e.g., "57–59." *Passim* is used for a cluster of references in close but not consecutive sequence. Book titles are listed under their author's name.

Library of Congress Cataloging-in-Publication Data

Mücke, Dorothea E. von.
   Virtue and the veil of illusion : generic innovation and the
pedagogical project in eighteenth-century literature / Dorothea E.
von Mücke.
       p.   cm.
Includes bibliographical references and index.
ISBN 0-8047-1865-2 (cloth : alk. paper) :
   1. European literature—18th century—History and criticism.
2. Bildungsroman.   3. Education—Philosophy.   4. Education in
literature.   I. Title.
PN751.M8 1991
809'.033—dc20
91–11112
  CIP

11. <the City> Mouse P. 8 | 12. Crow & Muscle. P. 10.

13. Fox & Ra... | P. 12.

15. Ass &... ...use P. 13.

17. Sick... ...low & ...

19. The Frogs de... ...a King P. 16. | 20. The Kite, ...awk & Pigeons P. 17.